# THE ELEMENTS OF THE SPIRITUAL
LIFE

*A Publication of the Literature
Association of the Church Union.*

# THE ELEMENTS OF THE SPIRITUAL LIFE:

## A Study in Ascetical Theology

*By*

### F. P. HARTON, B.D.
DEAN OF WELLS

*With an Introduction by*

### THE RIGHT REV.
### MARK CARPENTER-GARNIER, D.D.

LONDON

S · P · C · K

1964

*First published in 1932*
*by S·P·C·K*
*Holy Trinity Church, Marylebone Road, N.W.1*
*Printed in Great Britain by*
*Richard Clay and Company, Ltd.*
*Bungay, Suffolk.*

*Reprinted  .  1933*
*Reprinted  .  1934*
*Reprinted  .  1936*
*Reprinted  .  1939*
*Reprinted  .  1943*
*Reprinted  .  1947*
*Reprinted  .  1950*
*Reprinted  .  1957*
*Reprinted  .  1960*
*Reprinted  .  1964*

© F. P. Harton

# PREFACE

My aim in writing this book has been to give to my brethren of the Anglican Communion what we do not at present possess, a comprehensive study of the Christian spiritual life. The need of such a work is becoming increasingly clear; there are signs in many quarters of a real desire for the spiritual life, and priests are beginning to discover the vital and practical importance of a knowledge of ascetical theology. Whether I have been rash in attempting so difficult a task the event will show: I can only say that I have been led to place such knowledge as I possess at the disposal of others at the earnest request of friends whose judgment I respect and whose wishes I felt unable to disregard, and it is my hope that this book may be of real use to my fellow-clergy and theological students and not without interest to the laity.

The plan of the book is simple. Part I deals with the action of God in the soul by grace; Part II with the human resistance to the divine will and the means whereby that resistance may be overcome; Part III is a brief outline of the divine economy of the sacraments; Part IV is concerned with the life of prayer, and in Part V we consider the end of the spiritual life and the ways by which that end may be reached, concluding with a chapter on the guidance of souls with some consideration of the qualities of the ideal director. It is obvious that so wide a field can only be dealt with in outline, and perhaps somewhat unequally, in a work of this size; but I have endeavoured to make the book as adequate as possible. My aim has been to expound the teaching of the recognised masters of spirituality with the aid of such experience as I possess, eschewing alike speculation and controversy, and to make my exposition as simple, succinct and readable as I can.

A Bibliography has been added which I hope may be of service to those who desire to read more widely on the subject. It is not intended to be exhaustive, but is merely a list of the most important works under the headings of Patristic Authors; Classical Authors (by which term I understand the recognised authorities from the twelfth century to the eighteenth); Modern

Authors and Handbooks. Translations exist of most of the Fathers, but, with the exception of those noted in the Bibliography, are, unfortunately, out of print. Where translations exist of other works in foreign languages I have cited the English titles. The dates indicate editions which are now in print and obtainable in the ordinary way.

I wish to express my very grateful thanks to the Bishop of Colombo, who, with characteristic generosity, has found time in the midst of his arduous labours not only to contribute the Introduction, but also to read the whole manuscript and make many suggestions for its improvement. It is indeed probable that this work would never have been completed but for his constant encouragement.

My gratitude is also due to the Rev. Dr. W. K. Lowther Clarke, the Rev. Dr. Darwell Stone, the Rev. K. D. Mackenzie, the Rev. M. C. Petitpierre and the Rev. C. M. Stothert for kindly reading the manuscript and giving me much valuable help.

Chapter xiv, most of chapter xiii, the description of the Sulpician method in chapter xvii and the latter part of chapter xviii are derived from articles which I have contributed to *Theology*, and I would like to thank the Editor of that journal for permission to make use of them here.

I gratefully acknowledge the permission of the following publishers to use the longer quotations of copyright matter and would thank Messrs. Burns, Oates & Washbourne, Ltd. for *Holy Wisdom*, Dom J. McCann's editions of *The Cloud of Unknowing* and *The Secret Paths of Divine Love*, the translations by D. Devas of the *Treatise on Prayer* and by A. Ross of the *Devout Life*; Messrs. J. M. Dent & Sons for F. von Hügel, *Essays and Addresses* (second series) and E. G. Gardner, *The Book of S. Bernard on the Love of God*; Messrs. M. H. Gill & Sons, Ltd. for Dom V. Lehodey, *The Ways of Mental Prayer*; Mr. John Murray for R. C. Moberly, *Atonement and Personality*; Messrs. Methuen & Co., Ltd. for W. McDougall, *An Introduction to Social Psychology*, *An Outline of Psychology* and *Character and the Conduct of Life*; Messrs. A. R. Mowbray & Co., Ltd. for W. H. Longridge, *The Spiritual Exercises of S. Ignatius Loyola*; and Messrs. Sands & Co. for Abbot Marmion, *Christ the Life of the Soul*.

F. P. HARTON.

*Bristol,*
*Easter* 1932.

# INTRODUCTION

THE task of building up the Church in the midst of a non-Christian country leads one constantly to the consideration of ways and means. It may be taken for granted that there will be difficulties in securing the necessary funds; moreover, this problem will often assume such formidable proportions that the time and energy given to its solution might suggest that money is the one essential for the furtherance of the Kingdom of Heaven. But even if the necessary funds are forthcoming, much labour must be given to organisation. Within the diocese the work must be carried on in mission and parish, in groups of parishes and archdeaconries; and care must further be bestowed upon such important matters as the government of the diocese by the Bishop, with the assistance of Synod and Council. Moreover, these are days when great stress is laid upon the committee as an essential element in the Church's scheme of organisation. Consequently, in addition to the Sacred Synod and the Diocesan Council, a network of committees will be brought into being for the discussion and supervision of every department of the work.

However necessary money and organisation may be in the furtherance of God's Kingdom on earth, an obvious danger arises from the emphasis we lay upon such means. It may only too readily be supposed that they are all-sufficient; that the Church that is wealthy and efficiently organised must necessarily be adequately equipped for the tremendous task entrusted to it. Yet " not by might nor by power, but by My Spirit, saith the Lord of Hosts."

The works that are mighty, not only to the pulling down of the strongholds of heathenism, but also to the building up of the Church of God, are not of man's manufacture or devising, but are of God. Nothing but the grace of God is sufficient; only love can conquer; only through a deepening spirituality can grace and love express themselves and find freedom for their divine operation. This is the conclusion which experience teaches us, and it is one which too often we reach only after much waste of time and through disappointment and disillusionment.

The Church that is to be useful to God and a blessing to men must above all things be a spiritual Church. In other words, the only solid ground of hope we have of fulfilling our task lies in dependence upon God; and as to ways and means, long before adequate funds or efficient organisation, we need a true conversion ourselves; such a conversion as will make us place first the adoration of God for His own sake, and will create in our hearts a longing desire for spiritual growth. It has often been said that the greatest need in the extension of the Kingdom of God is not of more Christians, but of better Christians. We may be sure that this is true. Whether we are considering the work of the Church at home or overseas, the slightest capacity of spiritual discernment must reveal to us the pressing need of a deeper spirituality. The Church is the Body of Christ, and through the members of the Church our Lord has chosen to carry forward His Kingdom. It stands to reason, therefore, that He needs members who share His Spirit and are animated by His life. He stands in need of men and women who are concerned to fulfil His will and are determined to draw nearer to His Heart. Above all, He needs saints. As in ages past He was able most readily to express Himself and act through those who were heroes in faith, virtue and love, so now His most delicate tasks in the Church, as well as His most effective means of discharging them, wait upon the coming of such heroes. And how are saints to be formed? A beginning can be made in the glad recognition that the normal state of a healthy life in Christ is a state of growth and development. This cannot be stressed too often. Indeed, it is not too much to say that the greatest handicap which hinders the work and witness of the Church to-day is caused by the stunted and undeveloped lives of a multitude of her children and by the lack of vision and hope which makes such a state of things possible. The truth is, there are vast numbers of Christians who remain for a lifetime at the beginning of the way. Physically, mentally and in business or professional capacity they take pains to make steady advance; but spiritually they remain as little children, and, while efficient in worldly affairs, they are blind to the amazing possibilities of growth in spiritual life. This blindness, this lack of spiritual enterprise, is a very great hindrance, for it prevents the due development of the Christian community, and proportionately robs it of power and effectiveness. Moreover, it is a weakness which is shared by clergy and people alike. It is tragic to discover how abundant are the possibilities of spiritual advance and then to realise how widely such possibilities are ignored, how rarely the way forward is declared.

But there are signs around us that an awakening is taking place. A new interest is being shown in prayer, an interest that is prompted by a longing to draw nearer to God. The wholesome demand for reality and sincerity in religious belief and practice is driving many men and women to face principles and study fundamentals. There are many who can no longer be content with a formal and conventional religion. If they are to possess a religion at all, it must be one of personal experience. Above all, they must get right ideas about God and must know how He may be known and approached, loved and adored. This fresh movement towards vital religion has led to a considerable demand for instruction in the ways of prayer and of spiritual life; and so important is this movement and so momentous to the Church that few tasks could be more urgent than that of wisely and efficiently supplying this demand. A contribution towards this end is now before us in Fr. Harton's important book, and I count it a privilege to write a few words of introduction to such an admirable work. The author, who is very well qualified for his task, has first made a careful study of his subject, and has then set out its different parts with attractiveness and lucidity. The result is a book which is not only readable but instructive and stimulating, and which places valuable information and counsel within the reach of all in a form that is as easy to digest as interesting to read.

This study in ascetical theology is published at an opportune moment, for, if the movement towards prayer and a deeper spirituality is to find its true goal, it must be guided wisely and sympathetically. Above all, it must be directed by knowledge and sound learning. Such knowledge of the spiritual life is only too rare amongst us. Only too often the clergy go to their delicate task of dealing with immortal souls with their minds unprepared and their eyes closed to the issues involved. It is as if physicians went out to their work unskilled in technical knowledge; though ignorance of the proper treatment of souls may prove even more disastrous than similar ignorance in dealing with bodies. I commend therefore this book to theological students preparing for ordination; to the younger clergy entering upon their ministry; and indeed to all priests, of whatever age, who are called upon to deal with individual souls. The need to-day is that of skilled priests who know how to train their people in the spiritual life and how to lead them onward to make that progress which is God's purpose for all. If such priests are given to the Church, they are indeed a treasure, and the result of their labours is found in holy lives and a deeper spiritual perception and awareness. I trust that the study of this book may create and stimulate a desire to penetrate further into this important subject, so that there may be amongst us a more widespread knowledge in matters calling for spiritual counsel and direction.

But I am confident that this handbook of the Christian Way will prove of real value not only to the clergy, but also to those of the laity who are eager to press forward in the spiritual life. Further, I feel certain that those who study it will experience both encouragement in perseverance and a renewal of inspiration. It is unnecessary that I should comment in any detail upon the contents of the book. The line of thought is easy to follow and the chapters tell their own tale. I will content myself, therefore, by touching briefly upon the main theme and upon two points in connection with it.

The lesson of this book is a lesson of hope. It sets before us the wonderful possibilities which belong to the life in Christ; it leads us to think of that life in terms of vitality and progress. I have already touched upon the importance, even urgency, of the spiritual growth of the members of Christ in face of the tremendous task entrusted to the Church. In these pages we are given a sketch of the normal ways and methods by which such growth may be achieved, and our hearts will be dull indeed if they do not experience a fresh longing for progress and a sterner determination of concentrated effort. Certainly the goal that is set before us is attractive enough and, inasmuch as God wills and longs for our perfection, we can go forward joyfully towards it. But again and again we shall be reminded that there must be nothing selfish in our aim; indeed, selfishness and self-centredness will defeat their own object. Our strongest motive in pressing forward must be desire for God Himself, and secondary only to this a humble longing to promote His glory and serve His Kingdom. We shall rightly desire spiritual growth for ourselves, but at the same time we shall look beyond ourselves, and hope that

by the grace of God any progress that is ours may both redound
to His honour and stimulate the life and work of His Church.

The two points I wish to stress concern the teaching Fr.
Harton gives on mortification and prayer. I am very grateful to
him for his chapters on mortification. It strikes me that his
teaching on this subject is most opportune. Many of us are
being attracted now to the idea of spiritual advance and growth
in prayer, and nothing would please us more than to fly lightly
to the heights with the minimum of strain and effort. Moreover, for many people there is the temptation to imagine that
already they can recognise in their own souls the signs of advanced
mystical experience, of which they read in the Lives of the Saints
or possibly in books which not too wisely describe the mystical
life. The fact is, we have to learn that the only way forward is
the way of the Cross. Only by discipline and the government
of ourselves can we follow our Lord upward and onward; and
we must learn to entrust ourselves to mortification as to a dear
friend of our souls.

Secondly, I value especially the author's teaching about the
ways of prayer. I welcome his recognition of the Holy Spirit's
work in the soul, of His freedom and His spontaneity.

There are some books on prayer which seem to tie the soul
down to a hard-and-fast system, and suggest that progress can
only come by stages as rigid as cast-iron. There are other books
which offer only one way of mental prayer, and expect every
type of soul to respond to it and follow it. The truth is, every
soul represents a distinct personality, possessing its own characteristics and requiring personal treatment. The way of meditation
which may present the open door for steady growth in prayer to
one soul may be nothing but a prison house to another. We
dare not therefore propound our own theory of mental prayer
and set it before students as the only way. This is a truth which
experience brought home to me at Oxford. At one time I had
a good deal of contact with undergraduates at the University,
and it was my privilege to give what help I could to some who
were anxious to learn more about prayer. In this way I had to
teach the first beginnings of mental prayer. I found that some
types of mind took quite naturally to the Ignatian method, as
described in this book. But there were others who could make
nothing of this way, though they took readily enough to the
Sulpician method. Others again seemed to defy normal classi-

fication and to find their way at once to a kind of prayer, which in the ordinary course of events would be reached only through some earlier stage. The teacher has therefore first to study the mind of each student and then to offer the way of prayer which seems most suitable.

(Oxford folk will understand what I mean if I say that my rough division of types of mind was according to the " History " type or the " Greats " type, with the Ignatian method for the former and the Sulpician for the latter!)

Fr. Harton has provided in a convenient and adequate form an account of the common ways of prayer, and it is one which will reward careful study and quiet reflection.

It only remains to me to commend this book to the attention and consideration of all who are eager to go forward along the Christian Way, and to express the hope that the good things which it contains may be widely shared, carefully treasured and gratefully dispensed.

MARK COLOMBO.

*Colombo,*
  *November* 18, 1931.

# CONTENTS

# CONTENTS

# PART I

# CHAPTER I

# THE CHRISTIAN LIFE

*I live, yet not I, but Christ liveth in me* (Gal. ii. 20).

It is of primary importance at the outset of our discussion to arrive at some understanding of the nature of the Christian life. Much well-intentioned effort is rendered ineffective, and much criticism of the Christian Religion is entirely beside the point, because the worker or the critic has taken the Christian life for granted and omitted to form any clear conception of its nature.

We may perhaps assume the existence of the Christian life, distinct in kind from non-Christian life, a life of man which is *sui generis ;* the question we have to answer in regard to it is, What is the principle of this differentiation?

The answers which have been proposed to this question fall for the most part under three heads. The first is *morality*. Christian morality is, fundamentally, obedience to the revealed will of an holy God; an effort on the part of man, created in the image of God, to approximate to the character of his Creator.

An essentially practical race like the English is temperamentally apt to lay far more stress on the results of a thing than on the intrinsic truth or value of the thing itself; so it is hardly surprising that a number of people tend to find the essence of Christian life in Christian ethics and to regard such ethics as the *differentia* which we are now seeking. They would reduce essential Christianity to the Sermon on the Mount and the Ten Commandments.

Let us grant at once that Christian ethics, where they are truly Christian, are different from and higher than other ethical codes; we may go further, and claim that the imitation of Christ demands constant advance in holiness, without which the Christian life is a failure. The true Christian is not only not indifferent to ethical considerations, nor even mildly good, he is one of those who " hunger and thirst after righteousness "; but, even so, his life is something more than ethics.

3

Ethics depend upon law, but this conception is not specifically Christian, nor even Jewish; it is not even necessarily religious, since many high-souled philosophers of varying periods of history have endeavoured to practise a truly stern morality apart from all but a purely philosophical background and a conception of natural law.

People who do not want to practise the Christian religion frequently harass their parish priest on his rounds with the argument that many people who do not go to church lead better lives than many who do. Examination of this argument and of the assumptions which underlie it reveals the fact that it does not prove all that its exponents wish it to prove; but even if it did, that would not imply that the Church was a useless institution, for the Church exists for something beyond morality. The Epistle to the Romans is a constant reminder to those who would make morality the only test, that the Law, so far from being all, may, when isolated from other considerations, by itself be a cause of stumbling.

We may go further. Let us assume for the sake of argument that the Sermon on the Mount is the kernel of Christianity. Let us place that and that alone, as we are often asked to do, in the hands of a young man who is really in earnest and desirous of living the Christian life. He now knows what he is to do, and all that remains is for him to put it into practice. But it is precisely here that his difficulties begin; concupiscence, temptation, self-will, pride, covetousness, lust, accidie and all the hosts of hell besiege him and he is borne down. " Give us the Sermon on the Mount and all will be well " may be all right as a slogan, but as a statement of fact it is sheer nonsense. The truth of the matter is that to the natural man the ethics of the Sermon on the Mount are not only difficult, they are impossible. The beautiful practice of those ethics which we find in the lives of men and women depends on something else, for Christian ethics are the fruit, not the root, of the Christian life. We must look deeper for our *differentia*.

Many will now seek to find an *intellectual* basis for the Christian life; to them all depends on the preaching of the Gospel and the understanding of its implications. It is obvious that the gospel can only be brought to those who know it not by the ministry of the word, for " How shall they hear without a preacher? " It is also certain that our people need constant and systematic instruction in the truths of the Faith, far more indeed than they commonly receive, and it is further true that souls who are striving to live the Christian life need frequent help thereto by way of advice; but the apprehension of truth by the mind, vital though it is, is not the essence of the Christian life.

The Christian is striving after union with God, and all his necessary religious knowledge is strictly ancillary to this end. Knowledge, study, preaching, instruction are not finally directed to the enlightening of the mind, but, through the enlightening of the mind, to the directing of the soul towards God.

The Gospel which we preach is not merely a written or spoken message, it is the whole content of the Christian religion; the knowledge of Christ which we seek is not merely the assimilation of certain facts about Him, but knowledge won by experience of Him. It is quite possible for a man by careful and critical study of the texts and the arguments of theologians and thinkers to arrive at a nicely balanced belief in the Resurrection and yet to be far less *en rapport* with the Risen Life than a humble cottager who knows nothing of synoptic criticism.

Our Lord Himself preached the Gospel and gave commandment to His apostles to do the same, but the end of that preaching was never the satisfaction of intellectual curiosity—He was indeed content to leave many pressing problems unsolved; its end was the salvation of souls, and that end cannot be achieved solely by instruction.

Preaching, moreover, is not specifically Christian; Buddha preached, Confucius preached, Mohammed preached, and the advocate of every new religion does the like for obvious reasons; but preaching, after all, is but a means to an end.

Religion needs to be intelligent, and a knowledge of the truths of the Faith is essential to the Christian. An enlightened mind is the first requisite for a strong soul, but enlightenment is not life, and the speculative intellect is but part, though an important part, of the soul.

The Christian life is essentially spiritual life, therefore the *differentia* we are seeking must be spiritual, not intellectual.

Psychologists tell us that the intellect is not the ruling faculty of the human soul and that there are depths of our being which are little, if at all, subject to it. It has also been pointed out that the primitive reaction towards God is not intellectual and depends upon awareness rather than on thought. This all points towards a life of the soul which is larger than the simply intellectual processes, though it includes them. The spirit is greater than the intellect; and the Christian life if it is to be truly regenerative of the whole man must be a spiritual thing.

The great religious souls of all time have ever sought to develop the spiritual life as the fundamental necessity of all life, and that not merely in a visionary sort of way, but intensely practically. No one can accuse S. Gregory the Great, S. Bernard, S. Augustine, S. Catherine of Siena, S. Teresa, S. Paul or S. John of an obscurantist disregard of either morals or thought, but in all these cases, and in countless others, right thinking and living were strictly ancillary to the spiritual life with God.

We are on the way to our *differentia*, but have not yet discovered it, for spiritual life is no more exclusively Christian than moral or intellectual life. Buddhism, Sufism, *Yoga* and *Bhakti*, to name no more, are all attempts to live the spiritual life, attempts which not infrequently attain great heights and yet all fall short of Christian sanctity; for Christian life depends on a new principle peculiar to itself which is derived from Christ alone, a spiritual principle which is essentially " given " and essentially supernatural.

We must, at this point, carefully consider what we mean by " givenness " and the supernatural in religion. And first as to " givenness."

We must beware of too facile a distinction between " natural " and " revealed " religion. It is commonly assumed that natural religion is the upward striving of the unaided human intellect towards God, while revealed religion is the irruption into human consciousness of the pure action of God. While it is possible on this assumption to assert that the religions of the heathen are certainly false and Christianity alone is true, yet such clear-cut generalisations fail to agree either with reality or revelation. The ultimate fact is that there can be no upward striving toward God without the prevenient action of God Himself. God Himself is the Truth, Goodness and Beauty which attracts the soul of man, enlightens him and guides his endeavours. Human advance towards God is never self-initiated, it is always a response. All truth humanly perceived is divine, its existence is independent of human thought; all true spiritual life is the divinely initiated interaction of the divine and the human. The higher the religion the more all-pervading is its " givenness," until in Christianity we find a religion whose very life is divine. Insistence upon the necessity of the Christian Faith is no mere intellectual conservatism, but loyalty to given truth; insistence upon the necessity of the Christian Sacraments no mere delight in ceremonies, but the acceptance of given life; its emphasis from start to finish and in all departments is upon the action of God which is primary, not upon the action of man which is always secondary.

This doctrine does not in any way impugn the freedom of the human will—there must always be a human response to the divine action, a response which is real and not forced; but where it is right it is a response, and not self-initiated. When we come to the Christian Religion we find that which is uniquely given in the Person of Jesus Christ, Who is Himself the Way, the Truth and the Life.

If this is so it is clear that the Christian life is essentially supernatural. It is the ignoring or denying of this element which is the cause of most of the ineffectiveness of present-day religion. Supernatural religion is not popular, but that does not make it untrue. Protestantism dislikes it, the Reformation was largely a movement for its dethronement; Modernism dislikes it—the pathetic desire to find a merely human Christ and the condemnation of sacramental action as " magic " attest as much; Science dislikes it because it appears to the scientist to introduce an incalculable and undemonstrable element into Nature; the Man in the Street dislikes it because it is beyond his comprehension, and it is a common human weakness to fear and therefore to hate the unknown; it remains for the Catholic uncompromisingly to nail his colours to the mast and live supernaturally, confident that on that level alone will he find fully Him for Whom his soul thirsts.

It may help towards clarity if we observe at this point that the supernatural is not the same thing as the miraculous.

The essential characteristic of miracle, so far as our present knowledge goes, is a modification of natural law *ab extra* by the power of God; the scientist therefore dislikes miracles and often refuses assent to them because they seem to him to introduce the element of capricious interference into a universe otherwise uniformly governed by natural law. Now the Christian religion depends upon certain miracles which we believe to be consonant with a scientific view of the universe, but the defence of the miraculous is the province of dogmatics; ascetic theology is concerned with the supernatural, which is quite a different matter.

The physical life of creatures is natural, *i.e.* according to their physical nature as creatures, and the Creator alone is wholly above Nature, *i.e.* supernatural. Man, however, is created with more than a self-contained, physical nature: he is created by God for ultimate union with Him. This implies a supernatural action of God upon the soul, elevating it above its natural limitations to participation in His own Nature. Man lives in two worlds, the natural and the supernatural, and his supernatural life is initiated, maintained and developed by grace, working not capriciously nor even miraculously, but by a divine law which is comparable to the natural law. The fundamental religious action is continual response to the constant supernatural action of God on the soul by grace, and the primary purpose of the Church is to be the sphere of this divine action at its highest.

This conception of the supernaturalness of the Christian life is well brought out by Baron von Hügel in his valuable essay on " Christianity and the Supernatural," as follows:—

" We are busy here, not with the Miraculous, but with the Supernatural. When Bossuet and Fénelon had their celebrated controversy concerning the spiritual life, Fénelon, towards the end, insisted against Bossuet (who found downright miracle in the more advanced states of prayer and of self-surrender) that the entire spiritual life, from its rudimentary beginnings up to its very highest grades and developments, was for him, Fénelon, essentially and increasingly supernatural, but at no point essentially miraculous. Thus Fénelon found the human soul, at every stage of its spiritual career, to remain still within the characteristically human kind of freedom, our poor little liberty of choice; whereas Bossuet considered the soul, in its fullest supernaturalisation, to be, even in this life, literally established in grace, and to get beyond the imperfect liberty of choice. So too as to the operations of the mind: according to Fénelon the human mind, at least in this life, remains throughout more or less successive and discursive in its operations; with Bossuet, in the highest state, the mind becomes entirely intuitive and simultaneous in its action. I believe Bossuet, in this matter, to have been wrong, and Fénelon to be right. With Fénelon we will not deny the possibility, or even the actual occurrence, of miracle, in the sense just indicated, within the spiritual life. Still less will we deny historically attested miracles in the Bible and elsewhere. But we will simply hold with Fénelon that the spiritual life of Prayer, of Love, and of Devotedness is, even in its fullest Christian developments, essentially not miraculous but supernatural. Hence we can in the spiritual life more or less foretell its future operations, and we can very largely discover certain great laws and characteristics within its past operations, the limits arising here, not from anything really sporadic in the subject-matter, but simply from the difficulty, patent in every kind of human science, of bringing the analysis and theory of very certain, richly experienced facts, to a clearness at all equal to the vividness of the experiences; and again from the great need for the observing soul to be very pure from distracting or distorting passions and very docile to the delicate facts and their manifold implications." [1]

We have now before us the beautiful conception of the supernatural regularly completing, correcting and developing the natural life and commencing here the life of communion with God which we hope to complete hereafter.

We find the Christian life to be essentially spiritual and supernatural, a life whose real inwardness will never be known to those who neglect these levels, but we have not yet reached the *differentia* which we are seeking. Spiritual life and a supernatural working of God may be found πολυμερῶς καὶ πολυτρόπως among men outside the Christian dispensation altogether. May we then say that the Christian life is supernatural religion at its highest? Yes and no. If we understand by that definition a difference from other supernatural religion in degree only, No; the Christian life, flowing as it does from the Incarnate Christ, is and must be different in kind from all else. It is supernatural religion at its highest, but its supreme excellence and value result from the introduction of a new principle into human life which can be found nowhere else. In various non-Christian associations of spiritual people it is possible to detect evidences of divine action, and holy men of various faiths are conscious of the influence of the Spirit of God. The *differentia* of the Christian life is that it is a participation in the life of God, given by the Holy Spirit dwelling in us, in virtue of the merits of Jesus Christ. It may be summed up in the phrase from the Epistle to the

[1] *Essays and Addresses*, First Series, p. 279.

Galatians which stands at the head of this chapter: " I live, yet not I, but Christ liveth in me."

The Christian life is essentially God dwelling in us, and the fruit of that indwelling is the soul's participation in the divine life, but we must be careful not to interpret this fact in a pantheistic sense. Subjective and mystical souls frequently exhibit a tendency towards pantheism which is inconsistent with Christianity, and this needs to be carefully guarded against. Participation in the divine life does not mean participation in the divine essence; the indwelling of the Holy Spirit does not connote absorption in the Deity. Even the soul most advanced in the spiritual life, showing forth as it does more and more of the character of Jesus, does not become God. The divine nature is ultimate and infinite, human nature ever remains derivative and finite, man is still God's creature, even though the Creator in His love vouchsafes to enter in and dwell with him; and we must keep this sense of fundamental creatureliness ever before us. Union with God presupposes the continuous union of two beings, not the absorption of one into the other, the less into the greater. The Holy Spirit by His indwelling does not override " our poor little liberty of choice " or substitute Himself for any of the merely human powers of the soul; rather His presence is an objective reality within the soul to which there should be a more and more continuous response. The Christian life is not identical with the life of God, yet it is a finite though real participation in that life, which we must ever cultivate by our own act and choice.

This divine indwelling makes a fundamental difference in relationship between the soul and God. By nature man, in common with the rest of the universe, is God's creature, made in the image of God with a soul capable of response to the love of his Creator, but still a creature and a creature only. With his entrance into the Christian life he becomes something infinitely more: he is God's son and the eternal God is his Father. " Ye have received the spirit of adoption, whereby we cry Abba, Father. The Spirit itself beareth witness with our spirit, that we are the children of God." [1] We are then, according to S. Paul, made the children of God by a process of adoption. In human matters, adoption is a species of legal fiction by which a man takes a child and agrees legally to treat him as though he were his

[1] Rom. viii. 15–16.

child by nature and to give him the rights of family and property that would have been his had he been his natural child, and society accepts and enforces this arrangement; but when all has been said and done the child is no more the natural son of his adopted father after this legal process than he was before. In explaining supernatural matters one has constantly to use analogy and symbol, but the best natural analogy breaks down at some point when transferred to the supernatural, and it is at this point that we find the incompleteness of the Pauline figure. Protestant theology has constantly failed to recognise this fact by producing forensic theories of justification and imputed righteousness which represent God as a human potentate Who, in consideration of the Sacrifice of Jesus, agrees to treat the Christian as though he were His son and to impute righteousness to him by a legal fiction. We are not here concerned with the detailed refutation of this position, that being the business of dogmatic theology; what we are concerned to point out is that there is a fundamental difference between divine and human adoption. Human adoption does not effect a change in the nature of the adopted, because man is incapable of altering the laws of nature, the most he can do is to ignore them; God, however, can and does effect changes in the supernatural plane which radically affect the soul of man and bring him into new relationships with God Himself. Divine adoption actually does do what human adoption can only pretend to do. " Beloved, now are we the sons of God." [1] There is here no imputation of sonship, but actual sonship. We *are* the sons of God. Now how does this come about? Again the apostolic teaching is quite clear. " Ye are all the children of God by faith in Christ Jesus. For as many of you as have been baptized into Christ have put on Christ. There is neither Jew nor Greek, there is neither bond nor free, there is neither male nor female: for ye are all one in Christ Jesus." [2] The key phrase here is " in Christ Jesus." Jesus Christ is eternally by nature the Son of the Father, to the believer He grants by the grace of Baptism union with Himself, as is made clear by His own figure of the vine and the branches; and the fruit of this union is real participation in His own Sonship. There is here no question of imputation, we are sons of the Father because we are made one with Him Who is from all eternity His Son—our sonship is a spiritual reality.

[1] I John iii. 2.                    [2] Gal. iii. 26-8.

Once again we must remind ourselves of the distinction in being, mentioned above. Being " in Christ," we are sons of God, but not in the same sense that He is. We are still finite creatures, He is infinite God, and our nature is not metamorphosed into His. It is because He is Man as well as God that He is the " first-born among many brethren." [1] Had He not taken our nature there would have been no natural point of contact between God and Man, for it is in the Divine Humanity that we find the possibility of our own adoption as sons. He became Man in order that we might become the sons of God.

Through the grace of the Incarnate Christ we become the sons of God, filled with His life and conscious of His indwelling Presence; it is this fact which gives to Christianity its peculiar glory and it is the life in grace which we have now to consider.

[1] Rom. viii. 29.

# CHAPTER II

## HABITUAL GRACE

*If a man love me, he will keep my words: and my Father will love him, and we will come unto him, and make our abode with him* (John xiv. 23).

WE have seen that the basis of the Christian life is the indwelling of the Holy Spirit in the souls of the faithful, but, before passing on to consider grace, which is its fruit, we must pause to investigate a little more closely the character of the indwelling itself.

It is probably no exaggeration to say that to most people the divine indwelling is an extremely vague concept. This is due in the first instance to our very hazy idea of the Holy Spirit. Confirmation is still very largely regarded as the personal acceptance of the Baptismal Vows and the gateway to Holy Communion rather than as anything very definitely sacramental, and even where its sacramental character is recognised attention is frequently directed rather to the Gifts than to the Giver. The prayer of the Bishop before the administration of the Sacrament is theologically accurate, nevertheless, owing to our slipshod use of language, its significance is apt to be misunderstood. Praying for those to be confirmed the Bishop says: " Strengthen them, we beseech thee, O Lord, with the Holy Ghost the Comforter, and daily increase in them thy manifold gifts of grace; the spirit of wisdom and understanding; the spirit of counsel and ghostly strength; the spirit of knowledge and true godliness; and fill them, O Lord, with the spirit of thy holy fear, now and for ever." This is, of course, a prayer for the descent of the Holy Ghost *septiformis munere;* but we are so accustomed to speak in common parlance of a " spirit " of love, fear, or whatever it may be, when we really mean only an emotion or a gift, that it may be questioned whether many people attach any further meaning to the phrase in this connection.

The coming of the Holy Ghost is really a double gift, first of all the gift of the Third Person of the Blessed Trinity Himself, and then of the grace, infused virtues and gifts which He brings with Him. " The love of God is shed abroad in our hearts by

13

the Holy Ghost which is given unto us." [1]   We must then regard the indwelling of the Holy Ghost in the soul as a personal indwelling, and not simply as an infusion of divine characteristics or aids.

Another cause of vagueness is the difficulty most people experience of imagining the personality of the Holy Spirit.   It is a simple matter to imagine the personality of Christ owing to His Sacred Humanity, it is fairly easy to form some conception of God the Father by means of the human titles under which He is revealed, but it is by no means simple to grasp the personality of the Holy Spirit, for we can only apply to Him analogies which are themselves impersonal.   This fact, however, need not alarm us if we are prepared to resist an elementary tendency towards tritheism and refuse to fall into the heresy of dividing the substance of the Blessed Trinity.   The indwelling of the Holy Spirit in the soul is indeed the indwelling of the Blessed Trinity, for it is impossible to separate God from God.   It will have been observed that in the text at the head of this chapter our Lord speaks of the coming of Himself and of the Father; spiritual writers of various ages of the Church also speak indifferently of the presence of God, of our Lord and of the Holy Spirit.   Similarly, S. Paul speaks of the Christian as the temple of God and of the Holy Spirit indifferently.   "The temple of God is holy," he says on one occasion, "which temple ye are"; [2] and again, "Ye are the temple of the living God." [3]   And on another occasion, "Your body is the temple of the Holy Ghost." [4]   It is clear then that the indwelling of the Holy Spirit in the soul is nothing less than the personal presence of God, and not merely the gift of a spirit of virtue.   The whole possibility of Christian spirituality rests upon the fact that God dwells within the soul by the Holy Spirit filling us with His life, uniting us with Himself, and granting us intimate communion with the Blessed Trinity.

The fruit of the divine indwelling is *Habitual or Sanctifying Grace*.   Wherever God is, there is grace: He is the Eternal Giver. At all those moments of life when, raised above ourselves, we find God, we are conscious of an influx of grace; and such experiences should help us to realise that from the permanent presence of God in the soul there is ever flowing a continuous stream of grace, less sensible perhaps but nevertheless real and present. A particular grace is indeed given to us from time to time and for

[1] Rom. v. 5.      [2] I Cor. iii. 17.      [3] II Cor. vi. 16.      [4] I Cor. vi. 19.

particular purposes, called by theologians Actual Grace, but we are not now concerned with that. Habitual Grace is, as its name implies, a permanent, prevenient gift of God underlying and making possible our supernatural life, a new principle of life transforming the soul and making it and its actions godlike, a power which can only be quenched by mortal sin.

We have spoken above of the danger of a pantheistic interpretation of the divine indwelling and have pointed out that it is impossible for the soul to be united with the essence of God and so to become God in an essential sense; but with that caution in our minds we must grasp the real unity that grace produces between the soul and God. " God became man that we might become God " is true if rightly understood. True though the Pauline metaphor is, the soul is not *merely* the temple of the Holy Ghost. A temple is built as a House of God and is holy because the God Whom it enshrines is holy, but there is no personal coinherence between the temple and its deity; in the case of the soul, however, there is the closest connection between it and God, a connection which amounts in certain souls to actual union.

On the human plane we are familiar with instances of such close union between husband and wife or near relations, either natural or spiritual, that they may literally be said to think the same thoughts; and a similar union is to be found existing between the soul in grace and God. The continual actualisation of this union is the function of Habitual Grace.

The life of grace is indeed a new life into which we are born at Baptism, but it must not for that reason be set over against the natural life of man. By His indwelling the Holy Spirit interpenetrates the soul; in the same way the supernatural life of grace interpenetrates the whole life of its recipient. Once a soul is in grace we cannot say that there are certain levels of life in which the natural alone functions and certain other levels which are the province of the supernatural. It is indeed possible to shut away certain parts of life from the influence of grace, and this is frequently done by imperfect souls; the Holy Spirit never forcibly overrides the human will, but granted the acquiescence of the human will, there is no part of its activity which may not become supernaturalised by grace.

There is, then, no essential opposition between grace and nature; rather, grace is the completing, the directing, the healing of the natural by divine action. The Pauline argument is, alas, perfectly true, that " the flesh lusteth against the spirit, and the spirit against the flesh: and these are contrary the one to the other," [1] but the flesh here does not mean the natural man as God created him, it is the evil principle of concupiscence which is his through sin. The effect of grace is not the supersession of the natural, but its reorientation; grace directs the activity of the soul towards its true end, the will of God, which direction had been lost by sin, and at the same time gives the power to attain that end, thus enabling the natural to fulfil its true function and to overcome the intruding concupiscence which is no part of its original constitution. This is the introduction of a new principle into human life, but a completing, not an opposing principle.

It is important to insist on this fact because of the widespread notion that the asceticism which is inseparable from a spiritual life in this world is directed towards the killing out of the natural. This notion is responsible for much of the recoil from Christianity which is noticeable to-day among really well-disposed persons, but it is quite mistaken. Christian asceticism is certainly directed towards the killing out of the flesh (σάρξ) in the Pauline sense, in order that the natural (ψυχικός) may become more and more spiritual (πνευματικός) as the grace of God has progressively freer course.

Grace is essentially the principle of life, not death, and if we must die in order to live, as indeed we must, it is the false, self-willed self which must die in order that the true supernaturally natural self may live in God.

This is the work of grace, and it is clear that it can attain its completion only in heaven. " Beloved," says S. John, " now are we the sons of God, and it doth not yet appear what we shall be: but we know that, when he shall appear, we shall be like him; for we shall see him as he is." [2] On earth the work of grace is the continuous action of God on the soul, making it progressively more and more like unto Him, that at last it may be capable of the Beatific Vision. The perfect vision of God is impossible to the creature because it demands a quality of likeness which is foreign to the created nature, but God, by the free gift of grace, imparts His own likeness to the soul, which makes the Beatific Vision a possibility in heaven. " Now we see through a glass darkly, but then face to face." [3]

[1] Gal. v. 17.    [2] I John iii. 2.    [3] I Cor. xiii. 12.

Habitual Grace, then, is a preparation for heaven and a fore-taste here and now of the heavenly life. Heaven is where God is, and if God dwells in the soul, that soul must participate really in the life of heaven. When our Lord calls us out of the world into the Church it is to raise us above the flesh to the spiritual life of heaven on earth. This explains the " other-worldliness which is characteristic of true Christianity "; an other-worldli-ness which does not stand aloof from this world, but completes and sanctifies it; which is utterly alien to the world's evil, but which claims its good for God.

We have by grace an experience and a vision of God, obscure, indeed, and infinitely variable, but none the less real; an experience and a vision in which the soul truly lives.

Habitual Grace supernaturalises the powers of the soul, the intellect, the affections and the will. We shall have occasion hereafter to consider how these powers may and do go astray from God, it is enough here to remark that there is a natural level of their operation and a supernatural level; that the natural level is necessarily imperfect, being bounded by the human and unable to get above itself, while the supernatural, being divine, is only bounded by ultimate human incapacity and the will of God. Abandonment to divine grace renders the soul able truly to say with S. Paul, " I can do all things through Christ which strengtheneth me." [1] Habitual Grace enlightens the intellect and deepens its intuitive knowledge of God and divine things; it unifies the affections and centralises them upon the love of God; and it strengthens the will by aligning it with the will of God. Thus the soul in grace is enabled to grow to its full stature.

The effect of Habitual Grace on the soul is an interior trans-formation by means of a new, permanent and divine principle, so that a soul in grace is radically and permanently different from a soul that is not in grace. Holy Baptism, the sacrament by which souls are " born again " from the natural to the supernatural and become children of God, living with His life, confers " character " as the theologians say; that is, it makes a fundamental change in the soul itself, and for that reason it may never be repeated, no matter what may happen to the soul. It may be a Prodigal Son, but it is still the son of God; the Holy Spirit may be resisted and the channels of grace stopped up by continued and mortal sin,

---

[1] Phil. iv. 13.

C

but the way back is through the gate of Penance, not Baptism; and when the soul is happily restored, though it may and probably will have to learn to live over again, it is the same life and not a new one that it is learning.  It has come back to the old home, it has not gone out into a new country to find another.

This consideration brings us face to face with what is to many people a grave problem, the diversity of Christian souls, a diversity not merely of temperament, but of good and evil. Our Lord in two parables [1] has expressly prepared our minds for the existence of such a problem, nevertheless it is the cause of much perplexity.  There are two questions involved which may be briefly stated thus:—

1. If grace is what we have described it to be, why is there not an obvious generic difference between " the children of light " and " the children of this world "?

2. For the same reason, how is it possible for a Christian to fall away and be lost?

To these questions we may perhaps add a third:—

3. How is it that I am conscious of great differences in my own spiritual state, so that, at times, I appear to myself to be destitute of grace altogether?

The answer to these questions may be found in the consideration of the two factors which go to make up the life in grace, human will and grace itself.

Clearly, grace can only have free course in a perfectly surrendered will; every particle of self-pleasing constitutes an obstacle to be overcome, a resistance to be transformed.  Souls vary enormously in the completeness of their response to divine grace, but in none does it have a clear field.  There are the many and various movements of concupiscence, the passive opposition of habits formed by past sin, the active opposition of inordinate desires, weakness of will in some directions and, often, deliberate opposition to the will of God in others, as well as contentment with the simply natural.

We have already seen that grace does not normally work by way of miracle, so we shall be wrong if we expect to find absolute perfection in every Christian soul, for such a phenomenon would involve the miraculous extirpation of concupiscence and sin; what we should expect to find and what we do find is the possi-

---

[1] The Tares (Matt. xiii. 24–30) and the Drag-net (Matt. xiii. 47–50).

bility of perfection in such souls through participation in the divine life. This is a tremendous and fundamental difference between Christian and other souls, but it is a difference which must be actualised by the soul itself in correspondence with grace by mortification, by labour constant and unremitted, by true love of God. It is not enough that one should commit the day to God and hope that He will in some way or other see one through; perfection is only attained by constant self-discipline and surrender. It is then hardly to be wondered at that some Christian souls should fall short of perfection or that some should turn their backs upon it altogether. The whole purpose of Christian asceticism is to render the soul more and more responsive to the grace within it until at last it reaches perfection by way of ever-deepening surrender to the will of God. This is a gradual and progressive process by which the soul proceeds from stage to stage of the spiritual life, and the work of grace in the soul is, therefore, gradual and progressive, perceived now after one fashion and now after another, at times almost, if not quite, imperceptible. If then the work of grace is very variably perceptible to the soul itself, we shall not expect to see any particular degree of visible sanctity marking " the children of light " off from other people, even though interiorly they are different by the grace that is theirs; it is possible for a Christian soul to make the grace of God of none effect by its own will, because its will, even after the advent of grace, is free. The best that can be said of any ordinary Christian is not that he has attained to this or that height of sanctity, but that he is becoming, through discipline, more and more one with the will of God.

The life in grace is an advancing life. As the obstacles are removed and the soul becomes more uniformly united with God, so the action of Habitual Grace becomes more and more perfect and the grace itself appears to grow, not because the grace itself alters in character, but because the soul becomes more perfectly attuned to it. Because the Holy Spirit is Himself present in the soul He is present at all times with all the plenitude of His power; Habitual Grace is constant at all times, and the Infused Virtues and the Gifts of the Spirit are always present, but not always equally fruitful. At one period in the soul's development it is led by grace in the life of the virtues and at one time and another in one particular virtue more than the rest; later it is the Gifts of the Spirit singly and collectively which bear fruit in it, frequently the work of grace issues in an obscure leading. We must beware of conceiving of Habitual Grace as a static. quasi-material object which can be measured and is always, so to say, of the same size and weight. Habitual Grace is always present and always sufficient, having been given once for all, but it is dynamic, *immensus* with all the immensity of God, (ποικίλη χάρις, in S. Peter's phrase [1]).

Habitual Grace will appear to vary in the soul according to the variations in the soul's own life and its need of training. Mortal sin will choke it; preoccupation with sinful or inordinate desires or interests will reduce the responsiveness of the soul and so produce an apparent desolation (this is also one of the evils of worry), and so the soul may become " dry " from its own fault. The Holy Spirit Himself leads and trains the soul in the spiritual life; and this training, as we shall see in a later chapter, is, at certain stages, necessarily by way of darkness when the soul wanders, apparently alone, in realms unrecognised, when it seems as if grace has altogether departed. But at this very time grace may be working most freely. The Holy Spirit is treating the soul in the same way that a mother does her child when she stands out of the range of its sight and touch that she may teach it to walk; though all the time she is there ready to catch it should it stumble.

Habitual Grace works upon the depths of our spiritual being, unconscious as well as conscious; therefore the presence of this grace and its perception are two different things, and it is constantly necessary to remember that in the Christian life " we walk by faith, not by sight."

[1] I Pet. iv. 10.

# CHAPTER III

# ACTUAL GRACE

*My grace is sufficient for thee* (II Cor. xii. 9).

ACTUAL GRACE is for the Christian part and parcel of the larger life of Habitual Grace, but it is not confined to the Christian dispensation. Every movement of a human soul towards God is a response to Actual Grace working *ab extra* upon the soul. Any true knowledge of God is the fruit of revelation; any true devotion to righteousness is the movement of the divine will; conversion itself is nothing less than the call of God; and the moving power of all these things is Actual Grace. But for the Christian this grace is the movement of the indwelling Spirit.

We may define Actual Grace as a supernatural and transitory power which God gives us to enlighten the mind and strengthen the will that we may act according to His will. Whereas Habitual Grace is concerned with the soul's life as a whole, Actual Grace is directed towards particular acts and is called forth by individual occasions; whereas Habitual Grace is continuous, Actual Grace is transitory.

The action of Actual Grace is of two kinds, direct and indirect.

1. In the first place it acts directly and interiorly upon our spiritual faculties, the intelligence and the will, and moves them to grasp truth and perform the will of God. A great part of this action of grace is imperceptible, but from time to time one is conscious of it, and one frequently recognises on subsequent reflection that certain actions or courses of action were the result of the action of such grace. Sudden lights proceeding, as it were, from nowhere are perceived to be not simply the result of unconscious cerebration, but the work of Actual Grace. In cases of adult conversion not only the final call but a host of circumstances leading up to it are seen to be the work of grace, and the enlightenment of the conscience springs from the same source. To the Christian the working of Actual Grace in this way is an intense reality and a continual

21

source of wonder, and one realises that whatever progress one may have made in the spiritual life is the work of grace rather than of one's own efforts; indeed, the direct action of grace makes of one something very different from anything one would or could have made of oneself. In retrospect one finds at every point of the spiritual life the presence of Actual Grace. Through it the circumstances of life bring forth in us what God wills, and we are able to proceed with a sureness impossible to unaided humanity.

The Christian life is essentially supernatural, but constantly people revert to the natural, the upper air becoming too rarefied for them when they do not correspond to the special graces which God in His mercy gives them from day to day; this is, indeed, the tragedy of countless lives.

It has been said that a moderately good Christian is as unsatisfactory as a moderately good egg. The end of the Christian life is supernatural perfection, and yet many, perhaps most, Christians are content with natural respectability. They are righteous, but not righteous overmuch; their life is a compromise between God and Mammon. It is not that such people are bad or have succumbed to the lures of the grosser or more obvious sins; their overt sins may be few, but they are trying to live a supernatural life on a natural plane, and so withhold from God that which He most desires, their *whole* heart. Immersed in the world, they tend to conform to its standards, allowing public opinion to obscure the will of God; what is " done " becomes more important than what God requires, the daily movements of actual grace are disregarded, and the soul, thrown back upon itself, finds that it has lost its wings and so, in time, ceases all attempts to rise above the merely human level of its neighbours.

Correspondence to the daily pricking and aid of Actual Grace alone can save a soul from this nemesis, and such grace, if seconded by one's own will and desire, can and does supernaturalise the whole life.

2. As we have said, Actual Grace acts interiorly upon the soul, enlightening the mind that it may know God, kindling the heart that it may desire Him, and stirring the will that it may love Him in the individual happenings of life, but it also acts exteriorly through the senses, working thus upon the spiritual faculties indirectly

The normal methods of the Holy Ghost are *indirect*, so we are constantly conscious of the action of Actual Grace through physical media.

To many souls Nature is a real means of grace. The beauty of a spring morning, the glory of a summer sunset, the gentle melancholy of autumn woods, the grandeur of mountain snows truly lift up the soul through the visible to the invisible God. To the Christian this grace is the work of God, which is something far greater than what is commonly called Nature Mysticism. The attempt to rise " through Nature up to Nature's God " all too frequently ends in a vague pantheism, the man who prefers to seek God in Nature rather than in grace is generally actuated by an equally vague sentimentality; but for the Christian who simply seeks God, God uses all sorts of physical things and happenings as media for Actual Grace, media as various as the souls which they touch. Of course, to some souls Nature makes no such appeal, to others she makes too much, and then the love of Nature needs to be mortified lest it compete with the love for God.

Art, and particularly music, moves many souls towards God and may thus be a vehicle for Actual Grace, but it is of value in this way only as a vehicle. Nature and art may be, and are, sacramental, not because they are Nature and art, but because God uses them as means in the kingdom of grace; they do not of themselves produce revelation or even ideas, they become sacramental if and as the Mind of God employs them as symbols for interpretation by the mind of man. The action of grace does not end with the sensational, mental or emotional stimulus, but passes over into the direct action upon the spiritual faculties which we have already considered. Actual Grace working through physical media produces favourable impressions by which the mind and will are moved towards supernatural good, and the same grace working directly upon the soul enables it rightly to interpret those impressions. The exterior stimulus, having done its work, hands the soul over to the interior working of grace. One finds in Nature or art the God Whom one knows, and the work done in the soul is not the work of Nature or of art, but of God Himself through grace. For those who have ears for it there is no artistic means of grace so profound as some of the works of Bach: the sublime glory, say of the E major Fugue for Clavier, may, by the action of grace, so inflame the soul that it may be ravished with the beauty of God, but when that happens the beauty of the fugue is lost in the transcendent beauty of God, and He then deals directly with the soul.   God, Who knows that we move from the sensible to the spiritual, strengthens our weakness by means of sensible things conjoined with grace.

Nature and art can truly be used by the Holy Spirit as media for Actual Grace, but He also uses other and more definitely supernatural media: contact with a really holy person may and should be what we call an " inspiration "; and sermons, as well as the reading of Holy Scripture and spiritual books, may be definitely means of grace, for the purpose of religious instruction is not the satisfaction of intellectual curiosity, but the enlightening of the mind towards God.   The soul which keeps its spiritual faculties alert is frequently conscious of the action of Actual Grace in this way.   The sudden enlightenment in spiritual reading which has apparently nothing whatever to do with the sense of the passage that is being read, the strange applicability of *sortes liturgicæ*, or the general, obscure sense of God which is so frequently the result of such exercises are all cases in point.   But apart from conscious enlightenment or " uplift," which occurs with less frequency in some souls than in others and in the same soul at different periods of its development, there is the much less perceptible but more constant action of Actual Grace through these things and others, whereby in quite simple and ordinary ways the soul is enabled to find God.

We have been considering some of the many and various means by which God chooses from time to time to convey grace to souls—means which may truly be called sacramental; but these " sacramentals " are not truly sacraments.   To say that is not to depreciate their value, but merely to point out a very important distinction.   There is no such thing, strictly speaking, as a " natural sacrament," nor could such possibly take the place of the sacraments of the Church, because it does not fulfil the conditions that a sacrament does, the most important of which is certainty and indefectibility.   A sunset may convey grace if God wills it to do so, but not even the most confirmed Nature mystic will have the hardihood to suggest that every sunset invariably does so, even to his prepared and receptive soul; contact with a really holy person will frequently convey real grace, but not always; *sortes liturgicæ* occur only occasionally and are by no means always obvious. The soul living the life of grace needs more defined and certain means of grace than these. Rain water is a good thing, but no one would expect to gain a sufficiency of it by putting a bucket in the garden and hoping for the best. The God-loving soul will desire to " draw water from the wells of salvation " or, to take a more modern and less poetical image, from the main water supply, and to that end he will go either to the well-head or the tap, *i.e.* the sacraments.

We shall have occasion to deal with the sacraments in detail in a subsequent chapter, the important point upon which we must insist at this moment is that they are the covenanted, and therefore certain and permanent, means whereby grace may always be obtained. In view of what has been said above, it should be unnecessary here to refute the trite objection to the Catholic doctrine of the sacraments, that they tie God to certain means of conveying His grace to man. The whole position may be summed up quite succinctly in the statement that man needs a regular supply of grace in order to be able to live rightly, and this grace is given regularly by God in the sacraments under certain conditions; man has no right to expect God to give him a regular supply of grace if he wantonly refuses to use the appointed means under the mistaken idea that he is thereby being more spiritual. It is the divine certainty of the sacraments that gives them their unique position in the spiritual life, as well as the divine character of the gifts which they indefectibly impart. Extra-sacramental grace is, as the experience of every spiritual person attests, given by God to souls as He wills and as they need, but such gifts are of God alone and must not be presumed upon. Regular use of the sacraments is necessary for the obtaining of the grace necessary to true life, and we can be quite certain that, devoutly used, the sacraments do convey this grace. God regularly conveys natural life by natural means in accordance with natural law, and He equally regularly conveys supernatural life by supernatural means in accordance with supernatural law.

The sacraments, then, are the normal means of grace, by which the soul is united to God and the life of God is poured into it. Sacramental life is not something accidentally imposed upon the Christian life, but its natural medium; and the devout soul, realising the fundamental importance of its life with God, will make careful and regular use of the sacraments, not as uncomprehended forms or occasional aids, but as the constant means of its life and union with God.

A true sacramentalism is the best possible defence against a vague and sentimental mysticality and an unwise straining after mystical states which are out of reach. Through the sacraments God gives Himself, in them the soul is united to Him, they are the storehouse of Actual and Habitual Grace. These facts assimilated and acted upon are the foundation of a true and vigorous spiritual life, free from that uncertainty and feverishness which distinguishes so much of the religious effort of our day.

Theologians have separated the operations of Actual Grace into various classes, some of which it will be useful to consider here. I would reiterate what has been said above, that all grace is essentially one, and that any classification which may be made is an attempt to describe its modes of operation rather than to divide the indivisible; consequently we are here speaking not of graces, for that cannot be, but of modes of grace.

(a) Firstly, grace may be considered according to its purpose as *medicinal* or *elevating*.

The first effect of the outpouring of the Precious Blood is the healing of the wounds of the soul caused by sin, so that, viewed from this standpoint, divine grace is truly said to be *medicinal ;* and the sacraments which convey medicinal grace are Baptism, Penance and Holy Unction. Modern psychology, where it deigns to consider sin as sin at all, regards it exclusively as a disease to be cured. Without accepting this view as a complete statement of the problem, we must recognise that it does represent a very important part of it. The psycho-analyst deals with it, often very effectively, by purely natural methods, but fails to remove its evil effects because the root of sin can only be removed by grace. Sin is finally curable by grace, and by grace alone. The effects of the death of Christ are applied to the individual soul according to its need by grace, and it is important to realise the curative action of grace and the sacraments.

But it is not enough that the soul should be healed; it needs supremely union with God, to which its cure is a necessary preliminary, so grace is not only medicinal, but *elevating*, acting in this way not only through the sacraments mentioned above, but also through the others. Mystical union is given only to saintly and chosen souls after much purgation, but essential union with God begins in Baptism and is deepened, if the soul is faithful, all through the sacramental life. Superficial souls and souls in darkness frequently fail to realise the fact of elevating grace, but it is by its means that the indwelling Christ unites Himself to them. The soul is concerned not only with a transcendent, external Christ, but also with an immanent, internal Christ, Who is by elevating grace lifting it up continually to heavenly desires and to God Himself.

(b) From another point of view grace may be regarded either as *prevenient* or as *concomitant*. This distinction is of great importance, a fact which is attested by the variety of names which have been given from time to time to these forms of its working. Prevenient and concomitant, operative and co-operative, antecedent and subsequent, exciting and assisting are some of the pairs of adjectives used to distinguish these forms of the divine activity, of which we have chosen the first as being, perhaps, the most descriptive. From this standpoint grace is classified according to its effect upon the will. Much grace works unconsciously upon the depths of the soul independently of the will; it goes before the act of choice, and is therefore called *prevenient*—it is, in the language of the schools, *in nobis sine nobis*. Of such a kind was the guiding principle which brought about the spiritual *volte-face* which we call the Conversion of S. Paul; of such a kind is the operation of grace which produces the turning of any soul to God; very deep, mostly unconscious, often resisted, but quite sure, the action of the " Hound of Heaven " upon the soul. But its action does not cease with conversion; in vocation, and constantly in the major and minor crises of life, one is conscious, either at the time or subsequently, of a leading quite independent of one's own will, which does not supersede the action of the will in its proper place, but which, in the fullness of time, presents it with its prepared choice.

The moment the will comes into action grace becomes *concomitant* (*in nobis et nobiscum*), aiding, directing, but never forcing the will that means to give itself up to the leading of the Spirit.

The understanding of these aspects of grace is of the greatest assistance in realising the true dependence of the soul upon God and His unfailing care of it. It safeguards the essential responsibility of the human will and enables the soul to exercise that responsibility upon the background of the sure leading of God; it fosters the right use of the will in faithful abandonment to the will of God in all matters and at all times, and so deepens the union between the soul and God which it is the function of grace to actualise.

(*c*) From the point of view of its effects grace may be further classified as *sufficient* or as *efficacious*.

In all the events of life the faithful soul is always given grace *sufficient* for the matter in hand; there is no possibility of insufficiency of grace. The realisation of this truth adds greatly to the calmness with which one may face crises and enables one to accept the events of life as they come without undue worry. As the sense of one's own insufficiency deepens, as one realises that one's failures in the spiritual life are the result of one's own fault or weakness, and not of the failure of grace, so one is able to abandon oneself to the sufficiency of God.

But grace is not merely sufficient, but *efficacious* ; one may not only be certain that by grace an action may attain to a certain rightness, but also that it may, in union with the free action of the will, be efficacious to salvation. The end of grace is not merely abstract rightness, but salvation, and union with God which brings forth goodness.

It is clear, then, that grace is not merely valuable, but necessary to the spiritual life; we depend upon it for our conversion to God and our union with Him, for our perseverance in holiness, and for our soul's growth. It is essential that we should seek it and use it continually in the faithful use of the sacraments, and, so far as they are helpful and when they are helpful, in sacramentals; above all, by constant prayer. God gives His grace richly to those who ask Him, but the soul that does not pray is so shut up in itself that even the grace of God can hardly find an entrance. Yet the use of grace demands circumspection. If grace is to have free course and attain its end one must desire to do always the will of God and avoid exposing oneself wilfully to danger. It is precisely this holy circumspection which is so often lacking even in well-disposed persons, and which is responsible for so many grievous falls from God. There are many dangers in the world which cannot be avoided; if one loves God and desires to do His will one can rely on grace to keep one safe in these, but one has no right to presume on the grace of God by deliberately going into danger or by allowing oneself carelessly to drift. God will attain His ends in and by us if we are faithful, and only so.

# CHAPTER IV

# THE THEOLOGICAL VIRTUES

*Now abideth faith, hope, charity, these three* (I Cor. xiii. 13).

THE first-fruits of the entrance of divine grace into the soul are the three Theological Virtues of Faith, Hope and Charity; these are Infused Virtues, which term needs a little explanation. There is a sense in which all virtues may be said to be infused, inasmuch as our whole being is God's, and no beginning can be made in virtue without the movement of the Holy Spirit; there is also a sense in which all virtues are acquired, since none can come to perfection without the consent and labour of the human will. It may therefore be argued that all the virtues should be classed together, and their classification into the categories of " infused " and " acquired " may seem to be a distinction without a difference; we must, then, get our minds clear as to what is an Infused Virtue.

We have seen that the life in grace is an essentially supernatural thing demanding for its existence certain specific spiritual reactions towards God impossible to an unaided "natural" soul. The Infused Virtues are the spiritual faculties given by God which make these reactions possible: by them the natural life is supernaturalised, by them the Cardinal Virtues are raised above the merely moral sphere to the religious, by them the acquired virtues are made possible. Natural prudence is a great and wonderful thing, but it may go entirely wrong unless it is spiritualised and united with the wisdom of God by Faith, Hope and Charity. Natural prudence is God-given by reason of its "naturalness," and the ancient philosophers found it among the furniture of the human mind; but it may be developed on a purely natural and intellectual plane apart from religion of any kind. The study of ethics is a philosophical pursuit, but it cannot lead the soul to union with God without the truly Infused Virtues, though it may produce a very fine character. The Infused Virtues, then, are those given to us

through the indwelling of the Holy Spirit to unite us to God
and to enable us to live as members of Christ and bring forth
the fruits of the Spirit.

In considering Habitual Grace we tried to combat the view
which would regard it as a quasi-material something of
definite bulk, given to all alike and with invariable effects.   In
considering the Infused Virtues, which are the effects of Habitual
Grace, the same caution should be borne in mind.   Faith, for
instance, is connected with justifying and with Habitual Grace,
but the faith of a newly converted adolescent differs as greatly
from that of a middle-aged and worldly Christian as both do
from the faith of a contemplative nun;  yet it is the same divine
gift which is working in all.   The Theological Virtues are an
invariable effect of the presence of the Holy Spirit, but they
are increased by the soul's correspondence with them, and may
be lost by sin.   This explains the absence in many quite well-
disposed souls of one or other of the Theological Virtues.   To
many Faith means solely assent to certain intellectual propositions;  many have yet to learn the very rudiments of Charity,
and to many again the virtue of Hope is simply meaningless,
yet, once the right spring is touched, the soul is able to develop
the absent virtue, not of its own power, but because of Habitual
Grace, and the deeper its response to that grace the more perfect
becomes the flowering of the virtue.   If the virtue has been lost
it can be replaced in the soul by the ever-present Spirit;  but it
is not replaced full grown, the soul has to begin again at the
beginning.

In the regular progress of a devout soul the Infused Virtues
increase to such a degree as apparently to change their very
character, the sentimental and exuberant Charity of a beginner
in the spiritual life seeming to differ *toto cælo* from the strong
and disciplined Charity of the perfect;  but it is the same supernatural Charity in both.   Through suffering and discipline the
soul has grown in surrender, and Charity has therefore had her
perfect work.   It is, then, of the greatest importance that souls
should be encouraged to " covet earnestly the best gifts " [1] and
to foster their growth by their exercise, for the Christian life is
the life of the virtues.

[1] I Cor. xii. 31.

## I. FAITH

It is important to realise at the outset that Faith is a spiritual virtue, not a natural intellectual operation; therefore it does not oppose the rational processes of the mind, but completes them. Faith is not the negation of thought, but its perfection. We live in an age which is largely dominated by popular misconceptions concerning the infallibility of the intellect and the sphere of science, and Faith is regarded as an intrusive and illusive principle utterly alien to a world of hard, ascertainable and material facts and contrary to what is somewhat vaguely called " the scientific mind." There is no virtue of which people are so shy and none which is more fundamental to religion.

We must be clear, then, as to the purpose of Faith. It is not anti-intellectual, neither does it seek to invade the sphere of science or evade its conclusions. The field of thought may be divided into three parts, forming an ascending series:

(*a*) The investigation of physical phenomena and their classification. This is the province of science and is of very great importance. It is natural that in an age of unparalleled advance in this sphere science should seem to cover the whole field in popular imagination, but scientists themselves are by no means so sure to-day as they were half a century ago that it does so, and the symbolical character of scientific thought and its concern with what Professor Eddington calls " pointer-readings " rather than ultimate facts is becoming increasingly recognised. The dogma of the omniscience of scientists is out of date, and although this does not lessen their importance in their own sphere, it indicates that spiritual facts are not the same as physical and are not discoverable by experiment and measurement.

(*b*) The evaluation of the results of scientific experiment and the weaving of them into a coherent whole is the province of philosophy, which also takes cognisance, on the natural plane, of such spiritual facts as it can discover by intellectual means. One needs only to think of S. Thomas Aquinas in order to realise how much religion owes to the best philosophy; but this theologian reminds us that philosophy alone is unable, even intellectually, to produce a complete synthesis of all that is.

(*c*) Philosophy is completed by theology, which approaches the facts with which philosophy is concerned from the point of view of God and not of man, aided by a new set of facts given by revelation. The final resolution of facts must be supernatural and spiritual, and therefore religious; ultimate truths are all in the sphere of Faith, for they can be neither weighed nor measured, nor are they perceptible to the senses or comprehensible by logical argument: but they are perceptible by Faith and experienced in the life of grace.

"Spiritual things are spiritually discerned" and Faith is this spiritual discernment; there is therefore no necessary opposition between Faith and thought or religion and science. Human thought has, by observation, experiment and deduction, built up a wonderful knowledge of the material universe, a knowledge which is constantly increasing and being corrected, but behind and interpenetrating the universe at all points is God the infinitely Other and He is not susceptible of observation and experiment.[1] "Can man by searching (we should say, by scientific reasoning) find out God?" asks Job, and the form of the question "expects the answer, No," as the grammars say. Knowledge of God is revealed by God, and that not directly to the limited intellect of man, but through his spirit by the infused gift of Faith.

We must not be understood to suggest that there are two cognitive principles in man, intellect and spirit. Rather, the one intelligence acts at different levels in two different ways, mostly in various degrees of combination, rational and intuitive; the true intuition of the things of God which is Faith being the work of grace in the soul reinforcing and enlarging the intellect. Even on merely natural levels we are coming to see that we are not guided so exclusively by logical thought as we like to think we are, for the greatest scientific discoveries would appear to be intuitions based upon a foundation of hard thinking, *i.e.* revelations granted to a prepared mind. In the spiritual sphere the knowledge of God is an intuition granted to the soul through Faith. Such an intuition once granted, enlightens the intellect and is perceived to be true even though it transcends the processes of thought.

Faith is indeed far more than mere knowing, either rational or intuitive; it is the virtue by which we are united to God,

[1] "One of the greatest favours bestowed on the soul in this life is to enable it to see so distinctly and to feel so profoundly that it cannot comprehend God." S. John of the Cross.

D

Who is infinite Truth, and by which we are given, so far as we are able to attain to it, communion with the divine Thought, since by it God reveals Himself to us.

In purely human relationships we have faith in a person whom we believe to be true, honourable and of sound judgment, and because we thus believe in him we have faith in what he says and accept his word with our intelligence even though we may have no means of proving the truth of his words for ourselves; indeed, if we have a real faith in him we should not desire to prove his words at all.

The same is true of faith in God. The essential part of faith is a spiritual movement towards God, not, as many think, an unaccountable disposition to believe certain, mostly undemonstrable, statements. God is eternal Truth, and if I have faith in Him I shall certainly not be required to believe a lie, even though such faith leads me beyond the strictly limited field of ocular demonstration. The first article of the Creed is the foundation of all our knowing. *Credo in Deum:* I put my whole trust in God the eternal Truth, I place my little intellect in the hands of the divine Wisdom; of myself I can know nothing and therefore do nothing rightly, and so I submit my intelligence to His guidance and accept His word. The *abandon* of faith leads to truth, not credulity; because by it we are united to the divine wisdom and through it the thought of God is made known to us.

*Credo in Deum* is the language of the Creed, not *credo de Deo.* I come to know the truth about God and salvation later, through the revelation of Him Who is Truth, but my primary act of faith is one of blind trust in God Himself. It is essential to stress this point: by an act of faith one places one's mind in God's hands to be taught; which is the wisest thing one can do, but a difficult thing; that is why God in His mercy gives us at our Baptism the infused gift of Faith to aid our weak will and guide our faltering mind. The act of faith is an act of the whole being aided by grace; the mind perceives God to be eternal Truth, the heart trusts Him and the will makes the action, the whole being guided by the Infused Virtue.

Faith does not come into being full grown like Athene from the head of Zeus; complete abandonment of the intellect and the whole being into the hands of God is only possible to advanced and tried souls. Most people have to fight for their faith at some time in their lives, some for all their lives, and to many some part or other of the faith is a perpetual puzzle; these things are to be expected, and the faithful soul is perfected through trial. It is the habit of trust in God (*i.e.* the Infused Virtue) in which we must strive to grow by constant acts of loving, trusting, faith. After all, God is God and " all shall be well." " Lord, I believe, help thou mine unbelief."

The light of Faith is not the same as the light of demonstration, and the Apostle was but speaking the plain truth when he said, " Here we see through a glass ἐν αἰνίγματι." The light of Faith is fundamentally obscure, for it is impossible for our finite minds, darkened and twisted as they are by sin, to grasp the whole mystery of God in this life; though hereafter, if we are faithful, we look to see Him " face to Face." We must often be content to gaze and know and wait. The whole Truth can never be compressed into the most complete treatise of dogmatic theology, it must ever exceed our grasp, " else what's a heaven for ! " The most exhaustive treatise on dogmatic theology ever written is the *Summa Theologica* of S. Thomas Aquinas, and it is of perennial value; but it is said of the Saint that once, at the end of his holy life, God granted him a vision of His eternal Being, and the Saint ceased from writing for ever. The knowledge which comes by Faith is of the nature of obscure vision, which nevertheless enlightens the intellect in its limited understanding of God and His ways, and enables the soul to cleave to Him.

We have spoken of S. Thomas Aquinas; perhaps another story of him may be of assistance at this point: " After the death of the Doctor (S. Thomas), Brother Reginald, having returned to Naples and resumed his lectures, exclaimed with many tears: My brothers, while he was still in life, my Master forbade me to disclose the admirable things concerning him whereof I had been witness. One of these things was that he had acquired his science not by human industry, but by the merit of prayer, for whenever he wished to study, discuss, read, write or dictate, he first had recourse to prayer in private, and poured forth his soul with tears in order to discover the divine secrets, and by the merits of this prayer his doubts were removed and he issued therefrom fully instructed." [1] Here we see the prayer of faith enlightening and directing one of the acutest intellects the world has ever known.

[1] Peter Calo, *Vita sancti Thomae Aquinatis,* quoted by Maritain, *Prayer and Intelligence,* p. xi.

God does not leave the faithful soul without guidance on the way to Him, for Jesus Christ the Eternal Word is the perfect revelation of the Father. " God so loved the world that he gave his only-begotten Son that whosoever believeth in him should not perish b<sub></sub>t have everlasting life." [1] " Faith in the Divinity of Jesus is, according to the designs of the Father, the first thing needful in order to share in the divine Life; faith in the Divinity of Jesus Christ bears with it all other revealed truths.

All revelation, it may be said, is contained in this supreme testimony God gives us that Jesus Christ is His Son, and all faith is likewise contained in the acceptance of this testimony. If we believe in Christ's Divinity, we believe at the same time in the whole revelation of the Old Testament, which has its fulfilment in Christ; we believe the whole revelation of the New Testament, for all that the apostles and the Church teach us is only the development of the revelation of Christ.

Whoever then accepts the Divinity of Christ embraces the whole of revelation. Jesus is the Incarnate Word; the Word says all that God is, all that He knows; this Word is incarnate and reveals God to men: *Unigenitus qui est in sinu Patris ipse enarravit*.[2] And when by faith we receive Christ, we receive all revelation.

Therefore, the intimate conviction that Our Lord is truly God constitutes the first foundation of our supernatural life. If we understand this truth and put it into practice, our inner life will be full of light and fruitfulness." [3]

Faith in Jesus Christ is then the commencement of the spiritual life and, since two wills are involved in it, it has two sides. From God's side it is the mysterious means which He employs to initiate us into His life that we may know Him supernaturally; from our side it is the first supernatural act without which we can neither hope nor love nor make any advance in spirituality. " He that cometh to God must believe that he is." [4] It is for us the *possession* of God and of divine things and that knowledge of the supernatural whereby we grasp it and live in it. Evidently then it must be the foundation of the whole edifice of the spiritual life. Whatever virtues we may produce, whatever fruits of prayer may be ours, all springs from the divine gift of Faith.

[1] John iii. 16.
[2] John i. 18. " The only begotten Son, which is in the bosom of the Father, he hath declared him."
[3] Marmion, *Christ, the Life of the Soul*, pp. 129–30.      [4] Heb. xi. 6.

Indeed, the farther we advance the more profound must our faith become. The spiritual life of the soul is supported by the hidden workings of Faith, as a great tree is supported by its roots, which draw in from the earth the sustenance it needs and hold it firm against the winds' violence.

Faith unites us with God the eternal Truth, giving us communion with His thought and life, uniting our intelligence with the divine Wisdom, strengthening and consoling the will. By the light of reason we can know little of God and nothing of His *vie intime*, but by Faith we learn to know Him as He is. This knowledge deepens our understanding of truths already known; we know not only facts, but their meaning, and their meaning not only in natural sequence, but in the plan of God.

Faith imparts to the soul those profound convictions which alone can enable the will faithfully to persevere in well-doing; life is seen in the light of the purpose of God, and the will is thus strengthened to correspond moment by moment with that purpose. By Faith we understand what God has done and is doing for us, by Faith we realise the indwelling of the Holy Spirit in the soul and our incorporation into Christ by Baptism, not as statements of truth, but as experienced facts; and so we are enabled by God's grace to correspond with them.

We have seen that Faith, in common with all the Infused Virtues, has two sides; the " given " side, which is of God, and the " acquired " side, which is of man. In other words, the Infused Virtue must be practised if it is to perform its function in the life of the soul; it is this practice which we have now to consider.

At all stages of its growth the soul must use two means for its advance in virtue, namely prayer and effort. Effort is useless without prayer, but with it it is of great importance, and it is just because they are not prepared perseveringly to take trouble in this respect that so many souls become tepid and finally fall away; for our best efforts are unavailing in supernatural things without the simple adherence to the will of God which is actualised in prayer. In considering the practice of faith prayer must come first and effort second.

Souls may be divided according to their progress in the spiritual life into three classes: Beginners, Advancing and Perfect. The first two of these explain themselves, by the third we understand, not canonised saints, but those who have at least begun to attain to the Unitive Way.[1]  The full significance of this classification will become plain, I hope, towards the end of this book; for the present let us accept it and work on it as a convenient system of division.  It will be useful to consider the virtue of Faith as practised by each of these classes of soul in turn.

I. *Beginners*.  This class covers a great variety of souls, to each of whom Faith has to be made a reality.  There are the children of our Sunday and Day Schools, our Confirmation Candidates, our adolescents and many older people; in fact the majority of our people are in this state, though most are capable of advance.

It is important to disabuse these souls of the idea that Faith is a rare state of mind which can only be attained by a few, and to get them to realise that the gift of Faith is theirs by virtue of their Baptism.  In their prayer they should be encouraged to give thanks fervently for the gift which is theirs, with confidence that God Who has given them so great a thing and desires their perseverance so greatly will not fail them, and they should pray for grace to keep the faith.  Chiefly they should make constant forced acts [2] of Faith.  Simple short acts persistently used with humble submission build up the soul in Faith and enable it to approach God with that spirit of complete confidence which is the foundation of this virtue.

Besides prayer, beginners should be built up in the understanding of the faith.  It is astonishing how few of our people have a clear grasp of the fundamentals of the faith and an understanding of what it really is.  The result of this ignorance is distressing, as it stultifies their practice of Faith, with the result that they fall easy victims to the first clever sceptic they come across, or get lost in the wildernesses of private opinion.

The moral of this for priests is, teach, teach simply, and teach the faith, encouraging people to study and understand it.  It is not in the least necessary—rather, it is clearly undesirable—that our spiritual tyros should become budding theologians, but if God has vouchsafed to reveal Himself to man it is surely only courteous that man should grasp that revelation, or at least know what it is.  Much print is absorbed to-day, good, bad and indifferent; but the faithful, as a rule, read little or nothing about the faith, with the result that they have very little enthusi-

[1] cf. pp. 323 *ff. infra.*        [2] cf. p. 254 *infra.*

asm for it and are easily persuaded that it is unacceptable to the modern mind. Confidence in God and knowledge of His revelation are necessary to growth in the Infused Virtue of Faith.

On the other hand, there are certain dangers to be avoided or overcome. First of all the danger of sceptical literature. The *Index Expurgatorius* comes in for a good deal of abuse in these enlightened days and is not infrequently taken as the symbol of religious intolerance, but the principle underlying the formation of that work is a sound one and one in which our people should be trained.

It is commonly contended that the Index exists because the Roman authorities do not want their people to face the truth. That is not the fact. Rather do those authorities recognise that they have the greatest truth of all and are responsible to God for its guarding. In our own communion it is too commonly thought that the whole Faith is in the melting-pot and that individual thinkers are quite capable of deciding what is and what is not *de fide* and that what is vaguely called " modern thought " must be the arbiter of all things; thus the Infused Virtue of Faith disappears, and barren " views " take its place. We should be wise then to counsel prudence in reading and company. It is not " broad-minded " for untrained thinkers to read the latest *ipse dixit* of a fashionable sceptic, it is merely foolish. The " man in the street " is not capable of deciding between the theologians and scientists when they are in conflict, even though he be a Christian. Similarly, a beginner should avoid as far as possible the discussion of matters of faith with unbelievers.

We must, however, realise that our people live in the world and inevitably come up against its problems in newspapers, society and elsewhere and that the problems of the world are frequently their problems as well. Moreover, there is nothing that the modern world is so interested in as religion, so that a certain amount, and very often a large amount, of discussion is well-nigh inevitable. What is to be done about it?

We should seek to instil into our people from their earliest years an intense love of truth, as opposed to a passion for argument; and along with this a deep reverence for God and sacred things. *Magna est veritas et praevalebit*, and truth is God's truth. If by Faith we are united to God and if the faith is His revelation of Himself, we cannot possibly assent to the prevalent attitude of mind which considers all truth to reside in modern knowledge, and the faith to be either negligible or to be revised in accordance with the fashion of the day or each man's views. If God is God, He is Truth, and the faith is true, and if this or that advance in knowledge seems to contradict it one must not instantly assume that the new knowledge is right, but be content often to suspend judgment until it finds its place in the scheme of things. Humility is therefore necessary, which is a difficult virtue to come by. People are so fond of airing their views, so anxious to produce ripe conclusions on all matters, so fond of being up to date, that it is hard to get them to realise that all our boasted knowledge is as nothing in the sight of God and that the science of to-day may be, and probably will be, revised out of all recognition by the science of to-morrow, while the truth of the Lord remaineth for ever.

If the parish priest is to be truly the shepherd of his people he should encourage them to come to him in their intellectual difficulties, not to be " talked round," but to know what the faith is in that particular matter.

We should also seek to help our people to personal humility, and *per contra* to have a real contempt for a facile intellectual pride. It does not follow that because one has read a book by a sceptical physicist or an article about a book by such an one that one is in a position to understand what he is talking about, nor even if one is studying physics oneself that one is sufficiently learned to evaluate such conclusions as may result from such study. We live in an age when folk absorb opinions, largely without thought, from second-class brains, and think themselves clever enough to criticise the faith in consequence; the really faithful person is humble enough to realise the true extent of his own knowledge.

Temptations against Faith are frequent, and fall into two classes, General and Particular.

(*a*) General Temptations are, for the most part, moral rather than intellectual. The sort of vague questioning, " Is it all true? " is known to everyone and may be a direct diabolic temptation. In that case it should be brushed aside and the soul should betake itself to prayer, mainly of forced acts of faith in which it holds on to God with the will until this tyranny be overpast, and short stabs of prayer to Jesus for aid. It is well that souls suffering from temptation of this sort should be carefully instructed as to what it is and made to realise that it is not an intellectual " difficulty " to be argued with, but a temptation to be fought. They should be encouraged to hold on to God, come what may, and to trust Him personally. After all it is to be expected that the Devil should attack our faith by every subtle means in which he is adept, for if that should go we are completely in his power.

Another type of general doubt arises from a divided state of soul. This is the case of the soul that knows not whether to serve God or Mammon; the soul that desires to serve God on its own terms; the soul that knows the price of the Pearl and haggles about it; the soul that gives with one hand and takes away with the other; the soul that says deliberately *video meliora proboque*, on one day, and on another, equally emphatically, *Deteriora sequor*. There are numbers of such souls in our parishes, and they are not by any means bad, their chief fault being that they want to make the best of both worlds. The cure here is, once more, the prayer of forced acts and unification of the soul by facing the moral issue. This cure means hard work on the part of the director, and may take years to bring about; one must be prepared to go on hammering at such souls with endless patience, bearing with them in their tryingness, and fasting and praying for them oneself. Frequent confession is generally a source of much strength to both these classes of souls.

(*b*) Particular doubts, by which is meant doubts on certain specific points as against a general feeling of doubtfulness, may belong to one or other of the above classes or may be really intellectual, or they may arise from a desire to be interesting or shocking to oneself or others. All except the last class should be carefully probed to find out what is the root of the trouble. The last class will probably cure itself if we are obstinately neither interested nor excited.

A really intellectual doubt can be treated on intellectual lines, but not merely intellectual lines. A priest is not a lecturer and the Catholic Faith is not merely a series of intellectual propositions. Reasoning there must be, but it must be reasoning informed by a deeply spiritual Faith.

II. *Advancing Souls.* In process of time and often after much trial and temptation the soul settles down into the life of Faith.

The Faith which once had to be fought for gradually becomes " the master light of all its seeing." The life of such a soul has become altogether more interior, and Faith is the means by which it is constantly united with the Beloved. Jesus is the centre of thought and life, He is known as a Friend, not merely thought about, and the better He is known the more He is loved. The gospels are not merely instructions, or means of inflaming the soul, or vignettes of past history, but in them such souls follow Jesus step by step, listening to His teaching and entering into His Mind.

Everything is seen and judged from the point of view of Faith, *i.e.* with reference to God and His eternal purpose. The material universe is not merely " Nature," but the work of God, Who loves and cares for His Creation; circumstances are not fortuitous occurrences or the mere working out of natural laws, but the gift of God to be used according to His purpose; people are not merely troublesome or attractive men and women, but our fellow children of the Father, and Christians are our brothers and sisters in Christ. By Faith the advancing soul submits its judgments, words and deeds more and more to the will of Jesus, so that He may more and more live in it, and it seeks constantly by prayer, example, word and deed to bring others to Jesus, Who is its own life.

No two souls are alike, and this state of advance which we are considering is patient of infinite variety and many degrees, but it is a recognisable state of soul, and of more frequent occurrence than we often realise. It is the natural maturity of the earlier and distinctly different Faith of beginners, not an ideal condition restricted to the saints, and souls should be encouraged to persevere until they reach it, and further to persevere in it; for we may and should grow in Faith until it is " lost in sight," and Faith is the condition of that friendship with Jesus which is the heart of Christianity.

This state of soul is one of stability, when Faith is strengthened by long experience of God and His ways and the soul is, at any rate to some extent, unified by mortification; but it is not therefore exempt from temptations against Faith. In times of aridity, still more in those later crises of the spiritual life known as the dark nights, very subtle and frequently prolonged temptations occur. They proceed, for the most part, from the Devil and human weakness; they are less often intellectual, though such temptations do occur. In dealing with these souls as with beginners, the director must make up his mind as to the cause of the trouble before giving advice. What such souls need most is encouragement and a clear view of their state. In the case of diabolic temptation a return to forced acts is often efficacious, and instant flight to Jesus by means of the sign of the Cross, and repeated use of the Sacred Name, coupled with frequent Communion. It is frequently belief in the Blessed Sacrament which is attacked; in that case the soul should be encouraged to fling its " Credo " at the enemy by devout Communion, even though it feel dead and faithless.

In the case of temptations arising from its own weakness, the soul should be urged to greater generosity and a more complete surrender to the will of God.

Intellectual doubts, as in the former case, should be dealt with intellectually, and one should remember that these souls are worth considerable time and attention, especially in this fundamental temptation.

Sometimes one finds that the temptations of these souls spring from quite a small, ordinary and apparently trivial cause, but more generally their temptations are very subtle—far more so than those of beginners—and need considerable acumen in their diagnosis, and their director needs above all things prayer.

III. *The Perfect.* Souls who have attained to this, the highest, degree of the spiritual life have also advanced to a very deep and interior life of Faith, which is an exercise of the gifts of Knowledge and Understanding. It will conduce to clarity if we postpone the consideration of the Faith of such souls to the chapter on the Gifts of the Spirit (cap. VI. below), where the matter will be treated under the heads of the gifts just mentioned.


## II. Hope

Hope is, for most people, the Cinderella of the Theological Virtues. Faith we know and Charity we know, but with Hope it is different. It is true that the author of the Epistle to the Hebrews speaks of Hope as " an anchor of the soul, both sure and steadfast, and which entereth into that within the veil; whither the forerunner is for us entered, even Jesus," [1] and an anchor is a very necessary part of a ship's tackle, but, for all

[1] Heb. vi. 19-20.

that, many, perhaps most, souls have put the anchor in the hold and forgotten all about it.

Psychologists give us a rather poor account of hope. According to McDougall the poor thing has no independent existence, but is a " derived emotion," by which is meant one that " is not constantly correlated with any one impulse or tendency, but rather may arise in the course of the operation of any strong impulse or tendency; the emotion being dependent upon or derived from the working of the impulse under certain conditions." [1] He then gives it second place in a descending scale of five derived emotions: confidence, hope, anxiety, despondency and despair. He makes his meaning clear by means of an illustration. " Let us imagine ourselves," he says, " to be a party of Polar explorers returning from a dash for the Pole and making for a deposit of food a few days' march away. We have exhausted the supplies which we carried with us; but the conditions of travelling are good, we are all in vigorous health, and we know exactly where to find the hidden store of food. Then, though we all desire strongly to find this food, and though our minds may be much occupied by the thought of it, even tormented by ideas of succulent beefsteaks, we go forward in confidence. We do not hope for the food; we confidently look forward to reaching it. . . . But suppose that the sky becomes overcast, threatening a blizzard; or that the snow underfoot becomes so soft as greatly to impede our progress; or let any other difficulty arise that renders us a little doubtful of attaining our end. At once we begin to hope: we hope the weather will hold good; we hope the snow will harden; we trudge on, no longer confident, but full of hope, contemplating the desired end, enjoying in anticipation the food we desire and seek. But the threat, however faint, of some cause of failure leads us to concentrate our efforts a little more, keeps our minds more constantly occupied with the one all-important end, restrains us from all unnecessary dispersion of our energies. . . . Hope, then, is not a new force added to our desire; it is merely a new way in which the desire operates when confidence is no longer complete." [2] As the difficulties of the Polar expedition increase so their emotions descend through anxiety (which is regarded as a state of mind brought about by alternations of

[1] *An Outline of Psychology*, p. 338.
[2] *Social Psychology*, 20th Edition, pp. 370 f.

hope and despondency) to despondency and, finally, despair, which is the extinction of all hope.

McDougall is reacting from Shand, who, he thinks, gives hope far too many bouquets, and in the process of reaction he seems to have gone too far in his distinction between hope and confidence. His Polar expedition did not begin with confidence, but with hope. Confidence is impossible without, at any rate practical, certainty, and the odds were always sufficiently heavy against their reaching their food base to give their quest a large amount of uncertainty from the first; they must have hoped very strongly, but they could not have complete confidence. On the natural level confidence is the equivalent of faith, not a superior degree of hope.

Perhaps the real interest for us in this psychological exposition lies in the fact that it does exactly represent the popular notion of hope. " I hope it will be fine to-morrow," " I hope she will not be late," " We must hope for the best," (but of course we can hardly expect it to happen)—such banal phrases are the measure of this notion, and then there comes Dr. McDougall with his vision of hope as a pale and somewhat shaky wraith taking the robust though derived emotion of confidence by the hand and leading it down the initial steps of its inevitable *descensus Averno*.

Even on the purely natural plane hope is a much stronger and more definite thing than that. S. Thomas Aquinas [1] regards it as one of the four principal passions of the soul, the other three being joy, sadness, and fear. It is probable that few would assent wholeheartedly to the psychology of S. Thomas to-day; nevertheless he is far more often right, and fundamentally right, than his modern critics will allow, and here he certainly seems to be in a stronger position than the psychologists. Hope on the natural plane is a passion of the soul, a fundamental movement with which everyone has to come to terms, whereby one proceeds with ardour towards a desired object whose acquisition is possible though not certain, and a matter of some difficulty; a movement towards an absent good.

Without hope, directed and sustained effort would be impossible, and those who are deficient in this respect constantly fail to persevere in any continuous course of action. The farmer, when he sows his grain, hopes for a good harvest; the

[1] *Ia IIae. qu.* xxv. art. 4.

sailor, when he weighs anchor, hopes to gain " the haven where he would be "; the undergraduate, when he has matriculated, hopes at the end of three years to find his name in the final Honours list. It is true that the degree of hope habitually manifested by any particular individual varies according to temperament, this passion being excessive in the type of temperament called by the ancients sanguine and deficient in the melancholy; it varies also with the strength of the desire for the attainment of the particular thing hoped for at any given moment; but it is present in everyone, directing the action of each towards its desired end, and everyone is familiar with the difficulty of adjusting one's hope to further ends when previous ones have failed of fulfilment.

The motive power of hope is the imagination, which forms and keeps before the mind an attractive conception of the desired end, and by that means stirs the will towards its attainment.

To say that the end of hope is imaginary is not to say that it is false, for its truth or falsehood does not depend upon whether it is imaginary or not, but upon whether the imagination is working upon truth or fancy. Imagination and fancy, though often confounded, are not the same thing. The food desired by Dr. McDougall's Polar explorers really existed, it was in a known place, which it was possible, under certain circumstances, for them to reach, but until they did reach it it existed for them only in the imagination; nevertheless, the imagination was sufficiently strong to impel the will by means of hope to make every effort to attain the desired end.

So far we have dealt only with hope on the natural level, but in this chapter we are concerned with a higher thing, the Infused Virtue of Hope. This also is a movement of the will, informed by the imagination, towards a desired good whose acquisition is possible but not certain, but it differs from natural hope in its foundation, its object and its effects.

The object of Hope is God Himself, our eternal beatitude. We do not, or should not, hope for heaven, but for God, that we may possess Him eternally, and so attain to the happiness for which the soul was made. That happiness is heaven, but heaven is not desirable as an end in itself; our beatitude is not heaven but God, and if we attain to Him we shall attain to the joy of heaven and the family of the saints, for He is that Joy.

The desire to be happy in God is an interested desire, but it is a supernatural and a right one, for that is the end for which we were created, and it is that desire which Hope inflames in the soul. Hope then sets the course of the soul towards God, its eternal beatitude, and the joy of eternal union with Him.

Everyone naturally desires happiness, and the world seeks it in various ways and by many means. The craze for pleasure and amusement which is so obvious in every direction is the attempt of human beings to find satisfaction. Pleasure and amusement fail to produce happiness because, even when innocent, they are of themselves incomplete and transitory. They may produce a temporary sense of well-being, they may satisfy body, mind, or emotions separately or in combination, but earthly goods can never satisfy the spirit of man, for that was made in the image of God and can be satisfied by God alone, and can never be happy with a partial and transitory good. The desire for God is the fundamental desire of the soul. The virtue of Hope directs that desire towards its true end; it keeps before the soul the fact that union with the God Whom it knows by Faith is the end for which it was created, and is attainable through the merits of Christ; that the joy of heaven is not a pious imagination, but a literal certainty to the faithful soul.

Hope, then, settles the soul on God, our eternal beatitude and only true happiness, and directs the will towards its true end, which is the fulfilment of His will. Heaven is realised as the end towards which all our earthly life should be tending if it is to have any value at all, and this realisation gives a purpose and meaning to life which otherwise it could not have, and shows earthly and transitory goods in their true proportions. The effect of Hope is to produce in the will a fruitful and purposeful activity directed towards the attainment of God as our eternal and perfect joy; it is the source of that energy, courage and endurance without which advance and perseverance in the spiritual life are impossible. Faith sees God, Hope desires and seeks Him and renders practical the vision of God as our supreme good.

Like Faith, Hope is a virtue infused into the soul by God Himself, and its character alters considerably as the soul advances in the spiritual life and co-operates more and more with the divine action. The natural virtue of hope, as we have already remarked, depends to a great extent upon temperament; there are some people who are naturally hopeful and cheerful, and others who are quite the reverse, as well as a host of people who alternate between the two extremes. The supernatural virtue, on the other hand, is not temperamental, but an effect of Baptism, and therefore common to all Christian souls; but it may grow or decrease in any individual according as it is used or neglected. We must therefore consider the conditions under which the soul may advance in it, adopting the same classification of souls as in the previous section.

I. *Beginners.* Advance in Hope depends on the increase of depth and fruitfulness of the virtue. It is deepened by the increasing knowledge which the soul gains of its divine Object, it is therefore of the greatest importance that the soul should persevere in meditation, and in that particularly of the power, goodness and promises of God. If the soul allows itself to become detached from that degree of union with God to which it has attained, be it great or small, it inevitably falls away from Hope; if, on the other hand, it is beginning to catch a glimpse of God's eternal loveliness, if it is beginning to realise something of His love and care and eternal intention for it, its hold upon God and the eternal verities becomes surer, and Hope is deepened.

Priests cannot be too careful in training their people to persevere in the practice of mental prayer up to the limit of their capacity, and spiritual beginners should be most carefully instructed and observed. More advanced souls may be trusted to some extent to look after themselves, but beginners need training and encouragement in that way of mental prayer which is best for them, realising that growth in mental prayer means growth in the virtues.

The fruitfulness of Hope is gained by constant and faithful collaboration of the will with the means which God provides for our sanctification. The soul which neglects prayer and the sacraments, either from slackness or from the desire for the waters of Abana and Pharpar, must expect to become the victim of despair; but the soul which humbly perseveres in faithful use of the means of grace, and desires above all things that God's will may be done, will certainly be the child of Hope, and by the mercy of God attain in the end to that Joy towards which Hope tends.

Beginners in the spiritual life are apt to fall from Hope by two opposite faults: *presumption*, and *despair*, the one being the excess and the other the defect of hope on the natural plane.[1]

*Presumption* usually affects souls to whom religion is as yet easy and the horror of sin unrecognised. Such souls commonly regard themselves with some satisfaction as the elect, or truly spiritual people, who, either on their own merits and by their own efforts or by the certain grace of God, are quite sure of heaven; this leads to a subtle form of spiritual pride and a superior neglect of the sacraments as accidental or unnecessary.

Such an unpleasant state of mind is best corrected by the consideration that although eternal beatitude is certain, one's own attainment thereto is not, and that heaven must be won by penitence, mortification, growth in virtue and, above all, patient prayer and use of the sacraments.

*Despair* is produced by self-absorption, and the soul so affected cannot see the wood for the trees of its own scruples. It becomes obsessed with its own falls into sin and the sense of failure, and sometimes gives up all effort and sinks into a state of chronic spiritual misery. Frequently, especially among adolescents, sins against purity produce violent despair, which needs very careful handling.

Introspection should be guarded against as much as possible with souls of this kind. Self-examination must be thorough, but brief,[2] and the soul must be dissuaded so far as possible from self-contemplation. Instead of dwelling on its past sins, it should concentrate on what God wills it to do at the moment, and set itself simply, in union with grace, to accomplish it. Its gaze should be directed away from sin to virtue, away from self to God, Who is its Hope, with continual meditation on His love and power. Thanksgiving should be encouraged.

II. *Advancing Souls.* God is their Joy, and here and now their life is one with His life and is deepening into continuous companionship with Him; earthly life is for them the obscure beginning of the life of heaven; knowing and living in communion with God their eternal good, Hope has for them deepened into partial realisation and complete confidence.

As the soul advances, the essential difference between the

---

[1] " Virtue is a middle state between two faulty ones, in the way of excess on the one side and of defect on the other: and it is so, moreover, because the faulty states on one side fall short of, and those on the other exceed, what is right, both in the case of the feelings and the actions; but Virtue finds, and when found adopts, the mean." (Aristotle, *Eth. Nic.* II. vi.)      [2] cf. pp. 307*ff. infra.*

E

spiritual life on earth and in heaven diminishes.  A difference remains, because the life with God here is obscure and continually damaged by sin, whereas in heaven that life will be perfect and complete; but their life becomes more and more a heavenly life on earth; they have not to hope for an essentially other life, but for grace to enable them to be faithful that they may not lose that life which has already begun; in union with their Divine Lover, they await with confidence His call.

Hope when it has thus deepened produces an entirely new outlook on the earthly life.  It is seen consistently as a pilgrimage towards the heavenly country, and the suffering which it brings to the soul is seen to be incidental to its advance, and a means whereby it may be purified; while the incidental pleasures, the acquisition of which holds such a central place in the aspirations of most people, are seen in their true light, and found to be fundamentally unsatisfying, however delightful they may be when rightly used.

The soul that thus hopes in God refuses to be disquieted and disturbed by the power of evil in this world.  It knows the power of the Devil from experience and observation, but it refuses to get that knowledge out of scale by limiting its view to the life which is bounded by the grave.  It knows that over all God reigns, and that " the devil is come down having great wrath, because he knoweth that he hath but a short time." [1] This produces an essentially hopeful attitude towards the world which is impossible to a non-supernatural life.  It is not a shallow optimism which refuses to look facts in the face, but Hope which realises all facts, even the blackest, upon the background of the will of God.

The Hope of the advancing soul is, further, a defence against scruples and all that fussing about oneself which is so common among the devout.  Based on humility and penitence, Hope keeps the soul steady and undisquieted in view of its own sinfulness, for all ultimate issues are thrown into the will of God.

So in those times when the spiritual outlook is dark and heavy, times of dryness and absence of sensible devotion, when days and weeks pass with none of the happy experiences which once were realised; it is then that Hope is truly the anchor of the soul, keeping it steadfast when without it there might be despair, and enabling it to hold fast to God even though He hide Himself.

[1] Rev. xii. 12.

Hope then in this degree is a state of real joy and peace, often overshadowed, but nevertheless tranquil, and the life of such hoping souls is simple and right because always directed towards its true end. It remains for them to pray for final perseverance and a good death.

III. *The Perfect.* These souls attain to a still deeper level of Hope in complete abandonment to the will of God.

### III. CHARITY

Charity is the last and greatest of the Theological Virtues, the very spirit of the Christian religion, containing in itself all other virtues, and for this reason it is well to keep for it the ancient technical name of Charity, rather than the wider one of Love. The true Christian is in love with God, loving his neighbour in Him, but his love is Charity.

The contemporary use of the word Charity is an instance of the thoughtless prostitution of noble words which is so common amongst us. If I give a penny to a match-seller in the street or a similar alms to an organ-grinder for the purpose of securing his removal to the next street, I am said to be dispensing " charity," and, as is well known, a society formed for the purpose of co-ordinating voluntary relief has taken to itself the name of the Charity Organisation Society. It is clear that this modern charity is quite different from the Theological Virtue which we are discussing—it is, indeed, equivalent to alms-giving, and takes no cognizance of the motive from which the alms are distributed. It would appear at first sight that, this being so, it would be wiser for us to leave this degraded word alone and substitute for it the warmer one of Love, as has been done by the translators of the Revised Version, but here again we are in a difficulty, for Love is too wide a term for our purpose, and its use would introduce complications we should be wise to avoid. "Love" translates ἔρως, *amor;* φιλία, *amicitia;* στοργή, *benevolentia* and, sometimes, *dilectio;* it is therefore useless for our purpose, for ἀγάπη, *caritas* is none of these things. We shall therefore keep the term Charity to denote the Theological Virtue, as distinct from the natural emotion of Love, and endeavour to make the distinction as clear as possible as we proceed, resolutely banishing from our minds the modern philanthropic travesty of a sublime theological term.

Before passing on to our main theme it will be well to give some attention to Love.   It is difficult to know how to describe this phenomenon, for it appears in diverse forms at all levels of psychic life, and psychologists are by no means agreed as to their classification of it.   It has its roots in instinct, appears frequently as an emotion and gains its full stature as a sentiment.[1]

It is unnecessary for our purpose to trace the phenomenon of Love through all its stages and metamorphoses, it is sufficient to note that its origin is instinctive and that it is in itself emotive, an impulse towards a desirable object.   This impulse may be either sensible or rational or both.   Its end is union or possession, either physical or mental or both, and it demands a certain sympathy between its subject and object.

This natural sentiment is regulated, re-directed and elevated by Charity, but Charity is quite distinct from it.   The origin of Love is natural instinct, the origin of Charity is grace working upon the instinct and supernaturalising it.   The motive of Love is the possession of a created good, while that of Charity is self-oblation to God.   The object of Charity is the love of God for Himself and of creatures as the reflection of His infinite Being.   Charity is a virtue, not a sentiment in either the psychological or popular sense of the word, and it is dependent upon the free acts of the will, not on those of the emotions.   It is important to remember this distinction, because many people on being told that Love is the core of religion instantly imagine that religion is merely emotional sentimentality;   and many people in the practice of their religion become sentimental through a confusion of the supernatural virtue of Charity with the natural sentiment of Love.

The precept to love God is to be found deep in the heart of Judaism:   " Hear, O Israel:   the LORD our God is one LORD: and thou shalt love the LORD thy God with all thine heart, and with all thy soul, and with all thy might," [2] is the text of the whole book of Deuteronomy, and our Lord deliberately endorsed that precept.[3]   God has, then, quite definitely com-

---

[1] *Instincts* are " certain innate or inherited tendencies which are the essential springs or motive powers of all thought and action, whether individual or collective, and are the bases from which the character and will of individuals and of nations are gradually developed under the guidance of the intellectual faculties."   An *emotion* is the affective aspect of " the instinctive mental process that results from the excitement of any instinct."   A *sentiment* is " an organised system of emotional tendencies."   McDougall, *Social Psychology*, pp. 17, 40, 105.
[2] Deut. vi. 4–5.          [3] Matt. xxii. 37; Mark xii. 29–30; Luke x. 27–8.

manded us to love Him; not to think about Him, or argue
about Him, but to love Him. Charity, not thought, is the
fundamental activity of the Christian.

The precept to love God is preceded in the passage just quoted
by the solemn assertion of His Being. " Hear, O Israel: the
LORD our God is one LORD." Charity is the love of God as
He is in Himself in all the fullness of His Being. One is usually
led to the love of God by the realisation of one or other of His
attributes, but if we would love Him rightly it must be not
simply on account of that attribute, but for and in Himself.

Charity is also the love of God above all created things. The
second commandment with its solemn asseveration, " I, the
LORD thy God, am a jealous God," [1] drives this truth in upon
us. The love of creatures and the love of self are secondary
considerations which only find their right place in subordination
to the love of God.

Further, Charity requires the concentration of all the powers
of the soul upon this one point. " Thou shalt love the LORD
thy God with all thy heart, and with all thy soul, and with all
thy might."

The words used here in the Hebrew are *lēbhābh, nephesh,
m'ōdh,* " heart," " soul," " strength," but it is well to remember
that the Hebrew localisation of the powers of the soul was
different from that which has become traditional among us.
The Jew of the Bible thought with his heart and loved with his
bowels,[2] consequently LXX rightly translates *lēbhābh* here by
διάνοια, " understanding." The gospels give a conflate reading
of both διάνοια and καρδία, while *rachămim,* σπλάγχνα, " bowels,"
finds no place here in either Hebrew or Greek. This is to be
expected, as the love of the " bowels " is the compassionate
love of a mother for her child, but due consideration of these
facts makes it clear that Holy Scripture lends no countenance
to any sentimental view of Charity.

*Nephesh,* ψυχή, is the spiritual part of man, that in him which
is made in the image of God,[3] but it is also the seat of the emotions,
which are thus viewed as God-given rather than merely instinctive and so find their proper place in the hierarchy of Charity.

---

[1] Deut. v. 8-10.

[2] cf. Exod. xxxv. 35; Deut. xxix. 4; Judges v. 5; I Kings iii. 9; Ps. xiv.
1; Prov. xvi. 9; Matt. xv. 18; Luke ii. 19; Rom. x. 10; Phil. i. 8; Col.
iii. 12; also derivation of σπλαγχνίζομαι, Matt. ix. 36.

[3] Gen. ii. 7, καὶ ἐγένετο ὁ ἄνθρωπος εἰς ψυχὴν ζῶσαν. LXX.

*M'ōdh,* δυνάμις, ἰσχύς, "strength," stands for the whole soul driven by the will. It is clear, then, that the Charity which we are commanded to give to God is the action of the whole personality.

The precept is very wide—no limits are to be set to Charity, "the measure of loving God is to love without measure." [1] There should, then, be in the soul the constant desire to love God more and better, and self less.

S. Bernard distinguishes four degrees of love or, perhaps, one of love and three of Charity; these are best expounded in his own words:—

" Because we are carnal and born from the concupiscence of the flesh, it must needs be that our desire, or love, begins from the flesh; and if it is directed by right order, advancing by its several degrees under guidance of grace, it will at last be consummated by spirit. . . . First, then, man loves himself for his own sake; he is flesh forsooth, and can have no taste for aught beyond himself. And when he sees that he cannot subsist of himself, he begins by faith to seek God as necessary to him, and to love Him. Thus he loves God in the second degree, but for his own sake, not for Himself. But when, by occasion of his own necessity, he has begun to worship and approach Him, by meditation, reading, prayer, obedience; by a certain familiarity of this kind, little by little and gradually, God becomes known and consequently grows sweet; and thus having tasted how sweet is the Lord, he passes on to the third degree, so that he loves God, not now for his own sake but for Himself. Assuredly the abiding is long in this degree; and I know not if the fourth is perfectly attained by any man in this life, so that, that is, a man love himself only for the love of God. Let those, if any, who have experienced, tell us; to me, I confess, it seems impossible. But it will be beyond question, when the good and faithful servant is brought into the joy of his Lord, and inebriated with the plenty of the house of God. For, in a certain wondrous fashion oblivious of himself, and as it were utterly abandoning himself, he will wholly pass on into God; and henceforth, joined to the Lord, will be one spirit with Him." [2]

Thus we see the ladder of Charity set up from earth to heaven.

[1] S. Bernard, *De diligendo Deo,* cap. vi.    [2] *op. cit.* cap. xv.

Charity is the root of all virtues, and is thus itself the fulfilling of the law. As it grows in the soul it becomes more and more the motive power of all its acts, which, being thus done for love of God, are right and virtuous.

Charity unifies the whole soul; the mind loves to think of God, the will loves to submit to His will, the heart, loving Him above all things, subordinates all other affections to the love of Him, and the whole complex of energies of the soul functions rightly because all is done for God. We are speaking here, of course, of that Charity which has had her perfect work, the Charity of the saints, but every Christian should desire and strive after such love of God, however conscious he may be of his own failures in this regard. "For not what thou art, nor what thou hast been, doth God regard with his merciful eyes; but what thou wouldst be." [1] The patient and humble love of God transforms the soul and the life by uniting all to God. There is, indeed, no other way by which we may be united to Him than the way of Charity, and eternal blessedness, heaven, is none other than perfect union with Him.

One of the first effects of Charity is a new knowledge of God. The soul that loves him can say with Job, "I have heard of thee by the hearing of the ear: but now mine eye seeth thee." [2] It has tasted and seen that the Lord is good not only in his ways, but in Himself. Gradually it enters into a new and experimental knowledge of God, and a friendship with God springs up which is the most wonderful thing within the experience of man.

This loving knowledge of God increases the soul's energy for good. It may see little apparent result from its efforts to do good, but it gradually ceases to care about results; the one thing that matters is that the will of God be done by it from moment to moment, and so all its energies turn this way instead of being scattered about over a great number of secondary activities. All its energies and itself being turned towards their true end, the soul experiences a joy and peace which "passeth all understanding." "The noble love of Jesus perfectly printed in the soul maketh a man to do great things, and stirreth him always to desire perfection, growing more and more in grace and goodness." [3]

---

[1] *The Cloud of Unknowing*, cap. lxxv.
[2] Job xlii. 5.      [3] *de Imit. Xti.* III. **v.**

Love (*amor*) is essentially possessive and self-centred. It is true that in its higher manifestations (*dilectio*) this possessiveness becomes tempered with a large degree of self-sacrifice, and love is recognised as being ideally giving and not getting, nevertheless, both subject and object being human, possessiveness is never wholly eliminated. Charity, on the other hand, is founded on sacrifice. As soon as the soul begins to realise the infinite perfection of God, it realises also that He alone matters, and that the only love it can possibly render to Him is the love of self-oblation and, if it is generous, it desires to pour itself out in loving service and constant sacrifice.

The vision of sacrificing love is one which is frequently granted to generous souls in childhood or adolescence, and it is a vision which they can realise by the grace of God if they are faithful, but it is not attained all at once; the hardly won virtues of humility, self-control and self-forgetfulness have to be attained, the soul has to learn, often with difficulty, that Charity loves God for Himself, and not for His gifts, and often the dark descends and the vision is well-nigh blotted out; nevertheless the " generous love " of Calvary is always calling to the generosity of the loving soul and keeping it steadfast in the austerity of the spiritual life.

I. *Beginners.* There is but one foundation, as there is but one end of Charity, and that is God Himself, and souls should be trained from the beginning quite simply to realise God and love Him. We teach our children the Catechism and a good deal of assorted knowledge *about* God, but how much do we teach them to know, love and, therefore, to serve Him? Yet that is the end for which we were all created, and if it were really made the foundation and bed-rock of all religious training, as it should be, there would be fewer unsatisfactory and difficult Christians about. From the beginning, then, souls should be trained to contemplate the eternal being of God.

It may be objected that such contemplation belongs properly to a higher stage in the spiritual life, and, in a developed sense, it does; but children are capable of far more contemplation of this simple sort than we sometimes think, and many older people only need a little help to gain it. Let such souls meditate upon and frequently use Faber's beautiful hymn " My God, how wonderful Thou art," and such portions of Scripture as the Vision of Isaiah, and God will certainly draw their hearts towards Himself.

The first effect of the Vision of God upon Isaiah was the realisation of his own sin, so the soul that would grow in Charity must learn to hate and avoid sin and to grow in penitence. Penitence makes the soul see itself in its true condition as a sinner and causes it to realise afresh the amazing love of God for it, so that, seeing sin as it is, it comes to hate it and separate itself from it. Simultaneously penitence opens the heart to God and reconciles the soul with Him.

Along with the love of penitence there goes the love of the divine Will. The soul loves to do the will of God because it is His. God's commands are not an unwelcome imposition, but the way in which the soul may please Him, and so the soul gladly and lovingly submits itself to them and to the Church, which is the Bride of Christ, that so it may show its love for Him.

II. *Advancing Souls.* As the spiritual life advances, the knowledge of God that comes by Charity deepens, and the friendship between the soul and God becomes a settled fact which no longer has to be stirred up by acts, it is a fact which is the guiding and key fact of all their living. The soul rejoices in the goodness, beauty and infinite perfection of God, and finds its whole joy in bringing forth something of that perfection. By love it enters deeply into and shares the Sacred Passion by a true συμπάθεια. Instead of avoiding suffering, it accepts and eventually welcomes it as the one means whereby it may be united with Jesus crucified, the one thing of its own which it may offer Him and which, being offered, may become part of His atoning pain. This love leads on to an earnest desire for the accomplishment of the will of God by all creation, which desire is itself a sacrificial pain, for the soul in this degree of Charity feels in the depths of its being every insult which the sin or thoughtlessness of man offers to the Sacred Heart. It is by such souls that the world is converted, for their one desire is that God may be glorified by all His creatures and that every man may find his way home to the Heart of God. This degree of Charity expresses itself in constant love of conformity to the will of God. As the soul advances in this way self matters less and less and God more and more, so that finally it does not trouble about its own will, which is a thing of no moment, but gives itself constantly to the will of the Beloved; and it makes its own the great words of S. Ignatius that " we on our part should not wish for health rather than sickness, for riches rather than poverty, for honour rather than ignominy, for a long life rather than a short life, and so in all other matters, solely desiring and choosing those things which may better lead us to the end for which we were created." [1]

III. *The Perfect.* We have been treating of high things—the love of the friends of God for the Beloved, a good deal of which is " far above out of our sight "; what shall we say, then, of the love of these souls who are living in the Unitive Way? There is but one answer and that S. Bernard's:

> " Nec lingua potest dicere,
>     nec littera exprimere;
>     expertus novit credere,
>     quid sit Iesum diligere."

Still, even if the love of the perfect is unimaginable and that of advanced souls something to which we have not yet attained, in our best moments we realise that, poor though our love of God may be, the glorious virtue of Charity is in us by the grace of God, so that by faithful self-oblation the humblest lover of God may be led to the heights of heaven.

The precept of Charity is a double one, and the second commandment of Jesus is, " Thou shalt love thy neighbour as thyself," [2] which also is a quotation of the Law given by God to the Jews.[3]

Charity towards God and Charity towards one's neighbour are indissolubly bound together, and are indeed one thing, and not two, for Charity towards one's neighbour is the fruit of Charity towards God. Philanthropy is a great thing and has produced wonderful results, but it is not Christian. The Saints who have done most for their fellow-men did not set out to love man for his own sake, but because they were filled with the love of God. Christian Charity towards man is the measure of a soul's Charity towards God, but it is not independent of it. S. John's teaching is quite clear on this point: " We know that we have passed from death unto life, because we love the brethren. . . . Whoso hath this world's good, and seeth his brother have need, and shutteth up his bowels of compassion from him, how dwelleth the love of God in him? . . . If a man say, I love God, and hateth his brother, he is a liar: for he that loveth

---

[1] *Spiritual Exercises*, " The Foundation."
[2] Matt. xxii. 39; Mark xii. 31; Luke x. 27.    [3] Lev. xix. 18.

not his brother whom he hath seen, how can he love God whom
he hath not seen? And this commandment have we from him,
That he who loveth God love his brother also." [1]

One may love a man because he is personally sympathetic
or attractive to oneself, one may pity him because he is in need
or sorrow, and that is much, but it is not Christian Charity.
By Charity we love our neighbour in God and God in him,
and we love him whether he is personally attractive to us or not,
whether he be needy or self-sufficient, just because he is the
child of God. Such Charity does not proceed from natural
kindliness of heart, but is a supernatural thing, an Infused
Virtue.

None of those who heard it will ever forget Bishop Frank
Weston's wonderful appeal for Charity at the end of the Anglo-
Catholic Congress of 1923. "You must walk with Christ,"
he said, " mystically present in you, through the streets of this
country, and find the same Christ in the people of your cities
and villages. . . . It is folly, it is madness to suppose that you
can worship Jesus in the sacrament and Jesus on the throne of
glory, when you are sweating Him in the bodies and souls of
His children. . . . Go out into the highways and hedges, and
look for Jesus in the ragged and the naked, in the oppressed
and the sweated, in those who have lost hope, and in those who
are struggling to make good. Look for Jesus in them; and
when you have found Him gird yourself with the towel of fellowship and wash His Feet in the persons of His brethren."

That is a glorious hymn of Charity, but we must go a step
further still, and find Jesus not only in the poor and struggling,
but in every man, woman and child in the world, and pour out
upon them our Charity, which is not ours, but His.

I. *Beginners.* In this matter the vast majority of Christians
are beginners, and almost all of us have faults, and serious ones,
which must be rooted out before Charity can have its perfect
work, the chief among which is self-love.

Our Lord has commanded us to love our neighbour as ourselves. It is easy enough, too easy, to love oneself and claim
for oneself what one calls one's rights, but it is not so easy practically to concede to others just those same rights. Yet much
of our lack of Charity is due simply to the fact that we allow
people to irritate us because we allow our natural antipathies

---

[1] I John iii. 14, 17; iv. 20, 21.

full play and refuse to realise that they have as much right to consideration as we have ourselves.  Generous self-effacement is necessary if we are to have Charity one with another.

Rash, hasty and unbalanced judgments with imputation of uncertain motives are another frequent source of loss of Charity.  If we dislike a person very much, there is nothing that that person can say or do that is right, and we are perpetually on the look-out for faults, simply because we allow ourselves to be swayed by our instinctive self-love.

Self-assertion and rash judgment are alone fruitful sources of dispute and rivalry in which " all seek their own, not the things which are Jesus Christ's." [1]  Another sin against Charity which requires the closest watching is that of scandal in all its forms.  There is evil-speaking which is definitely untrue, and that should be impossible even to the tyro in the spiritual life; there is also evil-speaking which is half-true, which is extremely dangerous and not at all uncommon; there is evil-speaking which is true, but evil, because it is intended to damage the reputation of the person spoken about, or, at best, unnecessary; and besides all this there is that gossip, ῥήματα ἀργά, of which our Lord has solemnly warned us we must give account on the Day of Judgment, as well as those *jeux d'esprit* which, though sometimes witty, often cause pain to their subject, which is none the less for being hidden.

Obedience to this second part of the divine precept demands the greatest care in the discipline of the judgment and tongue and, besides that, great generosity in the pardon of real injuries. It is probably true that most people imagine, or at least exaggerate, two-thirds of the injuries which they think to be inflicted upon them by their neighbours, but even when the injury is real and unmistakable, the Christian must seek to forgive the agent of it.  The classical instance of such forgiveness is, of course, S. Stephen, but he does not stand alone in this, it is constantly to be found in the lives of the Saints; and anyone who, for love of Jesus, would be one with Him in His Passion should follow Him in the acceptance of injury, realising the force, in his own case, of the words of the dying Robber, " we indeed justly."

Above all, souls must learn to love supernaturally and to give themselves generously to their fellow-men because they love

[1] Phil. ii. 21.

God. Natural attraction and repulsion will always have their effect, but that effect can be very largely overcome by the deliberate practice of divine Charity; one may not like a person, but, nevertheless, one can and should seek to love him, giving oneself generously to be Christ to him.

II. *Advancing souls*, who are growing in union with the Divine Master, will strive to bring forth in themselves the dispositions of Jesus Himself, and to them Charity is the very breath of life. They need to be reminded that the command to love one another is His, directly and deliberately given to them; they should take to themselves and write upon their hearts His words: " A new commandment I give unto you, That ye love one another; as I have loved you, that ye also love one another." [1]

Such Charity is the very love of God and, like His grace, it must be *prevenient*. We must not wait to be loved or attracted before we ourselves love. " I say unto you," our Lord has said with all possible emphasis, " love your enemies, bless them that curse you, do good to them that hate you, and pray for them which despitefully use you, and persecute you; that ye may be the children of your Father which is in heaven." [2] Active love must be the habitual disposition of the Christian towards his neighbour, a love which is prevenient and God-giving.

True Charity is also *compassionate*. Loving God, the Christian feels the pain of humanity as no one else can, and with Jesus he suffers with those who suffer. There must be nothing detached, no *de haut en bas* feeling, about his Charity; he suffers with those who suffer because he is one with Jesus, Who suffers in them, and so he gives himself to the third note of Charity, which is *generosity*. The parable of the Good Samaritan, which our Lord has given us as an example, is a parable of generous love. The Samaritan might so easily have said that an injured Jew was none of his business and that he had his own work to do, and so had no time to take him to an inn and take care of him; but he did none of these things—he gave himself wholly to the loving healing of the pain of the world. This is the business of all who love Jesus, not only of priests and missionaries, and such love alone will bring the world to the feet of Jesus.

III. *To the Perfect* divine Charity is the devouring passion of their whole being, and life and self are swallowed up in it.

---

[1] John xiii. 34.        [2] Matt. v. 44–5.

## CHAPTER V

# THE CARDINAL VIRTUES

*Gracious and righteous is the Lord : therefore will he teach sinners in the way. Them that are meek shall he guide in judgment : and such as are gentle, them shall he learn his way* (Ps. xxv. 7–8).

THE Cardinal Virtues are commonly reckoned as " infused " and, indeed, they are such, but they differ considerably from the Infused Virtues *par excellence* of Faith, Hope and Charity.

The Theological Virtues are specifically Christian, the fruit of the Incarnation and Atonement and the result of the incorporation into Jesus Christ which the soul undergoes at Baptism. They do not introduce new faculties into the soul, but act upon natural faculties already in existence, raising them by grace above their natural limitations and directing them towards God, their true end, so that the soul in grace is by the sacraments and prayer raised above its natural limitations and united with the life of God through the practice of Faith, Hope and Charity.

How far the Cardinal Virtues are specifically Christian may seem to be debatable. As has been already remarked, they were discovered by the Greek philosophers among the furniture of the human mind, and may therefore be said not to be specifically Christian at all, but such a statement would appear to be far too sweeping. It is necessary for us constantly to emphasise the distinction between natural and supernatural, but we must be on our guard against a tendency to attribute the natural virtues to a power of nature virtually distinct from God, and the supernatural alone to divine agency. It may truly be said that the Cardinal Virtues are gifts of God infused on the natural plane, and at that level they are not specifically Christian, but broadly human. On that plane, too, they are not only capable of grave deflection from the *summum bonum*, but it is also at least open to doubt whether they ever have attained the full height of the theory of Aristotle or Cicero on this level. Socrates as a philosopher and Marcus Aurelius as an administrator certainly attained great heights in the life of the natural virtues, so much so that in them these virtues might perhaps be called preternatural, but such attainment was rare and not always rightly directed; moreover, the direction of the virtuous life being, at this level, human, there is no check on the *corruptio optimi pessima* resulting from ignorance or prejudice.

On the supernatural level the Cardinal Virtues are definitely Christian, not in the sense of being a new infusion, but as being the completion and supernaturalisation of the original infusion by grace, and, through the operation of the Theological Virtues, directing their exercise towards the only true and right end, which is God Himself. We view them, therefore, in combination with the Theological Virtues, forming with them a supernatural complex which, if freely responded to, will certainly produce sanctity, not merely in an aristocracy of " philosophic " souls, but in the humblest child of God.

It is a great mistake, but none the less one that is frequently made, to relegate the Cardinal Virtues to the sphere of Ethics, an abstract and popularly unknown branch of philosophy, and to depreciate them accordingly. They are, or should be, the backbone of the Christian character, fundamental qualities of the true manliness of the soul united to the perfect Humanity of Christ; and that pusillanimity which one has such frequent cause to lament among Christians is not seldom due to lack of instruction in their nature and exercise.

The complete discussion of these virtues would find its place in a treatise on Moral Theology, consequently we shall not attempt one here, but content ourselves with some consideration of them from the point of view of Christian asceticism. But it may not be altogether inopportune to remark here that the great value of the study of Moral Theology to the parish priest is not so much the understanding of how to deal with certain kinds of sin, though that in itself is of great importance, as the understanding of the integration of the various acquired virtues and their dependence upon the infused Cardinal Virtues.

The Cardinal, in conjunction with the Theological, Virtues build up the Christian character and regulate our action with regard to our fellow-men and ourselves. They are four in number: *Justice*, which governs our conduct towards others; *Temperance* and *Fortitude*, which concern ourselves; and *Prudence*, which governs the other three.

## I. Justice

In our modern use of it the word Justice has an exclusively forensic connotation which needs enlarging if we are fully to understand the meaning of its use to describe this virtue. The corresponding adjective has a wider meaning, but even so the just man may be no more than one who holds the balance level between *pro* and *con*, with no necessary reference to absolute rightness.

Fundamentally, Justice is the God-given love of right, which is in the last resort the will of God as expressed in the constitution of the universe and the end for which it is created. This is the fundamental meaning of that δικαιοσύνη of which not only Plato and Aristotle, but also S. Paul, S. John, S. Peter and S. James speak, and which our Lord bids us " hunger and thirst after." Δικαιοσύνη becomes in Latin *iustitia*, a word having a predominantly legal connotation that has been kept as " justice " in the English of the Douai Version. The translators of the Authorised Version attempted to reduce the legal and increase the moral connotation of the word by reading " righteousness " instead of " justice " in all cases, a rendering which is habitual to us to-day.

" Righteousness " is a good word, and, rightly understood, expresses well the fundamental meaning of δικαιοσύνη, but it is a misfortune that we have divorced it completely from the sense of " justice." There is too great an idea of freedom in the popular conception of " righteousness." It may truly be given or withheld, and, like all virtues, is valueless unless freely willed ; nevertheless it is not an act of grace on the part of the creature, but a debt which is due from him to his Creator, Whose will is expressed in the revealed Law.

The " justice " of the Jew and his insistence upon the paramount importance of the Law were not wrong in themselves and may be paralleled in Buddhism and Mohammedanism. It became wrong when the Law was no longer regarded as the unfolding of God's will and its moral implications were lost in a wilderness of interpretational subtleties, and legalism took the place of devotion to the all-holy will of God.

The love of right is, as we have said, the characteristic of this virtue, whether we regard it as " justice " or as " righteousness," and the just or righteous man wills to give to all their rights according to the will of God.

Towards God the virtue of Justice finds its expression in Worship. This is the primitive human reaction to any true apprehension of the divine; it is also the fundamental action of the most spiritual religion, because it is the fulfilment by the creature of his creaturely duty towards his Creator.

Once God is realised as God, worship is seen to be His right, and this conception lies at the root of true religion, expressed inwardly in adoration and outwardly in sacrifice and worship. Charity will, indeed, outstrip Justice here. The man who worships merely because he conceives it to be his duty because of the paramount rights of his Creator, has certainly not got very far in the practice of Christianity, but he has got somewhere, and this conception of duty is vital to true religion; and, inflamed by Charity, informed by Faith and idealised by Hope, it will be the directing force of his whole life Godward.

Towards man, Justice is the glad and constant rendering to others of their rights. The insistence upon one's own rights and the demand for freedom of self-expression is a common enough vice among Christians as well as others, the consistent recognition of the rights of other people is somewhat less general; nevertheless, there can hardly be a right practice of the Christian religion without it. It is a thorough, steady-going virtue, not exciting, but eminently necessary if the petition " Thy Kingdom come " is to have any meaning. It does not necessarily concern itself with public meetings or politics, but governs quietly all a man's relationships with his neighbours in the widest sense of that elastic term. Towards superiors it shows itself in respect and obedience, towards the unfortunate in compassion, towards the difficult in understanding, towards enemies in forgiveness, and in general in that level gentleness which is the mark of the Christian gentleman.

It is the virtue of order, for it seeks to restore to our topsy-turvy civilisation the order of God, and for the same reason it is the virtue of peace.

Justice is the negation of selfishness, for it is essentially other-regarding, but it is not merely other-regarding. It differs from philanthropy or social righteousness in caring for the rights of men not because they are the rights of men, but because they are the will of God for them. It desires that the will of God be

F

done for each because it is the will of God, and it causes the just man to fulfil the will of God for each in the daily relationships of life.  Justice produces in the soul ordinate affection (of which we shall have something to say later), broad-mindedness in its true sense and essential magnanimity.  The just man can never be small-minded or habitually bad tempered.  Most of the blame for the latter sin is commonly thrown upon that very convenient but elusive thing " temperament ";  and  " temperament," while admitted to be an evil, is regarded as a " necessary evil," whatever that may be.  In most cases, for " temperament " read " selfishness," and you find the true evil.  The just man cares for God and His will first, his neighbour in God second and himself last, and " temperament " or selfishness is seen to be but an intrusive element in a world which the Justice of God made right.

## II. Temperance

This is a virtue which has suffered much from popular perversion; it is a much bigger and more fundamental thing than is generally supposed, for it is only incidentally concerned with moderation in the use of alcohol, and not at all with abstinence therefrom.

S. Paul bids us regard the Christian as an athlete in  training, and this conception underlies the whole theory of asceticism; no virtue is more necessary to an athlete in training than that of Temperance; food, drink, tobacco, exercise, rest and a host of other things have to be subjected to a rigorous rule and used rightly, while excess in any of them must be avoided; indeed, as the Apostle says, " every man that striveth for the mastery is temperate in all things." [1]

The first purpose of this virtue is the keeping of the body in its right place, which is a matter of primary importance: " I keep under my body," says the Apostle, " and bring it into subjection: lest that by any means, when I have preached to others, I myself should be a castaway." [2]  Christian asceticism is not directed towards the destruction of the body, but its subjection to the Spirit, and this involves the careful regulation of the pleasures of sense.  These pleasures are of two kinds:  sinful and legitimate;  with the former the virtue of Temperance is

---

[1] I Cor. ix. 25.                    [2] I Cor. ix. 27.

not concerned, they have to be resisted, not used; it is concerned with the right use of legitimate sensible pleasures. It is not right to refuse to eat because there is a sin of gluttony, but it is necessary to use food temperately, whether one is tempted to gluttony or not. Temperance is, then, the right and ordered use of created things. This is such an important matter that S. Ignatius regards it as part of the foundation upon which the spiritual life is built; "Man," he says, "ought to make use of (created things) just so far as they help him to attain his end (*i.e.* the end for which God created him) and he ought to withdraw himself from them just so far as they hinder him." [1] That use and that withdrawal are of great importance and may, at first sight, appear to be regulated by the will of man alone: the action of the will is indeed essential, but guided by the unenlightened understanding alone it would and does make many mistakes. The right use of created things is inspired and guided by the Holy Ghost in the virtue of Temperance.

The purpose of the virtue is to enable man to attain the end for which he was created—that is to say, it is directed towards the fulfilment of the will of God, not simply towards the production of a strong ego, and therein lies the difference between the Christian and the pagan virtue; pagan Temperance is the austere man striving towards self-mastery, Christian Temperance is God bringing order into the Christian character. The aim of the Christian virtue is not to produce self-control but divine control, by it the spirit brings the body into subjection for God and in the power of God.

It is unnecessary to expound the details of the practice of this virtue here; in the struggle against sin it is active at every point, as will doubtless appear when we come to treat more fully of that struggle; but it will be well here to insist upon the fact that it is an Infused Virtue. The realisation of this fact is of immense encouragement in dark times when the passions are strong, desires raging and the will weak; at such times it is only too easy to imagine that God has omitted to equip us for this part of our struggle and that He is Himself afar off, and the soul is then strongly tempted to give up the struggle and embrace the easier gospel of "self-expression." It is precisely here that the grace of God working in the virtue of Temperance comes to its aid; self-control, to the Christian, is not a lone fight against

---

[1] *Spiritual Exercises*, "The Foundation."

heavy odds, but correspondence to a divinely infused virtue, for even fallen human nature is not wholly depraved, and the soul in grace, though often hard pressed, is aided in this matter by God.

The virtue is there and is powerful, but it must be practised. It is obviously absurd for one who refuses discipline to expect to be miraculously protected by the Infused Virtue of Temperance, which is the virtue of discipline; but those who are willing to persevere in the attempt to discipline self in the matter of sensible pleasure and use created things rightly, find that this virtue does bring divine illumination and power.

### III. Fortitude

We have seen that the object of the Cardinal Virtues is the direction of human activity towards its right end; thus, Justice is concerned with the right fulfilment of one's duty towards one's neighbour, and Temperance with the right government of oneself in regard to sensible pleasure and created things. These virtues are neither heroic nor showy, but are, as their name implies, the solid hinges upon which the character hangs. The heroism and glow of Christian character spring from the Theological Virtues, which unite the soul with God; but the Cardinal Virtues must not be decried on that account, for without them Faith, Hope and Charity would have no solid material upon which to work. Any priest of experience knows how impossible it is for him to do anything directly with a soul which has no conception of these moral virtues; he speaks a different language and has no point of contact; but given Justice and Temperance, even in a very rudimentary degree, a beginning at any rate can be made of better things. So in grace, Faith, Hope and Charity, working upon the Cardinal Virtues, do, in process of time, raise them above themselves and change them into the delicacy and strength of the developed character of the Saint. This metamorphosis is made possible by the virtue of Fortitude.

Justice and Temperance set us on the way to our right end with regard to God, our neighbours, ourselves and created things, but for the cultivation of these virtues and the pursuance of that end something more is needed.

The Christian Virtues are not popular, and he who is in earnest about his religion must expect to have every possible hindrance thrown in his way by his companions in the world; opposition, ridicule, often actual persecution are the world's reaction to Christ, and if the Christian is to persevere in the imitation of his Master he will need a strength of character more than his own. Such strength is also needed against the many wiles of the Devil and one's own weakness. The acquisition of virtue is no easy thing, nor is it accomplished all at once; much patient, hard work is necessary before the virtues begin to flower, and the soul is frequently tempted to give up. The middle-aged person who has lost the joy of fervour, who knows what it is to see ideals vanish and God hide Himself, as well as the discouragement of repeated falls into the same sin which takes the life out of his confessions, needs strength not his own, no less than the young man beset by the world and the flesh; the strength, that is, that perseveres quietly and steadily in the dark. Such perseverance is the fruit of the virtue of Fortitude, which, as it is practised, produces in the soul that level strength which is characteristic of the spiritual man.

We shall meet this virtue again in a higher form among the Gifts of the Spirit, which is a comforting reflection, for God at no time leaves the soul that desires Him without the strength necessary to attain its goal; Fortitude is always there; either as a virtue or a gift, enabling the soul to live constantly at the highest level of which it is capable and giving it the staying power necessary for its perfection.

The truly Christian character is neither weak, nor namby-pamby, nor prettily pious, it is essentially strong, as anyone may discover for himself by the investigation of the lives of the Saints. The Christian is strong because Jesus is so, for it is the very strength of Jesus which is his by the virtue of Fortitude.

## IV. PRUDENCE

Justice is the virtue by which our dealings with our neighbours are directed towards their right end; Temperance accomplishes a like regulation of ourselves with regard to sensible pleasure and created things; Fortitude is the persevering strength by which these and all virtues are brought to perfection, and Prudence is the guide which regulates conduct in regard to them.

Besides the virtue of supernatural Prudence there are also different kinds of natural prudence. There is a selfish prudence which seeks to regulate life with regard to personal comfort, ambition, success and other similar ends; there is also a worldly prudence which, though not blatantly selfish, is, nevertheless, the enemy of true religion. Whether good or bad, prudence always seeks to regulate conduct with regard to a definite end, and it is of vital importance that that end should be the right one. In the case of worldly prudence the end may frequently seem to be the right one, but its criterion is the world's standard of business, tactics, policy or what not, and it is that fact which vitiates it. It refuses to take risks or follow ideals; it is so eminently sane that the cross is to it as to the Greeks, " foolishness." In worldly affairs it is commonly successful and, for that very reason, it is in spiritual matters the Devil's favourite method of throwing dust in the eyes of the unwary. It " works," it is eminently successful up to a point, it appeals to " common sense," its motto is " be not righteous overmuch," and it seeks to balance the morality of Christ and the world.

Christian Prudence is the virtue of balance of another kind. It does not seek to reconcile Christ to the world, but man to God, and the scale whereby it weighs all things is the will of God. It directs the actions of everyday life not merely towards immediate and secondary ends, but towards the one primary end of the fulfilment of the purpose of creation.

It is therefore the supernatural directing power of the life of the virtues. Such direction is eminently necessary if the soul is to live its life aright, and it is also necessary that such illumination should come from God if the soul is not to lose itself in the complexity of life in the world as it is.

Prudence, therefore, sums up and directs all the other virtues and is the light by which the soul is guided until it comes more directly under the control of the Holy Spirit, as we shall see in the following chapter. The Wise Man remarks that " the wise in heart shall be called prudent," [1] and Prudence is truly the practical wisdom of Jesus; not a nice balancing of probabilities, but the discovery of the Father's will in the affairs of daily life and the doing of that alone which is consonant with it.

[1] Prov. xvi. 21.

# CHAPTER VI

# THE GIFTS OF THE SPIRIT

*The spirit of the LORD shall rest upon him, the spirit of wisdom and understanding, the spirit of counsel and might, the spirit of knowledge and of the fear of the LORD; and shall make him of quick understanding in the fear of the LORD* (Isa. **xi. 2-3**).

IT is a truism to say that the Incarnate Life of Christ did not end when He ascended up into heaven; but the implications of that statement are by no means so obvious, and we must face the question how we are to think of the present Incarnate life of the Son of God.

Incarnation demands a body, and the human Body of Christ is in heaven; so much is clear, but, if that were all, the Incarnation would have come to an end, so far as this world is concerned, 1900 years ago. That it has not done so we are conscious every time we offer the Holy Eucharist, for the sacred Host is, ineffably and sacramentally but none the less really, the Body of Christ by the power of His word. Yet even here we have not sounded the depths of His present Incarnate life, for S. Paul shows us a new Incarnation in His mystical Body, which is the Church; we are thus led to the final statement, that Jesus Christ is incarnate in this world to the end of time in His Church and in those human beings who compose the Church.

The purpose of Grace is the reproduction of Jesus in human souls, and the purpose of the life of the individual the reproduction, within the limits and under the particular circumstances of each soul, of His holy life.

To understand how this may be we must consider the human soul of Jesus. His human soul was holy because of its hypostatic union with the Eternal Word of God; His will had never been deflected for an instant from the will of God nor had it known sin in the slightest degree. His holiness was shown in complete submission to the movement and inspiration of the Holy Spirit.

The Conception of Jesus in the womb of the blessed **Virgin** Mary was the work of the Holy Spirit, and from that moment He desired no other will than that of God. We trace His

71

response to the Spirit's inspirations in the devotion of the boy of twelve to his Father's House, and we may see complete docility to the leading of the Spirit in the formative period of the hidden life at Nazareth.  With His Baptism the guidance of the Spirit becomes definite; behind the Baptist there stands the Power of the Highest, and the Holy Ghost descended upon Christ "in a bodily shape like a dove," entered into Him and immediately drove (ἐκβάλλει) Him into the wilderness.

No sooner does the ministry commence than we find our Lord insisting upon the fact of His inspiration by the Holy Ghost on the first sabbath morning in the synagogue at Nazareth (" The Spirit of the Lord is upon me . . ." S. Luke iv. 16 *ff.*), and all the way through it was the same, perfect docility to the inspiration of the indwelling Spirit, so that it could truly be said of Him that even the Son of God " learnt obedience."

It is clear, then, that the holiness of the human soul of our Lord depended upon two fundamental facts: the hypostatic union and the guidance of the Holy Spirit.  The holiness of the members of His mystical Body, the Church, depends similarly upon union with Him and the indwelling of the Holy Spirit.  Our holiness is the holiness of Christ and our life the imitation of His, not because we are trying to make them so, but because they *are* His holiness and His life, since we have been made one with Him in Baptism.  Union with Him, upon which all depends, is not the prize given to the few, though few attain to it in its wonderful completeness, but it is the condition of the super-natural life of all.  Sanctity is the effect of the grace of Baptism, and the development of this sanctity and this grace is the work of the indwelling Spirit, the fountain of grace, the giver of gifts, Himself *Donum Dei altissimi.*

We have already seen something of the effects which the Holy Spirit produces in the soul by His indwelling: Grace, which is nothing less than the life of God, and those spiritual and super-natural faculties which we call the Infused Virtues; but we have now to consider yet another kind of spiritual faculty which the Holy Spirit causes to grow in us, and which we call the Gifts of the Spirit.

These Gifts are usually regarded as seven separable and extremely vague things which are given by the Spirit and should be cultivated separately, but that is a mistake.  It is true that they will be developed differently in different souls and that different souls will incline to some Gifts rather than to others, nevertheless the *Veni Creator* speaks of them as one Gift which is yet sevenfold,[1] and if we would come to a clear understanding of this matter we must first of all realise their fundamental unity.

We have already noticed that the " manifold grace of God " is an unity; we shall do well now similarly to recognise the unity of the sevenfold Gift of the Spirit. To understand it and its place in the spiritual life we may borrow an illustration from the life of the musician. A musician, like his brother the poet, is " born and not made," which means that, from the beginning, he has certain instincts and capabilities, usually in a fragmentary condition and largely unrealised, but still there. These are comparable to the Gifts, which are present in the soul from the moment of Baptism, but in an undeveloped and unrealised condition.

In order that our tyro may become a musician in the true sense at all, he has to submit to a long course of training in technical exercises and long hours of practice at them, and his advance depends upon his own initiative and hard work, aided by his teacher and his God-given capacity. The purpose of this training is not that our musician may gain control over his instrument, as is thoughtlessly said, but over himself and over every part of himself, his eye, his ear, his hand, his whole body being in perfect control and harmony under his mind. This is the life of the virtues.

During this period of hard work there has been gradually growing that indefinable something which no amount of practice will give, that instinctive command over the instrument and understanding of music which make the musician. That is the gift of the Spirit. When it comes to its full growth the technical ability (the life of the virtues) is still there, and to lose it would be to lose the whole possibility of artistic expression, but it is functioning now not by separate acts of intellectually informed will, but by intuition and obedience to the Spirit, to produce what is truly called an inspired performance. The

[1] Veni, Creator Spiritus,
Mentes tuorum visita;
Imple superna gratia
Quae tu creasti pectora.

Qui Paraclitus diceris,
Donum Dei altissimi,

Fons vivus, ignis, caritas,
Et spiritalis unctio.

Tu *septiformis munere*,
Dextrae Dei tu digitus,
Tu rite promisso Patris
Sermone ditans guttura.

performance of a true musician is marked by delicacy of perception, sureness of execution and a real spirituality, which may also serve as the marks of the presence of the Gifts of the Spirit.

The Gifts are not inspirations, but intuitive dispositions of the soul which render it receptive to the inspiration of the Spirit and docile to His leading, and the characteristic of the soul in which they are developing is extreme suppleness in the Hands of God.

In the life of grace there is never a time in which the Gifts of the Spirit are altogether absent, nor is there a time in which the virtues are outgrown, but the method of operation of the Gifts differs from that of the virtues, and there are periods in the spiritual life when the soul acts predominantly under the influence of the one or the other.

In the life of the virtues God encourages the soul to act largely on its own initiative; it has to do its own practising and deliberately to cultivate the Infused Virtues according to the guidance of supernatural prudence, coupled with the aid of its director, if it has one, and aided by grace.  In the life of the Gifts, practice, though still necessary, has produced intuitive response, and God Himself takes control, asking of the soul that it allow itself to be guided, not by prudence, but by the inspiration of the Holy Ghost, Who operates in it largely apart from deliberation.

The life of the virtues is predominantly active and rational, the life of the Gifts predominantly passive and intuitive, and the latter, as a rule, presupposes the former.

The life of grace advances normally towards passivity, though many, perhaps most, souls do not arrive fully at that stage. This is not the passivity of emptiness and inaction, which is the Quietists' goal, but the passivity of constantly willed obedience to the guidance of the Holy Ghost, which is the active-passivity of the human soul of Jesus.  Such passivity is made possible by the Gifts; without them the soul would have no supernatural passive faculties, for the virtues work actively.  It is true that some souls are naturally more intuitive than others, and all possess natural faculties which form the natural basis upon which the supernatural Gifts work; but the Gifts are a distinct infusion given by the Holy Spirit, and progress in them is a distinguishing mark of souls which are going on towards perfection.

The detailed consideration of the Gifts emphasises the unity between the baptised and the Sacred Humanity of Jesus, for the Gifts which the Holy Spirit infuses in us are the same as those which Jesus brought forth in His human soul. The prophet Isaiah gives us the list in the passage which stands at the head of this chapter, and it will be noticed that there is one missing which is included in the Confirmation prayer; this has not been inserted by the mediæval Church to make up the mystic number seven, but is found in the LXX version of the passage of Isaiah under discussion.[1]

The fact that the enumeration of these Gifts occurs in a rhetorical passage of prophecy leads to the conclusion that it would be unwise to regard it as a scientific classification of separate Gifts, and we should rather recognise in it a description of the dispositions which the Holy Spirit implants in the soul, whose effect is mutual and cumulative rather than individual and separable. Once again we must remind ourselves that we are dealing with an unity, sevenfold indeed, but one, and thus we shall see the Gifts not as separate jewels, but as facets of the one ewel whose lights intermingle in the glory of perfection.

We must now pass on to consider each Gift in detail.


## I. HOLY FEAR

It seems strange, at first sight, to find fear among the Gifts. Fear, as commonly understood, is one of the great enemies of the spiritual life, and we have it on the authority of S. John that " perfect love (*i.e.* the Infused Virtue of Charity) casteth out fear ";[2] furthermore, we may ask what place fear had in the soul of Christ?

This difficulty rests upon a misunderstanding; the fear which it envisages is a passion of the soul to which the adjective " holy " can by no means be applied. We fear the unknown, suffering, sickness and death in a way which is certainly not Christ-like. Holy Fear, on the other hand, is that " fear of the Lord " which " is the beginning of wisdom," [3] and S. Augustine sees in it the crowning Gift to which all the rest are ancillary. It is, indeed, that reverence without which love cannot be: the reverence

---

[1] The LXX renders Isaiah xi. 2–3 as follows:—

καὶ ἀναπαύσεται ἐπ' αὐτὸν πνεῦμα τοῦ θεοῦ, πνεῦμα σοφίας καὶ
συνέσεως, πνεῦμα βουλῆς καὶ ἰσχύος, πνεῦμα γνώσεως καὶ
εὐσεβείας · ἐμπλήσει αὐτὸν πνεῦμα φόβου θεοῦ.

[2] I John iv. 16.          [3] Psalm cxi. 10.

of the creature for its Creator, of the son for his Father, which makes true friendship with God possible.  Holy Fear corrects that facile thoughtlessness which is characteristic of so much popular religion, which tends to become familiar with God and is generally easy-going with self.  To the soul that fears in this way the love of God is inseparable from His holiness, His home-liness from His majesty; its Fear springs from a living faith not a dead ignorance, and because it knows God it reveres and worships Him.  Thus the soul that fears cannot bear to speak the name of God lightly; religious ceremonial is to it not merely the per-formance of an external action, but the reverent service of the King, and natural science not the satisfaction of intellectual curiosity concerning an interesting " subject," but the seeking to understand the ways of God; to the fearing soul God, His works whatever they be, and all that concerns Him are essentially worshipful.

But the Gift contains also the fear of sin, not because of its possible or probable result in oneself or others, but because it robs God of that perfect obedience which should be His, and so we find the Gift cementing the soul to that constant obedience to the Holy Spirit which is the fruit of the Gifts.

To the soul that fears, irreverence, even the slightest, towards God, the Saints, holy things and places, causes pain, with the sting of a personal insult, and moves to the desire for reparation. Sin is not something to be minimised as much as possible, or even to be made the best of, but an insult to the love of God.

Holy Fear is, then, a supernatural disposition of the soul which colours the whole of our relationship to God, and through it we habitually reverence Him and live soberly, as in His sight. The Christian life is joyful and simple, so much so that in the eyes of the unwise its joy and simplicity seem excessive, the fruits of shallowness or feeble-mindedness; but it is not so; the truly joyful soul is so because at the bottom of its every thought is that Fear of God which keeps it in its place, brings forth obedience and makes it wise.

" My God," prayed Charles de Foucauld, " give me a perpetual sense of your Presence, of your Presence in me and all around me, and at the same time that loving fear one feels in the presence of him one loves passionately, and which makes one, in the presence of one's Beloved, keep one's eyes upon him with great desire and firm purpose to do all that may please him and be for his good, and greatly fear to do or think anything that may displease or harm him. In you, by you, and for you. Amen." [1]

## II. Godliness

Godliness is the complement of Holy Fear, as may be gathered from the beautiful prayer just quoted. If the latter is precious, the former is even more so, for it directs one's whole life and self towards God. The English word is the equivalent of the Vulgate; *pietas*. It may therefore be defined as adoration or devotion to God, resting upon reverence based upon that respectful duty which the child owes to his parents and family. Holy Fear then blends with Godliness, reverence with adoration, and the motive power of both is Charity.

To the soul which is guided by the Gift of Godliness adoration is its natural attitude towards God and the root and ground of its prayer, it is the loving response of the creature to the all-embracing love of its Creator; but that adoring response is not confined to the interior act of prayer, it passes into the exterior and common act of worship.

Ceremonial is not, to such a soul, an æsthetic delight, or even an aid to devotion—indeed it may not greatly appeal in these ways; it is the offering of an act, as beautiful and perfect as it can be, the lifting up of life and bodily activity to God in the ordered worship of His Church, the consecration of action, and the uniting of the activity of the individual with that of the Church and her divine Head.

Further, adoration passes over into life and makes every action, no matter how secular or commonplace, an act of worship, directed, not only to the practical end in view, but primarily to the service of God. To the soul guided by the spirit of Godliness scrubbing a floor or writing a letter is not just a tiresome incident or a boring detail of life, but an act of service to God, all the better for being ordinary, and so the Holy Spirit sanctifies the commonplace and directs the minor, as well as the major, activities of life to their true end, which is the fulfilment of the will of God. In the power of this Gift the soul turns instinctively towards God in all its activities; its life finds its

---

[1] *Meditations of a Hermit*, p. 41. "*In me and all around me.*" The English translation reads, "in all around me"; I have corrected it according to the original, "en moi et autour de moi."

purpose in Him and nothing less than Him; it is God-directed and therefore godly.

It is for the twin gifts of Holy Fear and Godliness that we pray in the seldom understood petition of the Litany: " that it may please thee to give us an heart to love and dread thee, and diligently to live after Thy commandments; We beseech thee to hear us, good Lord."

### III. WISDOM

Wisdom is " a certain divine light given to the soul whereby it both sees and tastes God and divine things." [1]  Like the two previously considered gifts its concern is with God; it is that savouring of God which is expressed in the invitation of the Psalmist: " O taste and see how gracious the Lord is." [2]

Wisdom is, then, primarily taste, a spiritual sense truly comparable with the physical one, and as ultimately indescribable. It is that fundamental experience of God which is the root of all personal religion, that experience of God which causes the soul to cry out, " I know," even though it is unable to describe what or how it knows.

Wisdom is not the fruit of thought, but of Charity, and describes in its fullness that state of loving God which is habitual to the perfect soul.  Founded on Holy Fear and Godliness, it is their perfection and the fundamental experience without which they can hardly exist and can certainly never attain perfection. The Fear of which we have written is not the fear of an unknown Potentate, the Godliness is not devotion to a distant Deity; alike they are the activities of the soul which has begun to taste God.

It should be noticed that this taste is not to be confined to a single experience.  Our realisation of it will vary in intensity, just as our physical taste does: it will very likely be specially connected with one or more moments in life when God made Himself unmistakably known to us; but, as the soul goes on living the life of the Gifts, the loving taste of God tends to become less a matter of conscious feeling than an unconscious spiritual sense.  Indeed, there are times when, to all conscious seeming, God has withdrawn Himself afar off, but all the while in the unknown depths of its being the soul tastes Him.  The possession

---

[1] qu. Holden, *The Holy Ghost the Comforter*, p. 51.    [2] Psalm xxxiv. 8.

of this Gift withdraws from the soul the need of excessive reliance upon sensible devotion and undue emotional striving after realisation of the divine Presence, giving it at the same time that savouring of God which is above sense or description.

If Wisdom is the taste of God, it is also the knowledge of Him which is comparable to sight; dim sometimes, as of a shape in a dark room, but nevertheless sight. We cannot look to see God face to face in this life, but we can see and know Him by the gift of Wisdom which the Spirit cultivates in us.

The gift of Wisdom gives pleasure in God, it leads the soul to find its true joy in Him Who alone can satisfy it. It was the experience of this Gift which brought to the pen of S. Augustine that cry of the devout soul of all ages: " Thou, O God, has made us for Thyself, and our heart is restless till it rest in Thee." [1] By this Gift the soul rests in God and has thus found that Wisdom which alone is true.

## IV. UNDERSTANDING

This Gift accompanies Wisdom, for God does not will to be known as a vague Something, even though that Something be All. The conception of the Absolute is philosophical, not religious, an abstraction from reality, and God does not will us to be saved by philosophy, however valuable a system of knowledge be in its right place, therefore He has revealed Himself to us in His Son.

The Catholic Faith is not the invention or discovery of man, but the revelation of God, and that revelation is in mysteries which are only partially intelligible to the intellect; by the gift of Understanding the Holy Spirit, Who " searcheth all things, yea the deep things of God," [2] gives to the soul a spiritual understanding of the mysteries of God which is the perfection of the virtue of Faith; by it the soul is able to say, " I know " not only God, but His Truth. As in the case of the Gift of Wisdom, this knowledge is not always clear, nor can it be confined within the limits of a syllogism, and the soul is not infrequently quite unable to argue about it or to convince others, but it is nevertheless a spiritual apprehension of truth and a fundamental reality to the experiencing soul.

The fact that it is an individual enlightenment frequently

---

[1] *Confessions*, I. i.          [2] I Cor. ii. 10.

leads those who do not possess it to cast doubts upon its validity, but they have no right to do so. All apprehension of truth is an individual experience, even the apprehension of such an universal axiom as that two plus two equals four, and spiritual things are spiritually perceived, ultimately by the revelation of the revealing Spirit.

The illumination of the gift of Understanding is not a revelation of new and different truths to each individual soul, it is no private revelation, and the soul which lays claim to such revelation is on a very dangerous road; rather it is an enlightenment which causes the soul to grasp and know the eternal truths, which change not.

It is a remarkable fact that many saints, though quite simple folk, have possessed a knowledge of the mysteries of the Faith to which theologians, if they are merely theologians, can lay no claim; that is the fruit of the gift of Understanding, and it is this Gift which gives to devout theologians their knowledge of things divine and their ability to teach them; it is the Gift of insight into the divine mysteries.

### V. KNOWLEDGE

The Gift of Knowledge is the completion of Wisdom and Understanding, by it we are enabled truly to know the universe in which we are and to see all things in their true proportion and relation to one another and to God; we may call it the Gift of supernatural vision with regard to things created.

It does not follow that the soul to whom it is given will become an expert physicist, astronomer, chemist or biologist, or even that he will have any particular interest in science, but it does mean that he will see all things *sub specie æternitatis*, *i.e.* with reference to God Who made them and to His will for them. To such a soul what we conveniently call secular knowledge is not an end in itself or the mere satisfaction of intellectual curiosity, it is rather a supernatural understanding of the plans of God, so far as they are comprehensible by the mind of the creature, and a knowledge of His mind as revealed in creation.

Without the key which this Gift provides, the proportion, orderliness and purpose of creation are easily lost, and cosmos becomes chaos; with it, though there will still be mysteries and problems, their final resolution is certain, and we can say with the true, deep optimism of Julian of Norwich, "All shall be well,

and all shall be well, and all manner of thing shall be well." [1]
The gift of Knowledge is, as a matter of fact, very marked in
Dame Julian, and she is abundantly worthy of study by those
who would attain to this gift.

## VI. COUNSEL

Counsel is the gift of practical wisdom, and is essentially the
intuitive government of the will in the light of the three previously
mentioned gifts. The practical outcome of the indwelling of the
Holy Spirit is holiness, and holiness is expressed in thoughts,
words and deeds which are wholly consonant with the will of
God. In the affairs of daily life the will of God is not infrequently
obscure, and even when it is clear, the natural man, although
he may not be moved by self-will or self-interest, is frequently
led to follow a secondary end rather than the true one.

The great lack in most lives is that of any really fundamental
principle of conduct. The Christian knows that the only true
principle is that of obedience to the will of God, his Creator
and Father. He knows that God made him for a purpose, and
he knows moreover what that purpose is; but the guidance of
his life in consonance with that purpose is not by any means a
simple matter. He knows, only too well, that the Fall has set all
his values wrong and that, only too often, he knows not how to
act as he should. It is here that the Gift of Counsel comes to his
aid. The indwelling Spirit does not only enlighten the mind
and warm the affections, He also guides the will; and the soul
that wills to obey Him is guided by the Gift of Counsel in his
choice of thought, word and action.

Counsel is also the great social Gift. Man as we are frequently
reminded by psychologists, is a social animal, and the Bible tells
us that " it is not good for man to be alone," yet our relationships
with our fellows are difficult and complex. Society, the nation,
the Church are not merely aggregates of individuals each going
his own way in complete independence; rather they are complex
organisms of which the individuals composing them are the
living, relatively independent cells. Our problem is not how
to live rightly as individuals, but how to live rightly as members
of the various human organisms in which we find ourselves,
and how to respond to our fellow-men within their unity.

[1] *Revelations of Divine Love*, cap. xxvii.

G

It is just here that the Holy Spirit aids us with the Gift of Counsel, which may be called in this connection the Gift of spiritual tact; the Gift which enables the soul to find Christ in his neighbour and to love Him when found.

## VII. Ghostly Strength

Lastly, the Holy Spirit grants us the Gift of Ghostly Strength. Human nature, even redeemed human nature, is weak, and incapable of rendering to God its reasonable service or of continuing in the rarefied atmosphere of the supernatural life without divine aid. The Gifts of the Spirit, wonderful though they are, would be of no practical avail without Ghostly Strength, for human nature could not rise to their practice; apart from this Gift they might illuminate, but could bear no fruit. Without it the soul might indeed make fitful efforts to please God, but it could not sustain them and so bring them to a good end. The Holy Ghost is truly the power of the Highest, and He gives His own power in the Gift of Ghostly Strength.

There are moments in the lives of us all when we dare not trust in our own strength, there are times when we know ourselves to be wholly unequal to the burden laid upon us; but the soul which gives itself to the leading of the Holy Spirit in humility instead of worrying, as most of us do, will simply throw itself upon the Gift of Ghostly Strength, and thus be carried by the Spirit through its crisis.

This Gift gives the peace of the strength of God to the soul, which no longer asks itself, " Can I do this? " when a difficult task is laid upon it, but " Ought I to do this? " and, if the answer is affirmative, goes straight ahead.

This Gift is also the earnest of final perseverance. " Shall I endure to the end and be saved? " This query is the source of desperate anxiety to many, but the soul which rests upon the power of the Spirit does not torment itself thus: it merely strives to hold itself from moment to moment in that power.

We must, however, guard against presumption. It would be wrong, because we have the Gift of Ghostly Strength, to seek tasks which are above us or for which we know ourselves to be unfitted. If they are laid upon us, well and good, we must do what we can, relying on the Holy Ghost; but they must not be sought, still less may we wittingly run into danger—this is the temptation of the Temple pinnacle. If we are conscious of the working of the Gifts of the Spirit we should rejoice, but with humility, realising that they are His and not ours at all; and with faithfulness, remembering that at any time He could remove His Gifts from the unworthy soul.

To the humble and faithful soul the Gift of Ghostly Strength is a priceless possession, because it is the power of perseverance. Many are the discouragements and falls of the soul on its pilgrimage to the Celestial City; often it feels itself surrounded and beaten down by the powers of evil and, realising its own weakness, it is tempted to give up; often the fight seems endless and monotonous: the same old sins, the same old self, the same old Devil, the same dull way. It is perseverance alone which will carry it through, and perseverance is but another name for the Gift of Ghostly Strength, the divine power of keeping on. This Gift is our aid in darkness, our armour in battle, and it is not ours, but God's, and can be completely relied on. It is the completion of the virtues of Hope and Fortitude.

Such, in brief outline, are the Gifts of the Spirit, the intuitive powers which He gradually brings to perfection in the faithful soul. In their completeness they are the powers of the most saintly, in their beginnings the unrecognised stirrings of the novice in the spiritual way. Their effect, as has been said, is to render the soul completely pliable in the Hand of God, to make it a delicate instrument which shall perform His will, not only in broad outline, but in every detail. They are truly gifts and cannot be acquired, but the soul can with the aid of grace render itself increasingly susceptible to them, and that chiefly by five means:—

(i) No life of advanced spirituality can be attained otherwise than by the love of those virtues which are its distinguishing marks and by hard and sustained labour in their attainment. The first means to the development of the Gifts of the Spirit is, therefore, *a persevering practice of the fundamental virtues*. We have seen that the Theological Virtues are completed by the Gifts, but that completion can only take place in a soul which lives by them. The effect of the Gifts is to render the soul completely supple in the Hands of God and perfectly surrendered to the power of the Holy Ghost; but this suppleness and surrender can only be gained by a soul truly humble which voluntarily surrenders itself to constant obedience to the will of God; the Gifts are the complete supernaturalisation of Justice, Temperance, Prudence and Fortitude, and imply their constant practice. In process of time the Spirit takes charge of the soul that works hard at the practice of these virtues in Faith, Hope and Charity, but this hard work is the foundation upon which He builds.

(ii) Further, there must be *a continual combat with the spirit of the world*. This spirit is around us and within us; we cannot evade its temptations, but there must be no compromise. There is nothing so dangerous as the worldliness of the spiritually minded, and there is no middle course which can be steered in regard to it. Worldliness must be distrusted, hated and fought, and one needs to be continually on the watch lest it find an entrance into the heart, praying at the same time for a deeper love of God. The Gifts of the Spirit can only come to perfection in whole-hearted lovers of Christ, and we must be on our guard lest we attempt to serve two masters.

(iii) The third necessity is *Recollection*. Something will be said of this later on; [1] it is sufficient here to point out that no soul can expect to be led of the Spirit, still less " driven " by Him, either into the wilderness or elsewhere if he allow large parts of his life to pass without any conscious movement towards God. One needs to be more than a Sunday Christian, and prayer must cease to be confined to two limited periods morning and night, if one is to be led of the Spirit: one needs the growing practice of recollection which fills all life with God and makes it a continual prayer.

(iv) Fourthly, there is need of *generous sacrifice whenever it is called for*. The spirit of sacrifice is the spirit of Jesus, and the obedience which we would give to the Holy Ghost is nothing less. This sacrifice is not always in what appear to us to be big things— the opportunity for such self-oblation comes but rarely—it is the constant willingness to sacrifice one's own personal desires and to accept hardship in small things that tests and strengthens the soul. The Saints were able to die for Jesus because they lived for Him, which living consisted mostly in constant sacrifice in small things; they were filled with the Holy Ghost because they were empty of self, and that means generosity of sacrifice.

(v) Lastly is needed *devotion to the Holy Spirit* Himself. It has been said that " devotion to the Holy Spirit is the supreme want of present-day Christianity." [2] Perhaps there are many

---

[1] cf. cap. XX *infra*.    [2] G. F. Holden, *The Holy Ghost the Comforter*, p. 1.

" supreme wants," but this is certainly one of them.  We can hardly expect to be inspired by One Whom we habitually ignore and barely know.  All orthodox Christians believe in the Holy Ghost, but often that is about as far as it goes.  We know the *Veni Creator*, but it does not mean much; we are accustomed to the use of certain collects at meetings of the Parochial Church Council or the Mothers' Meeting, and they hardly mean much more; the glorious phrases of the Creed leave us cold.  But the Holy Ghost is *Dominus Vivificans*; He moved upon the face of the waters and from chaos produced cosmos; in every movement of the human race towards God we see His Hand; and this great God indwells our poor souls.

If, then, we would be wholly given to Him we must enkindle within our hearts a real devotion to Him.

The Gifts of the Holy Ghost are, as has been said, intuitive dispositions of the soul which render it receptive to divine inspiration, docile to the leading of the Spirit and supple in the Hands of God.  The soul in whom they are at work is not idle, rather it brings forth acts of virtue of a far higher order than those of less surrendered souls; all its actions become marked by the impress of the Spirit of God and are truly the fruits of the Spirit.  We may expect such a soul to differ from others and to bring forth distinctive fruits.  Of fruits S. Paul enumerates nine: " love, joy, peace, longsuffering, gentleness, goodness, faith, meekness, temperance." [1]  As in the case of grace and the Gifts, we must notice an underlying unity here: the Apostle does not speak of the fruits, but the fruit of the Spirit.  Every soul in whom the Gifts are at work will exhibit their fruit in some way, but all will not exhibit each one in its fullness.  Further, we need not believe the Pauline list to be exhaustive: balanced it is, and nine is a perfect number; but, as in the case of Isaiah's enumeration of the Gifts, this list is far more rhetorical than scientific.  It is a wonderful basket of fruit: love, the characteristic of God Himself; joy, that joy which the world is ever seeking and never finds because it is found only in simple union with God; peace, which is the fruit of surrender; then the three social fruits longsuffering, gentleness, goodness; and lastly the ascetic fruits, faith, meekness, temperance.  Such fruits are the main characteristic of the soul in whom the Holy Ghost is working in His Gifts.  " By their fruits ye shall know them."

[1] Gal. v. 22–3.

# PART II

# CHAPTER VII

# HUMAN NATURE AND SIN

*I find then a law, that, when I would do good, evil is present with me. For I delight in the law of God after the inward man : but I see another law in my members, warring against the law of my mind, and bringing me into captivity to the law of sin which is in my members* (Rom. vii. 21–3).

REFLECTION upon human nature as we know and experience it reveals a fundamental contradiction, for we find in man two principles which are, apparently, irreconcilable. From our study of the gifts of grace we might expect *a priori* to find the nature of man an unity moving onwards without essential difficulty towards its end, but it is not so. S. Paul appeals to experience when he writes of his two laws, and the fact of their existence is a commonplace of saints, philosophers and poets of all ages. The Elizabethan poet Sir John Davies has put the situation forcibly thus :—

> " I know my soul hath power to know all things,
> Yet she is blind and ignorant in all :
> I know I'm one of nature's little kings,
> Yet to the least and vilest things am thrall.
>
> I know my life's a pain and but a span ;
> I know my sense is mock'd in everything ;
> And, to conclude, I know myself a Man—
> Which is a proud and yet a wretched thing."

In spite of all his knowledge, the philosopher knows himself to be blind ; the Christian, in whom are the gifts of grace, yet finds in himself " another law." It is clear then, that, if we are to get any further in our study of the elements of the spiritual life, we must gain some understanding of the facts of our condition.

The fundamental duality which we have noticed is at once the glory and the difficulty of man's position, for he is the meeting of nature and supernature, flesh and spirit, material creation and spiritual.

On the one hand, he is the highest development of animal nature, with all the characteristics which distinguish that level of life. Modern psychology has, indeed, taken the conceit out of us by showing alarmingly that not only our body belongs to the animal order, but also that our *psyche* [1] functions by means of instinctive processes which differ only in degree from those of the animal creation.

Man stands at the apex of that creation, but he does not consist only of body and *psyche*, as do the animals: in him there emerges that which we call spirit, mind, will. In him there appears for the first time in the material universe a created being who is fully capable of thought; of distinguishing between right and wrong; of deliberately willing to do this or that; and of union with God.

If, on the one hand, man is the highest of the beasts that perish, on the other he is cousin to the angels. Spirit is not simply *psyche* writ large, nor is the reasonable will but a developed form of instinct; the possession of spirit and all that it involves raises man above the animal creation to a new and very different level.

Nevertheless, spirit works through and in an animal organism without overriding its essential laws. Man does not leave instinct behind when he acts reasonably; rather, the higher forms of intuitive action are instinct sublimated by and united with mind. It is true that this view of human nature is not popular among psychologists at the present time, but the psychology of the day can hardly be said to have attained to its full scientific stature; it cannot yet see the whole tree, because it is still grubbing among the roots.

The old psychology studied man, as it were, from above, and regarded the whole of his mental activity as consciously governed by mind and will; the new psychology has discovered reflex action, instinct and the unconscious, and seeks to show that conduct depends wholly on these. The old psychology took man at his highest, in the philosopher or the good Christian, and sought to explain him as it saw him; the new psychology, taking man at his lowest, examines origins, and, by the study of reflex action and instinct in animals, the pathological reactions of neurotic human beings or the external behaviour of men in

[1] *Psyche*. I have retained the Greek word throughout in this connection, for two reasons: firstly because it is *psyche*, as distinct from spirit, which is the object of investigation of present-day psychology; and secondly because of the ambiguity of the word " soul," which is its obvious English equivalent. *Psyche* is the vital principle which we share with the animals, the principle of physical life and instinctive action, mental and corporal. The term " soul " is rightly used in this restricted and technical sense, but so to use it here would create confusion with its use in other parts of this book where I keep the popular and general sense and use it simply of the non-corporeal part of man as a whole.

general, seeks to explain man solely in terms of evolution and of his psychical reactions, without regard to spirit.

There is no doubt that in the old way of thinking the conscious processes of thought and will were believed to be the spring of much which we now see to be the result of instincts, emotions, repressed complexes and the like; moreover, the investigations of modern psychology are of real value in their own sphere. Nevertheless, man is not merely an animal, however superior; his higher mental processes are something *sui generis* which cannot be explained away by the lower processes,[1] and until psychology can give us, what at present she does not attempt to do, a synthesis of old and new, a synoptic explanation of spirit and *psyche*, she cannot be called a complete science of the human soul.

Animal behaviour is instinctive and unmoral: we find in animals something which corresponds to the beginnings of thought as well as a certain freedom of action and affection, but no animal is capable of abstract or speculative reasoning, so far as we are able to discover; he has no moral sense, nor is his will free in the sense that the human will is;[2] he is capable of affection but not of Charity. In man we find, for the first time, personality in its full and developed sense.

Catholic doctrine does not require us to agree with Doctor South, that " an Aristotle was but the rubbish of an Adam, and Athens but the rudiments of Paradise." [3] Our first parents were not necessarily very highly developed, civilised or cultured

[1] " To sum up, we cannot evoke or create emotions, but we can direct our actions, choose our goals and fix our purposes; and, in so doing, we form our characters and, indirectly and in the long run, determine the quality and intensity of the emotions with which we shall react to the incidents of the future. Hence the paradox, that, though what we are and what we feel is far more important than what we do; yet, in order to be what we would be and feel what we should, we must constantly act, and not merely feel."—McDougall, *Character and the Conduct of Life*, cap. xiii. pp. 167–8. 3rd Edition, 1928.

" Will, as I have said, is character in action; and in our most complete volitions, following upon deliberation, the intellect co-operates fully with character. . . . Does it then follow that we must accept the determinist position, must deny completely all freedom of the will, all power of voluntary decision to influence a course of events which has been pre-determined from the beginning of the world? . . .
The belief in ' strict determinism ' on the part of a man who actively pursues his goals, and puts forth strenuous efforts is, then, merely a symptom of mental disorder of so mild a nature that there may be good hope of recovery." —McDougall, *Outline of Psychology*, pp. 446–8. 4th Edition, revised, 1928. Section on " Freedom of the Will."
[2] Sin is impossible to the animal. He serves God by instinctively fulfilling the end for which he was created, and he cannot refuse that service.
[3] *Sermons*, II.

people, but they were different from the animal creation: they were responsible beings. They retained, indeed, their animal organism and instincts, but their use of those instincts was to be no longer blind, but deliberate and spiritual. In man we find the creature living on a new and higher plane, with new capabilities infused into the old structure. The animal has become, potentially, spiritual.

There are in man two principles, neither completely separate nor separable, but distinct: on the one hand his animal nature with its instincts, which the New Testament calls the Flesh, and on the other the rational, moral, thinking, willing, loving part of him which is the (human) Spirit.

We find here, as has been said, a duality. This, however, must not be understood to be a dualism: there is no more dualism in man than in God, Who created Him in His own image. Perfect man would be a perfect unity, the spirit working harmoniously in and through the flesh, the instincts guided towards their right ends by reason and will, and the whole man united to God by Charity. We have seen this perfection in Jesus, Who became for us, as Holy Scripture is careful to say, not spirit only but flesh, thus taking to Himself our whole nature perfectly.

Man was created to be an unity, uniting the lower creation with the higher, the physical with the spiritual, and both with God; but we find him still with his duality yet unresolved and his union with God by no means perfect.

The characteristic of spirit is Charity, for it is created in the image of God, Who is Charity. Man was created by God in order that he might love Him, and all other purposes which his creation might fulfil are strictly ancillary to this final end.

Science, because it is science and not theology, can give us no final answer to the fundamental and persistent question, Why did God create the world? Theology, however, gives us the vision of the whole creation finding its meaning in the response of love to the love of God. It would be interesting to speculate as to the way in which love enters into the response of the rest of the universe to the divine will, but, as we have no notion of the way in which spirit enters into matter in other worlds, or whether it does so at all, it would hardly be profitable. In this world creation enters the realm of potential Charity with man and attains fullness of created being in him: in him the response of physical creation to its Creator, partial but perfect in its degree, finds its completion and meaning in Charity.

This involves freedom of will: not, indeed, that complete freedom which pertains to the will of God, the freedom of uncreated and essential Being; but freedom of willed response to that Being, a response specifically human and spiritual, and not simply instinctive and animal.

Love must be free, or else it is no love; it cannot be wholly conditioned by circumstances external to the spirit. Whatever the previous evolutionary history of the organism or its present environment, the spirit, in order to love, must be capable of willing freely; and, indeed, the respect of God for the freedom of the human will raises problems in many minds.

The freedom of the will is of two kinds: first and highest, it is the freedom to love God. This fact is seldom realised at its full value, and frequently it is unrecognised altogether. The glory of man is that, in him, creation is free to love God and so to reach its perfection, and that is his true freedom which alone can unify himself and his life. True freedom is in loving, not in choosing whether one will love or not, and only by loving can one grow in knowledge and union with the loved one. The saints knew this on the supernatural plane, every true lover knows it on the natural. Freedom to love God is the greatest and most astounding freedom of the human will.

But along with that there goes another kind of freedom: freedom to refuse love. For love to be love there must always be the possibility of its refusal; it must be the act of free choice, or it ceases to be love, and the parlous condition in which man finds himself and the disintegration of his nature are due simply to the misuse of his freedom in this respect. The Fall is the refusal of love: by sin man deliberately chose self-gratification instead of the love of God and, leaving the freedom of obedience to the divine will, entered into the bondage of secondary ends and inordinate desires.

Taken at its lowest, the Fall was a regression; instinct, created to be the servant of mind, became its master. But man had emerged from the animal state, he could never return thither; *psyche* could not regain her independence of spirit: her rebellion made chaos of what had been created cosmos, and man, by his own act, had robbed himself of the power of attaining without struggle the end for which he was created and of tending naturally towards perfection. This was reversal of the divine intention which inevitably produced chaos.

Some scientists object to the doctrine of the Fall on the ground that regression from a higher stage of evolution to a lower is unknown in Nature, and therefore impossible. The answer to this objection is clear: such regression is probably impossible in Nature to all creatures below the level of spirit because they do not possess that freedom of will which makes such regression possible to man, to whom such regression is not only a possibility, but actually occurs.

The actual sin of the Fall, whatever it may have been, was the sin of its perpetrators, but its effects pass on to all mankind and are what we know as Original Sin. The act of one set up a fundamental discord in human nature which persists, and must persist until it is overcome by the power of the Cross, which is grace.

The coming of sin involved for human nature a *privatio*, a removal of grace with which man had been endowed. This was not arbitrary or the act of a vengeful God, it was inevitable. Leaving on one side its Godward effects, by sin man had reverted to a level on which grace could not function, and grace was therefore withdrawn. Man became natural and so lost the supernatural.

This had two important effects, the first of which is captivity to the instincts, of which we shall have more to say in the following chapter. We cannot properly speak of animals being captive to their instincts, for response to instinctive urges is their natural and right way of functioning; but for man response to instinct and the pleasure derived therefrom is not a final end, and is only right in so far as it subserves the spiritual end for which he was created. By making instinctive desires and personal pleasure ends in themselves, man became a slave to the flesh or the merely natural.

The second effect is man's imprisonment in the sensible. This is the result of the effect just considered. The spirit having been thrown out of gear and grace having been withdrawn, the flesh acquired a sway over the soul which it was not created to exercise. The flesh, with its instincts, has no cognisance of anything above the sensible; its life is sensible and its knowledge is sensible; in so far, then, as the spirit of man is subject to the flesh, it is imprisoned in the sensible and unable to fulfil its proper function.

This, however, is not all: had sin involved nothing more than the withdrawal of grace, its restoration through the death of Christ to those who are made one with Him by Baptism would perfectly restore human nature to its pristine integrity, whereas we know as a matter of experience that it does not do so, for even S. Paul found the law in his members warring against the law of the spirit. Original Sin, besides being a *privatio*, was also a *depravatio* : not only did it cause the removal of divine grace, it also made a change for the worse in the very nature of man. Human nature thus acquired a bias towards evil which vitiated it at its source; it did not become wholly evil (Total Depravity is not a Catholic doctrine), but it learned to take a delight in evil and to feel its attraction to the full, while at the same time imperfectly desiring good. Evil has a fatal attraction for fallen man, in consequence of this twist which his nature has acquired; even when he wants to be good evil attracts, and, apart from grace, conquers, and his " best-laid schemes . . . gang aft agley."

As man was created, the flesh was imperfect, *i.e.* in need of control, but not evil; through the Fall it has become evil in revolt. The principle of the lower nature, made really lower through sin, is opposed to the higher nature of the spirit and to God Himself; hence follows that fundamental duality for which we have been seeking to account.

It is this state of affairs into which all men are born. We have no experience of human nature as God created it, but only as twisted by sin; we do not know human nature in its integrity, but in its weakness; where it is seen to be strong and holy it is so, not by virtue of itself, but by the power of divine grace.

Much misunderstanding exists with regard to Original Sin. It is thought by many to be a kind of guilt which passes, most unfairly, upon children because of the sin of their fathers; while by others it is believed to be a kind of involuntary actual sin for which we are, equally unfairly, in danger of punishment. We should rather see it as the principle of sin which has passed upon our nature, because in his beginning man refused the height and joy of his vocation and made of self his God, thus putting asunder flesh and spirit, which God had joined together.

The Pauline teaching in this matter is plain, though perhaps the passage in which it occurs is not among his most lucid writings, at any rate in its English dress.[1]   He finds in fallen human nature a principle making for evil, which he calls sin (ἡ ἁμαρτία with the definite article).   This is something deeper than and different from actual sin (ἁμαρτία without the article), being, indeed, the disease of which actual sins are symptoms, the principle whence they arise.   The strange expression "another law in my members" suggests that this evil principle has its seat in the lower nature and is opposed to the "law of my mind," the spiritual law by which man serves God.   "So then with the mind I myself serve the law of God; but with the flesh the law of sin."

Man, according to the Apostle, is "carnal" (σάρκινος).   There are two senses in which the word "flesh" (σάρξ) is used in the New Testament: one in which it simply means man's physical nature, as in John i. 14, "the Word was made flesh."   The other sense is the one used here, meaning our lower nature organised in opposition to the spirit, much in the same way as "the world" in S. John usually means humanity organised in opposition to God.

In the flesh then, in this sense, "dwelleth no good thing," rather "sin dwelleth in me" and I am "sold under sin" and slain.   Sin dwelling in the flesh brings forth concupiscence (the Authorised Version translates ἐπιθυμία by "lust," but "concupiscence" is better), the desire for the satisfaction of one's lower self, and this concupiscence is the cause of our trouble, for if we did not desire sin there would be no conflict, whereas as a matter of experience, "what I would, that do I not; but what I hate, that do I."

By the Fall man has got himself into a situation from which he cannot of himself recover; he has regressed to the natural plane and cannot right himself, he can only be righted by the act of God, freeing his spirit and supernaturalising his nature by grace.   This is the purpose of the Atonement and the grace of the Christian dispensation, and this is its unique value.   There are other religions whose teaching is lofty and whose asceticism is severe, but they can never raise fallen man, because they are unable to break the entail of sin and fill man's spirit with the life of God; for that is the work of the Atonement of Jesus Christ alone.

[1] Rom. vii. 7–25.

It is clear, then, that the spiritual life is by no means so simple a matter as some of our latter-day prophets would have us believe, for it is not a continuous upward evolution, easily, gradually and inevitably attained by the shedding of imperfections and the enlightenment of ignorance, a natural human thing: rather it is a life of conflict, the constant effort, in union with divine grace, to bring the disorderly flesh under the control of the spirit and so of God. It is the discipline and methods of that conflict with which we shall have to deal in the subsequent chapters of this part.

H

# CHAPTER VIII

# THE ENEMIES OF THE SOUL

*Love not the world, neither the things that are in the world. If any man love the world, the love of the Father is not in him. For all that is in the world, the lust of the flesh, and the lust of the eyes, and the pride of life, is not of the Father, but is of the world. And the world passeth away, and the lust thereof : but he that doeth the will of God abideth for ever* (I John ii. 15–17).

*Your adversary the devil, as a roaring lion, walketh about, seeking whom he may devour : whom resist steadfast in the faith* (I Peter v. 8–9).

THE soul in its warfare against sin is beset by three enemies; or, to put it another way, all temptation can be ultimately traced to one of three sources or a combination of them, those sources being, the World, the Flesh and the Devil.

This fact is clearly implied in the first question which is put to the Catechumen (or, in the case of an infant, to the Godparents) at Holy Baptism. Were we (the clergy) not so accustomed to the rite for the administration of that Sacrament, or the laity so extremely unfamiliar with it, we might perhaps be tempted to wonder why it is that the neophyte is not required to promise to fight against sin or be watchful against temptation, since both these things are vital to the Christian life and essential to the Christian warfare. The answer to this hypothetical query is that Holy Baptism is a radical sacrament, and Holy Church is nothing if not radical in her administration of it; consequently, she assumes that the Christian soldier will wage unceasing war against sin and keep unsleeping guard against the temptations which give rise to it, because he *has renounced* " the devil and all his works, the vain pomp and glory of the world, with all covetous desires of the same, and the carnal desires of the flesh," which are the final sources of temptation.

To very many people, even assuming that they have overcome their initial repugnance to distinguish reasonably between its original and actual forms, sin is an extremely amorphous thing, and the distinction between mortal and venial sins and the seven capital sins merely a muddle; sin to them is just a number of wrong things of different kinds, and they habitually fail to distinguish between sin and temptation.

We shall have something to say about sin and temptation in later chapters; at the moment it is comforting to know that, however multiple our sins may be in form, the ultimate impulses to them all are but three in number, and it is in the completeness of our renunciation of these urges that the battle is won; moreover, it is to that renunciation that we are pledged in our Baptism.

It is comforting to realise this, because it clears matters up by showing us at once the spear-head of our attack on the forces of evil. We have to watch against temptation and resist sin; but these watchings and resistances are not merely unrelated and wearying acts, rather they are the activity of a soul which is interiorly renouncing the enemy. Before going any further, then, it is necessary to form a clear conception of the nature of our foes.

## I. The Flesh

The familiar order of the World, the Flesh and the Devil, which comes so trippingly off the tongue, is not the best for purposes of exposition; we shall therefore deal with the enemies of the soul in the less usual sequence of the Flesh, the World and the Devil.

We thus come first to the enemy within the gate, without which all the rest would be powerless. Were the intention single and the will steadfast, no temptation, however alluring, could have the least power: it is the weakness and vacillation of the will that is the cause of all our trouble. The enemy without can only take the citadel as he becomes the enemy within. The world may be very attractive, but unless we *want* the baubles of Vanity Fair, they are spread before our eyes in vain: the Devil may terrify and seduce the soul, but he cannot command. The disunion of the soul itself is our true weakness, hence the maxim of S. Catherine of Genoa is fundamental to the spiritual combat: " Ever fight self, and you need not trouble about any other foe." [1]

Now, Original Sin, as we saw in the last chapter, brings forth ἐπιθυμία which is the root of our disunion, vacillation and weakness. Ἐπιθυμία is translated in the Authorised Version, apparently indifferently, as " lust " and as " concupiscence "; the latter term, although the more unusual, is the more precise, and

[1] von Hügel, *The Mystical Element in Religion*, Vol. II., p. 35.

the one which we shall use in our discussion. It is the English form of the Vulgate equivalent for ἐπιθυμία, *concupiscentia*. This, like many another Christian theological term, is not a classical word, but was coined by that master-terminologist Tertullian from the classical verb *concupisco*, which means " to desire eagerly, to long for." Concupiscence is therefore an excessive and inordinate desire, longing or eagerness for personal satisfaction, primarily of the lower self. It is clear, then, that " lust " is too restricted a word for use in this sense, meaning, as it does for us, exclusively what the Prayer Book calls the " carnal lusts " of gluttony, intemperance and inordinate sexual desire; and being even more commonly restricted to the last-named.

Actually, concupiscence goes far beyond these, for the flesh seeks not only independence, but lordship over the soul. S. John distinguishes three kinds, which we will take as the basis for our discussion, " the lust of the flesh, the lust of the eyes, [" lust " standing in both cases for ἐπιθυμία] and the pride of life." [1]

### (a) *The Concupiscence of the Flesh*

We may define this as the inordinate desire for sensible pleasure. It is concupiscence on its lowest and simplest level, being directly instinctive and physical.

It goes without saying that sensible pleasure is not the highest form even of natural pleasure of which humanity is capable, but it is not necessarily bad; for it and the means of its gratification are God-given, in common with higher goods, and are intended for good and useful purposes. This is a fact which is frequently overlooked by enthusiastic moralists. It might easily be assumed, for instance, from the utterances of many good people, that the vine was created by the Devil, because a certain percentage of the human race habitually intoxicate themselves on the fermented juice of its fruit; but the root of the trouble here is not in the grape, nor in the pleasure of drinking wine, but in the concupiscence of man, which turns a good gift of God into a means of evil. Further, the facts of sex are frequently spoken of as though sex were a thing bad in itself, and this conception underlies many pronouncements made in the name of Christian morals; but sex is God-given and, as such, neither ugly nor evil; it is man's concupiscent defilement of it which is vile.

This is not merely an academic point. The soul has enemies

---

[1] I John ii. 16.

enough without making new ones. Brother Ass may be an ass, but he is a friendly one when well broken in; it is when he is allowed to have his head that he becomes dangerous. So sensible pleasure is good in its proper place.

If sensible pleasure is right in its proper place, it follows that desire for it is right under similar conditions. In a previous chapter we had occasion to allude to the strong desire for food experienced by an hypothetical body of Polar explorers who, having exhausted their supplies, were seeking their base. Nobody would wish to suggest that these men committed sin by desiring food under such circumstances, any more than we consider a labourer to be a glutton who, after a hard morning's work making a road, looks forward to bread and cheese and beer. The desire for sensible pleasure is part of man's animal nature, which was created good by God in order that he might naturally maintain himself and his race, and its right use is a matter of discipline or of sublimation, not of eradication.

Our trouble is that the desire for sensible pleasure has become our master instead of our servant, with disastrous results, and consequently good and evil have become apparently inextricably confused in us; but this fact must not lead us to over-statement. The Puritan, whether Catholic or Protestant, has always a tendency to repeat the Manichæan error that the flesh is evil in itself, and that the truly spiritual man lives as pure spirit. That is certainly the easiest way of disposing of the problem of the holy life, but, putting aside the fact that it does not work, which, to our pragmatist age, is apt to be conclusive in itself, it is neither Christian nor true. In the first place, our animal nature, no less than our spiritual, was created by God, Who made all things " very good," so that it cannot, in itself, be evil; in the second place, the second Person of the most holy Trinity, when He became Man, took to Himself not only the human spirit, but also " flesh," and He could not take to Himself an evil thing.

A further objection to this way of looking at things arises from the consideration of human nature itself, for such doctrine affirms the very dualism which in the last chapter we refused to accept; for God created our flesh, not that it might be eradicated by spirit, but that by unity with spirit it might attain its perfection. With regard to all " short-cut " theories, it is well to bear in mind Hooker's famous words on the mystery of the Incarnation : " Howbeit because this divine mystery is more true than plain, divers having framed the same to their own conceits and fancies are found in their expositions thereof more plain than true." [1]

We are now met by a further difficulty. Assuming that sensible pleasure and human desire therefor are both essentially right, is it not true to say that the *depravatio* of the Fall, imprisoning us as it does in the sensible, has made these things evil?

Our answer to this question is that the Fall has left these things exactly where they were before, but has made the human will susceptible of evil in regard to them. Hunger and the desire for food are neither good nor bad, but may become either according to circumstances and the attitude of the will towards them. The Fall has made their wrong use possible, and even probable, because by it concupiscence has acquired fatal sway over the soul.

Concupiscence is a disease of the imagination and of the will; it turns the ordered desire into a craving, the means into the end, putting sense in place of spirit, self in place of God.

What, then, is the test whereby we may distinguish concupiscent from rightful use of sensible pleasure?

The fundamental test is the end in view. The pleasurable use of God-given senses for God and according to His will is right; to desire pleasure for itself without relation to the will of God and to its right end is wrong.

The basic principle of the spiritual life is order—the order, not of man, but of God. As by the grace of God the soul advances in holiness, its whole life becomes more and more permeated by the will of God, and everything in it becomes by degrees ordered towards that end, thus finding its right place and use, until, in the saints, we find unity reigning in place of the chaos with which we sinners are familiar.

The Mosaic prohibition of idolatry was not simply directed against the worship of graven images, though that was its primary objective: it was the primary consequence of the commandment to love God with the whole being; for, if God is wholly loved, nothing may be put in His place. When a soul sins seriously, it means that something has got out of order and, for the time being, usurped the central place in the heart which belongs of right to God alone; the holy life is that in which every desire is kept in its right place and all in subordination to the will of God. The concupiscence of the flesh, being the most primitive and instinctive—in one way or another, usually gives most trouble in this respect.

[1] *Ecclesiastical Polity*, Book V. cap. liii.

God has attached particular pleasures to the natural processes of eating, drinking and sex for obvious physical reasons, but their effects do not stop short with the physical. Eating and drinking have been means of human fellowship in all ages, a fellowship which finally finds its spiritual expression in the greatest of the Christian Sacraments. Sex, as rightly used in Christian marriage, is more than procreation of children: it is part of that complete union of man and woman without which marriage is imperfect. Sensible pleasure is never solely sensible, for flesh and spirit are not separable; the use of it always involves considerations beyond and above itself. The sensible is not necessarily sensual, it becomes so when by concupiscence man takes it out of its place and abuses it, thus using unnaturally that which God created for a good and natural end.

Concupiscence, the craving of the flesh for that which is merely fleshly, without reference to the higher ends for which man was made, is dangerous, not only because it is a deordinating desire, but also because it alters all the values of the soul. This desire, by giving the soul a primary interest in the sensible, imprisons the soul in it, so that its conduct is dictated by considerations of sense which are often called " sensible " in a sense very different from the theological one. The soul led by concupiscence cannot love God otherwise than sentimentally, for it has turned away from Him to the love of the flesh: the things of the spirit fail to make any appeal, because, being no longer seen in their true light, they appear distasteful and the spirit becomes overlaid by the physical. Thus by imprisoning the soul in the sensible, concupiscence imprisons it in itself, making it a slave to its lowest self, and eventually, when it attains its full stature, it shuts out God and removes all desire for Him. Self has usurped the place of God and, like Narcissus, has fallen in love with its own image.

It might appear from these considerations that the urge of the flesh was an easily distinguishable thing common to those who practise the grosser forms of sin, but avoidable by the ordinary decent person: indeed, it is, or was, commonly supposed by parents that to send their children to good schools which would train their boys to be gentlemen and their girls to be ladies was a sufficient insurance against fleshly concupiscence. This idea is manifestly unfair to the schools concerned, because it assumes that, by some magic means, they can do what is beyond human power and change our fallen nature. The facts which must be faced are that concupiscence is common to every child of Adam, and that it is a very powerful and subtle thing.  The grosser forms of its indulgence may be relatively rare, though perhaps not so rare as we like to think, but the desire for them is common to all—latent, maybe, possibly working its way out in lines of thought and action not easily recognisable as concupiscent, but there and, like a tiger, ready to spring when disturbed.

The less gross forms of concupiscence are universal, and are responsible for the selfishness which rules the outlook and conduct of the unconverted, and often the converted also.  Petty selfishness, love of ease and physical comfort, daintiness and extravagance in food and drink, unnecessary eating and drinking, the use of religion as a spiritual anodyne, the habit of looking at everything from the point of view of one's own comfort—all these things and many others are the fruits of concupiscence.

If souls are to be led on in the spiritual life, they must be instructed in the nature, subtlety and malice of the concupiscence within them and encouraged to persevere, with the aid of grace, in those practices of mortification which alone can enable them to overcome it.

### (b) *The Concupiscence of the Eyes*

We have seen that the effect of concupiscence of the flesh is to imprison the soul in its worst self and so to separate it from God, leading it captive to the sins of the flesh.  The concupiscence of the eyes leads the soul to take a delight in the pleasures of the world and to desire them inordinately.

The concupiscence of the eyes touches the soul at a higher level than that of the flesh, and is consequently even more subtle and dangerous.  Everyone can distinguish sins of the flesh, and most people endeavour to keep themselves from any serious entanglement with them, but it is quite possible to become considerably involved in the concupiscence of the eyes without being in the least aware of the fact.

This form of concupiscence is of two kinds: curiosity and inordinate desire for the world's goods.

Curiosity is an inordinate desire to know things and, like fleshly concupiscence, it is the result of misuse of a good and necessary human function.  Without a desire to know and an interest in observation there would be no knowledge, for there would be no attraction towards discovery and none of that imaginative interest which is the mainspring of thought. All the inventions with which we are surrounded in this mechanical age, as well as the more abstract discoveries of science, have come about because men have been interested in examining the facts of Nature and curious to discover their meaning and possibilities. This scientific curiosity is a good and necessary thing, and a desire to know is as necessary to the philosopher, the theologian and the simple Christian as to the scientist, but it must not be a mere desire to know for one's own sake or for the sake of knowing. Intellectual curiosity, which leads to the amassing of knowledge for its own sake and unrelated to other mental activity, produces intellectual pride; the speculative intellect becomes the supreme arbiter, and the thinker tends to pride himself on his knowledge and capability of deciding all things thereby. This is a fruit of the concupiscence of the eyes, of which there is a very large crop at the present time. The knowledge of previous ages is rejected wholesale, because, owing to the great advance in knowledge of recent years, we like to think we know all things; the traditional teaching of the Church is likewise depreciated because it is said to be unacceptable to the modern mind; and so the poor little modern mind, which is really just as fallible as the ancient, puffs itself out with the conceit of its own curiosity.

Once again the trouble is lack of order. The knowledge of the world is made an end in itself, and desired accordingly. So knowledge becomes divorced from religion and Christian morality. It is right to know rightly, but merely to know is simply the satisfaction of the concupiscence of the eyes, and a degradation of knowledge.

The Christian should desire to seek God in all his knowing; if he did so it would make an incalculable difference to the world he lives in. It has been pointed out that man is incapable of adapting himself morally to the results of all the scientific knowledge that is rushing upon him, and that consequently it is well within the bounds of possibility that civilisation may eventually destroy itself with its own inventions. That, of course, is the inevitable end of a soul that is cut off from God, still more of a civilisation in which God is not the master light of all its seeing. The School-men, derided as they are by clever people to-day (though in some quarters the greatest of them is once more coming into his own), had a much truer idea of the function of knowledge than we have: they viewed all knowledge as one great scheme, beginning with the natural sciences and ending with theology.  That is a conception of ordered curiosity which has been destroyed for the majority to-day for two reasons: first, the field of knowledge has enlarged to such an extent that no one man can have any real knowledge of more than a corner of it, while science advances at such a rate that philosophy can hardly keep up with it, and thus there is produced a departmentalism and an inability to visualise a great structure of knowledge; secondly, civilisation tacitly ignores God and the possibility of any real knowledge of Him, still more the idea that science is in any way concerned with Him and His will, thus making human knowledge an end in itself.

Right knowing is the sanctification of the profane.  The separation between sacred and profane is not a division *in esse*, it is merely the reflection of the division in man caused by sin. To the Christian any fact about anything in the universe is sacred because the universe is the work of God; and all his knowledge, even of the least religious matters, should be not unmoral information, but knowledge to be used in fulfilment of the will of God.

But the inordinate desire to know shows itself in other and even less reputable forms when it becomes merely curious and idle.  The love of tittle-tattle and scandal, which is the bane of suburban drawing-rooms and even other places; the wild desire to know the future, which makes the fortune of crystal-gazers and spiritualists; the passion for news which causes the evening papers to blossom at mid-day and fills their columns with "sensations," are all instances of this concupiscence.

It results in a restless preoccupation with the world, which, feeding on itself, ever increases.  The curious soul is restless without a newspaper, its favourite topic of conversation is its neighbours, and all the time it is conscious that all is not well with it.  Its life is essentially superficial, and becomes more so as it continues in its concupiscence, and the things of the spirit, so far as they touch it at all, remain, if they are not put away on Sunday evening, quite separate from its real interests.

The concupiscence of the eyes also takes another form—that of inordinate desire for the world's goods.  Here for the first time we are concerned with an object of concupiscence which may not be right in itself.  The world's goods are partly natural and partly artificial: the goods which are made by man for man are not always legitimate objects of desire; many are innocent, but others are bad in themselves, and others again, by reason of the conditions of their production, are paid for by human misery. The Christian conscience on the whole is far too easygoing with regard to the last class, no doubt largely owing to defective knowledge and imagination, but no Christian has any right to condone sweating, whether he himself profits by it or not.

Money is a necessity of civilised life, nevertheless the love of money is, as S. Paul says, " the root of all kinds of evil "; [1] the desire for advancement subject to the will of God is right and healthy, but as an end in itself it leads to the most appalling selfishness and unscrupulousness, while the desire for possession puts the soul out of Charity both with God and man.

The desire for possession is, indeed, the root form of this kind of concupiscence and it puts self in the place of God in regard to external things, even as the concupiscence of the flesh puts self in the place of God in regard to internal, and produces that spirit of avarice which even the world abhors.

Essentially, man possesses nothing, as the Parable of the Rich Fool witnesses; actually he is always striving to possess. Those things which are " his " he holds, if he has come by them rightly, in trust as the steward of God, but he is constantly claiming to hold them absolutely and, as concupiscence grows, he lives more and more in order to increase them; thus they become ends in themselves for man's benefit without reference to God.

It is hardly necessary to point out to what great evils this concupiscence leads, yet it is so far unrecognised by the ordinary person as to be actually encouraged by many otherwise good Christians. A father will encourage his son to believe that the whole object of his life is to make his way in the world and amass a fortune, quieting his conscience the while with the consideration that " business is business " and is therefore quite independent of Christian ethics. This leads to divorce of life from God and something approaching terror of any religion which makes real demands upon its followers.

Public opinion on the whole can see no wrong in this con- cupiscence, but it is hardly too much to say that it is responsible for seventy-five per cent. of the misery of modern civilisation, and if the Church is to convert the world to the naked and crucified Christ Who alone can save it she must train her children to loathe and fight " the lust of the eyes."

[1] I Tim. vi. 10. (R.V.)

### (c) *The Pride of Life*

In considering concupiscence it is important to remember that it is not sin in itself, but the urge of our fallen and disordered nature which drives us towards sin.   Concupiscence of the flesh is not gluttony and sexual lust, nor is concupiscence of the eyes disordered curiosity and avarice, but they are the inordinate desires within us which make for these things; similarly, the pride of life is not pride properly so called, but the inflation of self which leads to it.

S. John calls this concupiscence ἡ ἀλαζονία τοῦ βίου.  Ἀλαζονία is translated in the Vulgate as *superbia*, because the Latin language has no exact equivalent for the Greek word; but it is not *superbia*, for that is the fully developed sin of pride, whereas ἀλαζονία is the characteristic of the ἀλαζών.   Now an ἀλαζών is a vagabond who wanders about the world living on his wits, and his ἀλαζονία is just empty swagger by which he tries to deceive himself and others into the belief that he is a very fine fellow.

This concupiscence seeks to put self in the place of God; not the worst self, but the most successful and, from the world's point of view, the most desirable self.   It is, as Bossuet says, " the most profound depravity: by it man, given up to himself, regards himself as his God by the excess of his *amour-propre*." [1] By it man, forgetting that God alone is the source of whatever is good in him, takes all his good qualities to himself and so becomes self-complacent.   This blunts his sense of sin and distorts his spiritual vision, thus leading to vanity, which, as its name indicates, is inordinate self-satisfaction founded on emptiness. Further, this concupiscence leads one to desire to do and obtain those things which appeal to self without regard to the will of God; it is thus the source of all sin, which is essentially the assertion of independence.   Self, as we have previously remarked, is, in the disordered state of our fallen nature, the root enemy; were we perfectly dependent upon God this would not be so, but we find within ourselves the constant urge towards independent self-satisfaction which is " the pride of life," and it is obedience to this urge which sets up that opposition to God which is the deadly effect of the Fall.

It is unnecessary to consider very fully the effects of this con-

---

[1] *Traité de la Concupiscence*, X. xxiii.

cupiscence in this place, as they will be dealt with at some length below, but we must point out the universal appeal and extreme subtlety of it. There are times in our experience when the concupiscence of the flesh or of the eyes ceases to attract, but there is no time when the pride of life loses its allure; egoism of one kind or another is our constant companion, and it is alarming to notice how often good and pious people, very often particularly good and pious people, fall under its spell, frequently without realising in the least that they are doing so, so insidious is its attack.

"The heart," as Jeremiah remarks, " is deceitful above all things, and desperately wicked," [1] and the tragedy is that, through the pride of life, it deceives itself, and sometimes its neighbours; it cannot deceive God and His angels nor yet the Devil, but it can and does deceive itself until it sincerely believes that some course of action is not only not wrong, but even pleasing to God, because it desires to follow it. Psychologists give us many horrid examples of this self-phantasy, and experience can generally supply others which demonstrate the extreme danger of this concupiscence to the soul. That it is subtle we need not wonder, for the self-assertion of pride is the fundamental sin of the Devil, and this concupiscence delivers us willingly into his power, who is the ancient enemy of all good

## II. THE WORLD

The threefold concupiscence is the enemy within, which, in our fallen state, predisposes the soul to sin; it is partly self-initiated and partly stirred up and encouraged by the enemies without. We have now to consider the first of these enemies which theology, following Holy Scripture, calls the world.

We must first of all carefully discriminate between the two uses of this term. The world, in the general sense in which the term is commonly used, is the globe on which we live and all that it contains. In so far as all things, even good things, *may* become means of temptation, the world in this sense, or some part of it, may become inimical to the soul, but not of necessity. The soul that would advance in the spiritual life needs to mortify itself in regard to the world, in this sense of created things, where it is good as well as where it is not; for, our nature being what it is,

[1] Jer. xvii. 9.

anything created may lead away from God.   The world as God
has created it is good, but it is evil in so far as it has been made
so by sin; in this sense, therefore, the world is a potential source
of danger.   But it is also a means of good, and so cannot be said
to be an enemy of the soul in the full sense of the word.

There is, however, a technical sense in which the world is
truly an enemy of the soul and, through concupiscence, a most
dangerous one : this sense is found fully developed in the writings
of S. John; for him the world means the *ensemble* of men opposed
to Christ, or rather that is one of the senses in which he uses the
term.   " In this sense the ' world ' describes the mass of men
(compare John xii. 19), distinguished from the people of God,
characterised by their peculiar feelings (vii. 7, xiv. 27, xv. 18*f.*,
xvi. 20, xvii. 14; 1 John iii. 13, iv. 5) and powers (xiv. 17;
1 John iii. 1) hostile to believers, and incapable of receiving the
divine spirit.   The disciples and ' the world ' stand over against
one another (xiv. 19, 22).   On the one side are the marks of
' light ' and ' love ' and ' life '; on the other ' darkness ' and
' hatred ' and ' death.'   The world has its champions (1 John
iv. 1 *ff.*), its inspiring power (1 John iv. 4, v. 19), its price (xiv. 30,
xvi. 11).   In the world the disciples have tribulation, though
Christ has conquered it (xvi. 33); and His victory is repeated
by them through the faith (1 John v. 4*f.*)." [1]

The world in this sense is in essential opposition to Christ;
this is its characteristic—the opposition of fallen humanity as a
whole to the Son of God.

The root of this opposition is not intellectual—though it is
prepared to make the most of any assistance the intellect may
give it—but moral; it is not the opposition of thought, but, as
S. John points out again and again, of passion.   Our Lord said
that the world hated him, not because it disagreed with His
teaching, but " because I testify of it, that the works thereof are
evil." [2]   The world is fallen and concupiscent humanity taking
combined action to preserve for itself its fallen way of living, its
inordinate use of the things of sense and its enjoyment of the
triple concupiscence.   Hence its power; it has all the strength
of combination and crowd suggestion reinforcing that of
individual concupiscence.

Much, perhaps most, of the unbelief and anti-Christianity of
our day is to be traced to this source.   Intellectual questioning

---

[1] Westcott, *The Gospel according to S. John*, Vol. I., p. 65.    [2] John vii. 7.

and uncertainty there undoubtedly is, but it is seldom the effective cause of active infidelity; at the root of which there is, as a rule, a moral difficulty.  There is a fundamental cleavage between the morals of the Church and those of the world : the Incarnate Lord came into the world " for judgment " and He judged it by His very presence, therefore the world crucified Him; the Holy Spirit came at Pentecost " to convict the world of sin," and the Church, living the Christ life, inspired by His Spirit, is, so far as she is faithful, a living witness to His holiness with which the world will have nothing to do.  It is hardly remarkable, then, that the world opposes Christ and that it opposes Him not because it believes His claim to be false, though, for obvious reasons, it maintains that it is, but because it fears His condemnation of its manner of life.

There is much worldly infidelity to-day, and it is probably on the increase, but a far commoner expression of the world's reaction against Christ is to be found in indifference.  People do not bother to crucify Christ, they just ignore Him; really fundamental matters do not interest them, they are just subjects for an occasional epigram.  Such folk cannot take the trouble to think; and as to their souls, they are not sure whether they have any, but, if they have, they do not propose to take them seriously until they are within sight of death.

This superficial *laissez-faire* attitude is very common and is due to the concupiscence which we have already considered. People are indifferent to Christ because, being shut up in sense, the pleasures of the world are to them the only real ones, the spiritual is for them the imagination of " religious " people; the pleasures of the world are real, full-blooded and desirable, the Christ is but a " pale Galilæan " Whom they will not allow to conquer.  They are satisfied by the world.

That is the active type of indifference; there is another, a passive sort, which is simply apathetic to anything which does not directly bear upon its immediate interests and pleasures.  It does not deny the truth of Christianity—it may, indeed, be quite orthodox so far as it goes—but it does not take " that sort of thing " too seriously.

Indifferent folk of this latter kind are frequently quite nice to the vicar, and even give him a subscription from time to time; they may be seen occasionally at Evensong and perhaps make their Easter Communions—charming people with strange and wonderful ideas on religion culled from their favourite news-papers and the inner consciousnesses of themselves and their friends, folk who would never dream of insulting Christ, but who never allow Him really to enter their lives. Their real interest is still the world, which is all the more dangerous for being a nice and rather benevolent world. They would treat S. Francis much as Assisi treated him in his day.

There is a further type of worldliness which is to be found within the body of the faithful—the worldliness of those who believe and practise Christianity with a view to their own pleasure or advantage. Some such treat the Catholic Church as a sort of spiritual insurance company to which they pay certain premiums in the way of church-going and the like in the hope of gaining substantial benefit hereafter; others fulfil their religious obliga-tions because they like the services or the clergy, but disappear altogether when something displeases them, or their consciences are in danger of being aroused; others again bring discredit upon the fair name of Christ by grave discrepancies between their lives and their profession. The call of present sensible pleasure is too strong for them.

The world is all-pervasive and no one but a saint is altogether free from its blandishments. Books, plays and newspapers are, naturally, full of its teaching and, now that lip-service to Chris-tianity is considered unnecessary to reputable literature, such teaching is becoming the more accepted; the maxims of the world are constantly on the lips of friends and companions, and even the Church is not free from their service.

As has been suggested, worldliness has many forms varying from open opposition to Christ, which is obvious, to the wiles of so-called prudence, which are not. It is always opposed to the spirit of Christ, but its opposition is often masked and its attrac-tions are extremely subtle. It is dangerous because it ministers directly to concupiscence and encourages the soul in indulgence therein, lowering resistance by the power of public opinion. Its maxims sound so wise, its " pomps " seem so alluring and its example is so infectious that it is hardly surprising that many souls are tempted by it and fall away from the hardness of the gospel to the comfortable hypocrisy of Laodicea.

The absorbing interest of the world is what the scriptures call the " vanity " of this life, and once again the Christian aim with regard to these things must be the order of the will of God.

Possessions and pleasure are not in themselves wrong, and when not wrong may be legitimate objects of desire, from which no one but a Religious can, or is required to, cut himself off, but they are means, not ends, and transitory at that.    If we would use created things aright, in the spirit of Christ and not of the world, we must always strive to see the temporal on the background of the eternal, and realise that *quod æternum non est, nihil est.*    Our interest in and desire for mundane things, to be right, must be ordered with regard to their eternal value and the will of God in regard to them; our use of them must be for the glory of God and the good of men, not merely for self-gratification, and we must be prepared boldly to forgo those pleasures which are contrary to the will of God for us.

The Christian is called to make a definite choice between God and Mammon.    Luxury is sinful [1] and not a thing to be desired, while luxury which involves suffering to other men is criminal. The days are gone when kings and nobles wore hair-shirts beneath their scarlet and ermine, and the spirit of that mortification has well-nigh gone too, but the teaching of the Christ who had not where to lay His head is still the same.    The spirit of the world can be exorcised by the spirit of simplicity and strictness of life, that spirit which is enshrined in the evangelical counsel of poverty, by which, having nothing, one yet possesses all things.    Simplicity and poverty of spirit are the marks of the true follower of Christ and the means whereby the joy and peace of God may be attained.    " How hard is it for them that trust in riches to enter into the kingdom of God !    It is easier for a camel to go through the eye of a needle, than for a rich man to enter into the kingdom of God." [2]

### III. The Devil

The last and most determined enemy of the soul is the Devil, and first we must emphasise the fact of his existence.    It is strange that we should be under this necessity, since every child of Adam suffers from his attentions, but one of the chief delights of the Father of Lies is to persuade men to believe the fundamental lie that *le Diable est mort,* and that, consequently, they have nothing to fear from him.    He loves to pose as a worn-out super-

---

[1] cf. p. 147 *infra.*              [2] Mark x. 24–5.

I

stition, a mere bogy with which to frighten children, disposed of by modern enlightenment.

We must admit that mediæval representations of the Devil do look very much like this to the superficial observer, and many a modern man is sceptical of his existence because he cannot bring himself to believe in his horns, hoofs and tail: however, it is not the Middle Ages that were mistaken in this matter, but ourselves. As we look more closely at the mediæval Devil we see that the details of his appearance which cause us such unnecessary hilarity were not intended to be taken literally, but are strictly symbolical. Now the essence of a symbol is not that it is a mere fancy, but that it is the clothing of a spiritual reality with conceptual vesture whereby its nature may be recognised by the mind: the mediæval pictures of the Devil are just that, and truly illuminating to the thoughtful observer.

Mediæval symbolism may fail to appeal to many minds in this prosaic age, but that is no reason for regarding the symbolism as valueless and for disbelieving in the reality symbolised.    The Devil is a reality, and a very formidable one—no invention of the desert and cloister, but the ancient enemy of God and of His Church.    In him we find the principle of deliberate evil.    In concupiscence we have seen the regressive movement of human desire towards physical satisfaction, we have seen that the world is the combination of humanity in the following of concupiscence, and that both are movements of imperfection, evil because opposed to the will of God; but in the Devil we find the deliberate working of evil for its own sake: he is truly the Evil One.

Belief in the Devil and his angels is, in one form or another, universal, a fact which is attributed by our modern theologians to primitive superstition.    This is one of those "blessed words" which are used with the utmost vagueness of content as a term of abuse.    Let us take a dictionary definition: Chambers defines superstition as "excessive reverence or fear, based on ignorance; excessive exactness in religious opinions or practice; false worship or religion; an ignorant and irrational belief in supernatural agency, omens, divination, sorcery, &c.: belief in what is absurd without evidence: rites or practices proceeding from super-stitious belief or fear [1]: over nicety, exactness, too scrupulous or morbid."

The term "superstition" may, then, be used in any of these

---

[1] This seems to come perilously near to a *circulus in definiendo!*

senses, and no doubt the list might be lengthened; we might add, for instance, " the beliefs and practices of those with whom we do not agree: the beliefs and practices of those who are ignorant of modern, Western and Protestant culture." The term is, of course, patient of an accurate, scientific and unobjectionable meaning, but it seldom receives it.

As will be seen from the definitions just quoted, the essential factors in superstition are not that it appears to be ridiculous to a mind reduced to agnosticism by a surfeit of comparative religion, but ignorance and irrationality. That these factors are and have been widespread in popular demonology we readily admit, but we must distinguish: the fact that a belief is mixed with superstition does not invalidate the belief, and the fact that belief in the Devil is universal to mankind, so far from demonstrating its falsity, should lead one to suspect that it is based on truth. It does not seem unreasonable to suggest that man believes in the Devil, not as an animistic explanation of physical forces, but because he has spiritual experience of his machinations.

But Christian belief in the Devil rests on a far more impressive fact than universal affirmation—namely, the teaching of our Lord Himself.

It is fashionable to-day to discount this fact by means of an exaggeration of the Kenotic theory of His personality, coupled with the idea that, so far from guiding the Church into all truth, the Holy Ghost led the apostles and evangelists into diverse misrepresentations. Granted that the second Person of the most holy Trinity " emptied Himself of His glory " and, becoming man perfectly, spoke as a Jew to the Jews of His age, we have no right to assume that He taught fundamental error. Granted that the apostles and evangelists were fallible men who admittedly misunderstood their Master on certain matters, we have no right to assume that the Holy Ghost caused them to mislead the whole Church in their inspired writings. In the New Testament, as in mediæval pictures, we find symbolism, for it is impossible to speak of spirit by any other means; but here, as there, symbol describes spiritual truth.

Our Lord found a belief in the Devil in Judaism, and it is noticeable that nowhere does He attempt to correct it, as He certainly would have done had it been false; rather, He adds to its content. On the threshold of the gospels we are met by the solemn story of His own temptation, which, be it remembered,

must have come to the disciples from His own lips; throughout
the ministry we find Him casting out devils and in an argument
with the Pharisees, against whom He could so easily have taken
up the Sadducean position had it been the true one, He claims
to cast them out by the spirit of God.   For Him the Devil is the
great adversary of God and man, who is constantly seeking to
frustrate His own work.   " The doctrine is not so much set forth
by way of dogmatic statement as assumed, taken for granted.
Jesus does not enlarge upon it, but quietly accepts it, presupposes
it as a matter about which there is no dispute.   The belief is there,
and Jesus sets upon it the seal of His authority." [1]

The Devil, then, is a reality, but he is not ultimate reality, he
is a creature.   The age-long war between good and evil in which
creation is involved is not a conflict between two gods, and the
ultimate issue is not in doubt.   It is this fact which leads to a
rather baffling feature of his mediæval representation.   The
makers of miracle plays, when they tired of representing the
horrid and terrible aspects of the Devil to their audience, would
change their tactics completely and make him a pure buffoon,
God's ape, and treat his servants in the same way.   They could
never be sure of taking Herod seriously, while Pontius Pilate was
eventually metamorphosed into Mr. Punch.   This peculiarity
is not due to misplaced humour or the dramatic need for a little
comic relief, but to the realisation that, in spite of all his present
power and subtlety, in the last resort the Devil is a bluffing liar,
limited by his creatureliness, conquered by Christ and unable
finally to withstand his Maker; so in the choir of Lincoln Cathe-
dral the calm angels barely notice the imp ineffectively grinning
among them.

The Church teaches that the Devil is by creation an archangel,
a pure spirit with the most penetrating powers of mind who fell
from his high vocation by pride, desiring himself to be as God;
or refusing to worship the Humanity of the incarnate Son.
The human race is the particular object of his envy because,
created lower than the angels, it is destined to fill the place in
heaven from which he himself has fallen, hence his continual
warfare against it.

There are certain facts about the Devil which we do well to

---

[1] cf. *e.g.* Mark i. 13; Matt. xii. 28; Luke xiii. 16; x. 17 *ff.*; Mark iv. 15 *ff.*;
Matt. xiii. 38 *f.*; Luke xxii. 31; Matt. xxv. 41.   I am largely endebted here
to H. H. Currie, art. " Satan," Hastings's *Dictionary of Christ and the Gospels*, Vol.
II., p. 570.

ponder; and first his essential evil. As self-knowledge increases we find within ourselves almost unlimited possibilities of evil, but these possibilities are only partially actualised and are mixed in a bewildering way with good desires as well as with actual good. The Devil is completely evil, he has said definitely " evil be thou my good " and translates every imaginable form of wrong into active energy. This active evil will is directed against God and His servants and is actuated by malice; with deliberate intent he wars against his Maker.

Further, although fallen from heaven and perverted from the purpose of his creation, he still retains the brilliant spiritual powers of the archangel; he is possessed of intense penetration and subtlety. The common expression " diabolical cleverness " is a true one; he is clever with all the brilliance of his spiritual nature perverted to evil use, and there is no end to his crafty deceptions; he is capable of counterfeiting even an angel of light to gain his own ends.

But his power is not only personal; he organises in his angels and, alas, in men a kingdom of evil, a love of evil for its own sake and a hatred of God, a complex, all the powers of which he can bring to bear upon the human heart in order to bring it to his own perdition.

If the Devil is what we have represented him to be, it is clear that we may expect his temptations to be of an extremely subtle character and definitely designed for the downfall of the soul: herein they differ from the temptations of concupiscence, which are rather those of imperfection and moral disease, and we must emphasise the importance of understanding their reality. There is a tendency to regard all sin as moral sickness; this is a half-truth and, like most half-truths, dangerous. Sin which proceeds from concupiscence is a spiritual disease which it is the business of the priest to cure by treatment, but sin proceeding from diabolic temptation is not susceptible to treatment, it must be fought.

The aim of the Devil is to detach the soul from God, and the more holy the soul so much the more incessant and subtle are his attacks upon it; but his power is not unlimited—he can only attack the soul in certain ways.

First, and most obviously, the Devil acts upon the soul through the *senses*, stirring up concupiscence and making the worst of our fallen nature. This is constantly occurring in small ways, and not infrequently in great, and especially do such temptations come when the soul is making a special effort towards God.  Souls are frequently distressed because there arise in them sensual desires, of a kind which would shock them at other times, at or immediately after their Communion; but such rising of desire is due, not to the inherent wickedness of the soul (save in so far as it encourages it), but to the Devil tempting through the senses.  Souls which give themselves to the exercises of a retreat not infrequently experience the same thing.

Further, the Devil acts directly through the *imagination*, that will-o'-the-wisp of the mind which is so constantly eluding our control; indeed, the imagination is in this respect the most vulnerable part of our being.  Here the Devil liberates all sorts of phantoms —concupiscent imaginings, doubts and worries of all kinds, which disturb the soul more than is generally realised.

The danger and fact of concupiscent imaginings is obvious, but they are not always easy to detect; the insatiable longing for some one thing, which we all experience from time to time, is often due, not to any need, but to the focussing of the imagination upon it in such a way that the whole desire of the soul is bent towards the acquisition of something (which not infrequently ceases to be desirable as soon as possessed), to the neglect of other and higher considerations; this is generally diabolic.

The Devil is master of the art of disturbing the soul.  With doubts we shall deal shortly, there remain worries.  Many souls are tortured and terrified by an inordinate fear of the unknown, the imagination dwelling without their own will or intention upon all kinds of tragic possibilities, ranging from the dark to Hell; such states of mind tend to render them incapable of any serious effort and disturb them to the foundations of their being, and in them, once again, we see the work of the Devil.

It is undoubtedly true that the imagination is, as we have remarked, singularly impatient of control; nevertheless many people, by allowing it to wander at will, lay themselves open to much temptation.  The practice of day-dreaming is dangerous for this reason.[1]  Day-dreams practically always centre round self, and, the mind being engaged in idly wandering among phantoms, it is easy for the Devil to slip in his temptations for its ruin.  It should be realised that the imagination is the Devil's

---

[1] This point is worthy of notice by those who have charge of children, for it is during childhood that the habit of day-dreaming most often begins.

point of direct contact with the soul, whence he attacks the mind and will.

It is impossible for the Devil to attack either the mind or the will direct. He may batter the will with all his wiles by means of the senses and the imagination until he finally wears down its resistance, but he cannot compel its surrender; God, Who created man with free will and Himself respects that freedom, does not allow His creature to override it.

In the same way, God alone can illuminate the mind. It is true that the Devil frequently attempts to undermine faith by suggesting doubts, but this he does through the imagination; for such doubts, despite their apparent speciousness, are ultimately found to be without foundation, either in revelation or thought, and whatever they appear at the time to be, they are not intellectual but imaginary.

We may ask, What are the marks of diabolic temptation? There are four chief marks to be noted. First, such temptation is vain, *i.e.* founded on emptiness: its attractions are imaginary and illusory, its doubts have no intellectual foundation, its worries concern what might be, not what is. Secondly, it produces pride and its antithetical consequences, presumption and despair, leading the soul to make self the object of its activity and either to presume on its own strength or to despair of God's grace. Thirdly, it tends to be violent and put the soul off its balance; and fourthly, it troubles and distresses the soul.

It is necessary clearly to distinguish this last mark, for frequently it is the only means of deciding whether an inspiration is good or evil. The Devil often poses as an angel of light, and to this end troubles the soul with thoughts of its own sinfulness, disturbing it with the thought that it is cut off from God and destined for Hell. Now such thoughts may be suggested by the Holy Spirit; a soul that is in need of conversion is frequently converted by just such realisation and fear, but the two suggestions are quite different in kind and effects. The inspiration of the Spirit is steady, leading the soul to repentance, to reliance upon the merits of Christ, to absolution and union with God, issuing in calmness, prayer and joy; the temptation of the Devil, on the other hand, usually troubles a soul which is already converted and causes it to doubt the efficacy of its absolutions, raising in it all manner of scruples which hinder it from prayer, and leading it to believe that it is useless for it to make any efforts in the spiritual life; whence issue gloom and distress of mind. Similarly the Devil will frequently twist to his own uses the inspired scriptures, as he did with our Lord in the wilderness, and the soul is violently disturbed by some text which does not apply to its condition. In all such cases it is well for the soul to seek the advice of its confessor, complete openness with him being often the cure of such visitations.

We have dwelt at some length on the reality of diabolic temptation, but one word of warning must be added. Eve, when convicted of sin, replied, " The serpent tempted me and I did eat," seeking thereby to avoid responsibility. What she said was true, for her temptation was from the father of evil, and we likewise frequently seek to avoid responsibility or to save ourselves trouble and shame by ascribing to the Devil what is the result of our own concupiscence. It is important in self-examination to try to distinguish between the sources of temptation, and always to remember that each sinner is responsible for his own sin, for the Devil cannot force the will.

The strongest defence against the wiles of the Devil is a humble spirit which puts all its trust in God; against such an one he can have no power, for his characteristic sin is pride and self-glorification. Such a soul will persevere quietly in the frequent use of Confession and Holy Communion and in prayer, striving to gain the habit of constant recollection, against which the Devil is powerless to prevail, though he may greatly disturb.

The struggle against evil is long and arduous, and often it seems as though the Devil must triumph, and, like the servant of the man of God, we lose heart. At such times there may come to us the words of Elisha, " Fear not: for they that be with us are more than they that be with them," [1] and we may see the horses and chariots of fire of the angels of the Lord.

[1] II Kings vi. 15 *ff.*

# CHAPTER IX

# TEMPTATION

*Blessed is the man that endureth temptation : for when he is tried, he shall receive the crown of life, which the Lord hath promised to them that love him* (James i. 12).

WE have now to discuss the large and difficult subject of temptation : a subject so large that there seems to be no end to it and so intangible that it seems impossible to pin it down.

The enemies which we considered in the last chapter are perpetually assailing the soul and presenting to it temptations of all kinds, small and great, spiritual and carnal, instantaneous and protracted, clear and obscure, delightful and repulsive—the pairs of adjectives might be almost endless. The beginner in the spiritual life, harassed by diverse and obvious temptations, looks forward to a time when they shall become less frequent and perhaps cease, but as he advances, he finds that they do but change their shape and become not less but more subtle and difficult to attack; he may get to that point, well known to the saints, when the whole power of Hell seems loosed upon him, and learn by sad experience that the saints are not the least but the most tempted of men.

The Christian life is one of progress in virtue, and because it is so it is also a perpetual conflict with temptation. When the world ceases to attract and the flesh to lose its hold the Devil becomes even more active, striving to detach the soul from God by means of the subtlest spiritual temptations.

The questions at once arise, Why does God permit this harassment of His servants? and whence comes it?

Temptation does not come from God. As S. James says: " Let no man say when he is tempted, I am tempted of God : for God cannot be tempted with evil, neither tempteth he any man."[1] God does, however, allow the Devil to tempt us, the world to entice us and concupiscence to urge us towards sin. To many people this thought of the divine allowing of temptation is difficult, a limiting of the almightiness of God. Actually it is because God

[1] James i. 13.

is almighty that He allows His servants to be tempted.  A conquering people that is not sure of its own strength refuses to the subject race any kind of independence at all and keeps it down with what it calls a strong hand, but the motive is fear.  God is not in that unhappy position, for the Devil is himself His creature; He therefore may allow men to be tempted, always giving them sufficient grace to overcome the temptation if they will.  " There hath no temptation taken you but such as is common to man: but God is faithful, who will not suffer you to be tempted above that ye are able; but will with the temptation also make a way to escape, that ye may be able to bear it." [1]  The realisation of the divine permission in this matter is a source of great comfort to the tempted at times when the power of evil seems overwhelming and the Devil tries to frighten him by making him believe that " there is no help for him in his God." [2]  It is, of course, always possible for the will to give way to temptation and fall into grave sin, but it cannot do so in spite of itself—such a fall is due to refusal of the divine grace, which is always offered; the Devil is strong, but he is not stronger than the will and grace together, he cannot bring so much *force majeure* to bear upon the soul that it *must* sin.

God does not allow the soul to be tempted without reason, and we must now pass on to ask why temptation is permitted.

First of all it is a test of character.  It is easy to imagine oneself to be the master of every virtue until one is submitted to searching temptation; the person who has never been tempted to intemperance finds it easy to condemn the drunkard and forthwith fall into the greater sin of pride, but let him be subjected to strong temptation of the same kind and he may fare no better than the man he despises, for he does not possess the virtue of temperance until he has been tested, though he may have the desire and intention of possessing it.  In this way temptation subserves the divine end of testing the soul and may be used as a means of strengthening the spirit.

Further, temptation may be a means of purifying the soul. Temptation not infrequently brings to mind the many times we have fallen into sin, and may be made the occasion of renewed contrition; indeed, an act of contrition is one of the best remedies against temptation, for contrition and sin cannot live together— one must drive out the other.  When He would cleanse the soul

---

[1] I Cor. x. 13.                    [2] Ps. iii. 2.

and lead it on to greater spiritual heights God often allows it to be the object of concentrated temptation; not because He wishes it to be lost, but because He wishes it, by triumphing yet more radically over self, to rise.

Temptation may thus be a means of spiritual progress, rousing the soul to watchfulness and energy, for through it the soul realises that virtue is not a happy state into which one may drift without much personal exertion, but something which is only attainable by hardness and labour. In this way fervour is stirred up and the soul deliberately sets itself to *attain* holiness. But not in its own strength: temptation is truly the school of humility, for through it the soul realises its own utter incapacity for good and the depths of its own potential sinfulness and learns to throw itself wholly upon the power of God.

There is much to be learned in the school of temptation, and for that reason God allows His children to be so sorely tried.

Temptation is made up of three successive phases; this is true of its most instantaneous as well as of its most protracted forms; sometimes the phases succeed one another so rapidly that they are barely noticeable separately and seem to be one, sometimes each phase is contested by the will.

The first phase is *suggestion* or *awareness*. This is simply the presentation of the sinful idea to the mind through the appetites or the imagination; somehow or other the idea comes into the mind, or the desire tickles the senses or the imagination.

This is succeeded by the second phase, which is *delight*. This is the more or less instinctive response of the soul to the suggestion. As yet it is but the lower part of the citadel in which the enemy has gained a foothold—the senses, the imagination, the temper, the memory, one or more of these has responded to the stimulus of the suggestion and is attracted by it.

It should be noticed that there is no sin in either of these phases, for the will has not yet declared itself. Many souls believe themselves to have fallen into grievous sin because evil suggestions form themselves in their minds and their senses desire their fulfilment in spite of themselves. It cannot be too clearly pointed out to them that the coming and going of such suggestions, even when there is an instinctive response of the lower self, is not sin unless it is consented to or encouraged by the will; it is on the presence or absence of the third phase, *consent*, that all depends.

The delight which is the second phase is involuntary, and

therefore not sin; the consent which is the third phase is voluntary, and therefore sinful.  The whole question of temptation has been dealt with at length and with the greatest lucidity by S. Francis de Sales in the fourth part of *The Devout Life*, and his exposition should be carefully studied.  We must content ourselves here with a short extract: " Though the temptation, to any sin whatsoever, should last all our life, it cannot render us displeasing to the divine Majesty, provided that we do not take pleasure in it (*i.e.* wilfully) and that we do not consent to it; the reason is that in temptation we are not active but passive; and since we take no pleasure in it we cannot be in any way blamed for it." [1]

We must consider the third phase with some care, for souls who fully appreciate the fact that all depends on this phase are frequently at a loss to know whether in a particular temptation they really sinned or not.  It should be said at the outset that sometimes it is impossible for the soul itself to know whether sin has been committed.  In that case, if the matter be weighty, it should be fully confessed, the doubt stated and the confessor's advice obtained; one of the great benefits of frequent Confession is the deliverance of the soul from scrupulosity or levity by the clearing up of such matters as this.  The first possibility is that consent may be refused and the temptation repulsed by the will; when this happens, even though there may have been some response by way of desire to the temptation, the soul has triumphed and refused to fall into sin.

In many cases such victory is perfectly clear and obvious, but in others it is less so.  With the attraction of the desire there should go the repulsion of the mind and will, and so long as this repulsion of the higher faculties from the temptation is there the soul has not completely consented.  " Never account yourself vanquished," says S. Francis de Sales, " so long as (temptations) are displeasing to you; noting carefully this difference between feeling temptations and consenting to them, which is, that we may feel them even though they displease us, but we cannot consent to them unless we take pleasure in them, because pleasure ordinarily serves as a step towards consent." [2]   If then the second phase is absent or unconsented to by the higher faculties there has been no fall into sin.

" As for the delectation which may follow the (first phase of)

[1] *The Devout Life*, Part IV., cap. iii.          [2] *Ibid.*

the temptation, inasmuch as we have two parts in our soul, the one inferior and the other superior, and since the inferior does not always follow the superior, but acts independently, it often happens that the inferior part takes pleasure in the temptation, without the consent—nay against the will—of the superior. . . . Though all may be troubled in our soul and in our body, yet we have the resolution not to consent to the sin or to the temptation, and the delectation which pleases the outer man displeases the inner, and though it be all about our will, yet it is not within it; and therefore we know that such delectation is involuntary and being such cannot be sin." [1]

There are many people who do not seem, at any rate to themselves, to react in this way to temptation but yet put up a very good fight. For them S. Francis' distinction between the outer and inner man does not seem to exist, for in time of temptation their whole being longs for the sinful object and there seems no attraction anywhere else, their only salvation being a dry and dogged acceptance of the Cross. In such cases there is truly a repulsion of the superior faculties from sin, though they do not realise it. It is not a repulsion from the particular matter of the temptation which S. Francis speaks of, but a desire and intention not to sin for love of Christ, even though the whole self be on the side of the concupiscence. Such temptation is great suffering, especially when accompanied, as it often is, by spiritual darkness, with no help of any conscious sense of repulsion or horror for the temptation and no realisation of the protection of our Lord; but the fight is won so long as the will holds on and the soul is being brought near to God through the depths of sheer self-denial.

The second possibility with regard to the crucial phase of temptation is partial consent. This may be of several kinds. Avoidable temptation is due to our own fault, and the deliberate running into temptation is of itself partial consent. It is not always easy to convince penitents of this or to persuade them to avoid temptation when convinced, for they frequently argue that circumstances or higher considerations prevent them from avoiding the occasions of sin. It is true that sometimes a soul must take risks, but it should never do so without the practical certainty that it is the will of God and should always seek the advice of its confessor. Such risks wrongly taken do not only provoke the sin towards which the temptation is directed, but also lead to

[1] *Ibid.*

presumption and spiritual pride, which may easily produce very serious consequences; it is therefore of the greatest importance that penitents should be warned of this matter.

Dalliance with a present temptation is also partial consent. As soon as its presence is realised, temptation should be repulsed at once, and so long as this is done even though it continue to return and entangle the lower faculties, there is no sin, but if the soul plays with the idea and fondles it, even though it does not propose finally to commit the sin to which the temptation leads, it has partially consented, and is therefore culpable.

Similarly, if the temptation is repulsed, but half-heartedly, wishing that it were possible to sin without blame, there has been partial consent. Further, when a soul is tempted to a sinful action it sometimes resists that temptation, but gives itself wholly to a sin of thought and imagination on the pretext that it must have some outlet for its desire and that the greater evil can be overcome by the less; that is a consent to sin which is none the less for being partial.

Such are the chief ways in which the soul partially consents to the solicitations of evil; there are, no doubt, many others, for temptation is often extremely subtle and the soul easily deceives itself in regard to it. It is very important that souls should be encouraged to be quite frank with their confessors in the matter of their temptations where there is the possibility of partial consent, and that the confessor should not dismiss all such matters as mere scrupulosity. Where there is scrupulosity he should be able to detect it and forbid the discussion of scruples, but levity is the more frequent disease.

The final possibility with regard to temptation is complete consent; in this case conscience is disregarded and the soul gives its whole self to the performance of that sin to which it has been tempted. There is no need to discuss it in detail, for it is quite easily recognisable.

Temptation may be, as we have seen, of great value to the soul, but it may also be a source of great danger—it is indeed always potentially dangerous; so God, Who allows us to be tempted, also gives us the prayer, " Lead us not into temptation." It will be well, then, to consider what measures the prudent soul should take against temptation.

Everything here may be summed up in our Lord's exhortation to the Apostles in Gethsemane: " Watch and pray." Watchful-

ness is not a virtue which is conspicuous in the majority of
Christians, and for this reason we are more frequently than need
be taken by surprise. " I did not think," " I did not intend,"
" I did not expect "; how often phrases of this kind are proffered
as excuses for some sinful lapse, but they mark " a sorry sentinel."
S. Paul pictures the Christian as a soldier on service,[1] and that
service demands watchfulness and resourcefulness as primary
desiderata, but few people bring them to bear on the spiritual
warfare; if they did there would be fewer sins of surprise. The
attacks of the enemy are frequently sudden and unexpected, but
that is exactly what one would expect the attacks of an enemy to
be. The spiritual man needs to be constantly on his guard lest
he be taken unawares.

This watchfulness must be coupled with humility. Past falls
should make one realise that, though the spirit may be willing,
the flesh is weak, and lead one to put one's whole trust in God,
praying with S. Augustine, " *Diffidam mihi, fidam in Te.*" Such
faith will be a guard against presumption, which is a most fruitful
source of sin, and that terror of the enemy which often hypnotises
the soul. These evils are complementary: in the one case we
have the fundamental sin of pride and in the other lack of faith,
both of which have the same effect of separating the soul from God
and thus rendering it an easy victim to suggestions of evil. We
need to strive to make the twin truths of our own nothingness and
God's almightiness fundamental to the spiritual life.

Further, it is important to avoid the occasions of sin, so far as it
is possible to do so. Danger commonly arises from circumstances
in which we have previously been led into sin, evil company or, at
least, dangerous company (it may not be evil in itself, but dangerous to one's own soul), idleness, softness of living, day-dreaming
and imprudent as well as evil imaginings.

Many folk encounter quite unnecessary dangers in the spiritual
life because they are afraid of being thought singular by their
fellows, and so they compromise with the spirit of the world and
lay themselves open to many temptations. Others fail to discriminate between recreation and idleness, with the same result;
they desire leisure in order that they may either do nothing or
else indulge in frivolous amusements, thus running into danger
through vacuity of mind. Others again become unduly attached

[1] II Tim. ii. 4. (R.V.) " No soldier on service entangleth himself in the
affairs of this life."

to the minor luxuries of life, which they quite innocently enjoy; but, being unwilling to sacrifice their self-love in small things, they become selfish and soft and unwilling to face the cross. Others again are entirely undisciplined in their imagination, very often believing that it is impossible to prevent it from doing what it will.

The cure for all these states of soul is a wise mortification, coupled with a true desire to love God above all earthly goods, and of this we shall have more to say hereafter.

It is particularly necessary to guard the weak spots of the soul. Everyone knows that these weak spots exist, but we generally either take them for granted as what we call necessary evils, or, being attached to them, we fail to probe them in any way. Much levity in this respect is the result of the use of that misleading term " besetting sin," which suggests that there are certain sins which we can hardly help falling into. Now sin is an act of will—an action, that is, of the soul itself—which cannot therefore " beset " the soul; we either sin or we do not—there is no " besetting " about it; what can and does " beset " the soul is temptation.[1]

Every soul is liable to certain particular temptations which make a special appeal to it; those temptations will therefore preponderate in its life—the attack, in other words, will be directed towards the weak spot and a besetting temptation set up. It is important therefore, if the soul is to overcome its spiritual enemies that it should, by careful self-examination, discover what its weak spots are and concentrate its energies upon building up the virtue which is lacking or weak and conquering the desire which leads to sin.

Watchfulness is of the greatest importance in the avoidance and overcoming of temptation, but it is not enough, it must be rooted and grounded in prayer. " As soon as you find yourself in any temptations, do as little children do when they see a wolf or a bear in the country; for straightway they run to the arms of their father or of their mother, or at all events they call them to their help and assistance. Have recourse in like manner to God,

---

[1] " Let us lay aside the sin which doth so easily beset us (τὴν εὐπερίστατον ἁμαρτίαν) " (Heb. xii. 1). This phrase does not contradict our assertion. εὐπερίστατος does not mean " besetting " in the sense in which the word is used above, but " readily standing around " (*circumstans* Vg.). Westcott in his note *ad. loc.* quotes Theopompus περίστατον βοῶσα τὴν κώμην ποιεῖ (' causes the village to *stand round* her ') and remarks that " The sin by which we are practically encircled answers to the cloud of witnesses with which God surrounds us for our encouragement." *The Epistle to the Hebrews*, p. 394.

imploring his mercy and his assistance: it is the remedy which our Lord teaches: *Pray, that ye enter not into temptation.*

" If you find that, notwithstanding, the temptation perseveres or grows stronger, run in spirit to embrace the holy Cross, as if you saw Jesus Christ crucified before you; protest that you will not consent to the temptation, and ask him for help against it, and so long as the temptation lasts, cease not to protest that you do not wish to consent to it." [1]

Watchfulness is impossible without prayer, for as soon as we cease to pray we cease to watch; the Devil, knowing this, frequently suggests to the tempted soul that it is unfit, by reason of its defilement, to approach God. This is an additional temptation and a subtle one, for, especially in temptations of the flesh, the sense of defilement is often strong in sensitive souls; but it must be remembered that, however horrible the temptation may be, it has of itself no power to defile the soul, for such defilement can only come by consent. The tempted soul should, therefore, brush away such suggestions as these, recognising them for the temptations they are, and, putting aside all other considerations, throw itself upon the mercy and power of God.

Victory over temptation is only finally possible in the power of divine grace, and the tempted soul should strive to be faithful in corresponding to grace, and regular and frequent in prayer and the sacraments. Regularity in these things is of primary importance, and here we find another frequent temptation—the suggestion, that is, that if spiritual exercises and the use of the sacraments become habitual they will become mechanical, and therefore worthless. But the spiritual life as it develops and becomes strong must become habitual; prayer and sacraments are just as necessary to the life of the spirit as food and drink are to the life of the body, and no one suggests that it is a bad thing to have regular meals on the ground that eating may become habitual and mechanical. The building up of the spiritual life is the formation of good habits to overcome evil ones and stablish the soul in virtue, for a virtue only becomes fundamental as it becomes a habit and part of the soul's life; irregularity is no virtue, but rather the reverse, and individual acts of virtue only become permanently valuable as they go to the formation of spiritual habits. The fallacy in this matter consists in treating the terms " habitual " and " mechanical " as though they were

[1] S. Francis de Sales, *op. cit.* Part IV, cap. vii.

K

convertible. A thing is not necessarily mechanical because it is habitual, but it may be. If one stupidly treats prayer and the sacraments as though they were charms without any intention of corresponding to the grace which they bring, the result is unintelligent mechanism, which produces its own nemesis; if, however, they are used regularly and devoutly, with wholehearted surrender to the will of God and a real desire to correspond to His grace, they are the fundamental means to the overcoming of temptation and advance in virtue.

When temptation is upon us, all the powers of the soul should be drawn to prayer and resistance. Resistance cannot be too prompt; many a fall into sin might be avoided if the soul would put all its power into immediate resistance instead of allowing the temptation to simmer within. S. Francis de Sales has a wise counsel here: " Do not look the temptation in the face," he says, " but look only at our Lord, for if you look at the temptation, especially when it is strong, it might shake your courage." [1] Looking thus at our Lord, we should then give our whole will to resisting the evil and so divert our mind from it by turning it to other things. In the case of temptations of the flesh, all spiritual writers are agreed that they must not on any account be parleyed with, but the mind should be distracted by other and, if possible, manual occupation. In the case of other sins, the consideration of the sufferings of Jesus will often bring peace and safety.

It is important not to make too much of temptations or to argue with them; often they are completely fraudulent in themselves, and only acquire power as we give it them. Temptations to doubt and mistrust, for instance, are frequently the hollowest of shams, which disappear at once on being ignored, but reduce the soul to chaos if taken seriously. We need to cultivate by prayer a sense of divine proportion and earnestly to give ourselves to the imitation of and friendship with our Lord and Saviour Jesus Christ.

One thing remains to be noticed: the wise conduct of the soul after temptation. It is not wise to institute a *post mortem*, and any self-examination which may be necessary should be kept till the proper time when one normally makes one's examen. If, however, the temptation has been overcome, one should make an act of thanksgiving, remembering that it is not in one's own strength

---

[1] S. Francis de Sales, *op. cit.*, Part IV, cap. vii.

that one has vanquished the enemy. If, unfortunately one has fallen into sin, one should instantly make an act of contrition. It is a mistake to postpone all contrition to one's evening prayer time or next confession, though, if the sin has been considerable, one must not imagine that a single brief act of contrition is sufficient for its expiation; what is necessary is to get right with God without delay, so that there may be no interruption of Charity, and one sin may not be allowed to draw others in its train. The service of God must not be interrupted even by sin; one must just pick oneself up and continue one's life with deepened humility because of one's own wickedness, but with a renewed confidence in God, which refuses to be discouraged by anything that befalls.

# CHAPTER X

# ACTUAL SIN

*All unrighteousness is sin and there is a sin not unto death* (I John v. 17).

IN this chapter we have to consider what sin is. That should be a simple matter, since everyone has a long and more or less varied experience of it and its effects behind him; but it is not so simple as it looks; indeed our general haziness as to the details of the subject is responsible for much ineffective direction and a great deal of obstruction to virtue.

Here we are not concerned with Original Sin, of which we have said something above, but with Actual, the sin which man commits. Such sin is easy to define, for it is simply disobedience to the will of God. It is necessary to keep this fact clearly in mind, for any experienced priest knows how frequently it is absent from the thoughts of his penitents. Quite a number of people have a conception of sin which is almost entirely limited to its temporal effects, and make confession because they realise that their sins have injured their own souls and damaged their neighbours. It would indeed be bad enough if that were all, but these effects are the least part of the dreadfulness of sin; far the most awful fact about it is that which it is in itself—an offence against God and a wounding of the Sacred Heart by disobedience to God's holy will—and it can never be known rightly until it is seen from the side of God. Man was created to do the will of God, and every act of sin is a contradiction of that creative purpose. That is fundamental.

Fallen human nature being what it is, it is possible for a man to disobey the will of God without knowing what he is doing, and therefore without intention to disobey, and it is possible to commit an act, which is in itself sinful, by accident. Such an act is sinful, for the will of God is disobeyed, but there is no guilt attaching to it, or perhaps only the guilt of a lesser predisposing sin. If a ship runs on a rock in a fog and several people are drowned, the captain is not guilty of murder, for he did not intend to kill them, but if the collision was due to his negligence he would be guilty of the lesser crime of man-slaughter; so, if a man is honestly and truly ignorant of the will of God and does not intend to commit sin, there is no guilt attaching to his action even if it be materially sinful.

This statement, it must be understood, applies only to *bona fide* ignorance of God's will. Much of such ignorance is culpable in itself, for it is the ignorance of a mind that has persuaded itself that such and such sins are not sins, or deliberately refuses instruction; and such ignorance is itself sinful.

In its full sense sin is conscious and voluntary disobedience to the will of God; for the act to be culpable the soul must know, or at least suspect, that it is sinning, and must will to do so. We are guilty in so far as we have light, and with the increase of light comes increase in the sinfulness of our disobedience. The believer in Mumbo-Jumbo may commit blacker sins than his Christian brother, but his guilt will be less because he has no clear knowledge of the will of God. "That servant, which knew his lord's will, and prepared not himself, neither did according to his will, shall be beaten with many stripes. But he that knew not, and did commit things worthy of stripes, shall be beaten with few stripes. For unto whomsoever much is given, of him shall be much required: and to whom men have committed much, of him they will ask the more." [1] It is no excuse for a Christian, to whom the revelation of God is given, to plead ignorance of the will of God if he refuse to listen to the promptings of conscience and to educate his conscience by prayer and instruction. Nevertheless conscience is to many but a name applied to an unaccountable spiritual discomfort, to which they pay as little attention as possible; and sin is crime, or, at most, those things which are "not done" in the circle in which they happen to move. Such people show a disregard for the law of God which is in itself culpable, and cannot claim their ignorance as an excuse for the sins which they commit. One of the most disquieting features of contemporary Christianity is the absence of a real sense of sin and an indifference to it which defies all the efforts of the preacher. Such indifference, so far from being a matter of little moment, is itself deadly sin.

S. John divides sin into two classes. "If any man see his brother sin a sin which is not unto death," he writes, "he

[1] Luke xii. 47–8.

shall ask, and he shall give him life for them that sin not unto death.  There is a sin unto death: I do not say that he shall pray for it.  All unrighteousness is sin: and there is a sin not unto death." [1]  There is, then, sin " unto death " and sin " not unto death," or, in the language of theology, Mortal and Venial Sin.  It is important to grasp the distinction between these two classes of sin.

Mortal sin is transgression of the known will of God, with full knowledge and consent and in a weighty matter, and its effect is to cut the soul off from sanctifying grace and to turn it away from God.

It is impossible in his fallen state for man wholly to avoid venial sin, unless he is sanctified by a special grace, as was our Lady, but the Christian who faithfully uses the means of grace and humbly desires to please God should never fall into mortal sin.  It is a sin about which there is no doubt, for the soul knows that the temptation presented to it is a grave one and, with that knowledge, deliberately wills to transgress God's will and resist the movements of His grace.  Such sin must inevitably cut the soul off from grace, for by it the soul contradicts the grace which it has and shuts itself up in itself against God, so truly committing spiritual suicide.

Venial sin, unlike mortal, is to be found in souls that love God, and even in saints, but it must not for that reason be thought of as consisting solely in " little " sins which are of no moment; indeed, that point of view which regards sins in terms of size needs radical alteration if it is to correspond to truth.  Every sin is an insult offered to the majesty of God, every sin added to the burden of the crucified Christ, every sin grieves the Holy Ghost, and we have no right to expect that God will not notice a sin because it is a little one and will allow us to indulge our petty foibles without check.  It is true that God is wonderfully long-suffering with our venial sins, but we may not presume on His loving kindness; most of the pain of Purgatory is the result of " little " sins.  Further, it is impossible for the sinner to judge whether his sin be little or great, for doubtless many of the sins which we commit light-heartedly enough cause the angels to weep.

We tend to take one-sided views of sin, generally regarding the sins of the flesh as the worst, and the more spiritual sins as

[1] I John v. 16–17.

being natural infirmities.  To some the only sin of real moment
is drunkenness, to others it is lust, while the " smaller " daily
evidences of pride and envy go unmarked, and anger is regarded
as inevitable.  Such classification of sin according to our own
bent is pernicious and dangerous, and ministers directly to the
most subtle and dangerous sin of all, which is pride.  We must
realise that no sin is negligible in the sight of God.

Complacency with regard to venial sins is a common temptation of the Devil, but it is entirely misplaced, for it is the " little
foxes that spoil the vines " and the vine of the soul has " tender
grapes." [1]

Venial sins are those of infirmity or surprise, into which even
holy souls may fall; sins in relatively unimportant matters, sins
of ignorance or thoughtlessness and sins which are the outcome
of particular temperament.  Such sins vary greatly in malice;
sins of surprise, the yielding to sudden temptation, the acting
on impulse or from natural imprudence, differ considerably from
those venial sins which are more or less deliberate and proceed
from unmortified self-will.

Venial sin is really sinful, and has far-reaching effects upon the
soul, besides being an offence against the love of God and a
real injury to one's neighbour.  In the first place, it reduces the
fervour of the soul and prevents that delight in the will of God
which is the distinguishing mark of the saint.  Venial sin is,
indeed, like dust on a mirror, which, settling on it gradually
in minute particles, dims its brightness and impairs its usefulness.
Secondly, although it does not, like mortal sin, cut the soul off
from sanctifying grace, it nevertheless hinders the operation of
grace by reducing the readiness of the soul's response to it.
Thirdly, it disposes the soul towards mortal sin and may, if
persisted in, become mortal.  Nothing is so blighting to the
soul or so difficult to eradicate as a habit of sin, be it what it
may, and habits of venial sin, which may, in themselves, seem
small enough, bind the soul in chains which need an infinite
outpouring of grace and almost infinite good-will and patience
to break.  Further, a small sin not infrequently prepares the way
to a greater one: small outbursts of temper may produce real
anger, which may deepen into hatred and even end in murder.
This fact in itself is sufficient to demonstrate the gravity of even
venial sin.  Fourthly, venial sin diverts the will from God

[1] Song of Songs ii. 15.

towards self and so ministers directly to that habit of self-pleasing, which is the essence of sin, and grieves the Holy Ghost by making impossible that relationship of love which should be between Him and the soul which He indwells.  To the soul attached to venial sin, the spiritual life becomes spasmodic, divided and lacking in attraction, because self-will is in competition with the will of God.

The purpose of Christian asceticism is the rooting out of sin and all that makes for sin from the soul; it is a work that is so difficult that without the aid of God it is impossible, and with the aid of God it demands the co-operation of all the powers of the soul.   In order to root out evil, the soul must desire good, in order to become detached from self, it must become attached to God;  therefore God puts into the soul the desire for Himself from which spring all the virtues of the Christian life.  We shall have much to say in the following chapters of repentance and mortification, and it should be borne in mind throughout this discussion that God does not will us to pull up weeds in order to produce a wilderness, but to pull up weeds and prepare the soil in order that He may plant the choice flowers of His virtues.  We need to encourage souls in the desire for God, for His holy will, for virtue, in order that they may persevere in the hardnesses of austerity and attain by the grace of God to true holiness.

We must now consider those distinctions in the manner of sinning which are none the less important for being elementary. We sin in four ways: by thought, word and deed and by omission. Sins of word and deed, being exterior, are easy to see, but something must be said of those in thought and omission.

Most people make little if any effort to control their thoughts; indeed, comparatively few realise that discipline of thought is possible: thoughts come into their heads and go, and that is all there is about it.   But thought is an operation of the mind, and can therefore be controlled by the will; so sin in thought is a possibility.  Nevertheless, not all bad thoughts are sin. Suggestions enter the mind through the senses and set up an attraction which, for a time, is involuntary;  that is bad, but not sinful.   If, however, the mind responds to the attraction and deliberately thinks about it there is sin.  We can choose to think about a thing or not to do so;  and it is important to avoid sins of thought, for such sins, far from being unimportant, poison the mind and result in wrong action, and even when their effect is less harmful than this, they set up a movement of the soul away from God or render the soul careless in regard to Him.

In spite of the fact that the Prayer Book causes us to confess them daily at Mattins and Evensong, many people hardly realise that there are such things as sins of omission; nevertheless they are of frequent occurrence. Such sins do not arise from definite temptation to evil; they are for the most part sins of laziness and tepidity, and may be very dangerous by slowly sapping the strength and energy of the soul. Many people who have, as they say, " never done anybody any harm," are often even less responsible for doing anybody any good; many who are innocent of grave sins are equally innocent of shining virtues, and so go on living a mediocre, negative sort of life, when they were meant to serve God with all their hearts. Sins of omission, by their very negativeness, militate against Charity, and are responsible for much of the flatness of contemporary religion. It is therefore foolish to say that sins of omission are unfortunate accidents which do not matter, for many a good rule of life has been ruined by them and many a promising soul has given up the struggle because it has never been taught to deal with them. Prudent self-examination as to what one has not done is just as important as self-examination as to what one has done, and much less frequently practised, and the wise confessor will keep his eyes open with regard to sins of omission and warn his penitents of the danger they run in allowing them to go on unchecked.

# CHAPTER XI

# THE CAPITAL SINS

*How many are mine iniquities and sins?   Make me to know my transgression and my sin* (Job xiii. 23).

SIN is a multiform and complicated phenomenon and, since it is essentially the principle of disorder, it is not easy to form a clear conception of it.   The same thing may, of course, be said of the diseases of the body, yet pathologists manage to discover their common causes and reduce them to at least a logical order. This chapter is concerned with spiritual pathology.   We shall not trespass upon the province of the moral theologian more than is necessary nor approach the subject from his angle; we are concerned with the spiritual effects, not the ethical culpability, of sin, and must therefore attempt to elucidate its root forms, which are commonly known as the seven Capital Sins.

Confusion is sometimes introduced into this subject by the application of the misleading appellation of " deadly " to these sins.   We have already attempted to define the nature of deadly sin properly so called, but commissions of the Capital Sins may be either deadly or venial, according to circumstances.   The Capital Sins are, in fact, the root forms of sin whence spring all its manifestations, either deadly or venial.

The list is very ancient, going back at least as far as S. Gregory the Great and coming to us by way of S. Thomas Aquinas and the Sarum Prymer, and is as follows: Pride, Envy, Anger, Covetousness, Gluttony, Lust and Sloth.

We have already seen that the triple concupiscence is the fundamental interior urge to all sin, and renders attractive to the soul the wiles of its three enemies, the world, the flesh and the Devil.   The Capital Sins are those fundamental forms of sin to which we are urged by concupiscence.   The lust of the flesh bringing forth Gluttony, Lust and Sloth; the lust of the eyes, Covetousness; and the pride of life, Pride, Envy and Anger.

We shall consider first the three spiritual sins of Pride, Envy and Anger.

## I. PRIDE

The chief danger of the spiritual life, due, surely, to the wiles of Satan, is the depreciation of the importance of spiritual sin. It is far more subtle than sins of the world and the flesh, and, consequently, far less obvious, and so it is often allowed to persist unchecked, and so work its ruin in the soul. Actually, spiritual sin is by far the most dangerous, and of all sin pride is the worst.

Pride is the root of all sins, for it is essentially the dethronement of God in the heart and the setting up of self in His place; it is the primary rebellion of the soul. Pride is the sin of the Devil, and it was to pride that he tempted Eve in the Garden when he said to her, " Ye shall be as God." [1] It was temptation to pride which our Lord had to face in the wilderness in the temptation of the temple pinnacle; and pride, in one form or another, is the root of all our self will. We fall into the sin of pride whenever we deliberately set aside the will of God in order to please ourselves; it is therefore the source of every deliberate sin, but it is also a definite form of sin in itself—an inordinate self-love.

It is exhibited in all forms of self-sufficiency and exaggerated ideas of one's own virtue, abilities or importance; in contempt for others; in looking at things and acting from the point of view of oneself, one's own comfort or advancement; the desire always to be thought well of, always to be the centre of attraction, to be constantly waited on and considered; confidence in the inerrancy of one's own judgment and opinion; the desire to impose one's own will upon others.

Pride has three children: presumption, ambition and vanity— unpleasant sins all of them. *Presumption* is the desire for things which are too high for us; it is shown in the spiritual sphere by a *penchant* for the more showy virtues and a strong distaste for hidden ones, the desire to be a mystic before one has begun to master the foundation virtues of the spiritual life; intellectually by an airy omniscience on all subjects, especially the most difficult. The presumptuous man has such a good opinion of himself that he never knows the limits of his own capabilities, nor

[1] Gen. iii. 5 (R.V.), *Elōhīm.*

realises his complete dependence upon God for any good that he does or is.

*Ambition* is the inordinate love of honours, dignities or authority over others. The ambitious man can never bear to be hidden or in a position of subordination, and he is frequently quite unscrupulous in regard to the rights of others.

*Vanity* is the inordinate desire to be thought well of. The vain man always wants to create a good impression, and not infrequently makes himself ridiculous in his attempts to do so, for nothing is so absurd, from the point of view of the observer, as the minor vanities. The man who always parades his own supposed virtues, who must be in the limelight, who always turns a story to his own advantage, is troublesome and silly, but he seldom realises the fact.

It is clear that all these sins are directly dishonouring to the majesty of almighty God. For man, who is but dust and ashes, to imagine himself to be something in his own right, to regard his virtues and talents (often grossly exaggerated) as his own, to aspire to heights which God does not will for him, to desire the emptiness of human esteem, to put his own will in place of his Maker's, would be ludicrous were it not infinitely sad. It is clear that by pride man inflicts upon himself the greatest injury that he can by separating himself from the loving will of God; but that is not all, for at the same time he injures creation, which can only find its true purpose and happiness in the fulfilment of the will of God, he spoils God's plan for His creatures, and, worst of all, he inflicts such injury upon the love of God as can only be known in the day of the revelation of all things.

The cure for pride is humility, a virtue against which most of our countrymen are unreasonably prejudiced. The genius of Charles Dickens has summed up this prejudice in Uriah Heep, but Uriah was not " 'umble," he was a canting hypocrite, and his sin was that dangerous " pride which apes humility," but is as far removed from it as mortal sin from sanctity. Humility is not hypocrisy, but sincerity; it does not consist in feigning oneself to be less than one is, still less does the humble man " fall down and humble himself: that the congregation of the poor may fall into the hands of his captains," [1] as the vulgar think. Humility consists in seeing oneself truly, as one is in the sight of God, nothing more nor less, realising that one's whole being,

---

[1] Psalm x. 11.

with whatever is good in it, is God's, though defiled by one's own sin; and in desiring that place and those things only which God wills for us, loving His will above all things and one's own not at all. A difficult virtue, and one we should not expect to be popular among the unconverted, but one in which the child of God must ever seek to grow.

The great danger of pride is its extreme subtlety and its Protean habit of masquerade. The forms to which we have alluded are easily recognisable, at least by others, but many symptoms of pride are extremely difficult to detect, and even the holiest desire to get their own way in some things. For those in authority it is not always easy to know whether one is seeking to require from others the will of God or one's own will, nor is it easy to avoid ascribing too much value to one's own judgment. We need to hate pride in all its forms as the hideous thing it is, to love humility, not to fear failure and hiddenness and, above all, constantly to pray to Him Who is " meek and lowly of heart " to give to us in increasing measure the true knowledge of the crookedness of our own heart and the priceless gift of His own humility.

## II. Envy

Like pride, envy, in its commoner forms, is a very subtle and hidden sin, and is often to be found disguised in the hearts of good people. It is a sin against our fellow-men, and consists in discontent with others' good. It proceeds from pride and the desire for one's own superiority; so the envious man is unhappy because another has something that he wants—wealth, comfort, happiness, goodness, it matters not what—or because another is preferred to himself. In this world material honours and happiness frequently go to the least worthy, and the good often feel, with justice, that they deserve better of the world than they get, and so the seeds of envy sprout in their hearts; for instead of accepting worldly inequality as a mortification and recognising the world's gifts as the unsatisfying good that they are, they allow the thought of others' good to rankle in their hearts, and so can never see or hear of one who is, for instance, " better off " than themselves without being hurt, saddened or uncharitable.

But the object of envy is not only the goods of this world, and anything which is or seems to be desirable—any way in which

one is made to feel one's own inferiority may become matter for
envy: so the man with the average brain envies the first-class
intellect of his neighbour; and even in spiritual matters we not
infrequently envy the person who is better than ourselves or
appears to be less severely tried.

Envy often produces dislike, or worse, of the person
envied, and so becomes *Jealousy*, which is made up of two
extremely dangerous components: self-love and fear of another's
superiority to oneself. Jealousy is the root of most of the strife
in the world, whether between individuals or communities, and
is all the more dangerous for being essentially unreasonable.
The jealous person is recognised as being a real danger to the
community of which he forms a part, for his sin reduces the
efficiency and ruins the peace not only of himself but of all with
whom he comes in contact; for jealousy finds continuous expression in all sorts of ways, most of them base and mean, and is a
fruitful source of greater sins.

S. James has remarked that " the tongue is a fire, a world of
iniquity: so is the tongue among our members, that it defileth
the whole body, and setteth on fire the course of nature; and it
is set on fire of hell." [1]   There are, of course, many ways in
which the tongue produces its evil works, but it is the special
instrument of envy and jealousy. The envious man does not,
and indeed cannot, keep his envy to himself; in all sorts of ways,
some of them unconscious, he tries to get the better of the object
of his sin and assert his own superiority; they range from small
expressions of dislike, innuendoes, half-truths, imputations
of unworthy motives, fault-finding, to real slanders; while
many apparently honest judgments of others are biassed by
this sin.

Where jealousy or envy exists just judgment is almost impossible,
for the envious man has always got some " wrong " whereby to
justify himself. In some cases this bias is hardly noticeable;
in others the intellect becomes so warped with passion that it
cannot form a right judgment even if it wishes to.

Apart from the effect which all sins against charity have upon
the soul's relationship with God, this has one in particular, for
the envious man tends to ascribe to God the harm which he
believes himself to suffer from the person whom he envies.
Many lapses from the practice of religion are the result of this

[1] James iii. 6.

sin alone, and, even where this does not take place, the soul cannot love God if he is deliberately envious of his neighbour.

The primary defence against envy is a real belief in the divine Providence. If God loves every soul that He has created and " divideth to every man severally as he will," [1] in that love, it is clear that He gives to each one what is best for him, even though the human idea of what is best may not be the same as the divine; we can therefore trust God, without whose will not even a sparrow falls to the ground, to give us what is really best. But the best for one is not the same as the best for another, and my good is by no means affected by what appears to me to be the greater good of another person. Further, we need to realise that those things in life which tend to lower our self-esteem are not evils but instruments of good, since without their discipline we should certainly find the doors of Heaven shut against us.

Trust in God's Providence leads to a holy indifference with regard to the things of this world. The will of God is holy and just and true; let us then accept what He sends with thankfulness and refuse to be envious of others who appear at the present moment to be happier than ourselves.

Further, we should strive above all things to " have fervent charity among " ourselves. Real Charity towards all men, whether we like them or not, is the virtue which exorcises this most obnoxious sin. If we truly desire the good of others as much as our own and truly love our neighbours as ourselves, as God requires of us, we shall have no room in our hearts for envy, though temptation knock at our door daily: we shall be able truly to " rejoice with those that do rejoice " instead of carping and criticising, and jaundiced jealousy will fly from us.

## III. ANGER

Anger has its roots in instinct and passion. This fact leads many people to believe that they cannot help being angry: they were, they will tell us, born with a bad temper, and so there is nothing further to be said. That suggestion would save much labour if it were true, but of course it is not. It is true that some people have naturally quick tempers which land them in difficulties before they know where they are, and so

[1] I Cor. xii. 11.

make the task of self-conquest difficult, but that is not the end
of the matter.

In its primitive form anger is a natural reaction against
something which thwarts us, but it soon passes beyond this
stage, and the man who raves for an hour because his breakfast
coffee was cold is, as we rightly say, " in a passion " no longer
instinctive, but emotional. The emotions may be joined by the
mind, as when we brood all day over a real or fancied slight,
and the sin reaches its height when the will goes over to the
enemy and we deliberately continue in a state of anger.

The preliminary stage of anger, impatience, causes trouble
to almost everyone and much to those who are naturally of a
quick temper; indeed it may never be wholly overcome. Its
chief danger lies in its suddenness—it has arisen and is over
almost before one is aware of it. That does not mean that
such outbursts are unimportant, for they frequently hurt others
extremely, and many a hasty sarcasm we would wish to have
unsaid. It is a common experience that the Devil frequently
attacks our morning prayers with greater vigour than he shows
towards any other devotion except our Communion, and the
reason is not far to seek; for if the soul has really prayed at the
beginning of the day it has, through recollection, a weapon
with which it may forestall all movements of impatience. This
trouble can seldom be directly attacked, but it may be overcome
by prayer and a strengthening of self-control in other directions.[1]

Impatience, if it is but transitory, need not do more than
ruffle the surface of the soul, but passion moves it to its depths.
Here we have vanity, self-will, pride and a variety of evils rushing in single spies or whole battalions to destroy that peace in
which alone the soul can keep near to God, and when the
passion passes, the soul is left weary and empty, at the mercy
of any desire that may be uppermost. The danger of passionate
anger is that it may be the bursting point of so many radical
sins; many a man has never realised what diabolical possibilities
there are within him until he has seen himself in a fit of passion
(for God in His mercy does sometimes allow the soul so to see
itself at such a moment). If impatience may cause hurt to
others, passion causes tenfold more, and moreover, the complete

---

[1] It is useful to practise making a deliberate act of acceptance of each circum-
stance which causes us impatience as it arises. This habit unites us to the will
of God and helps to form the habit of patience.

loss of self-control which strong passion produces may find its expression not only in words, but in deeds.

Many people are prepared to condone passionate anger on the ground that it cannot be helped (which is not true) or that it is soon over, but they do not approve a sulky temper; there is, indeed, little excuse for it. Impatience and passion may be more or less instinctive, but sullenness is deliberate, and so a more serious sin. In this kind of anger one broods over real or fancied injuries, or exaggerates the bad qualities, or what one regards as the bad qualities, of the person one is angry with, and deliberately encourages and prolongs the irritation and resentment, not infrequently planning, or at least desiring revenge; thus are born hatred and vendettas of all kinds.

Anger must never be encouraged or prolonged: " let not the sun go down upon your wrath." [1] It wants a large amount of humility and often courage to make up a quarrel quickly, but our Lord's words should be taken quite literally, " Agree with thine adversary quickly, whiles thou art in the way with him." [2] It is no excuse to say that we do not expect him to accept our apology; if he does not do so that is his responsibility; our anger is not cleared nor is reparation made until we have done all we can to make peace. How many family quarrels, estranging for generations those who should live in brotherly love and concord, were due in the first instance to nothing more than sullen anger and a pride that would not repent.

After Charity, which is obviously the root cure for this sin, temperance is the most necessary virtue [3] for its conquest. Self-control in the power and for the sake of Christ will ultimately break down the tyranny of instinct and passion; one should strive to build up a steadiness of outlook and deliberation of judgment with continual mortification of self-will, which will prevent one from being swept off one's feet by the unexpected onset of anger.

Further, one should learn to love and seek after patience with all one's heart. We live in an essentially impatient age; life is hurried; results must be instantaneous, and the patient man is considered to be rather a fool. This is not only due to the spirit of the age, but also to the virtual paganism of our civilisation, for patience is an essentially Christian virtue. The word does not occur in the Old Testament at all, but the New is full

---

[1] Eph. iv. 26.    [2] Matt. v. 25.    [3] *Vide* pp. 66 *ff. supra.*

L

of it.  The good ground of the parable " brings forth fruit with
patience," [1] and our Lord, giving counsel to His own in the
great apocalyptic discourse, says what is very germane to our
present purpose, " in your patience possess ye (R.V. ye shall
win) your souls." [2]  We speak colloquially of losing our tempers,
but when we lose our tempers we also lose possession of our
souls.  The sure way to gain command of them is patience, the
readiness to accept the will of God and wait for Him in calmness
of spirit.[3]

## IV. Covetousness

We have so far considered the three spiritual sins which are
the outcome of that form of concupiscence which is called the
Pride of Life; we have now to consider that which springs from
the Lust of the Eyes, the sin of covetousness.

We have already described the main features of this sin in
treating of the concupiscence which leads to it.[4]  It is the
inordinate love of worldly goods.  The goods of this world, in so
far as they are goods, and not evils which we mistake for good,
are given us by God in such measure as He wills for our need
and comfort *in via ;*  they are essentially transitory and applicable
to our mundane existence.  They are of three kinds:

(*a*) Those which are *necessary*, which God always provides.
These are, as a matter of fact, far fewer than any of us except
Carthusian monks, and others like them, suppose, being what
we call colloquially " the bare necessities of life."

(*b*) Besides these, there are goods which are *useful*.  Few are
capable of living fully on the bare necessities of life, the bodies
of most of us need a reasonable comfort, and the fruits of thought
and art are necessary to the development of mind and soul,
for " Beauty," as the Abbé Huvelin remarked, " is one of the

---

[1] Luke viii. 15.                    [2] Luke xxi. 19.

[3] In her excellent *Treatise of Prayer* S. Catherine of Siena, putting words
into the mouth of God, speaks of " Queen Patience, who is supreme over all
the virtues, because she is the mirror of charity.  She shows up in review the
virtues of the soul, and shows whether they are founded by me in truth or not.
She conquers, and is never conquered.  She is accompanied by perseverance
and fortitude, and when she comes out of the battle-field and returns with
victory to the house, to me, Eternal Father, the rewarder of every toil, she
receives the crown of glory."  Dialogue, p. 145.

[4] *Vide* pp. 106 *f. supra.*

proofs of truth." Here again we may be sure of having our needs provided for by the Providence of God, though He often requires hard work and spiritual progress as conditions of His gift.

(c) The third kind of worldly goods are *luxuries*. We have a way of talking airily about " little luxuries " as if they were quite harmless, the sort of things a generous mother sends to her child who is ill at school. A short excursion into etymology may give us cause to change our opinion. *Luxuria* is used in classical Latin to mean " debauchery," " extravagance," " excess," as applied to humanity; " rankness " as applied to plants; and, generally, " excess " or " superabundance " of anything; while in mediæval Latin it is the word whence we derive the English " lust," and the name of the sixth of our Capital Sins. This is hardly a respectable ancestry. Luxuries, then, are those goods which are in excess of our legitimate needs, or which minister merely to the satisfaction of the flesh; as such, they can never be right or desirable.

It is the third class of goods which the world desires and can never have enough of. History moves in cycles, and we see repeated again and again the same process: a civilisation is built up by discipline; it becomes powerful; then, sooner or later, sets in the process of decay; it becomes more and more luxurious and soft and then falls. Yet men do not learn that the luxuries of one age become the necessities of the next, and the vicious circle goes on; so men desire luxury for its own sake and are caught in the toils of covetousness.

It is not our business here to distinguish in detail between the useful and the luxurious—that is the province of the moral theologian—but we may make some discriminations. The desire of any good, even spiritual good, for its own sake and without reference to the will of God is covetous; the piling up of useful goods *præter necessitatem*, making the gaining of them the main object of life, is covetous; the acquisition of wealth without due care for the rights of others is covetous; the hoarding of goods which one cannot use is covetous.

Few people realise the evil of this sin, though most dislike it in others, as witness the contempt implied in the use of the word " miser " (which, by the way, really suggests that the covetous man is the most unhappy).

If we would be truly happy we shall keep our treasure in

heaven and in heaven only, living with the utmost simplicity, working for sufficiency but not superfluity, enjoying this world's goods as God means them to be enjoyed, but sitting quite loosely to them. "Having food and raiment, let us be therewith content." [1]

Covetousness is essentially selfish and produces a hard and grasping spirit, and its cure is generosity and largeness of heart. It is possible to find generosity combined with luxury, especially if the luxury is easily come by; but the covetous man is so busy amassing goods for himself that he has no room for generosity in his heart; he is so obsessed with getting that he has no desire to give—for that would take away from himself his possessions— moreover, he is commonly careless of the state of those less well off than himself. The spirit of Christ is utterly opposed to covetousness in all its forms, even the most apparently harmless; it was the danger of this sin that caused Him to require the Rich Young Ruler to sell all that he had and give to the poor, and prompted the sad reflection, "How hardly shall they that have riches enter into the kingdom of God." [2] Generosity in almsgiving is not only a great Christian duty, it is also a real aid to generosity of spirit, and a tried weapon against this fourth capital sin.

Above all things is it necessary to remember that all good comes from God and belongs to Him, that our possessions, be they great or small, are not our own, but held in trust for God, Whose stewards we are, to be used for Him and His glory and the good of our fellow-men, never merely for self; and that at the last day we shall be required to give an account of our stewardship.

## V. Gluttony

We come now to the last three sins—those which arise from concupiscence of the flesh, and, firstly, gluttony. This sin is an inordinate desire for the pleasures connected with the sense of taste and, as such, covers all sorts of excess in food. In colloquial usage, excess in drink is commonly called intemperance, but it is really part of the sin of gluttony, as has already

[1] I Tim. vi. 8.    [2] Mark x. 23.

been suggested in treating of the virtue of temperance, which is not specifically connected with this sin.

Food and drink being necessities of bodily life, it is to be expected that they will offer a very strong attraction to the natural man, an attraction which, in his fallen condition, he will tend to respond to excessively; in the case of alcoholic liquor there is the additional allurement of the sense of well-being produced by total or partial intoxication which may easily become an insatiable craving.

Minor excesses in food and drink are dangerous in that they tend insensibly to reduce habitual self-control. The woman who can never pass a box of sweets without nibbling, the man who can never pass his favourite place of refreshment without going in for a drink, do not sin gravely, but, by continually giving way to passing fancies or desires, they gradually build up a craving for sensible satisfaction which may become difficult to eradicate and they reduce their self-control not only in this matter, but in general.

In greater matters gluttony increases the disorder of the Fall, because the soul deliberately chooses to submit itself to the bodily instincts, and so becomes materialised in outlook and desire. The man who is constantly thinking about his food is not likely to rise to great spiritual heights, and the main danger of the habitual frequentation of bars is not intoxication (though that danger is real), but the materialisation of outlook which results.[1]

Gluttony inevitably exalts the flesh at the expense of the spirit and enfeebles the spiritual, intellectual and moral faculties of the glutton. It is, moreover, closely connected with the other fleshly sin of lust, and disposes the soul towards it by lowering the power of self-control and encouraging sloth.

There are, of course, many degrees of indulgence in this sin, some venial and even trivial, and others mortal; the latter need careful and wise treatment, and one needs to be on one's

---

[1] This must not be construed into an indiscriminate attack on public-houses. A badly conducted public-house is a menace anywhere, but such establishments are, happily, steadily decreasing in number. In the country the village inn is often in fact if not in name the local club, and the average amount of drinking is not excessive; it is the town public-house bar, where the social element is largely reduced, that exists almost entirely for the selling of drink, though there are exceptions here as well. Every parish priest knows the low mental, moral and spiritual level to which the habitual " pub-crawler " reduces himself.

guard against the former, for it is easy even for the best intentioned to become self-indulgent, and so soften the moral fibres of their being.

The Church gives us the keenest weapon against gluttony in the practice of fasting, and it can safely be said that the soul that conscientiously uses this weapon is unlikely to fall seriously into this sin. There has probably never been an age in which Christians as a whole treated fasting with such levity as they do in our own. Most people do not fast, and regard those who keep the Church's rules concerning it as freaks. Priests are frequently asked by penitents whether the Friday abstinence need be observed in a house at which they propose to stay, as their hosts, though good Church folk, " would not under-stand it," while some parents who do not fast themselves make it as difficult as they can for their children to do so. The parish priest, if he ventures to teach it, is not infrequently told that fasting is either " High Church " or " Roman Catholic." This, of course, is not true; our Lord fasted (and if He had need to, *a fortiori* the practice is necessary for us), the Bible has much to say about it, the Church has always required it and, in less self-indulgent days, it was not unknown among nonconformist bodies. Moreover, it is now commonly recommended by doctors, and so practised on medical grounds by those who may not be Christian at all.

The complete self-control at which the Christian soul should aim is practically impossible without fasting in some form, and the Church does not leave us in doubt as to her will for us in the matter.

It is necessary clearly to distinguish between fasting and abstinence. Abstinence consists in refraining from flesh food,[1] fasting in going without food altogether for a time, though in practice some food is allowed. The rule of fasting is that one full meal only may be taken during the day, usually at mid-day, and one half meal of not more than eight ounces of solid food (if the full meal is at mid-day this will be taken at supper-time, but the positions of these two refections may be reversed), and there may be a breakfast of not more than two ounces. Liquid food is not considered, as it does not break the ecclesiastical fast, though it does break the fast before Communion, with which we are not here concerned.

---

[1] Flesh food means meat, it does not include eggs or cheese.

" The Scriptures bid us *fast;* the Church sayes, *now,*" sang George Herbert, and we must ask when she does say " *now.*"

The Prayer Book gives a list of " Vigils, Fasts *and* Days of Abstinence " as follows: *The Evens or Vigils before:* Christmas, Candlemas, Lady Day, Easter Day, Ascension Day, Pentecost, SS. Matthias, John Baptist, Peter, James, Bartholomew, Matthew, Simon and Jude, Andrew, Thomas and All Saints. The forty days of *Lent; Ember Days; Rogation Days;* and all *Fridays* except Christmas Day.

This list is not only a long one, but it assumes that all the days included in it will be observed not only by abstinence, but also by fasting, a practice which would be impossible to many hard-working people to-day. We have to inquire whether we can legitimately distinguish between fasting and abstinence days. The 1928 Prayer Book like the 1662 one is ambiguous; it gives " a Table of all the Days of Fasting *or* Abstinence, throughout the year." This list is considerably shorter than that of 1662, as it *omits* the *Fridays* in the Octaves of Christmas, Easter and the Ascension and the *Vigils* of the Ascension, the Feasts of our Lady and all the Apostles except S. Andrew; but it gives no information as to which days are to be observed by fasting and which by abstinence, and so leaves the individual conscience without any guidance on the subject.

If we are to distinguish between fasting and abstinence, and so seek some alleviation of the heroic way of the Prayer Book, the only authority which offers any explicit guidance is the Roman. This rule prescribes *Fasting* on all the week-days of *Lent,* the *Ember Days,* the *Vigils* of Pentecost, the Assumption, All Saints and Christmas (except when these feasts fall on a Monday): and *Abstinence* on all *Fridays* (except Holy Days of Obligation and December 26th in England), *Wednesdays in Lent* (in England), *Ember Saturday in Lent, Holy Saturday* (until noon), *Ember Wednesdays,* and the *Vigils* of the Assumption, All Saints and Christmas (except when these feasts fall on a Sunday or Monday).

An ecclesiastical rule on this matter is of great importance, ruling out as it does all personal preferences, and the only rule which has complete authority over us is that of 1662; but, as we have seen, many people without any desire to shirk their duty in this matter find it a burden too heavy to be borne, while others, with the distinction between fasting and abstinence in mind, find it ambiguous. In such cases the wisest thing to do is to fall back upon the Roman rule until our own Communion discloses her mind more fully. This rule represents the minimum of fasting and abstinence which should be practised in normal circumstances by the ordinary healthy person. Dispensations are obtainable in cases of real need, and most Bishops habitually dispense from fasting the week-days of Lent except Wednesdays and Fridays. Fasting is not required of children or of persons over sixty years of age.

These fasts of precept should be kept with devotion, for without that they fail of their object, but so kept they are of inestimable value as real sources of strength to the soul. The person who is not afraid to fast and go against his natural inclinations in the matter of food learns to control the flesh in a way impossible otherwise.

Something must also be said of fasts of devotion. The custom of deliberately forgoing certain kinds of food which appeal to us for love of our Lord in a hidden and small way may be practised under all circumstances; abstinence from certain things (*e.g.* alcohol) for the sake of others is also praiseworthy if it be not done in a Pharisaical spirit; and in general the habit of eating and drinking what is set before one, " asking no questions for conscience' sake," helps greatly in the attainment of a spirit of holy indifference with regard to the pleasures of the table. Marked tendencies towards gluttony in any particular direction need to be counteracted by wise mortification, for the man who cannot willingly forgo certain forms of food is just as truly, though less obviously, a slave to his appetite as the drunkard.

## VI. Lust

It is unnecessary to catalogue the various manifestations of this sin, they are sufficiently well known and handled at length in treatises on moral theology and psychology: we must, however say something of the urges to it. If it is to be conquered it will not be by attempting to deal with its manifestations but with the impulses which precede the acts.

The first of these is physical. This should not be ignored, for, especially in adolescence, it is a force to be reckoned with whose sublimation is by no means easy. But as it is not easy, so neither is it impossible, as many think: work, healthy recreation and exercise all tend to reduce the physical urge.

The other impulse is mental, and is far the more important of the two, since, if the mind is right, the bodily craving will either not arise at all, or will be kept in check, and a careful guard will be kept over external sources of temptation. Much unnecessary temptation arises from vacuity of mind and the absence of mental and spiritual interest; if the mind is unoccupied and the life purposeless it is but natural that lustful imaginings should take possession of it, but the more the mind becomes active and interested in things that really matter, the less sway will this sin obtain over it.

Two elementary precautions are of primary value: a careful custody of the eyes, and, in time of temptation, flight.

The real defences, however, are positive and spiritual. To tempted souls frequent Confession is of the greatest value, together with regular Communion and constant prayer. This sin produces shame, and shame leads the soul to keep away from God, like Adam and Eve in the garden after the Fall, but nothing is so fatal as continuance in this isolation; the weaker the soul is the more it needs the help of actual grace and the more essential become Confession, Communion and prayer.

If other physical and mental interests are important for the overcoming of this sin, still more essential is a real spiritual interest. Lust, by its very nature, brings distaste for the things of the spirit, and the thought of chastity becomes a mockery; purity of heart, on the other hand, makes all impurity infinitely loathly. It is purity of heart which the soul must seek to desire and pursue. It is not difficult to lead the well disposed to desire purity of heart, however hard the fight may be to attain it, but it is undesired by many because they are imperfectly instructed as to its nature. Purity is not a pale, negative kill-joy virtue suitable only for the anæmic, rather it is the virtue of the valiant-hearted. It is very much more than endeavouring not to be impure; indeed, it colours every movement of the soul and claims the whole of life for its field: it is nothing less than the manful drawing of the whole self to the simple love of God, the consecration of the whole man to the Sacred Heart; the most positive, flaming, costing, giving, offering, worshipping thing that the soul can do. " Blessed are the pure in heart, for they shall see God;" they shall see because they love, and that love shall burn away all the dross. A simple thing, but a hard thing, and, because hard, infinitely worth doing.

## VII. SLOTH

This is the real canker of the spiritual life. Nothing can be done with the slothful man, all he wants is to be left alone to laze his miserable life away; all effort is distasteful to him and he fears anything which looks like discipline. Solomon says of him, "The slothful man saith, There is a lion in the way; a lion is in the streets. As the door turneth upon his hinges, so doth the slothful upon his bed. The slothful hideth his hand in his bosom; it grieveth him to bring it again to his mouth. The sluggard is wiser in his own conceit than seven men that can render a reason." [1] "The desire of the slothful killeth him; for his hands refuse to labour." [2] "I went by the field of the slothful, and by the vineyard of the man void of understanding; and, lo, it was all grown over with thorns, and nettles had covered the face thereof, and the stone wall thereof was broken down. Then I saw, and considered it well: I looked upon it, and received instruction. Yet a little sleep, a little slumber, a little folding of the hands to sleep: so shall thy poverty come as one that travelleth; and thy want as an armed man." [3]

Perhaps the truest thing that Henry VIII ever said was his assertion that "Idlenesse is chief mistresse of vices all"; for, in the words of the proverb, "Satan finds some mischief still for idle hands to do," and the slothful soul stands wide open and empty, ready for him to come in and work his will, which he is usually not slow to do. It is well known that unemployment weakens the moral fibre of a man and so degrades him by laying him open to the sin of sloth and the liability to evil suggestion that goes with it.

The slothful man accomplishes nothing and contemns the will of God, and his sin weighs him down to hell. It is clear then that it is a sin against which all should be on their guard, not only in bodily matters, but especially in spiritual, for it is possible to be very active externally and at the same time extremely slothful in spirit.

[1] Proverbs xxvi. 13–16.    [2] Proverbs xxi. 25.    [3] Proverbs xxiv. 30–34.

This sin attacks all parts of our nature, separately or collectively, and is to be found in many forms. Bodily sloth is obvious, but there is also intellectual sloth. This is extremely common in these days, when most folk are not trained to think and when they commonly prefer not to do so. It is slothful to take one's opinions ready made from the latest scientific oracle or from one's favourite newspaper, and equally so not to seek instruction in the truths of religion; yet how many people's opinions are based upon hearsay and the opinions of others, and how often religion is thought to have nothing to say for itself because one has never taken the trouble to find out what it does say. Most people talk loudly about politics and even louder about religion, yet one generally finds that those who talk most confidently have least right to an opinion, because, being intellectually slothful, they simply appropriate what someone else has suggested to them.

There is also moral sloth, which will never face a moral decision, but always take the path of least resistance until forcibly driven out of it. The morally slothful Christian likes to take refuge in the theory that one cannot apply the ethics of Christ as they stand to the conditions of the twentieth century, and thus excuses himself from taking the Christian ethic seriously at all; so we have a whole army of formal Christians who never attempt to live the Christ life and would be very much surprised if anyone suggested that it was their duty to do so, regarding the saints, if they regard them at all, as cranks. The slothful person will never face a final issue if he can help it—it is much too uncomfortable in its demands.

The last and worst kind of sloth is spiritual, and to it is applied the special name of *accidie* (ἀκηδία). This is a spiritual gloom and heaviness, which takes the life out of our prayers, kills devotion, implants a distaste for spiritual things and renders the soul restless and unhappy. It is impossible within the limits of this chapter to attempt an adequate exposition of this sin and its effects, nor is it necessary to do so, since this has already been done so completely and beautifully by Bishop Paget of Oxford in a book which should find a place on every priest's book-shelf.[1]

From what has been said and one's own experience, it is clear that sloth is dangerous, as predisposing to all sin and cutting the soul adrift from its loyalties. It holds the will and binds

---

[1] *The Spirit of Discipline.* Introductory Essay.

it down to the moods of the flesh and prevents it from rising up to God.

Of remedies, the first is simple, being merely hard work. S. Benedict says in his Rule,[1] " Idleness is an enemy of the soul. Because this is so the brethren are to be occupied at specified times in manual labour, and at other fixed hours in holy reading." This rule is fundamental to the Religious Life, and no less so to all fruitful life in the world.   Without spiritual, mental and corporal work the soul inevitably becomes soft and slothful.   The proportion between the three must, of course, vary according to the individual requirements and, if the soul is to keep a healthy balance, due provision must be made for recreation, but mere idleness, the just doing nothing, should be eschewed at all times. Many people spend the major part of their lives, when they are not obliged to be working, either in frivolous amusement or in what is called " killing time," a barbarous phrase describing a barbarous thing; such people become bored because they are slothful and wasting the life which God gave them for better things.   Willing work brings happiness and slays sloth.

> " Ydelnesse " (as Chaucer remarks)
> " Is the porter at the gates of sin,
> Eschew her, and by her contrary her oppresse,
> That is to say, by lawful besynesse,
> Wel oughte *we* our business to fulfil,
> Lest that the Fiend thurgh ydelnesse us spill.
> For he that with his thousand cordes slye
> Continuelly wayteth us to get,
> When he may man in ydelnes espye,
> He can so lightly catche him in his net,
> Til that a man be caught and sure beset,
> He is nought ware the fend hath him in honde;
> Wel oughte we werk, and ydelnes withstonde.
> And though men dredde never for to deye,
> Yet see men wel by resoun douteless,
> That ydelnes is roten sloggardye,
> Of which ther cometh never good increase;
> But sin that sloth ay holdeth in a leash,
> Only to sleep, and for to drink and ete,
> And to devouren al that others get." [2]

[1] Cap. xlviii.        [2] *The Seconde Nonnes Tale.*

Further, "agains this horrible synne of accidie, and the braunches of the same, ther is a vertu that is cleped *fortitudo* or strengthe, that is, an affeccioun thurgh which a man despiseth alle noyous thinges." [1] We have already discussed this " vertu," and need say no more here. The man who would overcome in himself sloth, and be by way therefore of overcoming those sins " that sloth ay holdeth in a leash," has need of strength and perseverance in serving God with all his might in the small things of daily life, so may he despise " alle noyous thinges " as he ought and attain to the joy of freedom in well-doing. His motto might well be the sturdy words of Pére Coton: " Let us go to Him, O my soul, *with giant strides*."

[1] *The Persones Tale.*

# CHAPTER XII

# REPENTANCE

*Now when they heard this, they were pricked in their heart, and said unto Peter and to the rest of the apostles, Men and brethren, what shall we do? Then Peter said unto them, Repent, and be baptized every one of you in the name of Jesus Christ for the remission of sins, and ye shall receive the gift of the Holy Ghost (Acts ii. 37–8).*

MAN was created in the image of God that he might know, love and serve his Maker according to His will. But sin is essentially rebellion against this purpose of his creation. We are born with a nature into which, by the Fall, sin has already entered, a nature which needs purification before it can begin to fulfil the purpose of its creation and purification from those sins into which it falls by the way. This purification is the work of God through the Sacred Passion, given to us in the sacraments of Holy Baptism and Absolution; it is given by no merit of ours, but because of the prevailing merits of the sacrifice of Christ, for apart from Him we can merit nothing, apart from Him there is no remission of sins, apart from Him there is no flowering of virtue. The power of Christ lifts us out of the sin-ruined natural life of the flesh and enables us to live in the Spirit, as God means us to do. But the divine purification demands a human response if it is to be effective, and that response is Repentance, without which the life of the virtues is impossible.

Repentance is the one essential condition upon which God opens to us the treasures of His grace. The message of S. John the forerunner was, " Repent ye: for the kingdom of heaven is at hand," [1] and repentance was the solitary condition upon which he baptized; when " Jesus came into Galilee, preaching the gospel of the kingdom of God," His message was the same, " Repent ye and believe the gospel." [2] Later on when, full of the Holy Spirit, S. Peter preached his first sermon on the day of Pentecost; his answer to those who asked him, " What shall we do? " was identical with the teaching of his Master, " Repent, and be baptized." [3] Neither Christ nor S. John the Baptist

---

[1] Matt. iii. 2.  [2] Mark i. 15.  [3] Acts ii. 38.

nor S. Peter required holiness of their catechumens, but repentance.

"Repentance from dead works " is, according to the author of the Epistle to the Hebrews, " the foundation," the first of " the principles of the doctrine of Christ," [1] and the foundation must be well and truly laid if the house is to stand; without a sound foundation and a deep one the building develops cracks in various places and eventually shows signs of falling, which is exactly what happens to the religion of those who try to be good without coming to terms with their sins.

Repentance is essentially a change of mind (μετάνοια), a turning away from the mind of the flesh, which delights in sin, and a hatred of sin in itself; but it is just this change of mind which is so conspicuously lacking in the average Christian. Sin is, for the most part, taken for granted as an unfortunate accident of human existence, a thing in itself delectable though forbidden, and it is not surprising that while this attitude of mind persists little or no headway should be made against it. Not until sin is realised as hateful is there any possibility of overcoming it. It is this change of mind which marks the difference between the Spirit and the Flesh; repentant souls may fall, as the result of temptation or infirmity, but they will not want to, neither will they continue in sin; they may feel the attraction of sin, but they will not love it.

If, however, Repentance were no more than this, it would be of little avail; it would, indeed, produce in the soul a divine discontent with evil, but would not materially assist in the production of anything better. This negative side of Repentance is of the greatest importance and must in no case be slurred over; the soul, if it is to attain to virtue, must face sin in all its native hideousness and realise that the Christian life is infinitely more than academic morality. But sin cannot be recognised for what it is until it is seen against the background of the love of God, and for the gaining of a new mind with regard to sin (μετάνοια) the soul must turn to God (ἐπιστροφή, conversio). The Evangelical Revival fixed upon conversion as the starting point of the spiritual life and the supremely important Christian act, and rightly so. It is true that in process of time conversion became a fetish, certain of its more emotional forms being regarded as essentials, which they are not, and man's act in

---

[1] Hebrews vi. 1.

conversion being made to take the place of the act of God in Baptism.  Probably few souls are " converted " in the Methodist sense, but unless they are converted in the true sense their religion is sterile.  Conversion or Repentance, for the two terms are nearly interchangeable, is simply the turning away from sin to God; to souls brought up in the practice of the Catholic religion this does not necessarily involve any violent emotional upheaval such as is frequently the prelude to better things for those who have been less fortunate, yet to them, as to others, there comes a moment of personal apprehension of Jesus which changes all the values of life.  The Saviour may come so quietly that the meeting is only known for what it is in retrospect, His coming may be by way of a sudden revelation or a gradual process, He may speak predominantly to the emotions, the intellect or the will, but in one way or another there comes to the soul an intuition of God to which its reply is either conversion or rejection.  Francis Thompson's poem " The Hound of Heaven " makes its appeal to religious souls of widely diverse Christian bodies not only because of its inherent beauty, but because it represents an experience which, in one form or another, is common to them all.

The primary business of the parish priest is to convert; it is useless to exhort people to be good, or moral, or mystical if they are not (let us frankly use the Evangelical phrase, for it is a good one) " converted souls."  S. Paul preached Christ crucified and so did S. Peter, and the practical result which each desired to bring about was Repentance; but their latter-day followers are often so preoccupied with the desire to be " up to date " and in touch with the modern mind, that the primary message of our holy religion is well-nigh forgotten. Frequently, too, we tend to believe our people to be much more " converted " than they really are, and so " leave " too soon and too frequently " the principles of the doctrine of Christ."  S. John Baptist was not afraid to preach the doctrine of Repentance in season and out of season, and we shall do well to follow in his footsteps, even though, like his own, our message should be unpopular.

The immediate incentive to Repentance is *Compunction.* This term is derived from the Latin verb *compungere* " to prick," and signifies a pricking of the soul.  We are told that S. Peter's audience on the day of Pentecost " were pricked in their heart," and the Apostle recognised that pricking as the first sign of the Repentance to which he desired to bring them. If the priest does not move his people to Compunction, his best instructions on Repentance will be sterile.

The human body is extremely sensitive to the pain of a prick, so we call small spiritual pains " pin-pricks," not because they are small, but because they hurt and irritate; in such wise Compunction hurts, which is one reason why so many refuse to face it.

I. The pain of Compunction is caused by the dart of God, and brings us to sorrow for sin, which is the first part of Repentance. There are many considerations which may lead us to grieve for sin; some of them are frankly self-regarding; these are not to be despised if they lead the soul to Repentance, but they are not adequate in themselves. We may sorrow for sin because of its ill effects upon ourselves, and the consequences of sin here and now frequently lead souls to try to get right with God, and in so far as they do that they are valuable; the fear of Hell also operates in the same direction. We may also seek Repentance because of the injury which our sins cause to others; this is a higher motive, but still inadequate. In fact, sorrow for sin based on merely human considerations may operate in either of two opposed ways: it may lead to remorse which partakes of the hopelessness of Hell and has led many a soul to despair and, in extreme cases, to self-destruction, or it may lead to *Attrition*, which is real Repentance, for moral theologians tell us it is sufficient for absolution, but inadequate.

The only really adequate sorrow of Repentance is caused by the pain of having offended God and caused, in our measure, the Passion of our Lord. This is *Contrition*, which is the movement of divine Charity in relation to our sin. Face to face with Christ crucified, the soul realises the heinousness of its sin; it is no longer a question of ethical theory, it realises the cost, not of sin, but of its own sin, to the Sacred Heart, and it is pierced with sorrow. It is the breaking of the alabaster box that the ointment of Charity may be poured out at the feet of God.

II. Contrition leads necessarily to *Confession*, which is the supernatural offering to God of a natural human urge. The child that has been naughty is unhappy until it has told its mother (though she knew all about it before) and been forgiven; the Prodigal Son naturally resolves to make his Con-

M

fession as soon as he has "come to himself" after his sin; and in both cases full and expressed forgiveness follows the Confession, and does not precede it, nor does the love of the parent make the Confession unnecessary, though that love has been there all the time, for the child has not become completely "forgivable," in Dr. Moberly's phrase, until it has confessed its sin. Similarly with the soul and God, the Bible bears witness to the fact that, in the dispensation of God, Confession is the necessary condition for the divine forgiveness, for, until the soul has nerved itself to make that offering of humility and, be it said, honesty, its Contrition is not complete.

III. The third part of Repentance is *Satisfaction*. This is begun in Confession, for by Confession we seek to make such amends to God as we can for the wrong we have done Him by our sins. The act of Confession is, however, but the beginning of our Satisfaction; there must be further the intention to make *reparation*, and this is done by the acceptance of a penance. In the formula of Confession used in the sacrament of Penance the penitent is required to *ask* of the confessor not only absolution, but also penance, which penance is not remedial, but reparatory; but we are struck at once by the apparent inadequacy of the penance ordinarily imposed. It is well that this should be so, and it is ordinarily a great mistake for confessors to bind penances heavy and grievous to be borne upon their penitents, for the very lightness of the penance compared with the sin is a reminder that the very heaviest penance which we could undertake would be entirely inadequate as reparation for the smallest sin, since that sin caused the death of the Saviour. The essence of our acceptance of penance is the offering of obedience, by asking for it we place ourselves unreservedly in the hands of our confessor to do exactly what we are told, whatever that may be, and that is real reparation; then we are told, maybe, to say a prayer with which we are perfectly familiar and which perhaps we are accustomed to say, and it seems almost paltry; which it is, as is all our own reparation, but it becomes of infinite value when united with the reparation of the Cross, which alone can really avail. So the simple act of penance nails us with Christ on the Cross and gives us a true part in that atoning offering. The acceptance of penance means that we are willing to be crucified with Christ, and is efficacious in that it is united with His perfect offering.

Further, Satisfaction, if it is to be real, requires the intention to forsake sin, and it is of no use to confess our sins in order to quiet our conscience if we intend to return to them as soon as temptation assails us; if we are truly contrite we are desiring to be done with sin for ever and intending the will of God only, and there may be no mental reservations. We know from sad experience that even with the grace of God we shall fall again into sin, but we must neither desire nor intend to do so; there must be the intention to fight against sin and advance in virtue, otherwise there is no true contrition.

Repentance is an act of reparation to God for the dishonour we have done to Him by sin, but it is not solely a transaction between the soul and God. Man is not simply an individual, he is a member of the human family and, if he is a Christian, also of the Church, which is the family of God; to these families he is bound by the most subtle and fundamental bonds, so that, as S. Paul says, " If one member suffer, all the members suffer with it." [1] Sin, even the most personal, injures creation, humanity, the Church, as well as God, and true repentance includes reparation to these as part of our reparation to our Creator and Father. In the sacrament of Penance the Confessor is the representative of God, but he also, by his priesthood, represents the Church and, by his manhood, humanity and creation. In sacramental Confession the soul does what it cannot do in any kind of confession to God alone—the confessor is the proxy of all who have been injured by the soul's sin, and the soul in confessing its sin to him confesses it to all whom it has injured. This is an aspect of the sacrament which is very generally overlooked, but it is of great importance: often it is the only reparation that can be made to others for sin, and, in any case, any other reparation that can be made is incomplete without it. The child that, in a fit of temper, has broken its sister's doll may save up its pence and buy her a new one, but if it has not confessed its fault and expressed sorrow the new doll is but a present. So with the children of God, restitution is a necessary part of penance where such restitution is possible, but for many sins restitution is not possible, and even where it is, the making good is secondary to the change of heart and offering of charity which is expressed by Confession and sorrow for sin.

[1] I Cor. xii. 26.

Contrition, Confession and Satisfaction are the three necessary parts of Repentance, and they are inseparable; we cannot have one without the others—Repentance is, indeed, a real trinity in unity. Some people feel a certain sorrow for sin, perhaps as the result of a moving sermon, and think that that is enough, but without the other parts of repentance that is merely emotionalism without any real movement of the will, and produces no results; others think that if they make their Confession that is all that can possibly be required of them, but that is formalism; few attach right importance to Satisfaction. It is not enough to preach Confession, the priest must preach Repentance whole, in all its parts, and seek to pierce the hearts of his people with the divine dart of Compunction by lifting up before them Christ crucified.

It is a noteworthy fact in the lives of the saints that the more they advance in holiness so much the deeper does their Repentance become, and if we would be like them we shall not merely strive to imitate this virtue or that, or to frame our lives on the external manifestations of theirs, but to grow as they did in Compunction. We have spoken of Repentance as synonymous with conversion; this does not mean that it is a single act which, once done, is finished. In many lives there is a crisis which is never repeated, but Repentance in all its parts is continually necessary while there is sin in us; and even were we to attain to perfect sanctity, that attainment would bring with it such a realisation of the horror of past sin that we should feel that we had only just begun to be penitent. Everything that we learn of God, all that we come to know of ourselves by the light of the Holy Spirit, should go to the increase of Compunction and the deepening of Penitence. The monks of S. Benedict wear black habits because they are penitents, S. Francis called his Third Order an order of penitents, Penitence is the mark of the saints, that has, indeed, made them saints; and for all it is the way to the Heart of God.

# CHAPTER XIII

## MORTIFICATION (I)

*Ye are dead, and your life is hid with Christ in God. When Christ, who is our life, shall appear, then shall ye also appear with him in glory. Mortify therefore your members which are upon the earth ; fornication, uncleanness, inordinate affection, evil concupiscence, and covetousness, which is idolatry : for which things' sake the wrath of God cometh on the children of disobedience* (Col. iii. 3–6).

THE subject of this chapter is of the greatest importance, for apart from mortification the spiritual life is impossible; but it is a subject which is very widely misunderstood and feared. To many the term simply connotes a masochistic tendency cultivated to an unhealthy degree by the monks of the dark ages which should be discarded by all healthy-minded people. Others, with their eyes firmly fixed on the unessential, believe it to be concerned wholly with terrific austerities, and so turn away from it through fear.

As a fact, both of these ideas—they can hardly be called views—are wrong and spring from entire misconceptions of the nature of mortification, which is a necessity to all serious life (and *a fortiori* to all spiritual life, whether Christian or otherwise), and is clearly laid down as a fundamental principle of the Gospel by our Lord Himself. The contemporary notion of free self-expression as the ideal of life is pernicious and untrue, and produces nothing but unscrupulous egoism. For serious progress in any walk of life mortification is necessary if a man is to be anything more than a piece of mechanism—the doctor, the scientist, the lawyer, the soldier, the sailor, the business man must all learn to " scorn delights and live laborious days " if they are to accomplish anything; free self-expression is of no use whatever to them. And the same thing is true in a far deeper degree of the life of the spirit: those who would serve God must refuse to serve self, those who would be one with Him must be empty of self, and the means thereto are mortification and prayer. The undisciplined soul cannot be the instrument of the Holy Spirit, and the means of attaining to self-discipline is mortification.

Much opposition and indifference towards mortification are due simply to concupiscence: the self does not want to be disciplined, and so maintains vigorously that mortification is either unnecessary or mischievous or both, but the Christian way is the way of Christ, and no soul was ever yet perfected without the Cross. It is therefore of first importance that we should face the fact and necessity of mortification.

Even among the pious this fundamental need is often set aside, and so we see the unedifying spectacle of people who are probably an immense trial to their relations and friends, desiring to be " mystics," and absorbing multitudes of little books which purport to teach them how to become such in six months or so, at the same time showing no desire for confession and making no notable attempts to curb their concupiscence or extirpate their sins. To such people the love of Jesus crucified is pure sentimentality, producing no fruit in their own lives, but rather resulting in self-deception; they should ponder well the words of an old spiritual writer who says that " to aspire to perfection without the serious practice of mortification is merely to nourish self-love, and to feed our imperfections without making any progress." [1]

It is greatly to be desired that priests should teach their people constantly, clearly and wisely on this most important and necessary matter. Realising one's own great lack of mortification, it is right that one should feel considerable diffidence in this, but such diffidence should lead not to avoidance of the subject, but to greater strictness in one's own life.

People rightly look for a greater measure of strictness of life and a more serious purpose in a priest than they expect to find in the laity, and if these things are absent, though they may flatter us as " good fellows," they will not respect us as ambassadors of Christ: the priest needs real mortification in himself if his ministry is to be of any value whatever. Further, souls need, as we have said, teaching on this matter. There is amongst us a widespread desire for real and costing religion, and this desire needs detailed guidance in the ways of mortification and prayer above all things; but, alas, such guidance is seldom forthcoming, and those who seek it are, only too often, urged not to take such things too seriously, but just try to be good.

It is not for the writer of such a book as this to beat his fellow-

[1] Barbanson, *The Secret Paths of Divine Love*, Part I, cap. iv.

servants, but he may perhaps be allowed to remind them of a passage from S. Peter's speech in " Lycidas," which, learned at school, has ploughed upon his own back fairly often " and made long furrows " :—

> " Blind mouthes! that scarce themselves know how to hold
> A Sheep-hook, or have learn'd ought els the least
> That to the faithfull Herdmans art belongs!
> What recks it them? What need they? They are sped;
> And when they list, their lean and flashy songs
> Grate on their scrannel pipes of wretched straw,
> The hungry Sheep look up, and are not fed,
> But swoln with wind, and the rank mist they draw,
> Rot inwardly, and foul contagion spread:
> Besides what the grim Woolf with privy paw
> Daily devours apace, and nothing sed."

There is also a contrary danger against which we should be on our guard, a danger which arises, not from neglect of mortification, but from an enthusiasm which is not according to knowledge. It is of the greatest importance to the director of souls that he have a clear grasp of the nature and balance of mortification, combined with a real knowledge of human nature, but there are directors among us to whom mortification means only extraordinary austerities and who, with more zeal than sense, would urge all pious souls to such austerities whether they are ready for them or not. Such direction may do untold harm, and we shall have more to say on this point later on. To regard all our geese as swans is a human failing, but because S. Therèse of Lisieux is a saint it does not follow that all our pious women are " little victims."

Mortification is for all, but there are different kinds of mortification, some of which are universal, and others particular. Souls require training separately, with careful attention to their personal *attrait* and circumstances, and we need greatly to be on our guard against broadcasting for the multitude teaching which is intended for the few.

The chief concern of the parish priest is the multitude; he has, for the most part, to lead a number of everyday people in the ordinary ways of the spiritual life, to teach them to love God and their neighbour and to mortify themselves. These things are for *all*, and mortification, with which we are at present concerned, is not a close preserve of favoured souls, but a means of the sanctification of all. It is, for the most part, a simple, costing and everyday thing, not a rushing after novelty; and, if we are to commend it rightly to our people, we must commend it as the simple, costing and everyday thing that it is, without hysteria or mysticality.

Fundamentally, mortification is the necessary condition of living the gospel life. For this reason, the great Evangelicals, no less than great Catholics, have been people of great mortification; we must therefore look in the gospel for the root of the matter.

Our Lord teaches us quite unmistakably that the Christian vocation is the love of God (" Thou shalt love the Lord thy God with all thy heart, and with all thy soul, and with all thy mind. This is the first and great commandment "),[1] and the end which we are to seek is nothing less than the perfection of God. (" Be ye therefore perfect, even as your Father which is in heaven is perfect.") [2] This vocation and this end are a pearl of great price, the value of which is not something, but everything. (" The kingdom of heaven is like unto a merchantman, seeking goodly pearls: who, when he had found one pearl of great price, went and sold all that he had, and bought it.") [3] This teaching is universal; our Lord does not confine it to the few; it is a principle of the kingdom of heaven. God asks all men to love Him and, as a necessary consequence, to leave all else for the sake of that love. In order to be attached to God by love we must be detached from all things created; that is why our Lord required of the rich young ruler, who was, after all, a good and pious young man, that he should sell all that he had,[4] and said to the multitude, " Whosoever he be of you that forsaketh not all that he hath, he cannot be my disciple." [5]

Detachment is fundamental to the spiritual life; thus S Ignatius makes it the foundation of his Spiritual Exercises: " Man was created," he says, " to praise, do reverence to and serve God our Lord, and thereby to save his soul. . . . Hence it follows that man should make use of creatures so far as they do help him towards his end, and should withdraw from them so far as they are a hindrance to him in regard of that end. Wherefore it is necessary to make ourselves detached in regard of all created things." [6]

But detachment must go further than things, and extend

---

[1] Matt. xxii. 37–8.  [2] Matt. v. 48.
[3] Matt. xiii. 45–6.  [4] Mark x. 17–22.
[5] Luke xiv. 33.  [6] *Spiritual Exercises*. Rickaby's edition, p. 18.

also to persons. " He that loveth father or mother more than me is not worthy of me: and he that loveth son or daughter more than me is not worthy of me. And he that taketh not his cross, and followeth after me, is not worthy of me." [1] This is a hard saying, and one that is so frequently misunderstood that the majority of Christians tend to put it aside altogether; yet it is fundamental to true Christianity. It should be noted that Christ does not tell us to cease from loving others—rather He says that we shall love our neighbour as ourselves; but the love of our neighbour is subordinate to the love of God and springs from it, it becomes sinful when we love him more than God; in a real sense we must, if we would love God truly, leave all other and cleave unto Him alone. " The spiritual man must learn to leave himself and all other things for the love of God. He must possess nothing with any tenacious affection of heart. He must hold fast to no visible and perishable thing, to no passing and created object. He must not seek the friendship, familiar intercourse or presence of anyone, however holy, for any mere natural gratification. He must remember that not only bad things, but even those that are good, may become hindrances if they are loved or sought inordinately." [2]

By detachment we strive to give our whole self to God, that all our willing, loving and desiring may be in Him. This involves the discipline of the whole man and the collecting of all the powers of the soul into one, that, being detached from the pursuit of pleasure for its own sake, the soul may find pleasure in God alone. " As a stream which divides its waters into many channels, cannot communicate itself so plentifully to all as it would to one, if all the others were stopped up: so it is absolutely necessary that we set some stops or bounds to our hearts, that so, having checked all corrupt inclinations and inordinate love of ourselves, we may with greater freedom apply the whole current of our affections to the only object of all our good, God and His love.

" *Humanum cor* (says S. Thomas) *tanto intensius in aliquid unum fertur, quanto magis a multis revocatur :* Man's heart adheres the more intensely unto one thing, by how much the more it is withdrawn from all others. Wherefore one of the principal means of gaining the divine love is the collecting of all the powers of the soul into one, so that they may be able to fix

---

[1] Matt. x. 37-8.    [2] Blosius, *Spiritual Instruction*, cap. II, Sect. i.

themselves on God alone, exercising themselves day and night in whatever may stir them up to love him. For as long as, being full of the love of earthly things, we let our understanding, will and memory dissipate themselves upon exterior things, we shall never attain true introversion, nor that unity and simplicity of spirit which is the immediate disposition for the presence of God in our souls." [1]

This detachment and gathering the soul into one can only be attained by constant mortification. " If any man will come after me," says our Lord, " let him deny himself, and take up his cross daily, and follow me." [2] Mortification is just that denial of self and daily bearing of the cross.

Our Lord Jesus Christ is our example in mortification, as in all else; in the sacred Humanity we find perfect detachment, perfect mortification, perfect devotion to the will of God, perfect love of the Father; but He is more than our example—He is our life. S. Paul, in writing to the Colossians of the Christian life, reminds us of this fact, and, further, that we are here and now " risen with Christ." " If ye then be risen with Christ," he says, " seek those things which are above, where Christ sitteth on the right hand of God." Seek God and His love and the obedience and joy of heaven. " Set your affection on things above, not on things on the earth." Not only seek God, but steadfastly love Him. " For ye are dead, and your life is hid with Christ in God." The Christian lives by the risen life of Jesus, but that life is only attained through death to sin and self. " Mortify therefore your members which are upon the earth." [3] You are dead, therefore put to death the old man, the concupiscent longings, the merely earthly desires and loves, because you are living the risen life. There is mortification: the crucifixion of the old man that we may be filled with the life and love of Jesus.

Quite simply, mortification is nothing more nor less than the daily bearing of the Cross. For this reason we can hardly expect it to be popular among unconverted Christians. On the other hand, we must not be surprised if generous souls who long to give themselves wholly to Jesus crucified tend to rush to extremes in their penances. The priest's duty is, in the first case, to do all he can to move his people to the love of God,

---

[1] Barbanson, *Secret Paths of Divine Love*, Part I, cap. iv.
[2] Luke ix. 23.                    [3] Col. iii. 1 *ff.*

and, in the second, wisely to guide that love that it may grow to perfection.

We must now pass on to consider in what mortification consists.

I. First, it consists in the avoidance of sin and its occasions. Continuance in wilful sin is incompatible with true love of God; consequently any soul that really wishes to love Him, or even one that merely desires to live rightly, will strive to eradicate not only mortal, but also venial sin. This is not an easy matter, as we have seen; it involves a very real bearing of the cross, and severely tempted souls need great encouragement to persevere. It is so hard to struggle against one's sinful desires, and so very unromantic, that we often long for more interesting and self-sought means of mortification; nevertheless no soul can be saved without this cross, and there is no point in the spiritual life at which it may be abandoned.

To each soul some sins make more appeal than others, each has its own vulnerable points where self-will must be mortified by self-abandonment, and much of the wearisomeness of the spiritual life is caused by the necessity for continual strife against one particular temptation: too often this strife is unnecessarily protracted and the soul depressed because it is thought sufficient to go on producing general, unpractical or merely formal resolutions at intervals, without any clear perception of the cause of the danger or any real attempt at mortification in regard to it. It is useless to go on saying, " I resolve to fight against my besetting sin," if one is neither attempting to build up the opposite virtue nor to discipline the interior irregularities which lead to it.

The mortified soul will seek to discipline itself with regard to its known weaknesses and the sins into which it naturally tends to fall, and it will be found that persevering mortification of one sinful tendency will bring with it the mortification of others as well and strengthen the character in often unexpected directions. Let us take, for example, a case of chronic bad temper. A person may go on all his life saying, " I resolve not to lose my temper to-day," and be nothing bettered, but rather grow worse. There must be a positive force behind the mortification— the force of a peaceful spirit, which must be deliberately cultivated, as though there were no contrary temptation there at all, with prayer and recollection and real desire. It may then be discovered that certain persons " get on one's nerves." It is of no use to argue with a reaction of that kind—one must search for the cause, which is often enough that one is looking at them solely in the light of one's own moods, and not at all from the point of view of God's will; that means mortification of what the old writers called the " irascible appetite." Further examination may reveal the fact that certain people arouse one's anger with great frequency and vehemence, which may lead to the discovery of springs of hitherto unrecognised envy, jealousy, pride, self-will and the like which require deliberate mortification. Thus it may be found that the real remedy against one's bad temper is deliberate mortification of a particular kind of pride, and that the root of the matter is not in one's " nerves " or irascible appetite, but in the mind and the will.

II. It will thus be seen that particular mortification in regard to sin is of the greatest importance in the spiritual life, and it leads on to the second form of mortification, which is the general mortification of our " members which are upon the earth."

It is a matter of experience that our whole selves are disorganised and thrown into confusion by concupiscence; if, then, it is to be possible for us to attain to any real unification of this complexity and make any real offering of self to God, a general self-discipline of this kind is a necessity.

It should be noticed that the aim of mortification is the discipline of the whole soul, and not its destruction. We are to put to death, not the soul or any part of it which God has created good, but the sinful tendencies of the old man, the concupiscences of fallen nature. We are to root out the desire for self-gratification and plant in its place loving self-surrender to the will of God and the fair flowers of God-regarding virtue.

First of all there is need for the mortification of the *senses*, which by their disorderly clamour lead the soul to a divided allegiance and many sins. The root of this mortification is simplicity of life and the avoidance of what is merely luxurious and superfluous. This is attained in the Religious life by the vow of poverty, by which the Religious possesses literally nothing, in obedience to our Lord's command, " Sell whatsoever thou hast, and give to the poor, and thou shalt have treasure in heaven: and come, take up the cross, and follow me." [1] It may be thought that this principle is possible only to Religious; S. Francis, however, thought otherwise, and proved that he was

---

[1] Mark x. 21.

right by the establishment of his wonderful Third Order, which has done so much for the training of saints, and humble followers of Jesus, in the world. The key-note of the spirit and rule of this Order is the following of Christ in self-chosen poverty, yet it has contained kings like S. Louis of France and great land-owners like the Lady Giacoma, as well as humble souls like the Curé d'Ars; but the Lady Giacoma administered her family estates as a trust from God, and without any thought of personal magnificence, and S. Louis wore a hair-shirt beneath his purple and ermine. The principle of evangelical poverty is essential to the following of Christ; to some it will mean what it meant to the rich young ruler, to others it may mean that far harder thing, the stewardship of riches for the glory of God, to all it means that detachment from created things which we have seen to be fundamental to the Christian life, and constant refusal to cultivate softness of living and to make bodily luxury and self-gratification even minor ends of life. If we would but come back to the following of Jesus in poverty of spirit we should cure, not only the ills of our own souls, but also those of our sick and pleasure-seeking civilisation.

It is through the senses that external impressions enter the mind, so, since these impressions are of different kinds, good, bad and indifferent, the use of the senses is in need of mortifica-tion. A multitude of sense-impressions are constantly clamouring for admission to the soul, but only those to which we pay atten-tion actually find their way within. In the normal course of events our selection of sense impressions is more or less fortuitous. The untrained listener at an orchestral concert hears a great deal of noise going on, but is quite incapable of distinguishing between the trombone part and that of the French horn, though if there should be " a tune " he recognises it and is happy: out of, say, sixteen sets of noises he has heard, by good fortune, part of one. With the trained musician the case is different: he will be able to keep clear in his mind the lines of the various instruments, or, if he will, follow the movement of a hidden part—say the viola—in its setting as though it had no competitors. Really to listen to music one needs to mortify one's sense of hearing and hear what one needs to hear. The same thing applies to reading a book in a train; in order to accomplish that difficult feat one has to prevent one's eyes from wandering over the landscape, one's ears from taking in one's neighbours' conversation, and, very often, one's nose from being distracted by the pipe of the man opposite.  If mortification of the senses is necessary for such very ordinary things as reading and listening to music, it is still more so in the spiritual life, but it is very seldom practised.  As we go about we allow our eyes to take in a thousand unnecessary and distractive impressions, and then wonder why we get tired and disinclined for any spiritual effort; what is needed is careful custody of the eyes and ears, by which we only allow ourselves to attend to those things which concern us.

It may be objected that such custody of the senses leads to lack of observation and absence of mind.  This is not so. Observation is not the taking in of any and every impression, but attending to the significant; which involves custody of the senses in regard to the insignificant, and such custody, so far from making the mind absent, renders it more collected.

Custody of the senses is a very real mortification, for it is a direct attack upon concupiscence; for that reason we constantly try to persuade ourselves that it is either undesirable or impossible.  Concupiscence of the eyes leads us to uncurbed curiosity, concupiscence of the flesh to worse things; both gain full sway over a soul that has not got its attention under control, hence the importance of this mortification.

Further, S. James tells us that " the tongue is a fire, a world of iniquity," [1] and here we find a further need of mortification. " Especially needful is a guard over the tongue, for it is written that life and death depend upon it.  And silence is at once the secret and the safeguard of devotion, innocence and a pure conscience.  How much harm is done to the spirit of recollection by unnecessary discourses, idle words, calumny, detraction, murmuring and lies! " [2]  There is little doubt that most people talk far too much and far too carelessly even when they do not consciously speak ill.  The love of silence, the habit of speaking as in the presence of God are great needs, and they can only be attained by careful watchfulness and mortification of speech.

" The servant of God must keep an exceedingly careful watch over his senses.  As far as possible he must take care not to use any of his senses for mere self-gratification—that is, not to look at, hear, smell, taste, say or touch anything merely for the

---

[1] James iii. 6.
[2] Barbanson, *op. cit.*

pleasure of doing so; and when he has slightly offended in such things he must severely reprove himself. He must not desire to see, hear, smell, taste, speak or touch more or otherwise than God interiorly permits. For if he seeks delight in creatures, he will not be able to find true delight in God." [1]

[1] Blosius, *op. cit.*, cap. II, sect. ii.

# CHAPTER XIV

# MORTIFICATION (II)

*Our old man is crucified with him* (Rom. vi. 6).

THE exterior mortification of the senses which we have been considering is of the greatest importance to the spiritual life, but the interior mortification of the mind and heart which we have now to consider is even more so.

It should be noticed at the outset that these two forms of mortification go together, neither being complete without the other. S. Vincent de Paul remarks somewhere that interior mortification is the soul of piety, but we must not on that account neglect exterior mortification, without which it is a soul without a body. Simplicity of life and custody of the senses are the outer defences of the castle of the soul, and must be securely kept if the castle is to withstand invasion and maintain its loyalty to its Lord; but the keep of the castle is the will, which we must seek to keep whole and entire in its allegiance.

Allegiance to God is shown by a pure intention to love and serve Him in all things, which involves detachment from all things created, and this requires a rigorous interior mortification. It is not enough to keep from overt sin if one is still desiring the forbidden fruit in one's heart; the desire must be mortified, as well as the sense, and the will must be kept steady in its love of God. The purpose of interior mortification is to make the will, united with the will of God, master in its own house, and the intellect (by which we understand the higher intuitive faculties as well as the conscious intellective ones), enlightened by the Holy Ghost, the keeper of its conscience. This mortification is nothing less than the continual application of the will of God to the movements of the soul, and it depends on the enlightenment of the intellect by prayer and the strengthening of the will by grace. It is essentially a continuous response to the leading of God, not a self-actuated movement; were it otherwise it would be an impossibility. The interiorly mortified soul intends the will of God in all things, seeks of Him grace to perform his will and guidance thereto. Interior mortification seeks to bring all the powers of the soul into obedience to the will of God that He may do what He will with and in it.

The essence of the matter is the constant intention to abandon at once whatever is evil or dangerous for the love of God.

(1) This involves, first of all, mortification of *thought*. The imagination is constantly at work presenting to the mind thoughts of all kinds, indeed it is probable that the majority of what passes for thought among people with untrained or only partially trained minds is imaginative rather than intellectual, and the imagination is, as we have seen, notoriously impatient of control, though it is capable of education. The important matter here is the mortification and unification of interest. It is impossible to prevent wrong suggestions of the imagination, but it is possible to reject them, and such rejection becomes progressively easier as the soul loses interest in them by reason of its increasing interest in the things of God: therefore S. Paul says, " Whatsoever things are true, whatsoever things are honest (σεμνά), whatsoever things are just, whatsoever things are pure, whatsoever things are lovely, whatsoever things are of good report; if there be any virtue, and if there be any praise, think on these things." [1] But such interest in the things of God implies constant rejection of all imaginings which are contrary or dangerous to them, which is mortification, and such mortification must not be confined to the imagination, but extend also to the intellect. The intellect is easily absorbed by self-interest, warped by prejudice and passion and inflated by pride, and the man of God needs to mortify his mind that he may see all things *sub specie æternitatis*. God asks not only for acute, but also, and chiefly, for consecrated thinking.

(2) Perhaps the most essential part of interior mortification is the mortification of *desire*. Here again we have a movement which begins in the dim instinctive recesses of the soul and surges up into consciousness, bringing with it much disorder. Those natural attractions and aversions with regard to people and causes, fear and hope with regard to the future, instinctive depressions, unreasoning anger and the like, which disturb the peace of the soul and drive it into sin. How many souls fall away from God through lack of mortification in such things. How much is the Church weakened by the same cause.

[1] Phil. iv. 8.

N

It is essential that the servant of God should realise that his life is supernatural, and not merely natural, and that the supernatural life involves a real ἀπάθεια with regard to the instinctive desires. The natural desires are essentially self-regarding and need to be subordinated to the love of God by constant mortification. All desires can be sublimated to the love of God, but such sublimation involves a radical mortification of self. Desires must be mortified quickly before they attract to themselves the higher powers of the soul, and their mortification requires constant watchfulness and prayer.

(3) The final interior mortification is that of the *judgment*. Our life is determined by our judgments; we have to make a judgment on every choice that is offered to us and everything that we consider, but unfortunately we too often regard the faculty of judgment as an automatic part of our soul, which does its duty without need of care from us. Too many people believe that what " I think " is right because " I " think it, and it never occurs to them that their judgment may be warped by a multitude of prejudices, imaginations and desires. We need to realise that our judgment is only right so far as it is consonant with truth and righteousness, or, in other words, with the will of God; we need, therefore, unity with the indwelling Spirit and a rightly informed mind. Here again is room for much mortification: in important judgments we should be sure that we are fully informed about the matter, in all things we should seek deliberation. A momentary pause and lifting of the soul to God before coming to a decision will save the soul from many errors.

A further means of mortification is the acceptance from the hand of God of all the adversities which may happen to us. These range from the little accidents of daily life to great trials.

(*a*) We have been considering various means whereby the unruliness of the soul may be mortified, we now come to that whereby everything that happens to the soul in its earthly pilgrimage may be a means of purification and union with Jesus.

All pain may be a means of such purification and union, but it does not necessarily follow that all pain is that. A painful disease, for instance, may be the means of complete purification of a soul and a real share in the Passion whereby one is allowed to " fill up that which is behind (τὰ ὑστερήματα) of the afflictions

of Christ," [1] but it may also be the occasion of grave selfishness
and rebellion against God. All depends on the intention of the
soul: the mortified soul will accept its pain with joy or, at least,
fortitude, the unmortified soul will resist and resent it with all
its might.

Eliphaz the Temanite remarked that " Man is born unto
trouble as the sparks fly upward." [2] This saying is capable of
great exaggeration and, if regarded apart from the love of God,
may lead to pronounced pessimism, nevertheless it is true.
God tests the soul daily by pain, not in order that He may hurt
it (such a view of God is unworthy to the last degree), but that
He may purify it and give it somewhat to offer to Him in union
with Jesus crucified. Religion is essentially the offering of the
soul to God, not the gaining of happiness from Him, though the
way of faithfulness leads to eternal joy; but the soul is bankrupt,
it is nothing and has nothing save what God made and gave it;
by sin it has made itself unworthy even to approach God. But
God gives it through the Precious Blood firstly pardon and then
grace, and then pain, that it may itself be crucified with Christ
and have " somewhat to offer " in union with its Lord.

The statement that our pilgrimage through this world is a way
of daily pain seems to some people profoundly depressing and
to others unhealthily exaggerated, but in truth it is neither. The
thought of the suffering of pain is always depressing to the
selfish and unmortified, as well as to the well-meaning but ignorant soul. So long as pain is meaningless it is the most terrifying
fact in the world, but to the Christian it should not be
meaningless; so long as our best energies are devoted to having
what we call " a good time," so long will the thought of pain
depress, but the moment we face the love and will of God and try
lovingly to accept and offer the pain He gives, then " perfect love
casteth out fear."

There are people who enjoy bad health with an enthusiasm
worthy of a better cause, similarly in the spiritual sphere there
are those who would have us believe that life is nothing else than
pain of the most crushing kind, so they go through life wrapped
in a gentle melancholy.

Such a view is wickedly exaggerated; the spiritual life is one
of joy, which, at times, is intense and leads to a joy which shall
be eternal; and pain, even when crushing or prolonged, is

[1] Col. i. 24.        [2] Job. v. 7.

ancillary to joy.   Our blessed Lord was truly " a man of sorrows
and acquainted with grief," but that was not all; it was " for
the joy that was set before him " that he " endured the cross,
despising the shame."   Pain is neither the whole of life nor an
end in itself, but it is our daily trial.

Now, some people, mostly superficial folk in easy circumstances, take a directly opposite view to that which we have just
criticised, and regard pain as an occasional intruder into a life
which is predominantly happy.   Incidentally such people have
but to exercise a little imagination with regard to others less
happily situated than themselves to be convinced of the inadequacy of such a view; but, leaving that consideration on one
side, it is essential for our purpose to realise that there are many
kinds and degrees of pain.   In the physical sphere pain may be
occasional or chronic, general or localised, subdued or acute, an
ache or a stab; in the spiritual sphere it is similarly diverse,
and when one says that pain is the daily trial of the soul, one has
in mind pain in its widest connotation.   We may suffer in any
part of our complex being, from a great variety of causes, and with
very various degrees of intensity.   God gives us physical pain,
but not always; grief is an occasional and dreaded visitant; the
great spiritual trial of apparent separation from the Beloved
tests the love of interior souls.   But these great sufferings are not
all.   No day passes without those minor pains which are none
the less searching for being what we call small.   The little
accidents of life, trying, stupid or bad-tempered people, minor
hardships, anxieties, irksome occupations, little ailments, inter-
ruptions, " pin-pricks " and the thousand other small things
which wound self-love and against which one's natural tendency is
to rebel, are all pains, as well as the burden of the world's sin
which lies so heavily upon the hearts of Christ's lovers.

There is no lack of pain in daily life, and the more sensitive
and Christ-like a soul becomes by so much the more does its pain
increase in depth and intensity.

" Properly speaking, there is nothing either little or great
with regard to the things of God.   Everything that bears the
impress of His Will is great, however small it may be in itself." [1]
The little pains of everyday life as well as the great pains which
are of less frequent occurrence are sent or permitted by God and
are His means of fashioning the soul into His likeness.   Consider

---

[1] Grou, *Manual for Interior Souls*, p. 115.

the art of the sculptor: he takes a rough and unfashioned block of marble, neither beautiful nor shapely, but with potential beauty; with a chisel he cuts away a good deal of his marble, and out of what is left fashions a statue. If one were entirely ignorant of the process and the end in view, one would say that this cutting-away process was wasteful and meaningless, but in fact every blow of the mallet is designed to produce a particular effect, to form a certain part of the work of art, and when at last the statue is finished it stands forth in all the beauty of the marble, a perfect expression of its maker's thought.

That is a parable of the discipline of pain. The soul at the beginning is rough and unfashioned, but its end is to be the perfect expression of the thought of God. This end is attained by pain, by the blows of the mallet and the cutting of the chisel; but this pain is not fortuitous, for every part of it is co-ordinated to the end in view: so, sometimes by heavy blows, more often by light ones, the process goes on, while the statue, now in one part and now in another, begins to show forth the thought of God, until at last, if not in this life certainly in the next, it is fashioned into His image.

As with all parables, there is a point in this similitude at which it ceases to be adequate, for marble is, by reason of its nature, both passive and insensible, whereas the soul is neither. The fashioning of the soul into the image of God demands a response if it is to be effective, the constant intention of accepting all pains, whether great or small, as from the hands of God, that thereby self-will may be mortified and the soul more and more wholly abandoned to the will of God.

This mortification is one of the great tests of true spirituality. There are many people who " seem to be religious " who nevertheless are constantly complaining over the slightest discomforts, rendering all about them unhappy by their minor selfishnesses; such people are lovers of self and not of God, and for that reason their religion, tried by the touchstone of mortification, is vain. Others desire, or believe they desire, extraordinary mortifications which lie outside their state of life, but make little attempt to accept those lesser ones (or apparently lesser ones) which God sends them within it; that is pure self-will and a sign, not of devotion, but of lack of true mortification. They are like those folk, against whom Spurgeon inveighed, who sing lustily

> " Were the whole realm of nature mine
> That were an offering far too small,"

what time they search their pockets for the least valuable coin they can find to put in the collection bag.

This way of mortification is most precious, for it is the work of God Himself; it involves no straining of desire after ways which are not ours, for it lies wholly within " that state of life into which God has called us." It leads the soul to place its whole will and desire in the hands of God; for it is not self-imposed, and therefore accomplishes, if we will, just what He wants, which is all that matters.

(b) In discussing this way of mortification, we have, so far, only indicated exterior pains; but it should be realised that God also disciplines the soul by interior pain, which the mortified soul must learn to accept and offer. Some souls, especially beginners, are but little tried in this way; but, as the soul advances, God commonly sends it spiritual desolations and trials, that it may be drawn to love Him for Himself apart from any joy or gifts that He may give it. At the beginning of its course the soul often experiences fervent happiness, but this is subsequently withdrawn and the soul learns, if it does not fall away, to go on with very little sensible consolation in prayer, and frequently has to face shorter or longer periods of time when its prayer is just hard work with no apparent movement from God at all; later on perhaps it may be called to undergo real desolation, so that it cries out with its Lord, " My God, my God, why hast thou forsaken me? " All these things are the deepest pain, but, when they are not the result of sin, they should be accepted as the most searching means of mortification, for by them God is leading the soul from sensible to truly spiritual devotion, from love of His gifts to love of Himself, from the darkness of light to the light of darkness.

In setting itself to accept with joy these God-given spiritual mortifications, the soul should root itself deeply in the soil of faith. God may lead one into a dark room where one can neither see nor touch Him and may have, apparently, little attraction towards Him; nevertheless, one does desire Him, or one would not feel the lack of fervent love, and He has not withdrawn Himself from one, though one has no sensible perception of His Presence. One must be content to suffer, that His will may be done, confident that this most intimate cross will work His will in us more effectively and more costlily than any other.

It may be well to remark that not all souls are tried by God
in this way; indeed some souls seem to attain to a considerable
degree of sanctity without, apparently, suffering very severe
spiritual trials.   God has His own purposes with regard to each
soul—some He leads by one way, some by another; but it is
well that devout souls should know that spiritual suffering of
one kind or another is almost inevitable at some periods of spiritual
advance, and so not be taken by surprise when and if such
trials occur to themselves.   The soul should strive to be detached
from spiritual joy as from other sources of self-satisfaction, and
be ready to give itself peacefully into the hands of God should
He remove it.

There is yet one more way of mortification which differs from
all the rest in one important respect—namely, that it is wholly
voluntary; it is a cross of devotion, and not of necessity.   This
way includes all austerities and penances which the soul *imposes
upon itself* for the love of God.

We have considered the ordinary ways of mortification by which
the soul becomes purified and united with our Lord: the detachment of the will from all things created, in order that it may be
perfectly obedient to the will of God; the mortification of the
inordinate movements of the senses, heart and mind by discipline; the acceptance of every pain which God sends as a means
of mortification and union.   In the lives of the saints we find a
further and even more radical mortification in suffering raised
to the heroic level, terrific austerities voluntarily undertaken and
prayer to God for the quintessence of suffering.

The austerity of the saints is a fact which flames across the
history of the Church and which should be faced by serious souls,
and, like all such facts, it either repels or attracts powerfully.
Many souls are so repelled by the austerities of the saints that
they throw over all idea of mortification of any kind; others,
fewer in number, are moved by a sentimental and morbid
interest in suffering to desire to emulate the saints in this matter;
others again—and these are very few—are moved to heroic
austerity because the hand of God is upon them and they cannot
do otherwise.

We are mainly concerned with the first two classes, and into
both we should seek to instil a little humility and respect for
hard facts.   The austerities of the saints are the austerities of the
saints, but these souls are as yet far from sanctity, and the ways

of advanced spirituality are, as yet, " far above out of their sight." Souls which are repelled by these austerities need to realise the intense beauty of sanctity as revealed in those who are likest Jesus, and to learn that such beauty of soul is only attained and maintained by mortification which, for themselves, means the ordinary ways which we have considered.

It is right that souls which desire to love God should be attracted by the saints who are His friends, but they must realise that they are not themselves saints, and that they have to learn to love God within the limits of their own capacity and state of life: it is rash in the extreme for a soul living in the world, possibly married, with a husband and children to care for, to emulate the austerities of a Carmelite nun because S. Teresa used and counselled such austerities. The call to self-imposed suffering seldom comes in the early stages of the spiritual life. " The desire of doing and suffering great things," says Père Grou, " is very often, indeed almost always, an illusion of self-love and an effort of presumption. I should like to practise great austerities, like such and such a saint; I should like to bear great crosses: this is all pride, all vain-glory. The saints never formed such desires. Now, what happens to us when we do? We try of our own will to perform great austerities; then our fervour cools down, and we give them up; then some very ordinary crosses present themselves to us, and the soul, which thought it could bear such great things, finds it cannot bear the very smallest." [1]

Pride, self-will and presumption; these are hard words, but true of the souls which the great director had in mind. It is pride in this matter to say that what the saints have done I will do. We should indeed desire the heroic virtue of the saints— would to God it were more desired—but the more whole-heartedly we desire it the more clearly we shall see our own glaring failures in the ordinary ways of love, and fear to lay hold of the sufferings of the saints before we have learned to mortify ourselves in lesser ways. The saints undertook greater austerities not because they were less mortified than we are, but because they had learned, what we are but striving after—the complete obedience of self to the will of God—and could therefore proceed to greater lengths in the extermination of self-love than the ordinary soul dreams of. No soul should dare to take up

[1] *Manual for Interior Souls*, p. 117.

extraordinary mortifications until it has gone very far in the ordinary ones.

We must here guard against a misconception. The Religious Life is a life of mortification voluntarily undertaken; are we therefore to say that only advanced souls have a call thereto? Such a statement would be manifestly absurd; we must distinguish. God calls souls to the Religious Life at all stages of spiritual advance; it is a call to a complete renunciation of the world and to a life of voluntary mortification, but, the surrender once made, the austerities of the Religious Life are not extraordinary to the Religious, however much they might be so to the ordinary Christian, but are incidental to his state and rule, and therefore are part of our third means of mortification. There is a sharp line of division between the cloister and the world here.

It may seem strange to say that a desire for pain is due to self-will, but so in some cases it is. It is often noticeable that souls who desire to practise voluntary austerities of various kinds are singularly impatient of the little crosses of everyday life—a sure sign of self-will. Some souls, of an unhealthy and sentimental tendency, make a real cult of pain, magnifying the most ordinary sufferings into mystical ones, and believing themselves to be victim souls, when they are only beginning to be purified; so they become self-absorbed and, instead of falling deeper in love with God, they make an idol of their own imaginings. That is self-will of a most subtle and dangerous kind: the saints who, being throughly purged, really did suffer with Jesus for the sins of the world did not contemplate themselves suffering; pain, especially imaginary pain, was not the centre of their universe, their sacrifice of self was complete, being actuated only by the costing love of Jesus and compassion for the world.

A further mark of self-will which is not altogether unknown is the refusal either to ask or accept direction in the matter of voluntary austerities. It is quite certain that no voluntary austerities should be practised unless permission has been asked and obtained from one's director and his ruling has been accepted without argument. Souls of the kind we have in mind frequently think they know better than their director and, if he refuses to allow them to do whatever they like, decide at once that he does not understand them, and absolve themselves from obedience on that account. The ruling of the director on a matter of this kind must be accepted as the will of God, and independence or contempt is a sure sign of self-will.

The desire for extraordinary mortification is presumptuous when it arises from the notion that the ordinary ways by which God mortifies the soul are insufficient, and therefore one must do something about it oneself. Such a notion is only possible to an unmortified soul, and is itself a sure sign that it is not ready for voluntary mortifications, but it is not uncommon. Perhaps a woman living at home in the world disregards the sufferings of her state and longs to be an enclosed Religious, though in fact she has no vocation to that state; she then decides to adopt certain exterior mortifications of the Religious Life, hoping thereby to become a Religious in the world; but the unexpected result is that she becomes " difficult," her home is spoiled, and her health injured because she tries, quite unsuccessfully, to combine two entirely dissimilar manners of life with a marked contempt for one of them. God has intended her to find her mortification in a life to which He had called her, but which she did not desire; she tried to mortify herself by imitating the life which she did desire and despising the mortifications of God. Nothing could be more foolishly presumptuous, but it happens, and is sometimes encouraged by directors.

In writing thus we do not mean to suggest that the way of voluntary mortifications is proper only to canonised saints, and that no ordinary souls are called to it, still less do we wish to discourage the completest self-oblation and the love of heroic virtue, but it is necessary to point out that voluntary mortifications undertaken by those who have no call to them, and from any but the purest motives, so far from being acts of divine love, militate against it.

Directors of souls need to exercise the greatest care in the discernment of spirits in this matter. It is necessary to be quite sure of one's ground before one gives permission for any extraordinary mortifications, and it will do the soul no harm to be kept waiting for a while. If its desire is of God it will certainly persist, if it is self-initiated it may evaporate; a hasty decision will probably be found afterwards to have been wrong. Such souls as we have criticised are often very deceptive; they frequently read books written for souls of quite a different kind, and believe themselves to be far more advanced than they are; they have acquired a way of talking which may beguile an inexperienced director into agreeing with them, and generally there is real, if misguided, piety behind their desires. It is necessary to look for signs by which we may know the soul that is really called to mortifications of devotion.

In the first place, we should expect to find great strictness of life in that state in which the soul finds itself, combined with a considerable measure of interior mortification. Secondly, we should look for an ardent love of Jesus crucified, leading to a loving desire to share His Cross in all mortifications, small as well as great; for the secret of mortification is not the love of pain, but the love of Jesus; it has no meaning apart from Him. Thirdly, the sure call of God. This is essential, and brings this way of mortification into line with the rest. Père Grou says, truly but unexpectedly, " The saints never formed such desires "; yet they performed the austerities, and they were self-inflicted. In truth, the mortifications of the saints were not self-inflicted; God asked, the saint gave; the mortification was not his desire, the will of God was his desire; the baptism wherewith his Lord was baptised not infrequently caused him a hard struggle, and therefore he was able to be baptised with it. So, truly, the great mortifications are not self-inflicted, but God-inflicted, and are the necessary response of the soul to the love that will not be denied; they are not sought, but given. The fourth sign is a proof of this, and is complete candour with and obedience to the director. To the soul that Jesus calls to share His Cross in this voluntary way it is sorrow unspeakable to be kept back from that drinking of the cup of His Passion; but it is willing to bear even this, and suffer for Him in another way, rather than encourage self-will in the slightest degree.

Mortification in all its forms is the irresistible outcome of the love of Jesus, as is well brought out by Dr. Moberly in his profound book on the Atonement, and we would close this chapter with his quiet yet moving words. " It is difficult," he says, " for our imagination to emphasise too strongly what the meaning would be of ' being in love with ' Christ, crucified and risen; or to how much it would be the practical key in the way of the translation of the spirit of Calvary into the animating spirit of individual Christian life. What engrossing of faculties, what absorption of desire, what depth of thought, what wistfulness of kindness, what strength of will, what inspiration of power—to endeavour or to endure—would forthwith follow, with spontaneous, silent, irresistible sequence, if once we were ' in love ! '

" So all-inclusive indeed is the meaning of love, that it is needless to distinguish from love, as though it were a separable point, the effort of personal imitation and approach. Consciously or unconsciously, love is imitative. What I am really in love with I must in part be endeavouring to grow like; and shall be growing like, if the love is really on fire, even more than I consciously endeavour. What I am really in love with characterises *me*. It is that which I, so far, am becoming. *In* love then, at least, though perhaps not separably from love, there is much imitation, conscious and unconscious, of the Spirit which revealed itself to the world on Calvary. There may be no inherent beauty in asceticism. There may be no form of asceticism which is not, sometimes, the product of mean and selfish impulses; which does not, sometimes, draw justly upon itself the condemnation, and even contempt, of healthy consciences. But alas! for us if we cannot also, in this context, see how directly the ascetic spirit may be the irresistible outcome of pure love. The daily unselfishness —more and more smiling and spontaneous—the quiet stringency and gladness of detailed self-discipline; do we not see how this, as the unconscious, or the conscious, imitation of the Cross, by one who is in love with the Crucified, may be just the natural homage, the relief which *will* not be denied, of a devoted love, welling up and bubbling over in act? Be it what it may as cold self-conscious rule, at least as the expression and relief of overflowing love, asceticism, even the exactest, is not only blameless but beautiful. It is also, in very large measure, a practical token of the thing we are looking for: a secret of the process of the real translation of Calvary, contemplated *and loved*, into the inmost characterising reality of the spirit of the loving worshipper." [1]

[1] R. C. Moberly, *Atonement and Personality*, pp. 147-8.

PART III

# CHAPTER XV

# THE SACRAMENTS

*He shewed me a pure river of water of life, clear as crystal, proceeding out of the throne of God and of the Lamb* (Rev. xxii. 1).

THE Christian life is the life of grace, and its growth depends upon grace freely received and responded to; we must therefore now give our attention to the normal means of grace, which are the sacraments. We shall not attempt to treat of the dogmatic theology of the sacraments—that necessary groundwork must be sought elsewhere; even from our present point of view any adequate treatment of the sacraments would demand a book to itself, and any compressed treatment must be but partial. We shall content ourselves with drawing attention to such facts as seem most important, showing at any rate something of the relationship of the sacraments to the needs of life.

## I. BAPTISM

Baptism is the sacrament of birth into the life of grace; by it we are " born again " into the mystical Body of Christ. (It is impossible to avoid mixing metaphors here.) Its essential effect, from which all else follows, is union with Christ in His Body the Church: Christ does not merely do something for us, He unites us with Himself; being baptised into Him, we are henceforth " in Christ," as S. Paul so frequently reminds us, and the whole Christian life is made possible by this fact. Advance in the Christian life is the development of the essential union with Him which we have by virtue of Baptism, not by setting ourselves to attain states of rapture or ecstasy. The Spiritual Marriage is the fulfilment and completion of the union with Christ already present in Baptism, and is the highest manifestation of that union. The union of the saint with the Divine Lover is an infinitely closer and more wonderful union than that which ordinary Christians know or can imagine, but it is not different in kind from ours; it is truly given over and above the common grace of Baptism, and few receive it, because few love our Lord so completely as to make the perfect human response to the grace of Baptism, but it is made possible by that grace, and is not independent of it. The point we would make here is that union with Christ is ours as a present fact by virtue of our Baptism; we are by that sacrament united to Him, whatever use we may be making of that union and in whatever stage of the spiritual life we may be.

Baptismal union with Christ produces two effects in the soul, which S. Paul calls death and life. " Know ye not," he says, " that so many of us as were baptised into Jesus Christ were baptised into his death? Therefore we are buried with him by baptism into death: that like as Christ was raised up from the dead by the glory of the Father, even so we also should walk in newness of life . . . our old man is crucified with him, that the body of sin might be destroyed, that henceforth we should not serve sin. For he that is dead is freed from sin . . . reckon ye also yourselves to be dead indeed unto sin, but alive unto God through Jesus Christ our Lord." [1]

The first effect of Baptism is, then, the death of the " old " man, the fallen, natural man. The waters of Baptism wash away all sin, original as well as actual, and thus potentially slay the old man and deliver us from the power of sin. But notice here that S. Paul says, " Our old man is crucified with him." Being crucified, he is as good as dead—potentially dead, but not actually so; the old man has to be kept on the cross if he is completely to die to sin, and that is the business of the ascetic life: to unite the soul by will and desire to Jesus crucified, that sin may be actually slain in it. The entail of original sin with which we are born is broken by Baptism, so that we are no longer captive to fallen nature; but its effects remain, as we know only too well, in sinful tendencies which the sacrament gives us grace to keep nailed to the Cross, or at least to re-crucify, enabling us to fight temptation in the power of Christ.

Death to sin makes us capable of " newness of life," the natural man gives place to the supernatural, union with the vine makes it possible for the sap of grace to flow into the branches continually; so the other effect of Baptism is the infusion of Habitual Grace. There is no need to labour this

---

[1] Rom. vi. 3, 4, 6, 7, 11.

point, for the matter has been fully treated above, but it should be noted that it is the possession of Habitual Grace which makes the resurrection life of the baptised possible. The union with Christ which is ours is not the harnessing together of two entities which remain separate, but the joining of the soul to Christ in such a way that it becomes part of the mystical Body in which His life flows without at the same time losing its individuality. The old man is fallen man alone, the new is redeemed man with Christ, filled with His life.

Such are the effects of our baptismal union with Christ considered in itself; but union with Christ comes about by means of a further union, which is with the Holy Spirit. If the baptised soul is truly said to be " in Christ," it can, by virtue of that union, be equally truly said to be "in the Spirit." It is filled with the life of Christ through His Spirit and the great gift of the Infused Virtues.

Further, united with Christ and indwelt by the Holy Spirit, we are by Baptism brought into a new relationship with the Father, and made " sons of God " in a truer and deeper sense than that in which all men are His sons by creation. God loves us in Jesus, and pours forth upon us the riches of His love unchecked by the barrier of original sin. Baptism opens to us " eternal life," which is life with God begun here, and opening out hereafter, if we are faithful, into the life of heaven and the Beatific Vision.

Again, our union with Christ in Baptism is also a real and living union with the rest of the Body of which we are part. We are no longer merely individuals, but one with the whole Church on earth, in purgatory, and in heaven, and have our part in the life and love and holiness of the Body of Christ.

The grace of Baptism is a great and wonderful thing, given to us by God freely and without any personal meriting of ours; it comes to us, as the theologians say, *ex opere operato*, by virtue of the action of the Church, not by virtue of any act of ours; nevertheless, if this grace is to have its perfect work in us and accomplish in us that which God wills, we must make to it the completest response of which we are capable. Baptism gives to us inexpressible blessings, but it also lays upon us the gravest responsibility, a fact which is very insufficiently realised by most baptised people.

The fact that they were baptised in infancy, when, from the

O

nature of the case, they could know nothing about it, means for the majority of Christians that they take their Baptism for granted, and seldom stop to consider what is the nature of the life which they are living; hence there is far too little attempt to actualise that union with Christ which is theirs and to correspond with the grace that flows from it. In order that the grace of Baptism may have full course, certain dispositions are necessary, the chief of which are:—

(a) *Faith.* " He that cometh to God must believe that he is," [1] says the author of the Epistle to the Hebrews, and faith is the antecedent condition of the grace of the sacraments. By faith we accept the grace of God offered to us, and without it the life in grace is impossible. The apostles were unable to do the very works which our Lord sent them to do because of lack of faith; [2] it is faith as the grain of mustard seed which works the works of God. The Christian life depends on a living and growing faith in Him with Whom we are united.

(b) *Charity.* The realisation of God as our chief good and the centring of the heart and will on Him.

(c) *Hope.* The committal of self and life to God, in Whom one trusts.

(d) *Repentance.* The change of mind in regard to sin which marks the difference between the " new " and the " old man."

(e) *The removal of obstacles.* It is obvious that the gift of grace is limited by the soul's capacity to receive it; nevertheless it is seldom realised how greatly we can interfere with the action of grace in the soul by our own fault, through interposing obstacles or failing to remove those that are there. If grace is to have full course in the soul, there must be at any rate the desire to mortify the soul in regard to all that opposes it.

(f) The negative removal of obstacles is completed and made possible by the *desire for holiness.* At the beginning of the spiritual life this will no doubt be a somewhat vague thing, but unless the soul at least wants to please God it

---

[1] Heb. xi. 6.
[2] Matt. xvii. 20. " Because of your unbelief (ὀλιγοπιστίαν) : for verily I say unto you, If ye have faith as a grain of mustard seed, ye shall say unto this mountain, Remove hence to yonder place; and it shall remove; and nothing shall be impossible unto you."

will be opposing a fundamental resistance to the grace of the sacrament.

Of these dispositions the first three are the root virtues of the Christian life; the next two are concerned with the cruci- fixion of the old man, and the last one with the growth of the new. None of them is ever outgrown in the spiritual life, but rather deepen with the growth of the soul; for just as Baptism is the fundamental sacrament upon which all the others rest, so the dispositions which are necessary to the fruition of that sacrament are fundamental to the whole spiritual life.

If the soul is to advance rightly in the spiritual life it is of the utmost importance that it should realise the effects of Bap- tism, and endeavour to make the fullest possible use of the grace given thereby.


## II. Confirmation

Confirmation is the completion of the sacrament of Baptism. This does not mean that the latter sacrament is in any way incomplete in itself, but that in the former God completes what has already been done by the gift of special grace.

Confirmation is analogous to Ordination, in that it is a special outpouring of the Holy Ghost, Who is already present in the soul by Baptism, for a particular purpose. This is a difficult truth to grasp, and it is necessary to remember that we are dealing with mysteries so great that they elude all attempts at exact expression in human language. The Holy Ghost is given in Baptism, He is also given in Confirmation and again in Ordina- tion; it is the same gift in each case, but with a difference. The gift in Baptism is a general one, the gifts in Confirmation and Ordination are particular ones for special purposes applicable to certain states of life in the Church.

When a man is ordained he is set apart by God to exercise certain functions in the Church, and is given a special gift of the Holy Ghost to enable him to do so. It is no otherwise with the boy or girl, man or woman who is confirmed, for with Confirmation he or she attains his full status as a member of Holy Church, and receives a special gift of the Holy Ghost to enable him to discharge the functions of the priesthood of the laity, and to be a good soldier of Christ.

It is so frequently assumed that anyone can be a Christian and that the laity have no responsibilities to the Church, save such as they choose to incur by sitting on Parochial Church Councils and the like, that the importance of Confirmation for the adequate living of the Christian life is well-nigh lost sight of, and so parents have their children " done " as a matter of course, and no attention is paid to the matter once the special course of instruction and the ceremony itself are over.   Confirmation should, however, be a reminder that the layman, no less than the priest, has a definite spiritual responsibility towards the Church which he cannot adequately bear without the special aid of the Holy Spirit Who indwells the Church.

But the special gift of Confirmation is no less necessary in the individual life.   As the child comes to " years of discretion " he discovers that the crucifixion of the old man and the putting on of the new are by no means easy, and that he needs all the aid that grace can give in order to give a creditable account of himself in the spiritual combat, and it is precisely at that moment that the eternal wisdom of the Holy Ghost comes to him with just that grace which is necessary to victory.

In Confirmation the Holy Ghost shows Himself as the guidance and strength of the Christian in the daily vicissitudes of his warfare against evil, enlightening his mind, firing his heart and moving his will by His Gifts, that he may be a good soldier of Jesus Christ.

A word must be said here on the vexed question of the age of Confirmation.   There is a widespread notion that thirteen to fifteen are the ideal years for the reception of this sacrament, but psychology and experience alike seem to suggest that, whatever age may be right, this one is certainly wrong, and that, owing to the upheaval of adolescence, the years from twelve to seventeen should be avoided.   If Confirmation is postponed to the latter age, we incur the responsibility of leaving the boy or girl without the particular gift which they most need at that time, and the risk of losing them altogether from effective membership of the Church; it seems then that the years from seven to twelve are to be preferred.   At what particular part of this period we should present children for Confirmation depends upon circumstances and individuals, and the exact moment for the administration of the sacrament can only be rightly determined by observation of the individual child.   The ultimate test is a spiritual one. Candidates for Confirmation are not required by the Church to be theologians, their intellectual knowledge is to be simple and fundamental, for they are to know " the Creed, the Lord's Prayer and the Ten Commandments," or, in other words, what they are to believe, how to pray and what to do, " and to be further instructed in the Church Catechism set forth for that purpose." A working knowledge of these things is not difficult of acquisition if the child is adequately instructed before the period of Confirmation Classes, for they are the foundation knowledge which a child should be taught so soon as it be able to learn; an adequately brought up child should then be brought to Confirmation when it is spiritually ready to receive that sacrament.[1]

Confirmation is the sacrament whereby the Christian is given strength to fulfil his office in the Church and to live the Christian life, and the strength thus conferred is adequate to all the various vicissitudes through which the soul may pass. The realisation of this truth will give poise and steadiness to many a soul which otherwise frets against its own weakness and the power of the enemy, and increase its sense of unity in and responsibility to the Body of Christ. It should also lead to a deepened devotion to the Holy Spirit. Unfortunately the Holy Spirit is gravely neglected by those in whom He dwells, and this neglect results in much weakness and loss of spirituality; what is needed perhaps more than anything else is a revival of devotion to Him and a more active correspondence to His presence in the soul. This can be attained by stirring up the gift that is in us, there is no need to strive after new forms of devotion; the Holy Spirit is there and will teach us all things; all that is necessary is that

---

[1] Lest the preference for an early age for Confirmation should seem to be merely personal, one may remark that the mind of the Church as expressed in the Book of Common Prayer seems to contemplate no other. The pertinent passages are as follows:—

" Ye are to take care that this Child be brought to the Bishop to be confirmed by him, *so soon as* he can *say* the Creed, the Lord's Prayer, and the Ten Commandments, in the vulgar tongue, and be further instructed in the Church-Catechism set forth for that purpose." (Publick Baptism of Infants *ad. fin.*)

" *So soon as* Children are come to a *competent* age, and can *say* in their Mother Tongue, the Creed, the Lord's Prayer, and the Ten Commandments: and also can *answer to* the other questions of this short Catechism: they shall be brought to the Bishop." (Catechism, 3rd Rubrick *ad. fin.*).

The words italicised seem to suggest that the " competent age " is not a very late one, and the " years of discretion " mentioned in the sub-title of the Order of Confirmation need not mean more than an ability to distinguish between right and wrong (*i.e.* to commit or not to commit mortal sin) and to grasp the meaning of the elementary instruction required by the rubric.

the faithful should live in the power of the Confirmation gift, simply submitting themselves to the indwelling Spirit. Such submission would lead to such quickening of prayer, such a flowering of the Infused Virtues and Gifts as no power of evil could withstand, and the wilderness of semi-converted hearts would blossom as the rose with the sweet fruits of the Spirit.

### III. PENANCE

Baptism, as we have seen, purifies the soul from all sin, original and actual, and so far as original sin is concerned, what is then done neither needs nor is capable of subsequent repetition; but with actual sin it is different. Baptism, while providing the powerful aid of grace and incorporation into the Body of Christ, does not abrogate the freedom of the will; consequently baptised souls no less than others may fall into mortal as well as venial sin, and, as a matter of experience, we know that they do. Mortal sin is an important matter to any man, but to the Christian it is even more serious, for he has been redeemed by the Precious Blood, united with Christ and filled with grace, and mortal sin, besides its universal evil effects, renders nugatory this great work of God.

Mortal sin does not terminate the fundamental union between the baptised soul and Christ, but it makes it ineffective, because it separates the will of the soul from the will of Christ. The same thing happens more gradually when the soul gives way persistently to venial sin, or becomes obsessed by the material: it ceases to desire the will of Christ, first of all in a particular matter, then, perhaps, more generally, until the things of God cease to attract because its desire and will are elsewhere. It may not definitely desire evil—indeed, its intentions may be quite good—but its life in Christ has become ineffective through sin. Mortal sin by itself and venial sin by its cumulative effect separate the soul from any effective union with Christ, and reduce that union which should be effective and actual to a more or less inoperative potentiality.

Similarly, sin chokes the channels of divine grace in the soul and renders impossible that active co-operation which should be between the soul and the Holy Spirit. Grace, the sap of the vine in our Lord's figure, is essential to the living of the Christian life, but its effectiveness is limited by the capacity of the soul; consequently if the soul is choked with sin and its effects, the living of the divine life is impossible and the soul reverts to the merely natural.

A further effect of sin is the separation of the soul from active participation in the common life of the organism which is the Church. This is a very serious matter for the soul, and it also injures the Church, for the vine which contains withered branches is not likely to bear much fruit.

It is clear that post-baptismal sin is even a more serious matter than pre-baptismal sin, and that a soul that so sins, besides bringing itself into a parlous state, injures the Church, grieves the Holy Spirit, wounds the Sacred Heart of Jesus and sins against God by neglecting the responsibilities of sonship.

The soul that sins after Baptism throws away by its own act the redemption which Christ died to give it, but even here the love of God will not be denied, for, knowing our human frailty, He meets our feeble penitence with the sweet grace of Absolution. In the sacrament of Penance that which had been given in the sacrament of Baptism and lost by subsequent sin is restored; it is therefore the sacrament of restoration of lost life. There are three persons concerned in it: God, the priest who ministers the sacramental gift, and the penitent. We must first of all consider this sacrament from the point of view of the priest who ministers it. He has to give (or withhold) three things, absolution, penance and counsel.

(a) *Absolution.* This is the grace of the sacrament, the reply of God to the confession of the penitent, the pouring out of the divine forgiveness upon the soul; and there are three points which we should note in regard to it.

1. By absolution the soul is completely forgiven and restored to that integrity which was originally given to it in Baptism.

2. This forgiveness restores it to a state of grace and gives an actual grace and impetus towards holiness and renewed union with Christ. This positive end of absolution must not be overlooked. Absolution is truly and fundamentally forgiveness of sin past, but it is forgiveness in order that the soul may increase in grace, which increase is begun in absolution itself. We are forgiven not only that we may find peace, but that in that peace we may find God. The point is well put by an old spiritual writer thus:

" The principal part of the intention (in Confession) must be the increase of Grace and love of God, by which, formally infused or poured into ourselves, God Almighty doth blot out sins and wipe them away. Now although absolution from sin is never given without infusion of Grace, yet ought the intention of the penitent to be principally the obtaining of Grace; for if he principally intend the absolution from sin, it is a reflection of the soul upon its own profit by self-love, desiring to avoid the wrath of God and punishment due to sin, and to be freed from the deformity of guiltiness; which, though it be a good desire, yet is but a property of beginners in love, and nothing comparable to the intention of Grace, which is the perfect love of God, and is an elevation of the soul to transcend itself and all creatures, to live only in God." [1]

This thought may appear rather startling to those unaccustomed to it, but it will repay careful consideration. The point is that absolution does not stop with forgiveness, but goes on to give grace to enable the soul to rise up to God; consequently while the penitent should desire forgiveness, he must not stop at that point, but desire even more the grace of self-oblation to God which is the fruit of that forgiveness. Absolution not only restores Baptismal innocence, but also builds up the soul in Christ, and souls which use this sacrament faithfully experience positive grace as well as cleansing.

3. Absolution readmits the soul to the unity of the Church and restores it to the harmony of her organic life.

(b) Having absolved the soul, the priest must assign to it a *Penance*. Some confusion of mind exists among confessors as to what the penance really is, and it is necessary to underline what has been said above in our chapter on Repentance, that penance is reparatory and not remedial; while, therefore, in some cases it should contain an element of comfort, the penance selected should be primarily an act of worship, praise, thanksgiving or self-oblation. The penance is an act of reparation addressed to God, not an ascetic remedy to be applied to the soul; it should, then, be simple and capable of immediate fulfilment.

[1] Fr. Leander de S. Martino, " A Memorial," in Fr. Augustine Baker, *Holy Wisdom*, p. 557.

(*c*) The third responsibility of the priest in the administration of this sacrament is *counsel*. There is an idea prevalent among us that counsel is just a pious talk, in consequence of which some confessors pass on to their penitents the first ideas that come into their heads; the fruits of a recent meditation or retreat of their own, an abstract of next Sunday's sermon, or some ideas that have struck them in a book. The confessor certainly gains much help for this part of his ministry from meditation, retreat and spiritual reading, but such fruit of his own spiritual life must be applied to the needs of the penitent, and used only so far as it may be helpful.

The purpose of counsel is to guide the soul in its struggle against sin, the acquirement of virtue and the development of the spiritual life; it should therefore not be casual and general, but directly applicable to the particular penitent at the particular moment.

Adequate counsel demands a real knowledge of human nature, understanding of the principles of ascetic theology, real humility, and a deep personal life of prayer, and it is greatly to be desired that priests should take every care to prepare themselves for this most responsible part of their work; it is still far more difficult than it should be to find a priest who can direct a soul wisely in any but the most elementary ways of the Christian life.

Counsel is not always necessary, and where there is nothing to be said it is far better to say nothing, or at most to limit one's remarks to a few words of encouragement,[1] than to launch forth into generalities. The soul comes to the sacrament of penance to receive absolution, and any advice which it may receive depends upon the needs of the case. Where the confessor is not also the director, counsel should only be given when asked for, though if the soul is clearly in need of particular guidance it should be advised to consult its director.

We have considered the part of the priest in the sacrament of Penance; we have now to consider that of the penitent. The essential disposition is Repentance, which we have already considered[2] in its three parts of Contrition, Confession and Satisfaction. Of these, the first has been sufficiently considered above, but something more must be said of the other two.

---

[1] It may be noted that there are times when encouragement given discreetly is of great value; especially is this so with advancing souls suffering from interior trials and desolation.   [2] *Cf.* cap. xii. *supra.*

In order to receive absolution it is necessary to make one's confession, and that demands as a preliminary an adequate examination of conscience. To many people this means running through lists of sins in a devotional book and noting those which seem to fit one's case; children particularly adhere so closely to the printed list that it is possible to discover the book they use from the language of their confessions, and adults are often hardly more adequate; and it may be well, therefore, to make a few practical suggestions on this important matter.

In the first place, we must realise that as we are entirely dependent upon the Holy Spirit for a real self-knowledge, our first action in preparing for confession must be most devoutly to place ourselves in His hands that He may show us ourselves.

(a) In the case of the *first confession*, examination should be made leisurely and without strain. First of all the whole of one's life should be gone over, and those sins which come to the memory noted. In the case of an adult, it greatly assists the memory (to say nothing of making the resulting confession intelligible to the priest) to divide one's life into sections (*e.g.* school-days, subsequent life at home, life after leaving home, married life, or whatever divisions are applicable) and examine each separately. When this method has yielded all that it will, then, and not till then, one may take a good list of questions to aid one's memory and direct one's attention towards hitherto unrecognised sins. The purpose of the question list is not to be the foundation of one's confession, but a sieve to catch those sins which have slipped through the larger mesh of memory. This done, the written confession should be put away for a few days, during which time other sins coming to mind casually should be added, and finally the confession may be gone through again and completed. If this has been done conscientiously, one may be sure that, though it is doubtless still inadequate, one's confession is as complete as one can make it, and one may proceed trustfully to the sacrament, eliminating, so far as possible, all fuss and scruple.

(b) With *subsequent confessions* the matter is simpler. The difficulty of preparation can be considerably reduced by the habit of daily general examen recommended below.[1] This examen should consist of a rapid review of the day past, noting any sin that should be subsequently confessed. If this is done

---

[1] *Vide*, pp. 307 *f. infra*.

regularly, all that will be necessary before confession will be the gathering up of these results of previous examens, and perhaps the application of the sieve of the question list to the whole period since one's last confession. If the daily self-examen has not been regularly practised, then it will be necessary to go over the whole period, first of all in memory and then with questions. In any case, the examination should be careful, but not protracted, realising that while God asks of us the best confession we can make, He does not expect impossibilities.

Since the daily examen has been considered in this connection, it may be well to point out that, although it is of great value in the examen before confession, its purpose is different. The purpose of the examen before confession is to discover one's sins, that of the daily examen is to know oneself and one's spiritual life as a whole; the latter must not therefore stop at the cataloguing of sins, but take account of the whole of life.[1]

The examen completed, confession must be made to a priest before we can be absolved. This is of the greatest value to the soul in ensuring a certain care in preparation and deepening humility, for it is a far harder thing to confess one's sins to God before His priest than to do so alone; there is also a great psychological value in admitting one's sin to a person who is commissioned to receive that confession under the proper safeguards.

Apart from that, the priest receives our confession on behalf of God, Whose representative he is; thus we are assured that confession really has been made to God : further, he receives it on behalf of the Church that we have injured by our sin, and so we are able to make some reparation to that Church.

A word must be said with regard to the third part of Repentance. If the grace of absolution is to have its perfect work there must be a firm purpose of amendment in the penitent; all is not done when one has said one's penance—rather that is the beginning of a renewed life. To the soul that is in earnest every confession marks a step further on the road towards perfection, because with every confession its firm purpose of amendment is deepened.

---

[1] The instruction of the Ancren Riwle may be commended to penitents: " Confession should be accusatory, bitter and sorrowful, full, candid, frequent, speedy, humble, with shame, anxious, hopeful, prudent, true, voluntary, spontaneous, steadfast and premeditated." If this advice were followed there would be fewer scruples.

The confession may, and very likely will, show that the soul has many things to do, but of them all one should be selected as the centre of its efforts and a definite resolution made in regard to it. The resolution need not be a new one at every confession—indeed it is often best to keep to the same one for a considerable time—but whether it be new or old, a resolution at this point is of great value in re-directing the soul's effort. If the priest thinks it well to advise remedial exercises, it is in this connection that he should do so, not prescribing them as penances; on the whole it is, however, well not to interfere too much with the actual resolution, which loses much of its force if not spontaneous.

The general question of direction is a large and difficult one, and little can be said upon it here. Broadly speaking, there are two obvious errors which the director can make—he can direct too much or he can direct too little. It is to be hoped that, with all its faults, this book may at least suggest to directors of the latter class that there is more science in the direction of souls than they had previously realised; to those of the former I would suggest that they should realise before all things that the Holy Ghost is the true Director of souls, and the priest's business is to do His will and get out of the way himself. A soul placed in our hands to train for God is not our property, but a precious responsibility for which we shall be required to give account at the last day; and the motto of the director may well be that of S. John Baptist: " He must increase, but I must decrease." [1]

The following advice of a great director may well be laid to heart by all who are called to this ministry. " The priest," he says, " is the minister of Jesus Christ and the more he identifies himself with his divine Master the more he enters into His dispositions towards His Father and souls—the more, too, his ministry will be blessed. It is most important (1) before beginning to hear confessions to humble oneself profoundly in the presence of God and confess that one is incapable of doing the least good to souls without Him. (2) To offer this holy work as an act of love to our Lord. (3) To efface oneself as much as possible so that Christ alone acts. To speak and act in the name of Jesus Christ and with a great dependance upon His Spirit. (4) Not to desire to attach penitents to oneself but to direct them towards God alone with great detachment from every creature." [2]

---

[1] John iii. 30.    [2] Dom Columba Marmion *qu.* Thibaud *Un Maître de la Vie Spirituelle*, pp. 267*f.*

A word may be said about casual confessions. If a penitent who is unknown presents himself, the confessor needs to ascertain whether the penitent has a director or not; if he has, the confessor should normally give no counsel, and if counsel is imperative, he should carefully avoid usurping the authority or contradicting the ruling of the director; if he has no director, the confessor is, of course, free to give what counsel may seem good to him. It is necessary to be careful about this matter, as penitents sometimes avoid their normal director if they have a somewhat inconvenient confession to make or are displeased with him; and the casual confessor is sometimes so sure of himself that he throws the soul into confusion by making demands he has no right to make.

The same difficulty may occur in an intensified form in retreats. The conductor of a retreat is in a peculiar position, inasmuch as retreatants often come to him with a more or less general confession and ask his advice in detail in the ordering of their life. It is of the greatest importance that the conductor should realise that he is an external adviser, a specialist adviser truly, but having no authority over the retreatant and, if the retreatant has a director, he must be most careful not to interfere with his ruling and authority. One has known great damage done to souls by retreat conductors who presumed to direct where they had no right to do more than advise.

Our last consideration must be the frequency of confession. Absolution is necessary for the restoration of the soul after mortal sin; it is not a necessity after venial sin, and spiritual writers from Augustine Baker to Baron von Hügel have pointed out the dangers of a scrupulous hunting for minute sins and the unnecessary use of confession for them; nevertheless almost all souls who desire to advance in the spiritual life would do well to make their confession at regular intervals. We are not ourselves the best judges of our spiritual state, and some sins which we cheerfully put down as venial may be great obstacles to the grace of God, and need the grace of absolution for their removal; further, the dust of even venial sin dims the brightness of the soul and needs to be removed by the grace of the sacrament.

The use of the sacrament of Penance should be as normal as the reception of Holy Communion, and to the soul that uses it normally and regularly it is a great guard against preoccupation with self, for one has no need to be continually considering whether one is in need of absolution if one regularly seeks it.

The frequency of confession will vary with individual souls, and no hard-and-fast rule can be laid down. It will vary, naturally, with the frequency of Holy Communion. For some souls a quarterly confession is perhaps enough; most will probably need rather more than that. With Holy Communion monthly or weekly, monthly confession is probably normal; with daily, or almost daily, Holy Communion most souls will probably need confession fortnightly or weekly. The exact degree of frequency must vary, as we have said, with the individual, but the rule once made, regularity in its observance is of the greatest importance.[1] Sin is an act, and sinfulness a state of rebellion; it is necessary that the soul be brought back to the way of obedience to God by regular, unhurried, persevering use of the means that He has provided.


## IV. HOLY COMMUNION

Our Lord is present in the Holy Eucharist for two purposes—sacrifice and communion. The first of these is considered in a later chapter, the second must be discussed here, but we must first notice the close connection that exists between the two.

In the plan of this book it has proved most generally convenient to consider the sacrificial aspect of the Holy Eucharist last, but its right place is first, for the Sacred Mysteries are primarily sacrifice, and secondarily communion. The Mass is the most perfect act of worship possible to man, and as such its action is essentially Godward, the offering to the Father of the sacrifice of Christ; and the inestimable benefits which the worshipper receives in Holy Communion are consequent upon this. There can be no Communion without the sacrifice, but the act of worship is complete whether the individual worshipper makes his communion or not. Our Lord is present in the Blessed

---

[1] It should be noted that when sin has been committed which is certainly mortal, confession of it should be made without waiting for one's accustomed time. In such cases confession is of necessity not of devotion and it is most important that souls should grasp this distinction. There are, of course, scrupulous souls who have to be restrained from rushing to their confessor every time a scruple presents itself, but there are others who keep their rule of confession carefully but yet do not realise that in the case of mortal sin the rule must be superseded by confession of that particular sin as soon as a competent confessor can be found.

Sacrament as Victim, the " Lamb as it had been slain," and the communicant in receiving Him receives the Body broken and the Blood poured out on Calvary, and is thus himself united with the sacrifice of Christ in the most complete way.   Holy Communion springs from sacrifice and consummates sacrifice, and so, while it is the greatest gift which we can receive on earth, its end is not the benefit of man, but the worship of God.

In Holy Communion our Lord gives Himself to be our spiritual food, " My flesh," He says, " is meat indeed, and my blood is drink indeed." [1]   It is true that in this sacrament we receive an increase of habitual grace and very many actual graces, but the sacrament itself is more, infinitely more, than these, being nothing less than Christ Himself.

Further, in receiving His Body and Blood we possess the whole Christ, His very soul and divinity.   This is an elementary truth, and yet one which, owing to the weakness of our human imagination, is sometimes overlooked.   We can realise that we have received a tremendous Gift, we may realise clearly that we have received the Body and Blood of the Lamb of God, but that we have received Jesus, that His love and virtues and mind are ours, that we go forth from our communion bearing Him is less easy of realisation, yet it is the truth.   Holy Communion is the centre of the Christian life because in it the soul receives Jesus.

It is a most wonderful thing that the Second Person of the Holy Trinity should take our flesh and become man for us, and it is even more wonderful that for us He should take bread and wine, man's ordinary daily food, and give Himself to us in them; and the divine purpose underlying the two acts is the same, the sacrament flows from the Incarnation.

The Word became flesh in order to redeem the whole man; had He not done so man could have been but partly redeemed.  Similarly our Lord takes to Himself bread and wine that He may become the Food of the whole man.   He might have communicated Himself to our souls apart from material means, but He could not so have been the Food of our whole being.   The tremendous fact that the Blessed Sacrament is the food of the whole man and not just a convenient symbolism, is brought out in the Words of Administration: " The Body (Blood) of our Lord Jesus Christ, which was given (shed) for thee, preserve thy *body and soul* unto everlasting life."   In the Blessed Sacrament

[1] John vi. 55.

our Lord gives Himself to the communicant in the most fundamental and complete manner possible, and thus unites the whole
man to Himself.

Our union with Christ in the Blessed Sacrament is an actual
and not merely a symbolical union, a union which not only
promises, but gives life. " As the living Father hath sent me,
and I live by the Father: so he that eateth me, even he shall
live by me." [1]  The life of Christ is built up and sustained in
the faithful communicant by the heavenly food which is Christ
Himself.  The life is there by virtue of Baptism, but it is sustained by the food of Holy Communion, so the vitality of the
Christian depends upon the regular and devout use of this
sacrament.

By the food of the sacrament our Lord strengthens our weak
souls, enabling us to overcome sin and grow in virtue;  moreover, by it He gradually transforms us, if we will, into the likeness of Himself.  S. Augustine has a remarkable phrase which
well expresses what takes place.  He represents our Lord as
saying to him: " I am the food of strong men, grow apace, and
thou shalt feed on me;  nor shalt thou convert me like common
food into thy substance, but thou shalt be changed into me." [2]

It is well that we should ponder this transformation into
Christ which is ours by devout communion.  We become like
Christ not simply by imitating Him, but by union with Him;
we can only think His thoughts, say His words and do His
deeds if He will think, say and do them in us;  through Holy
Communion He repairs, strengthens and increases our spiritual
perceptions and powers, transforming us gradually into likeness to
Himself and, dwelling in us, He directs the soul which is His home.

But Christ does not accomplish all this in us without our
desire and consent.  Many regular communicants show very few
signs of advance in grace;  they do indeed receive Christ, but
selfishness and sloth interpose such barriers to grace that He
can do but little with them.  Very much then depends upon
the dispositions of the communicant, for if the soul be full of
self there is little room for Christ, if it have little desire, even
heavenly Food cannot tempt its appetite.  We must consider
what dispositions Christ would find in the soul to whom He
comes.

[1] John vi. 57.
[2] " *Cibus sum grandium :  cresce et manducabis me.   Nec tu me in te mutabis sicut
cibum carnis tuae, sed tu mutaberis in me.*" *Conf.* VII. x.

(*a*) *Preparation*. In approaching the altar the soul needs first of all *Faith*. The intensity of the virtue will vary in different souls, but the virtue itself must be present, otherwise there is no contact between the soul and God, and any real participation in Christ is impossible.

Secondly, the soul should have a *loving desire* for Christ. This is the spirit of devotion without which the soul is cold and hard. It varies greatly in intensity according to the spirituality of the individual and in the same person at different times: with some people and at some times it is a deep thirst for God, while with others and at other times it is no more than a quiet wish for Him. This intensity of desire is only partially under one's own control and should never be " worked up." The root of the matter, which is in one's own hands, is that one should desire God and none of His goods, and fixing the whole of one's love and attention upon Him, quietly remove from the heart all that distracts.

As regards self, two things are necessary, *penitence* and *humility*. The thought that one is to receive Jesus should deepen in one the realisation of one's own sinfulness and unworthiness. If one has sin on one's conscience one should make a confession before one presumes to approach the altar, and if not, the near approach to the sinlessness of Christ should make one realise one's own sinfulness the more and deepen one's penitence by acts of contrition.

Penitence leads on to Humility, for if one realises one's sin aright, one passes on to the realisation of one's own nothingness, and, acknowledging one's true state to God, proceeds to put self out of the way; indeed, the whole ascetic preparation for Communion may be summed up as the putting of self away that Christ may be all.

(*b*) *The Communion*. Being prepared, with what dispositions should we approach the altar? There are two persons concerned, Christ and myself, and there are two fundamental dispositions of soul at this moment, *adoration and self-oblation*. As regards Christ, the Charity which began in desire has now become in His Presence adoration—one simply loves and worships; as regards self, Humility has become self-oblation. We receive Christ in Holy Communion in order that we may give ourselves to Him more wholly; our reception of the sacrament should never be merely self-seeking. We need Him more than

P

we can say, and we need much from Him, which He gives us in full measure in giving us Himself, but Holy Communion is far more than the satisfaction of our own needs, however pressing they may be. The completeness of Christ's gift of Himself to us demands an equally complete giving of ourselves to Him; we receive Him in order that we may be more wholly given to Him. So with a prayer for generosity there must be in the heart at that moment the desire to give Him the most complete offering of self of which we are capable. We may not have reached the heroic self-oblation of the saints, but we are commonly capable of far more generosity than we realise if we will only stir ourselves to desire it; and, if we want it to do so, the grace of the sacrament increases this generosity in us. The one thing needful is that we open our heart wide to the divine Guest and that there be no closed doors in it.

(c) *Thanksgiving*. The fundamental dispositions after Communion are *praise* of God for Himself, *thanksgiving* to Him for His inestimable Gift and wholehearted *Charity* to God and one's neighbour. The time after Communion is an exceedingly precious one, when we are very near to our Lord and may rightly speak to Him freely of all that is nearest to our heart, but we should not be in a hurry to talk about *things*—it is *Himself* with Whom we should be occupied, not ourselves and our needs. He will " give more than either we desire, or deserve " if we trust Him, but in Holy Communion He has just given the most glorious Gift of all; our immediate desire should then be to praise and thank and adore Him Who is ours, and centre upon Him our whole heart and mind and will, so that we may go forth from our Communion bearing Him within the shrine of the heart with renewed Charity to God and man. Christ moves about the world daily in the persons of His people, and the world is sadly little bettered, because His people leave their remembrance of Him at the Church door; if every communicant were to carry Him forth in a simple, adoring and loving heart, all men might soon be brought to the feet of Christ the King.

Souls in different ways of prayer will have different methods of preparation and thanksgiving for Holy Communion and of assisting at the Holy Mysteries. If vocal prayers are used, the ancient offices of preparation and thanksgiving make an excellent foundation, either as they stand or adapted to individual needs. We would also plead for a greater use of liturgical prayers as the foundation of private prayer at Holy Communion itself. We shall speak of liturgical prayer in a later chapter; here we are thinking of individual prayer at Mass, when one is not deliberately following the liturgy and when one's great objective is Holy Communion. Our books of devotion give many prayers which may be used, many of them good, others not so good, but the great mine of ancient liturgies eastern and western which lies ready to hand is but little worked; indeed, we can think of only one popular manual which provides a good store of liturgical prayers.[1] It would be a great blessing if communicants could be led to use the ancient prayers of the Church as the basis of their own, for, with certain great exceptions, no others satisfy so completely.

Those who use affective prayer will in course of time make their own collection of useful acts,[2] while contemplative souls can be trusted to look after themselves. It should, however, be said that, for all, Holy Communion is a precious jewel which should be set in the pure gold of silence. It is unfortunate that our social habits, which make Saturday evening as well as Sunday essentially a time of recreation, make a quiet preparation rather difficult, but the soul that is in earnest will, nevertheless, seek to still itself for its preparation, and endeavour to keep as quiet as possible, realising Who is coming to it, from the time it goes to bed till its Communion next morning. The most precious times of silence are those just before and just after Holy Communion. There should be no hurry and no talk on the morning of Communion, but quiet waiting on Him Who is coming, and when He has come one should guard one's silence with Him with the most jealous care. There may not be much time, but there will be some—at any rate one should not rush away the moment the priest has left the altar unless there is a really urgent cause, as it is then that we are closest to Him Who is our Life.

---

[1] *Before the Throne*, by W. Bellars. For the construction of a book of prayers from the ancient sources there are, of course, the editions of ancient liturgies of Neale, Brightman and Hammond, while Dr. Bright's *Ancient Collects* (now, unhappily, out of print) is a storehouse of immense value to the priest for all sorts of purposes. *Ancient Devotions for Holy Communion* by S. A. C. (Burns, Oates and Washbourne) is a handy and useful collection of liturgical prayers.

[2] Fr. Augustine Baker, *Holy Wisdom*, Gertrude More, *Writings*, and Fr. Gilbert Shaw's *Burgh Booklets* contain general collections of acts. Fr. Roche's *Mysteries of the Mass in Reasoned Prayers* is a book of great value which can be used with but little adaptation and supplies a real need. *Reasoned Prayers for the Lord's own Service*, by A. K. Bostock, is an Anglican book on similar lines.

A word must be said as to the frequency of Communion. There can, of course, be no hard and fast rule on this matter which can be applied to everyone; what is important is to encourage souls to make their Communion as often as their spiritual state allows, and to realise that advance is always a possibility.

At Confirmation we commonly encourage our adolescents to make a rule of monthly Communion, and this is in most cases right, but there is a real danger of making a fetish of " the first Sunday in the month." Monthly Communion is a beginning, but it is only a beginning, and we should never be content or allow our people to be satisfied with that; the norm for ordinary people is once a week, and for the more spiritual, twice and thrice a week, until daily Communion is reached. It is probably true that in most churches there should be more weekly and daily communicants than there are.

People need great encouragement in this matter. Our Lord did not institute the holy Sacrament for saints only, but for sinners who want to be saints. Many people stay away from Holy Communion because they feel they are not good enough, though they want to be, and by doing so they are depriving themselves of the very means of advance. Temptation, trial, weakness are not barriers to communion, but signs of need; the only barrier is sin, and the remedy for that is repentance and absolution.

While encouraging souls to advance in the spiritual life, and so to come frequently to the Holy Sacrament, we must remember that Communion must on no account be made cheap. Many people refrain from coming to the altar often not because of indifference, but because of reverence, and this reverence is a very precious thing which must on no account be broken. It should, however, not be allowed to separate the soul from its Lord, but rather lead to a deeper love and desire for Him and a longing for greater holiness, that it may approach Him rightly.

A real, not merely sentimental, desire for Jesus is fundamental to Holy Communion; where this is present, hypocrisy and formalism, those bugbears of the sincere Christian, cannot flourish, without it they may become rampant.

We should seek to guide our people as to frequency of Communion according to their spiritual state and their conditions of life; it does not follow that every pious lady is ready for daily Communion, nor should one who works twelve hours a day always be allowed to make it—a wise discretion is necessary. Communion should be made regularly, and so become a regular part, and the most important part, of life, but we must be ready to advise a change of rule when the soul is ready for it, and avoid separating people into classes. Many adolescents who are rigidly confined to " once a month " really need and are ready for a weekly Communion, while some older people need a change in the opposite direction. We have to guide souls, not classes, and, on the whole, their chief need is encouragement to advance in holiness by means of sacramental grace.

## V. Holy Matrimony

The fundamental fact of Holy Matrimony is that it is not only a contract, but a sacrament. Non-Christian marriage is essentially a contract between man and woman; in Christian marriage the contract is still there—indeed, it is the sacramental action—but the parties do not simply agree to live together, they marry " in Christ " with the blessing of His Church, and their subsequent relationship is not merely natural and dependent upon human good-will, but supernatural and dependent upon the grace of God. In Christian marriage the parties do not make a mutable contract, but take vows for life which are immutable, not merely because they are vows, but because the supernatural effect of the sacrament is to make man and wife " one flesh."

From this essential unity everything else flows. Holy Marriage is not merely a conventionalising of concupiscence or a convenient partnership for the procreation of children; it is far more than that—it is the supernaturalising of that most beautiful thing, human love. The natural tendency of love is to unite, and in Holy Matrimony God takes the naturally uniting love of the man and woman and makes of it a supernatural union, making them one in Him and giving them grace to love one another not merely naturally, but supernaturally, and from this union of love spring children, if it be the will of God, and so human life is maintained through the sanctified love of the parents.

Those who approach the sacrament of Holy Matrimony need to realise these facts and come to it with reverence, and if their marriage is to be a right one there should also be certain dispositions of soul.  First of all, true *love for each other*.  Love is not merely a desire to possess, but also, and chiefly, a desire to give, and those who would marry must be prepared for sacrifice not only for the other, but also for that unity which is their joint life in God.  It is lack of sacrificing love which causes most matrimonial shipwrecks.

Secondly, there should be a sense of *vocation*.  Those who marry rightly do so not merely because they want to, but because they believe it to be God's will for them, and if marriage is to be really raised to its true supernatural level it will be because it is accepted as the soul's vocation.

Thirdly, there should be *love of God*.  Human love is a beautiful thing, a most wonderful and compelling thing, but, just because it is so fine, it can be most dangerous if pursued as a final end. The one final end is the love of God, and it is in this love that Holy Marriage is perfected.

Christian marriage is a wonderful thing, but because it is so wonderful, those who are not prepared to pay the price find it hard, and are tempted to say it is impossible; so we find on all sides compromises with the spirit of the world.  But we must not compromise or allow the ideal to be in any way diminished. Christian marriage is for Christians; we have seen that the Christian life demands the offering of self and ever-increasing charity to God and man; we cannot allow that the only place where discipline is unnecessary is the home.  But to the soul that truly gives itself, the grace of God makes of marriage not a bond, but an ever-increasing wonder.  There is, then, no need to compromise the ideal; it is within our grasp if we are faithful to God; it is not something made by man for himself, but given by God to those who ask Him, and the transforming grace of Holy Marriage should be sought, not merely by each alone, but by both together.

With not a few so-called Christian marriages the actual ceremony is the last appearance of the pair together in church, except perhaps at the Baptism of their children and the funerals of relations; but married life cannot be supernaturally lived unless both are at one in the deepest thing of all, which is their life in God.  The married life in which husband and wife kneel together at the altar Sunday by Sunday, in which they share their religion as well as their amusements, in which they are both trying to live the Christian life as well as they can, seldom goes wrong. The union which is marriage must be lived, and lived in God, if it is to attain its fullness and produce new generations of the lovers of God.[1]

## VI. HOLY ORDER

The special grace of Holy Order, like that of Confirmation, is the outpouring of the Holy Ghost for a special purpose—in this case, the conferring of spiritual functions and the grace to perform them.

The sacraments are divine gifts, of which the primary minister is Christ Himself, but His ministry is mediated to us by men, and, in so far as the sacraments imply material media, necessarily so. It must always be remembered in regard to the office of the priesthood that no priest (and *a fortiori* no Bishop) attempts to suggest that the authority which he holds is his own, but that it is the delegated authority of Christ given to him by the out-pouring of the Holy Ghost at ordination. The priest does not, for instance, absolve in his own right—the " I absolve thee " is not that of the individual man, but of Christ, Whose absolution he ministers.

It is necessary, if sacramental grace is to be bestowed, that it be bestowed immediately by a human being, and if it is to con-fer grace it cannot be bestowed by any human being, but by one to whom Christ has delegated His authority for this pur-pose. The minister of the sacraments must then be authorised by Christ, and not merely self-appointed; hence the sacred ministry is appointed and given authority by the Church, the mystical body of Christ.

But the authority to minister the word and sacraments is more than merely human, it is supernatural, and needs the gift of grace for its fulfilment, and so the grace of Holy Order is given by sacramental means by the special outpouring of the Holy Ghost, Who unites the ordinand with Christ as His minister and bestows upon Him the grace of Christ to fulfil the ministry committed to him.

The ascetical preparation for Holy Orders is too great a sub-ject to be dealt with here, involving as it does special spiritual and

[1] Those who wish to pursue this subject further cannot do better than study *In Defence of Purity* by von Hildebrand. This is a small book which does far more than its title suggests, being in fact a brilliant exposition of the Catholic ideals of sex, purity, marriage and consecrated virginity.

intellectual training, but the sacrament must be at least referred to for the sake of completeness.

Just as the natural life of the Church is maintained by the sacrament of Holy Matrimony, so its supernatural life is maintained by the sacrament of Holy Order, so from generation to generation fresh supplies of men are raised up by the power of the Holy Ghost to perpetuate the teaching and life of the Church, to convert and to build up.

Much is heard to-day of the shortage of clergy, and one cannot help feeling that one reason why this is so is that the true significance of the ministry is insufficiently explained to our people, especially to our boys.  In these days the parish priest is far too apt to be thought of as a chairman of committees who also officiates in Church, and his spiritual vocation, which is, after all, his *raison d'être*, is insufficiently understood.


## VII. UNCTION

This is the last sacrament of all, and it fulfils a very important function.  Its purpose is not, as is often supposed, simply bodily healing by spiritual means; the Christian sacraments do indeed benefit the body, and this one does so very greatly, but their end is never bodily but spiritual: so the purpose of Unction is to restore that harmony of organisation between soul and body which has been disturbed by evil, so that the soul may best fulfil its vocation, whatever that may be.

Unction then restores a right relationship between soul and body, and for that reason its effect is frequently curative, but it may also be a preparation for death; all depends upon the will of God for the soul.

Unction should never be given lightly or as a last resort when other cures have failed, and it may only be given in cases of serious illness; ordinarily not more than once in the same illness, though it may be repeated in a further crisis of the same illness or a subsequent attack of the same disease.

This sacrament does not deal with sin, but with the disorganisation introduced by evil in the world, it is therefore always preceded by Penance, and should be prepared for as carefully as may be, having regard to the physical condition of the patient.

The administration of this sacrament is attended by two contrary dangers: in the first place a desire simply for physical healing may lead to its use only as a physical cure; this, as we have said, is too light a use of the sacrament. In the second place, people frequently put off this (and the other last sacraments) until the patient is *in extremis*, which is the contrary abuse, and is sanctioned by no ecclesiastical authority. It is true that the Western name of the sacrament is *Extreme* Unction, but that does not mean that it is only to be used *in extremis*. The sacrament should be used in all cases of grave illness when the patient needs its grace to help him in his struggle for health or preparation for death, and people should be encouraged to receive it with the same devotion that they receive other sacraments.

It is a wonderful thing to see in this sacrament the loving care of God for the weak and suffering bodies of His children, as in the others His particular care for their souls, but we must keep in mind the fact that, just as in Holy Communion our Lord is the food of body and soul, so in Unction He gives grace to soul and body. When, then, the reception of this sacrament brings healing, it should be realised that such healing is the result of a restored balance of soul and body involving a new life spiritually as well as physically; and when it is the preparation for death, we find in it the fortification of soul and body in the last agony.

PART IV

# CHAPTER XVI

# PRAYER AND ITS DIVISIONS

*Let my prayer be set forth in thy sight as the incense* (Ps. cxli. 2).

THE Christian life is essentially a life of union with God, a union given to us in Baptism by no merit of our own, but by the infinite love of God. This union is potentially ours by virtue of our incorporation into Christ in Baptism, it is deepened by the continual partaking of the sacrament of the Body and Blood of Christ, and actualised in prayer.

It is to be feared that to the " ordinary Christian " prayer is an occasional and more or less irregular exercise which has no very obvious connection with life at all; such a phrase as " the life of Prayer " has no meaning for him whatever. He " says his prayers " morning and night and when he goes to church and receives Holy Communion; they are an occasional exercise depending for their sanction on custom and a vague hope of an " answer." There is probably some idea of keeping touch with God, but God is apparently very far off and well-nigh unknown; the conception of prayer as converse with a present God is lacking.

This unfortunate view of the characteristic religious activity seems to rest on certain fundamental misconceptions. There is first of all the idea of a distant God, Who for some inexplicable reason requires to be propitiated by the regular recitation of some formulæ; in consequence of this it is not uncommon to find grown men who still recite night and morning the prayers they learnt as children.

It is normally the mother's business to teach her children their first lessons about God and how to pray, and this is admittedly difficult. It is necessary to lay stress upon the transcendence, the majesty and the " otherness " of God, but it should always be seen through His love. God, the infinitely Other, should always be approached through the incarnate Son. The child should be taught to pray not to a distant, unapproachable and unknowable Deity, but to a God Who, while dwelling eternally in heaven, is, nevertheless, near and present; a God Who is love and Who wants the child to talk to Him about its rocking-horse as well as the more important matters of life, Who wants the child's love and loving talk just as the mother herself wants them, only much more so.   The Lord's Prayer and other forms must, of course, be taught, for prayer is not merely chatter, and the child must learn to pray well and rightly, but they should not be taught simply as forms.   One has early recollections of being made to say the hymn " Gentle Jesus " night by night without the slightest idea of why one did it or what it meant.   The child should be taught not only forms, but what they mean and how they are to be used, as it grows.

Another misconception is the idea that prayer consists only of petition.   The result of this is that prayer becomes very fervent in times of need and tends to contract to bare formulæ at other times, and, if the suppliant does not get what he wants, frequently is given up altogether.

This again is often the result of imperfect teaching in child-hood.   Of course the child should be encouraged to ask for what it needs and often for what it wants, still more it should be encouraged to pray for the needs of others; but its primary idea of God should not be that of an ideal Uncle Whose chief purpose is to produce presents at all times.

Other popular misconceptions of the very fundamentals of prayer are common, and any priest with ordinary parochial experience could produce many.   Fallen human nature being what it is, prayer is not the simple natural activity which it no doubt should be.   It is as natural as walking or eating, but it has to be learnt laboriously, just as those simple natural functions have to be learnt.   It is not enough for the priest to exhort his people to pray—he must teach them what prayer is and how to exercise it, he should train in the life of prayer his children, his adolescents, his young men and women, even his middle-aged and old ones.   Nothing can take the place of this training, and it should be very carefully adapted to individual needs.

We must pass on now to consider what prayer is.   S. John Damascene has given us a definition which has become classical and penetrates to the root of the matter.   Prayer, he says, is " the lifting up of the mind to God." [1]

Ordinarily our thoughts are occupied with a variety of matters

---

[1] *De Fide Orthod.*, III, 24.

of greater and less importance; in prayer we deliberately put
all these aside and " lift up our hearts " above all that is created,
even above the angels and the saints, to God Himself and,
gathering the whole self together, we enter into loving converse
with Him.

In prayer the soul comes to God, not to " say its prayers," not
to " make a meditation," not to think or rest, nor to ask, but to
find Him and be with Him.   With Him it may speak or be silent,
it may make a meditation or contemplate, it may ask or wait;
the action of prayer differs with each individual soul and in the
same soul at different times, but its essence is always the same—
" the lifting up of the mind to God."

This simple act is divisible into four parts:

(1) *Adoration.*   Baron von Hügel, being asked on one occasion
to distinguish between religious and non-religious activity,
replied in an often-quoted phrase, " Religion is adoration." [1]
Adoration is the true and instinctive response of the creature to
the presence of its Creator, and as a truly religious life is one lived
for and with God, its chief characteristic, as the Baron truly says,
must be adoration, which *a fortiori* must be the chief characteristic
of true prayer.

It is well to realise far more than we commonly do that in
prayer we enter the presence of God the Eternal King, our
Creator, our Lord.   It is true that He is also our Father and that,
of His boundless love and condescension, He allows us and
desires of us a great familiarity;  but familiarity is of two kinds,
bad and good, the bad kind that breeds contempt and is itself
wholly contemptible, which is a kind of snobbish self-assertion,
and the good kind that proceeds from true love.   The first kind
is that of the *parvenu* who behaves after the manner of his kind
in the palace of the King;  the second is that of the King's son.
Worship is adoration, not patronage;  love has always in it the
element of respect, and respect as applied to God is nothing less
than adoration.

The soul when it comes to prayer is truly the son in the Father's
house, but it is also the servant in the presence of the King, and
that side of the truth needs far more stress than it commonly
receives.   God is Love, not good nature;  the Lord Christ has
humbled Himself to the manger and the cross, but that very act
makes Him more and not less adorable.   He calls us His friends

[1] *Selected Letters*, p. 51.

and has made us the sons of God, He has brought us home; but we are infinitely unworthy of Him. It is possible even for a Christian to be guilty of the sin of *lèse-majesté* towards God, and when one rushes into His presence, prefers a request or a demand, and rushes out again, or, more sophisticatedly, enters into His presence and talks about oneself, one commits that sin. God loves me and desires to give me Himself and His gifts; I may talk to Him about myself. Yes, but He is God.

In coming to prayer one should realise where one is. "I saw the Lord," says the prophet, and the realisation of the presence of God is the foundation of good prayer. Adoration springs from looking at God, but this look must be at God Himself. We are not at the moment concerned with Thanksgiving, which is another part of prayer, we are not now loving God for anything that He has made or done, but we are loving Him for Himself. "The lifting up of the mind to God." God the Eternal, the Incomprehensible, the Perfect; God Who is Himself Holiness, Love, Beauty, quite apart from particular manifestations of His attributes. Realise God and adore.

Realising God we adore Him also in His acts, and here the Church's collects, for the most part, give us excellent instruction. "Almighty God, who hast given us thine only-begotten Son to take our nature upon him, and as at this time to be born of a pure Virgin;" [1] "Merciful Lord;" [2] "Almighty and ever-lasting God, who dost govern all things in heaven and earth;" [3] "O God the King of glory;" [4] "O God, the strength of all them that put their trust in thee;" [5] "Lord of all power and might, who art the author and giver of all good things;" [6] "O God, our refuge and strength;" [7] "Almighty God, whom truly to know is everlasting life." [8] The list might be considerably lengthened, but it is long enough to indicate a way of adoration for those who find it difficult to centre their soul directly upon God in His eternal and transcendent Being. It is a way of adoration through His acts or His attributes. Taking one of these, the soul looks at God in it and adores the God Whom it reveals. Some souls can use Nature in this way, but not all: the glory of a sunset, the beauty of a bird, the majesty of the sea and the wonder of the simplest creatures may lead at once to an act of adoration of their

---

[1] Christmas Day.  
[2] S. John's Day.  
[3] Second Sunday after Epiphany.  
[4] Sunday after Ascension Day.  
[5] First Sunday after Trinity.  
[6] Seventh Sunday after Trinity.  
[7] Twenty-third Sunday after Trinity.  
[8] SS. Philip and James.

Creator. By whatever means it is reached, it is clear that adoration is the fundamental act of prayer to a soul that knows into Whose Presence it has come.

(2) *Thanksgiving*. This is the second part of prayer the subject of which is God. It will not necessarily follow immediately upon Adoration in practice—indeed many souls will put it habitually in the third or fourth place—but it is convenient for purposes of exposition to place it here. In whatever order they may come in practice, the various parts of prayer are closely interrelated and flow from one another in various ways. Thanksgiving flows from adoration because it is God Whom we are thanking, and we are thanking Him first of all for Himself, which thanksgiving becomes Praise.

One's usual list of subjects for thanksgiving is normally so narrow that this statement may seem rather strange, but naturally if God is God and one is adoring Him, one may very well begin one's thanksgiving by thanking Him that He is. The openings of collects which we considered under the last head lead imperceptibly into thanksgivings, and as the Festivals of the Church come round they are all opportunities for the same act.

Giving thanks to God for Himself, for His mercy, for His love, for giving His only-begotten Son; giving thanks to Jesus for His Incarnation, for the Blessed Sacrament; giving thanks to the Holy Spirit for His brooding on the face of the waters, for His indwelling of the Church, for His presence in one's own soul: these thanksgivings and others like them are a very precious offering to God, and will also have the effect of making the truths of religion living and real to oneself and of increasing one's love for and trust in God. Thanksgiving so conceived vitalises the virtues of Faith, Hope and Charity almost more than anything else.

Nevertheless, it will hardly be contested that no part of prayer is more consistently neglected, largely because the majority of people do not even realise that God may and should be thanked for these things; they are just taken for granted, and thanksgivings are limited to answers to prayer and one's own personal blessings, with the result that they tend steadily to decrease. The religion of many is depressed and joyless because they have never learnt to thank God for everything, and consequently do not realise what they have to thank Him for.

(3) *Penitence*. This part of prayer springs likewise from adoration. The soul, looking at and adoring God in His per-

Q

fection and holiness, sees itself as it is in its nothingness and sin-fulness, and from this sight spring humility and penitence. It was because Isaiah had seen the Lord and heard the angelic hymn of adoration that the cry of penitence was wrung from his lips: " Woe is me! for I am undone; because I am a man of unclean lips, and I dwell in the midst of a people of unclean lips : for mine eyes have seen the King, the Lord of hosts." [1]  The sight of God comes first, then the sight of self, and all holiness springs from these two sights. Our Lord said to S. Catherine of Siena, " Knowest thou not, daughter, who thou art and who I am? If thou know well these two words thou art and shalt be blessed. Thou art she that art nought; and I am He that am ought. If thou have the very knowledge of these two things in thy soul, thy ghostly enemy shall never deceive thee, but thou shalt eschew graciously all his malice; and thou shalt never consent to any-thing that is against my commandments and precepts, but all grace, all truth and all charity thou shalt win without any hardness." [2]

Humility and penitence bring forth confession; without it all one's prayer is on a wrong level. I may strut and posture before my neighbour and he may think me a fine fellow, but in God's sight I know myself a sinner, and a bankrupt sinner, and all I can do is to throw myself upon the mercy of my Saviour.[3]

(4) *Petition.* The soul is now in a position to ask of God rightly, to ask His favours as of grace and not as of right. We may never demand. Petition is essentially an act of homage. Seeing God and oneself, one places oneself wholly in the hands of God. He is all powerful, we cannot live for one moment or make one single movement towards Him without Himself, our very prayer is the movement of the Holy Spirit within us, we rely from moment to moment upon His prevenient grace, and yet He waits for our prayer before He can impart His best gifts—we must open the window before the fresh air can come in. This reciprocal action between the human will and the Will of God is a great mystery, but it is fundamental to the plan of Creation. God loves to communicate Himself to man, " His delights are with the sons of men." [4]  The whole Bible, Old Testament as

---

[1] Isaiah vi. 5.

[2] *The Cell of Self Knowledge,* Edmund Gardner, p. 37.

[3] The wise man says, " the prayer of him that humbleth himself shall pierce the clouds." We do not sufficiently abase ourselves before God.

[4] Prov. viii. 31.

well as New, bears witness to this truth, the very existence of the Church and the Sacraments testifies to it, but He so limits Himself, He so respects the freedom of His creature, that His desire must stop short of fulfilment without ours.

If we are to exercise the privilege of petition rightly it must grow out of the other parts of prayer. Adoring God, we realise that He is the source of all being; seeing self in His sight, we realise that without Him we are nothing and worse than nothing, and so, abasing ourselves in penitence, thanking Him for all He is and does, we are encouraged to act upon the evangelical promises of our Lord and ask for the supply of our needs, confident that He is but waiting for the co-operation of our desire to " give more than we ask or think."

Our greatest need—indeed, our only ultimate need—is God Himself, consequently the fundamental petition is " O God, give me Thyself." We need God far more than His gifts, and in Him we have all else. The desire for God is the secret of all good prayer and right life, and this desire should be expressed not in many words, but in much prayer. " All the life of a good Christian man is nought else but desire," says S. Augustine.

Our petitions, then, should cover all our spiritual and physical needs as may be necessary, not leaving out those the supply of which we commonly take for granted. It is the placing of every part of life in the hands of God. This is a very different thing from just asking for what we want at the moment (which is perhaps the most common form of petition), and the principle behind it is quite different. It is commonly supposed that " ask and ye shall receive " means " ask for whatever you want, and God will give it you, and if He does not He has not answered your prayer," but our Lord's promise is : " Whatsoever ye shall ask the Father in my name he will give it you." That is prayer in union with Christ—the Son asking the Father that His Will may be done in this individual case; its formula is, " Thy will be done." If this fact were recognised there would be fewer difficulties about answers to prayer.

But, besides being directed to the fulfilment of the will of the suppliant instead of the will of God, petition is commonly far too restricted. Recovery from sickness, aversion of threatened ill, success in a venture, are all legitimate objects of prayer, but are not the only ones, or even the most important; they must be kept in their place. Spiritual gifts—grace, the virtues, the gifts of the Spirit—are far more important, and far too frequently taken for granted. The apparently automatic things of life— food, safety and the like—should also find their place in our petitions; and in proportion as our petition covers the whole of life, instead of being restricted to the more obvious or pressing parts of it, will it attain to its right dimensions.

But petition should not be confined to one's own needs, there is a larger field still to be covered, a field as large as creation; and this involves *intercession*.

Now if petition is apt to be haphazard, intercession is often more so. We can rise to prayers for father, mother, husband, wife, son, daughter and special friends at special times; the Church may find some place in our prayers; perhaps if we are keen on social work or some like activity we shall also pray for that; but even in these intercessions there is often little regularity and considerable vagueness as to what is to be asked. We must try to get back to first principles.

True prayer unites the soul to God, Who is the Source and Sustainer of all being; consequently, the nearer the soul comes to Him the closer it is to all creation, the more vital becomes its relationship to the whole Church. The praying soul therefore comes before God not as an individual, but as part of His creation and family, not merely as an individual, but as having its part in the priesthood of our Lord, praying in union with Him. In prayer, the Christian is exercising a priesthood, he is the priest of creation, because to man alone, in this world, has God given the power to pray and the responsibility to exercise that power. As a member of the Body of Christ he has his part in the priesthood of his Head. In intercession the suppliant considers the needs of creation and the eternal desire of God to satisfy those needs, and brings the two together in Christ.

In true intercession, then, there will, of course, be petition for special needs and special persons, but behind that there will be much general intercession; special needs and persons will be lifted up to God, but so will all mankind, and indeed all creatures. There must be the double action, of contraction to special needs and expansion to all needs.

This does not, of course, mean that prayer should be made in detail for every need that we can think of—all life would be too short for such prayer—but it does mean that every need must find its place in general in the heart and be offered to God.

The use of intentions for this purpose—an *Our Father* for the world, for mankind, for the Church, for sinners (the list may be infinitely extended), is of great value. Those who are required to say the Divine Office may and should offer it with definite intentions of this sort, and the Holy Sacrifice in particular should be offered for specific intentions. As this sort of praying becomes part of one's prayer life one is learning to be an intercessor.

A danger to be avoided in petition and intercession is that of absorption in the person or object for which one is praying, instead of in God. If one feels very strongly about a thing or is very worried about a person, one's feelings or worry frequently go on in one's prayers, not only unchecked, but even encouraged by the notion that one is talking to God about it. One is indeed talking about it, but generally more to oneself than to God, with the result that one rises from one's knees more agitated than when one knelt down. It is, of course, right to pray a thing out with God, but one should always be looking at God, and not at the thing; otherwise the subject of one's prayer becomes merely a distraction, and one ends by making a lengthy meditation on the distraction. Once again we must get back to fundamentals. Prayer is " the lifting up of the mind to God "; in petition we make a connection, as it were, between the matter of our prayer and the will of God, and in doing so our mind must be occupied not with the thing we are praying about, but with God and His action upon it.

We have now considered the parts of which prayer is composed:

1. Adoration.
2. Thanksgiving.
3. Confession.
4. Petition.

Some people would speak of Praise as a fifth part; but praise, blessing and worship are really aspects of adoration and thanksgiving. The more deeply these are understood, the more it is seen that they are all facets of one jewel, which is the act of prayer itself, the more they are seen to be organically connected the one with the other, so that the simplest act of prayer would appear to contain them all. It is not to be imagined that every time one comes to one's prayers one would express them all in the same words, the same order or with the same degree of emphasis. At first some plan and some explicit form of prayer is necessary;

gradually, however, prayer should become more flexible and exercised with increasing freedom.

In the earlier stages of prayer, books of devotions need to be used almost as they stand; later on, however, they will not be so used.   Prayers which express what the soul would say will be used frequently, those which make less appeal more rarely, others not at all.   Priests can give much useful help here.   The Confirmation prayer-book, for instance, should be chosen with great care.   It is a mistake to give a book because it has been the custom of that particular church to give it for years, or because it is published by Messrs. So & So, and therefore must be all right.   The priest should satisfy himself that it is, if not all right, at least the best that he can obtain.   As time goes on he would do well to advise his penitents, guild members and others to look further afield for their prayers and show them where to look. A small MS. book of prayers gathered by oneself is of far more value than all the printed manuals, because it is one's own, and the search for its contents accustoms the soul to the prayers of the saints, which are of inestimable value in themselves, and still more valuable as guides to the making of one's own.

But books of prayers, however valuable, must never be a substitute for the soul's own prayer and converse, either with words or without, with God.   It is well to accustom souls to a great freedom in the use of forms, using them as crutches or props to support the halting soul or as matches to set light to its loving desire for God, never as chains.   Many excellent souls never have time to pray because they have so many prayers which they make it a rule to say, and when they go into Retreat they almost need a pantechnicon to carry their little books.   Never let us teach people to say prayers, but always teach them to pray; it will take longer and need great care and patience, but it will be worth it.

# CHAPTER XVII

# MEDITATION

*Lord, what love have I unto thy law : all the day long is my study in it* (Ps. cxix. 97).

MENTAL Prayer is the primary necessity to all those who desire seriously to live the Christian life. It is not merely a fad of a certain number of pious and leisured people who have a liking or facility for it. Reduced to its simplest terms it is just that converse with God in which the soul truly lives, and it is as necessary to the ploughman as to the philosopher, to the factory girl as to the nun. There is no baptised soul which is incapable of mental prayer, though many, through ignorance, defective will or desire, may think they are.

It is probably true that the mental prayer of no two souls is exactly the same, because no two souls are exactly the same.[1] The director of souls should carefully consider this fact. There is a great temptation, especially to busy priests, to separate people into classes, or more often herds, and treat them as if every member of the herd were alike. That is fatal. In training souls in the spiritual life and in instructing in prayer, each soul must be considered individually, and instructed so far as possible individually. Class instruction is useful and, indeed, necessary when there are great numbers of people to be instructed; sermons on prayer should be far more frequent than they are, but the real work is done in the confessional or the study. No habit is of more value to the priest than that of studying each soul separately, and if he is to guide them rightly through the ways of the spiritual life it is essential.

No two souls are alike, and the prayer of every soul is, consequently, different. Nevertheless all souls are human; underlying all their manifold diversity there is a fundamental unity of nature, and the prayer of each soul is the lifting up of that soul to God, Who is changeless. Souls do fall into fairly well-defined classes, for God's creation is cosmos, not chaos, and those

---

[1] " God leads every soul by a separate path, and you will scarcely meet with one spirit which agrees with another in one half of the way by which it advances." S. John of the Cross, *Living Flame*, Stanza III, p. 98.

231

classes have in broad outline certain defined ways of prayer. The way of the spiritual life is a defined way though different souls are at different stages on it, and advance in it is normally by a beaten track.   Two things therefore need study: souls and the experience of the saints in the way of prayer.   In these chapters we are about to consider the way of prayer.   It can only be done here in outline, but the priest who is in earnest about the direction of souls will read as widely as he can on the subject.   It is never wise to attempt to direct souls by rule of thumb derived from one's own limited experience.   How many priests attempt to direct souls in mental prayer by means of a hazy recollection of a method of meditation which they once attempted and subsequently gave up!   No, the subject should be studied seriously and in good authorities.   Little books should be avoided at all costs, and by little one does not mean little in size, but in matter.   One good text-book should be mastered to show the way, and then as wide reading as possible in the great masters, the old masters.   It is not books about the masters, but the masters themselves that should be read.

In these chapters we are concerned with two things which should always be kept distinct—namely, varieties of prayer, and the methods by which they are exercised.   Both must be studied in order to help souls, but they must not be confused.   We may be able to say of a soul that its prayer is meditation, but it does not therefore follow that the Ignatian method as commonly understood is therefore right for it.   A good method is capable of great variety when used by differing souls, and it is the director's business so to study the tried methods that he can guide souls rightly in their use until they are able to discard them.

The whole purpose of method in meditation is to enable the soul to get into converse with God, just as the purpose of scaffolding is to enable one to reach something that is out of one's reach without it.   Method should therefore be subordinated to prayer.

In practice the soul may find itself drawn to God at any part of its meditation, and when that happens it ought at once to lay aside its preconceived plan and give itself to the leading of the Holy Spirit, reverting to its method when the " leading " ends. This sense of God and movement towards Him Himself is the thing which should be nourished always, so that even the most unbending of the methods of S. Ignatius should lead not only or chiefly to the deepening of intellectual perceptions, but always, as its chief end, to converse with God and personal devotion to Him.

Souls should normally begin the practice of mental prayer with *some form* of meditation. It is true that exceptional souls sometimes begin naturally with a higher form of prayer. When this happens it is clearly the work of the Holy Ghost, and is recognisable as such; the director should not attempt to force such a soul to meditate, but, since such souls are the exceptions which prove the rule, it is a sound principle always to begin the spiritual life with some form of meditation.

## I. The Ignatian Method

The most usual form of this exercise, indeed almost the only form which is at all widely known in the Anglican Communion, is the Ignatian, and it is right to consider this method first.

Prayer is the lifting up of the whole soul, the whole being to God—imagination, intellect, affections and will. In the earlier stages of the prayer life this has to be done explicitly and deliberately, and it is the purpose of this method to do this.

It brings into play, first the imagination, then the memory and intellect, then the affections, and finally the will, the whole being pervaded with the desire for God.

It is at least doubtful whether S. Ignatius ever intended this method to be the cast-iron system which so many people make it. On paper it necessarily looks complicated, because it deliberately brings into play all the powers of the soul, and at first this is a complicated business, and its apparent complexity frequently discourages a soul which wants simply to pray. No method needs such careful explanation or greater discretion in use, but if used with common sense and perseverance no one can doubt its great value.

### (1) *The Preparation.*

Prayer is a serious act, the approach of the soul to the eternal God, and as such it should be prepared for with the greatest care. Unprepared prayers easily become slipshod, haphazard, formal or irreverent, and yet they are all too common. People are far too apt to think that the meditation itself is all that matters, and that the preparation is unnecessary or at best unimportant and may be omitted or reduced at will. No greater mistake could be made. It is certainly possible to over-prepare the immediate preparation so much as virtually to make two meditations, but that is the result of misunderstanding what is meant by it. One must beware of careless preparation.

There are three parts in the preparation of the soul for meditation:—

1. Remote.
2. Proximate.
3. Immediate.

1. *Remote.* This is simply the constant effort to keep one's life habitually in harmony with one's prayer. The desire to pray at all systematically means that one wants to take the Christian life seriously, and no advance is possible in prayer unless one does. What one is in one's life one is also in one's prayer; there is no magic about it. The life of prayer consists in the union of prayer and life, and if one is making no effort to approximate one's practice to the will of God, one can hardly expect to pray.

The remote preparation, then, is of fundamental importance. It consists of three things:—

(*a*) *Mortification.* This is dealt with elsewhere, so there is no need to enlarge on it here except to remark that it is the twin wing by which, no less than by prayer, the soul rises to God.

(*b*) *Habitual recollection.* This also is considered in another place; it is enough here to say that advance in prayer is marked by increase in recollection at all times.

(*c*) *Humility.* The realisation of one's true relationship to God and one's absolute dependence on Him.

2. *Proximate.* This also consists of three parts:—

(*a*) *Consideration of the subject.* The best time for meditation for most people is first thing in the morning as soon as one is up. For some people this time is unsuitable, and they must find another. I would merely point out that the early morning is not necessarily unsuitable because it involves rising half an hour or an hour earlier than one is accustomed to. I am assuming here that the meditation will be made at the beginning of the day; in that case the consideration of the subject of the meditation will be made over-night. It is really a very simple operation, and consists in reading over or thinking over what we propose to meditate on. It should be done quite quickly and generally, the object in view being not to make one meditation in order to prepare for another, but merely to get the subject of to-morrow's meditation clear in our minds in advance. This enables the unconscious mind to get to work during sleep, so that when we come to our meditation in the morning we are familiar with it and able to enter into it as we could not do if we were approaching it then for the first time.

(b) *Recalling the subject* first thing on waking. This is the work of a moment and turns the mind towards God straight away.

Most people find that when they wake, their mind resembles R. L. Stevenson's world in being " full of a number of things," mostly dim and shadowy things half realised, but active enough to produce an unsettled and often depressed state of mind, possibly definite and worrying things tending to the same end, or exciting things tending to distraction. A moment's recollection now will concentrate the mind and the will on God.

(c) *Consecration.* The giving of oneself to God with enthusiasm. This also is the work of a moment, and may make all the difference between not only a good meditation and a bad one, but between a good day and a bad one.

3. *Immediate.* This is the commencement of the meditation itself. Again three parts:—

(a) *Recollection of the Presence of God.* This is vital, and in connection with it we may recall the words of our Lord, " Thou, when thou prayest, enter into thy closet, and when thou hast shut thy door, pray to thy Father which is in secret." [1] We must enter into the closet of our soul and resolutely close the door upon all that is not God, for, if this is not done, the subject of meditation will be but one of the many subjects of thought or desire which will jostle one another in the mind. If we are to keep our attention fixed, we must consciously drive out all objects of attention save one, and when we have shut the door we shall be able to give all our attention to God and pray to Him. Detachment first and then attachment; having shut the door we look at God and contemplate Him present in the secret chamber of the soul. We are not coming to meditation to preach ourselves sermons, but to lift up the mind to God; He alone must reign in the heart. At first it may take some time to centre the soul

[1] Matt. vi. 6.

on God; if it does one must be patient with oneself and give as much time as may be necessary to this act; even if it takes the whole of one's prayer time, that time will not have been wasted; sometimes, indeed, such preparation *is* the prayer. But it will not always take as long as that—on our best days it should only take a few moments.[1]

(*b*) *Act of humility.* All prayer is the action of the Holy Ghost in the human soul, without Him we cannot make even the first movement towards God; we should frankly realise this, and make now an act of humility and penitence acknowledging our own inability. Sometimes, especially in a progressing soul, this may be no more than a swift movement of the spirit.

(*c*) *Prayer to the Holy Ghost.* This follows naturally from (*b*). We are unable to pray of ourselves, and so must ask the aid of the Holy Ghost, Who alone can help us to pray. This should be done quite shortly, as also should the preceding act of humility, but with great fervour. This prayer, as Fr. Longridge remarks, " should never be omitted. In it, besides asking for divine help, without which all our efforts would be in vain, S. Ignatius would have us earnestly protest before God that we come to our medita-tion not to receive consolation or for any motive of self interest, but purely for the service and praise of His Divine Majesty. To enter upon prayer in this spirit of detachment and self-surrender is one of the great secrets of making it well, as also of persevering in times of dryness and desolation." [2]

We now come to *the Meditation itself.*

(1) *The Preludes.*

(*a*) *Composition of Place.* This is the exercise of the imagina-tion, and its importance will vary with different people, for to some whose imagination is vivid it will be the life of the medita-tion, to others whose imagination is less active it will be rather difficult. " The composition of place is an act of the imagination by which we represent to ourselves the place where what we are about to meditate upon takes place. If, however, the subject of our meditation is something abstract and invisible, we should make use of some corporeal object as a symbolic representa-

---

[1] We should never force the soul to a *sensible* realisation of God's presence which He may not will to give. Realisation of God depends upon Him, attention and love upon us: it is these that we are here concerned to gain and give.

[2] W. H. Longridge, *The Spiritual Exercises of S. Ignatius of Loyola*, p. 53.

tion. . . . The object of this prelude is to restrain the wanderings of the imagination by binding it down to some definite picture which illustrates the subject of the meditation, and may often of itself suggest helpful considerations and pious affections. Those who cannot thus work with their imagination, as indeed many cannot, should pass over this prelude lightly; it is just an expedient which some may find helpful, others not. In any case there must be no straining of the mind." [1]

(b) *Petition.* A short prayer that God will grant us to find in our meditation the fruit which is pleasing to Him.

(2) *The Exercise of the Powers of the Soul.*

(a) *The Memory.* This is a twofold operation: firstly, the operation of the memory pure and simple in recalling the subject of meditation, and then the thinking about it in general, what it is, what it means, which involves a simple and general use of the intellect. There is here no hard and fast distinction between the action of the memory and the intellect, both are being used and each should help the other.

(b) *The Intellect.* We now reflect in detail upon the subject of the meditation and apply it to our own soul and its needs, trying to discover its practical consequences in our own case. The object of these considerations is not to think things out or to work out theological problems to our own satisfaction, but so to reflect upon the truths of our holy religion that they may become part of ourselves and issue in the activity of love. We are not exercising the mind for its own sake, but in order that it may set the heart afire.

(c) and (d) *The Will.* (c) This is the real centre of the meditation, though the fact is often lost sight of. The common use of the word meditation to describe quiet thought and the large place assigned in this type of prayer to discursive thinking easily give rise to the idea that meditation is just holy thinking, but thinking is not prayer, though in this case it should conduce to it; prayer begins when the soul turns from its considerations to speak to God, and the first act of the will is just this speaking to God. In this section of the meditation the soul gives itself in love to God and speaks to Him. As soon as the soul has been led to do this, the intellect has done its work, and all further considerations may be suspended, unless the soul flags, when they may begin again.

[1] Longridge, *op. cit.*, p. 54.

(*d*) The colloquy with God to which the soul has now been led should itself give rise to a resolution. This should be simple, definite and such as can be put into practice at once; abstract and general resolutions, such as " I will love God more," and the like, should be avoided at all costs, the resolution should be practical and concrete. Another point which is worth consideration is that it is unnecessary, and often inadvisable, to make a new resolution with every meditation. The making of such new resolutions may be an excellent exercise of ingenuity, but it does not always help forward the spiritual life, because nothing is ever finished. We begin with a resolution of one kind, and next day shoot off on quite a different one, having kept the first very indifferently; then we wonder why we make no progress in the spiritual life, and say that resolutions are no good. It is often far better to go on driving in the same resolution day after day with hammer-strokes of the will, thus we may find one day, to our surprise, that the nail has gone home.

## (3) *The Conclusion.*

The Meditation should end with a quiet gathering up of the fruits of our prayer. S. Ignatius says, " For the space of a quarter of an hour, either sitting or walking, I will examine how it has gone with me in the contemplation or meditation; if badly, I will look for the cause whence it proceeds, and when I have discovered it I will be sorry for it, so as to amend in future; if well, I will thank God our Lord, and proceed in the same manner another time." [1]

In the " Exercises " S. Ignatius is, of course, thinking primarily of a retreat in which a quarter of an hour would not be too much to add to an hour's meditation, but in using his method for ordinary meditation it would not be necessary to give more than a few minutes to a brief examen and a prayer for grace to keep the resolution we have made, though this examen and prayer should not be omitted.

Set out thus, the ordinary Ignatian method of meditation, as has been remarked, looks very complicated and formidable, but it must be remembered that it is always a much more complicated matter to explain a thing than to do it when explained. The complication here is due to the fact that every power of the soul is deliberately, individually and explicitly exercised. The

---

[1] *Op. cit.*, Addition V of the First Week.

method should not, however, be applied with cast-iron rigidity to all souls or to the same soul at all times; it must be made flexible by use. The imagination may need little attention, then do not trouble overmuch about the composition of place; the heart may be burning, then do not linger over the considerations, but, using them so far as may be necessary and helpful, pass on to the colloquies which are the apex of the prayer. The purpose of this, as of all methods of mental prayer, is to bring the heart into converse with its God. Learn to pray by method, but do not be a slave to the method by which you learn.

### Scheme of the Ignatian Method.

(1) *The Preparation.*

> *Remote.*
>> Mortification.
>> Recollection.
>> Humility.

> *Proximate.*
>> Consideration of the Subject.
>> Recalling the Subject.
>> Consecration.

> *Immediate.*
>> Recollection of the Presence of God.
>> Act of Humility.
>> Prayer to the Holy Ghost.

(2) *The Exercise.*

> i. Composition of Place.
> ii. Petition.
> (*a*) Recollection.  (The Memory.)
> (*b*) Considerations.  (The Intellect.)
> (*c*) Colloquies.  (The Will [affective].)
> (*d*) Resolution.  (The Will [conative].)

(3) *The Conclusion.*

> Gathering up of the fruits of the meditation.

### II. The Salesian Method.

The method of meditation advocated by S. Francis de Sales in his *Introduction to the Devout Life* is based on the Ignatian, but is sufficiently original to merit description. The Saint explains it so clearly and gracefully that it would be an impertinence to describe it in any other words, and I shall therefore let him speak for himself.[1]

---

[1] The passages quoted will be found in *The Devout Life*, Part II, chapters 2–7.

### (1) *The Preparation.*

(a) *Of the Presence of God.*　Four principal ways.

The *first* consists in a lively and attentive apprehension of the omnipresence of God.　Everyone knows this truth, but everyone is not attentive to grasp it.　Therefore, before prayer we must always stir up our souls to an attentive thought and consideration of this presence of God.　When therefore you come to prayer, you must say with all your heart: O my heart, my heart, God is truly here.

The *second* way of placing yourself in this holy presence, is to think that not only is God in the place where you are, but that he is in a very special manner in your heart and in the depth of your spirit, which He quickens and animates with his divine presence, since he is there as the heart of your heart, and the spirit of your spirit.　In the consideration therefore of this truth, you will stir up in your heart a great reverence for God, who is so intimately present there.

The *third* way is to consider our Saviour, who in his humanity looks from Heaven upon all persons in the world, but particularly upon Christians who are his children, and more especially upon those who are in prayer, whose actions and behaviour he observes.

The *fourth* way consists in making use of the imagination alone, representing to ourselves the Saviour in his sacred humanity, as though he were near to us, just as we are wont to represent our friends to ourselves saying: I imagine that I see such a one who is doing this or that; it seems to me that I see him, or some such thing.　But if the most holy Sacrament of the altar be present, then this presence will be real and not merely imaginary; for the species and appearances of the bread are as it were a tapestry, behind which our Lord really present sees and observes us, though we see him not in his own form.

You will make use, then, of one of these four ways of putting your soul in the presence of God, before prayer; and you must not seek to make use of them all together, but only one at a time, and that briefly and simply.

(b) *Of the Invocation.*　The invocation is made in this manner: your soul having realised that she is in the presence of God, prostrates herself with profound reverence, acknowledging her unworthiness to appear before so sovereign a Majesty, and nevertheless, knowing that his goodness desires it, she asks of him the grace to serve him well, and to adore him in this meditation. You would do well also to invoke your good Angel, and the holy persons who are concerned in the mystery upon which you are meditating.

(c) *Of the Setting Forth of the Mystery*. This is no other thing than to represent to the imagination the scene of the mystery upon which the meditation is made, as though it were actually taking place in our presence. As regards mysteries such as the greatness of God, the excellence of virtue, the end for which we are created, which are invisible things, there is no question of making use of this kind of imagination.

Now, by means of this imaginary scene we confine our spirit within the mystery upon which we intend to meditate, so that it may not range hither and thither, just as we confine a bird within a cage, or as we put jesses on a hawk so that it may remain upon the fist.

### (2) *The Considerations*.

One or many considerations may be made in order to stir up our affections towards God and divine things: and herein meditation differs from study and from other thoughts and considerations which are not made to acquire virtue or the love of God, but for other ends and intentions, as, for example, to become learned, to write, or to argue. Having then confined your spirit, as I have said, within the enclosure of the subject upon which you intend to meditate, either by the imagination if the subject be something perceptible to the senses, or by the simple setting forth thereof, if it be something imperceptible, you will begin to make considerations on it. And if you find sufficient relish, light and fruit in one of these considerations, stay there without passing on to another, acting like the bees, who do not leave a flower so long as they find any honey there to gather. But if you do not find anything to your liking in one of these considerations after having dealt with it and tried it for a little while, pass on to another; but proceed quite gently and simply in this matter, without undue haste.

### (3) *The Affections and Resolutions*.

Meditation produces good movements in the will or affective part of our soul, such as the love of God and of our neighbour, etc.

R

However, Philothea, you must not dwell upon these general affections to such an extent that you omit to convert them into special and particular resolutions for your correction and amendment. For example, the first word that our Lord spoke on the cross will doubtless stir up in your soul a good affection of imitation—namely, the desire to pardon your enemies and to love them. But I say now that this is of little value, if you do not add to it a special resolution to this effect: Well then! I will not hereafter be offended by such or such annoying words, which such or such a person, a neighbour of mine perhaps, or a servant, may say of me, nor by such or such an affront which may be put upon me by this person or by that: on the contrary, I will say and do such or such a thing to gain him, and appease him, and so also in other matters. By this means, Philothea, you will correct your faults in a very short time, whereas by the affections alone you will do so but slowly and with difficulty.

## (4) *The Conclusion and Spiritual Nosegay.*

Finally, the meditation must be closed by three acts which should be made with as much humility as possible.

The *first* is the act of *thanksgiving*, by which we thank God for the affections and resolutions which he has given us, and for his goodness and mercy which we have discovered in the mystery upon which we have been meditating.

The *second* is the act of *oblation* by which we offer to God this same goodness and mercy of his, the death, the blood and the virtues of his Son, and, together with these, our own affections and resolutions.

The *third* is the act of *petition*, by which we demand of God and implore him to communicate to us the graces and virtues of his Son, and to bless our affections and resolutions, so that we may be able faithfully to put them into practice; then we pray in like manner for the Church, for our pastors, relations, friends and others, availing ourselves, for this purpose, of the intercession of our Lady, and of the Angels and Saints. Lastly, I have noted that one should say the *Pater Noster* and *Ave Maria*, which is the general and necessary prayer of all the faithful.

To all this I have added that one should gather a little *nosegay of devotion*. My meaning is as follows:

Those who have been walking in a beautiful garden do not leave it willingly without taking away with them four or five flowers, in order to inhale their perfume and carry them about during the day: even so, when we have considered some mystery in meditation, we should choose one or two or three points in which we have found most relish, and which are specially proper to our advancement, in order to remember them throughout the day, and to inhale their perfume spiritually. Now we should do this in the place where we have made our meditation, either staying where we are, or walking about alone for a little while afterwards.

S. Francis lived in more spacious times than our own, and his bouquet would seem to be rather larger than we need; but the spiritual nosegay which he so beautifully advocates is a conclusion which may and should be made to any kind of meditation, though most people will find it most useful to confine it to one point instead of the two or three suggested by the Saint. Those who have practised it know the extreme value of this custom in deepening recollection and supernaturalising life.

### Scheme of the Salesian Method.

(1) *The Preparation.*

    (*a*) Recollection of the Presence of God.
    (*b*) The Invocation.
    (*c*) The setting forth of the Mystery.

(2) *The Considerations.*
(3) *The Affections and Resolutions.*
(4) *The Conclusion.*

    (*a*) Act of Thanksgiving.
    (*b*) Act of Oblation.
    (*c*) Act of Petition.
    (*d*) The Spiritual Nosegay.

### III. The Method of S. Peter of Alcantara

The *Treatise on Prayer and Meditation* of S. Peter of Alcantara is far less known among us than it deserves to be. The late Fr. Hollings, S.S.J.E., edited a translation of it by the Rev. G. F. Bullock and introduced it to Anglican Catholics as *A Golden Treatise of Mental Prayer* (which it truly is) in 1905, but this edition has unfortunately been out of print for some years; another edition has recently been published by Fr. Dominic Devas, O.F.M., in the " Orchard " Series of Messrs. Burns, Oates and Washbourne.

S. Peter's method of meditation may be summarised as follows :—[1]

(1) *The Preparation*.    The Saint very beautifully remarks in this connection that " it is necessary to prepare the heart for this holy exercise, as one might tune up a guitar for playing on it " (p. 84); it is a phrase which may well be treasured by all who desire truly to pray, whatever their way of prayer may be.    Too many souls simply tumble into prayer without staying to tune the instrument, and the result, naturally, is distraction and ineffectiveness.    The soul that would speak with God needs to be tuned to Him.    The tuning, according to S. Peter's method, consists of three acts.

(*a*) *Recollection*.    " Begin," says the Saint, " with the sign of the Cross, and get your imagination under control " (p. 86). Here again we have a piece of penetratingly wise counsel, for if the imagination can but be controlled, most of the difficulties of prayer are overcome at one blow.    The Saint would have us control our imagination by " withdrawing it from the affairs of daily life, raising up your soul on high and considering how our Lord is watching you.    Maintain in yourself the same attention and respect as if you saw him actually present."

(*b*) This act of Recollection leads naturally to one of *Contrition*, which S. Peter says should be in the morning the *Confiteor* and in the evening a general examen of the day past.

(*c*) The third act is one of *Invocation* of the Holy Spirit, begging Him for enlightenment and grace to pray rightly.

(2) *The Reading*.    This corresponds to the Consideration of the Subject in S. Ignatius' scheme, and consists simply in the reading of the subject-matter of the meditation.    " This must not be done hurriedly nor in cursory fashion, but with attention and calm, applying thereto not merely one's intelligence, so as to understand what is read, but, above all, the will so as to relish it: and when one alights on some moving passage, one should pause

---

[1] *A Golden Treatise of Mental Prayer*, by S. Peter of Alcantara.    A new translation edited by George Seymour Hollings, S.S.J.E.    Mowbray, 1905.    *Treatise on Prayer and Meditation* by S. Peter of Alcantara.    Translated by Dominic Devas, O.F.M.    Burns, Oates and Washbourne, 1926.    The method explained here is to be found in Part I capp. v–xii.    The quotations are from the latter edition.

a little so as to appreciate it better.   The reading should not be
very long " (p. 88).

(3) *The Meditation.*   This is of two kinds: either Imaginative
or Intellectual.   In the Ignatian method, while there are naturally
some subjects upon which the imagination cannot be used, yet,
where possible, both faculties are brought into operation, the
former in the Composition of Place and the latter in the Considerations.   S. Peter, on the other hand, seems to expect that our
meditation will be either imaginative or intellectual, but not both,
though he leaves the soul free as to its movements.

In *imaginative* meditation, *e.g.* on the life or passion of Christ,
he says, " We must figure each detail as it actually exists, or
actually happens, and must consider it as taking place in the very
spot where we are, and in our presence.   Such a representation
will make our consideration and appreciation of the mystery more
vivid.   It will be even better to imagine all as taking place
within our own hearts.   If cities and kingdoms can find a place
there, how much more a representation of these mysteries.   This
will help a great deal in keeping the soul recollected, by occupying
it within itself (like the bee in her hive, busy over her honey) "
(p. 90).

In *intellectual* meditation, *e.g.* on the perfections of God, S.
Peter wishes us to strive to avoid " an excessive use of the speculative intellect, endeavouring to treat the matter in hand with the
affections and sentiments of the will rather than with speculative
reasonings of the intellect.   Beyond all question, they miss the
way who set themselves to meditate in such fashion during prayer
upon the divine mysteries, as if they were studying them for
preaching purposes.   That tends to scatter the powers of the soul
rather than to recollection, and far from making us enter into
ourselves, tends to carry us without.   Thus it comes about that,
when prayer is over, one is as dry and indevout, and as prompt
and ready for every triviality as one was before.   To speak truly,
such have not prayed at all, but simply composed phrases and
studied, which is a very different thing from praying.   They should
bear in mind that in this exercise we should listen rather than
speak " (pp. 104 *f.*).   This is most important advice for all ways
of praying which involve the conscious use of the intellect or are
founded upon intellectual considerations, and should be most
carefully noted by all who use such ways or train others in them.

(4) *The Thanksgiving.*   This may seem at first sight rather an

early place for this most important act, but in reality it is not so. The thanksgiving flows naturally from the meditation, for in it we lift up our heart to God and thank Him " for the benefit conferred on us in the mystery we have been considering." Thus our consideration becomes an act of worship and joy. S. Peter would, however, have us go further than this, and enlarge our act of thanskgiving to cover all the benefits of the General Thanksgiving and " summon all created things in heaven and on earth to help you in this work."

(5) *The Offering.* If the Thanksgiving is the natural completion of the Meditation, it also leads on, equally inevitably, to an act of Self-Oblation; realising the infinite perfection, love and goodness of God, and thanking Him for all the good which He gives, the soul, realising its own nothingness, is led to make an offering of itself into the hands of God, resigning itself wholly to His holy Will and offering, " at the same time, all his words, actions, thoughts and toils, all he may have to bear and suffer, that all may be to the honour and glory of God's holy name " (pp. 93 *f.*).

But that is not all: this offering of self only attains its full stature in union with the offering of Christ our Head, so S. Peter would further have us " offer to the Father all the merits and good works of his Son . . . for it is all our treasure and heritage which he has bequeathed to us in the New Testament by which he has made us heirs to all this great wealth. For just as what is given me by grace is no less mine than what I win myself by my own efforts, so the merits and rights which he has given me belong to me as much as if I had myself sweated and laboured to secure them. Thus may a man make this second offering no less than the former, counting up as his own all the services and labours and all the virtues of that most holy life . . . This is the richest and most precious offering we can possibly make to God " (p. 94).

(6) *The Petition.* This consists first of an act of *intercession;* for the whole world, the whole Church, Kings, Bishops, all in authority, the poor, prisoners, the needy and the dead. This should be followed, not preceded, by petition *for one's own needs*: pardon, contrition, grace, virtues and all needs. All is concluded with a *prayer for the love of God.* It is this act towards which the whole exercise has been tending. " Dwell upon this," says S. Peter, " occupy with this the greater part of your time, demand of our Lord this virtue with feelings of the most ardent longing,

for herein lies all our good " (p. 97). His own " special prayer for the love of God " is too long for transcription here, but it is of the greatest value and beauty.

It will have been noticed that this method of meditation differs a good deal from those we have so far considered. S. Peter himself regards it as a method for beginners, but it is a very flexible method, and one which may be used in various ways by a variety of souls, many of whom may be by no means beginners. The Saint himself insists upon this flexibility: " I know quite well," he says, " that all these acts, and in the order given, are not always necessary, but still they serve as a start for beginners, by giving them a definite order to follow and a scheme by which they may direct themselves. Again, in all I have said so far, I would not be considered as laying down a permanent rule or general law, for my intention is not to legislate, but to introduce newcomers into this path. Once they have entered upon it, use and experience and, most of all, the Holy Spirit will teach them the rest " (p. 85). His purpose is to secure devotion, the expressed love of God, and all means are to be subservient to this end. " When we set ourselves to consider any one of the subjects treated of above, at the time fixed and according to the scheme determined on, we should never tie ourselves down so completely as to think it wrong to pass on to some other, in which we find more devotion, more relish and more profit. Since the purpose of our efforts is to secure devotion, that which helps us the more towards this end we should look on as being, for us, the better. This, however, should not be done lightly, but only where there is a clearly recognised advantage.

" Similarly, if at any given moment of our prayer or meditation we experience more relish and devotion than at another, we should pause as long as this *affection* lasts, even though it continue during the whole time of our recollection. As we have said, the purpose throughout is *devotion*, and it would be a mistake, in consequence, to seek elsewhere, and with doubtful hope of success, what we already hold securely in our hands " (pp. 103 *f.*).

The Ignatian method, as has been said, aims at the deliberate exercise of each one of the powers of the soul; it is therefore maimed if it is not practised according to the rules laid down; this renders it peculiarly valuable to some types of beginner, whose souls need exercise. There are, however, other types of beginner to whom the more definitely affective method of

S. Peter will be of more use from the beginning, and it is often very valuable to those who, having used S. Ignatius for some time, find his way cramping. It is possible that S. Peter's plan is the most valuable of all, as it provides a complete way of praying without tying the soul at any point to the method.

In Part I, Chapter xii, S. Peter sets down eight counsels for the practice of prayer, some of which have already been quoted. Despite their value it is impossible to deal with all of them here, but, since we have spoken of devotion as the end of this exercise, the fifth Counsel must be quoted. He is speaking of those times, distressingly frequent in the experience of most of us, when, do what we may, the soul remains cold and without conscious feeling of God. He counsels us at such times not to abandon our prayer, but to wait for some little while. " If our Lord comes, thank him for his coming; if it seems to you that he is not coming, humble yourself before him, knowing you do not deserve that which is not given you and content yourself with having made the sacrifice of yourself, renounced your own self-will, crucified your own natural inclination, struggled with the demon and with yourself, and, at the least, done what you could. If you have not adored our Lord with such fervour of devotion as you would wish, it is enough to have adored him in spirit and in truth, and it is he who would have it thus. Believe me, it is certain this is the most perilous spot in the voyage, and the place where those who are really devout are proved. If you come well out of it, all the rest will go prosperously " (p. 108). In another place the Saint points out that devotion is our Lord's gift, and not the fruit of human effort; and that to the faithful soul He will give either that " or some even greater grace " as He will.

The last point to which we must draw attention is the completeness of this method: it is far more than a plan of meditation, it comprehends in one act examen of conscience, contrition, spiritual reading, meditation, thanksgiving, self-oblation, union with our Lord, intercession and petition, thus drawing together into one all the various activities which we call " our prayers." In learning to use this method the soul is not only learning to meditate, but, in the widest sense, to pray.

SCHEME OF THE METHOD OF S. PETER OF ALCANTARA.

(1) *Preparation.*

> (*a*) Act of Recollection.
> (*b*) Act of Contrition.
> (*c*) Invocation of the Holy Spirit.

(2) *Reading.*

(3) *Meditation.*

> (*a*) Imaginative.
> (*b*) Intellectual.

(4) *Thanksgiving.*

(5) *Offering.*

> (*a*) of self.
> (*b*) of the merits of Christ

(6) *Petition.*

> (*a*) Intercession.
> (*b*) Petition.
> (*c*) Prayer for the love of God.

## IV. THE SULPICIAN METHOD

A fourth method of meditation must now be considered; a way which is simpler and less intellectual than any of those which we have so far studied. Essentially it marks an advance on at any rate the first two, as will be seen in the next chapter, but for many people it is the beginner's method.

People tend to fall into two classes : intellectual and affective. For the affective mind the Sulpician method gives, as a rule, all the help that is necessary in meditation, for it contains little or no discursive reasoning, but, rather, a simple concentrated attention to God with acts of the affections.

The Ignatian method tends sometimes to become rather superficial through overmuch attention to the external actions of the gospel story. The Sulpician method seeks to enter into the spiritual reality of which they are the expression, and so to enter into communion with our Lord Himself, and by that communion to become like Him.

The preparation may be the same as that for the other methods. That being done, the meditation consists of three very simple and sustained acts, of which our Lord Himself is the sole object:

(1) *Jesus before the eyes* (Adoration).   The soul, having placed itself in the presence of Jesus, contemplates Him in one of His virtues, *e.g.*, humility, obedience, love—looking at some of the incidents in the gospels which illustrate it, or at some of His teaching upon it, but in quite a general sort of way—*e.g.*, it looks at Jesus humble before Pilate; it does not try to argue about the scene or draw out explicitly all its implications, it looks and adores.   It is concerned with Him, not with a subject.

The intellect, like the tongue, is an unruly member.   It loves to work out its own ideas about God, and in its own place such intellection is right and proper; but in prayer it needs to learn the illumination of adoration, its attitude should be " Lord, enlighten me, show me Thyself."   That is the attitude here.

(2) *Jesus in the heart* (Communion).   The soul now draws into itself, as it were, the virtue which it has seen in our Lord.   It sees that virtue in its beauty and its own lack of it, and desires, with all the intensity of which it is capable, to be like Jesus in this thing; it desires His purity, His love, His humility or whatever it may be, and prays earnestly for it.   " As the hart desireth the water-brooks, so longeth my soul after Thee, O Lord."   Through His virtues it desires Him and finds Him.

(3) *Jesus in the hands* (Co-operation).   Here the will comes into play, and the soul lays itself whole in the will of God.   " My God, I give myself to Thee, Thine ever, only Thine to be."   All right action is the result of co-operation between the human will and the will of God.   It is evident that this act is most important and most full of love, and it will usually issue in some simple and definite resolution.

This simple plan is patient of almost infinite variation to suit the needs of different souls and the same soul at different times, and, like that of S. Peter of Alcantara, it is a ladder, by means of which souls may climb freely to the prayer of contemplation, if it be God's will to call them thither.[1]

---

[1] This chapter was completed before the publication of Fr. Bede Frost's valuable book *The Art of Mental Prayer*.   I would advise those who may wish to explore other methods of meditation to study this book carefully.

# CHAPTER XVIII

# AFFECTIVE PRAYER

*I will love thee, O Lord my strength* (Ps. xviii. 1).

In the latter part of the last chapter we considered a method of meditation differing materially from the better-known and more elementary Ignatian model. In so far as it is a method of meditation, it was convenient to discuss it in connection with other methods; considered as a way of prayer, its place should rather have been at the head of this chapter, for, as was indicated in its discussion, it marks a distinct advance in the prayer life. Perhaps it may most usefully be visualised as a bridge leading from discursive meditation to affective prayer, but a bridge constructed, as it were, from the affective side.

I am inclined to think that one reason why there is not more advance in prayer among us is that the characteristic English distrust of affection and fear of sentiment flourish unchecked, especially among men. Contemporary English religion on the whole tends to be intellective—the faith must be in all ways interpreted in terms of modern thought, the individual must think out his religion and express it in terms which seem true to him. The craze for a late age for Confirmation which is not even yet dead rests on the assumption that the child must *understand* what the sacrament is, in the sense of assimilating certain arguments about it. Discursive meditation makes a certain appeal to this intellective type of mind because it deliberately gives a good deal of scope to purely reasoning activity. Rightly understood, it is not an intellective exercise, for intellection should lead on naturally to the more important affection and conation; nevertheless, as it is commonly practised, this type of prayer is almost entirely thinking or speaking.

There comes a point in the history of most souls when this type of prayer ceases to satisfy; it is then commonly dropped, and if distrust of the affections is operative there is nothing to take its place. Incidentally, this is generally an opportunity for Christian

Science or Spiritualism or for one of the other affective aberrations in our midst, which mask their emotional appeal with a scientific jargon, to capture the soul; or else it may slip into indifferentism. Actually the Englishman is not the severe intellectualist he would have people believe him to be, he is an incurable sentimentalist, consequently he fears the affections.

No wise man wishes to depreciate the work of the intellect in its right place—it has its part, and a very fundamental part, in all true religion—but it must be pointed out that religion, which is life with God, and prayer, which is the expression of that life, are fundamentally the work of the will and the affections. God has not commanded us to understand Him or argue about Him, but to love Him. "Jesus said, Thou shalt love the Lord thy God with all thy heart and with all thy soul and with all thy mind." [1] The mind's action is strictly ancillary to the love of God.

If the soul is to avoid the nemesis which is apt to attend on a one-sidedly "intelligent" religion it is necessary to master two facts:—

> (a) that "the lifting up of the mind to God" is fundamentally an act of love.
> (b) that in this act of love the intellect has its part and is not stultified thereby.

"Why did God make you?"

"God made me to know Him, love Him and serve Him in this world, and to be happy with Him for ever in the next." [2]

Love, as we have seen elsewhere, is the motive and purpose of creation, prayer is essentially an act of love. Knowledge there must be, and that is the province of the intellect, but it is knowledge which proceeds from love and produces love. There is ever-deepening knowledge in prayer, but the higher the prayer the less purely intellectual that knowledge becomes. It is more and more the intuitive knowledge of love.

True love is not sentiment—let us lay that bogy at once—it is the action of the will desiring God and surrendering itself to Him.

It is the habit of modern psychologists to heap scorn upon the faculty psychology of the Schoolmen. As a matter of fact, the Schoolmen and the mystical saints, or at any rate the best of them, were very much better psychologists than is generally allowed. Nevertheless the moderns are right in refusing to allow that "the

---

[1] Matt. xxii. 37.　　　　　[2] Penny Catechism, Q.2.

mind," " the heart," and " the will " are separate entities, though it is at least open to doubt how far the scholastic philosophers really thought they were.    They did not, for instance, mean by the term " mind " the discursive intellect, as we do, and it is necessary to remember this in considering the definition of prayer which we have adopted.    Blosius (sixteenth century) puts the matter clearly, " The highest part of the soul, called the mind, is the simple and God-like basis or groundwork of the soul—that is, the simple essence of the soul sealed with the image of God. . . . From the mind itself the three higher powers flow and re-flow again into it, as rays of light emanate from the sun.    Here, in truth, the likeness of God shines out in a wonderful way.    For as the Father and the Son and the Holy Ghost are three Persons but one God, so the memory, intellect and will are three powers but one mind.    And just as the three Persons of God work together in inseparable union, so do those three powers of the mind.    The memory recalls nothing without the intellect and the will; the intellect does not understand or know anything without the memory and the will; and the will desires nothing without the intellect and the memory.    One consequence of this union is that the term ' mind ' is often used to denote the higher powers as well as the essential basis of the soul." [1]    No doubt we should put matters differently to-day.    For one thing, our habitual trichotomy being different, we should not speak of memory, intellect and will, but prefer to say mind, heart and will, thus separating heart and will, which the older writers preferred to treat as one, and treating as one memory and intellect, which the older writers preferred to divide.    But the real point of interest here is Blosius' insistence on the essential unity of all the powers of the soul in every mental act.    If then prayer is love, it is an act of the whole being, and not merely of the affections, as so many believe; indeed, the point to be grasped in this connection is that love is not a sentimental working of the affections at all, but the act of the will, which is nothing less than " character in action." [2] In passing, then, from intellectual to affective prayer we are not exchanging a dependable faculty for one which we instinctively distrust, but we are making our prayer consciously and simultaneously the act of the whole being.

Affective prayer is so called not because it is a bubbling over

<hr/>

[1] Blosius, *Spiritual Instruction*, Intro. pp. 4–5.
[2] McDougall, *Outline of Psychology*, p. 442.

of sentimental affections, for it is not such, but because it consists of acts of loving desire.   It is well to remind oneself that the old trichotomy of the soul is memory, intellect and will, as we have seen, and Fr. Augustine Baker speaks of this prayer as "affective prayer of the will." [1]   It is well for us to think in this way of affection and will as one, remembering that the affections which we should desire to pour forth in prayer are not chance ebullitions of sensible devotions, but deliberate loving acts.   Sensible devotion is accidental to true prayer, it comes and goes, often long periods pass without its ever coming at all, but affective prayer should still go on, being made by the will based on the simple and contemplative action of the intellect.

There are three distinct kinds of prayer comprehended in this way, which are not wholly separable and frequently mingle; these are forced acts, affections and aspirations.

1. *Forced acts.*   These are deliberate acts of the will, generally with little or no emotion in them, " made in and by the superior will only, without any concurrence of sensitive nature." [2]   In these the soul worships God very simply, holding itself to one act, as long as it may, by repeated strokes of the will.   These are the forced acts of which we have spoken from time to time in the course of our previous chapters.   " These are called forced acts, because after that a soul is become indisposed to prosecute the exercise of meditation, it will be long before that good affections do, as it were, naturally flow from her, so that she will need to use some force upon herself for the producing of the said acts of the will." [3]   As time goes on, however, they will become less forced and more spontaneous.

2. *Affections.*   These are not necessary to this prayer, indeed, many people experience them very little, for they are, as a rule, the overflowing of a naturally affectionate nature which must express itself thus, being simply the pouring out of the affections towards God in acts of love, joy, hope, desire and the like.   It is clear that the soul to whom such affections are natural should exercise a wise restraint in regard to them, for otherwise its prayer may become merely sentimental.   Such affections should be balanced and spiritualised by acts of humility, penitence and self-oblation and by a careful mortification of life.

3. *Aspirations.*   These, "though they be in substance little

[1] *Holy Wisdom*, Tr. III, Sect. I, cap. iii. 15.
[2] *Ibid.*, Tr. III, Sect. III. cap. i. 4.          [3] *Ibid.*, cap. i. 2.

differing from the former, yet by reason of the facility wherewith
they are produced without force, foresight, or election, purely
flowing from an internal impulse of the Divine Spirit, we therefore give them another name." [1]  They are the infused element
in this way of praying, and are in no way under the control of the
soul.  When they are given they should be followed so long as
they last.

It will be useful to gain some general idea of the practice of
this way of prayer; we will therefore append Fr. Baker's description, which is clear and succinct.  "The soul's aim," he says,
" is to recollect herself by that general notion that faith gives her
of God; but being not able to do this presently, she doth in
her mind, and by the help of the imagination, represent unto
herself some Divine Object, as some one or more perfections of
God, or some mystery of Faith, as the Incarnation, Transfigura-
tion, Passion, Agony or Dereliction of our Lord, etc.; and there-
upon, without such discoursing as is used in meditation, she doth
immediately, without more ado, produce acts or affections one
after another towards God, or upon herself with reference to God,
adoring, giving thanks, humbling herself in His presence,
resigning herself to His will, etc." [2]

We have drawn our exposition of this way of prayer from Fr.
Augustine Baker's *Holy Wisdom*, Treatise III, Section III, Chapters
i–iii, which should be carefully studied by those who have to
train others in prayer.  It is also invaluable to those who pray in
this way by reason of the large number of affective acts which it
contains.[3]  As souls advance they are able to make their own
acts, and should do so, but the difficulty for a beginner is that
there are so few books of prayers which can give him any help.
One may mention Fr. Roche's *Mysteries of the Mass in Reasoned
Prayers* and Fr. Gilbert Shaw's Burgh Booklets, which are very
valuable, also a small book called *Ascensiones in Corde*.

In affective prayer the action of the intellect is always of a
simple perceptive sort; indeed, it tends to become still simpler,
for some souls do not seem to themselves to be using their intellect
at all, so much does its action become second nature and so
quickly does the soul pass to acts of love.  Some spiritual writers
do indeed speak of the paralysis of the mind which takes place in

---

[1] *Ibid.*, Tr. III, cap. i. 2.                    [2] *Ibid.* cap. i. 11.
[3] These acts have recently been reprinted separately in a convenient form
by Dom Weld-Blundell, O.S.B., under the title of *Acts and Affections for Mental
Prayer*.

certain stages of the prayer life, and those who have practised such prayer know what is meant; nevertheless, it is certain that the intellect is not really paralysed, but actually working unconsciously and without hindrance, absorbed with God. The central activity of prayer now is in the affections.

Affective prayer is the prayer of Christ's lovers. For them the truths of religion do not require perpetual argument and restatement, for they have deepened into profound convictions, and become the truths by which the soul lives. They know the truth, and the truth makes them free—free from deliberate delight in sin, free to love God; and their prayer is the action of that love. This prayer is expressed in repeated acts of the will. Words are reduced to a minimum, often the same phrase is repeated over and over again. This is not a vain repetition, for the sole purpose of the phrase or word is to direct the action of the soul and hold it in the presence of God, and the real work is being done underneath without words.

For souls who are drawn to this kind of prayer it is useful to keep a note-book into which can be copied phrases which may be useful in prayer. Scraps of the gospels which have become luminous by meditation, words of our Lord, or the apostles, or the saints, bits of the psalms, hymns, all short and such as may be used in a breath. " Short prayer pierceth heaven " not, in this case, because it is short, but because it may be used over and over again.

Some people prefer to use more extended prayers, not continuously, but repeating each phrase until its sweetness has all been extracted, and then passing on to the next. In this case the soul should move freely, not feeling any necessity to use the whole prayer, but only so much of it as it needs. The formula is a vehicle of the soul's love, its act, not a substitute for effort, or a cage.

Some people, again, prefer to have a method, especially at first, because the simplicity of this way of prayer is apt to be deceptive, and to give the impression that the soul is doing little or nothing, when it is probably doing exactly what God requires of it. The experience of most people, however, is that the more this way of prayer is used the less possible or desirable it is to bind the soul down to any method at all. Prayer becomes more and more a loving converse between the soul and its God, a converse of speech and silence, of stammering words oft repeated, as the child in its mother's arms cannot and need not say more than, "I love you . . . I love you."

For those who do need a scheme it is possible to make one something on the lines of the methods of meditation which have been already considered.

All prayers should begin with God, continue with God and end with God. If the whole of one's prayer time is spent in quietly closing the door of the soul on all else and looking at God only, so far from its having been wasted, which some would think, it has been very perfectly occupied; indeed, the final simplicity to which many attain is nothing more than this. On the other hand, many people spend their prayer time in great activity, praying earnestly for a variety of objects, persons and virtues, and yet have really hardly prayed at all, because they have been occupied with *things* rather than with God. In this method, then, the soul should begin by looking straight at God in *adoration*. Seeing God, it then sees itself truly, as it is in His sight and realises its own nothingness and creatureliness, which leads to an act of *humility*. Further, in the light of the infinite Purity of God it sees its own sin, and falls before Him in an act of *penitence*.

We now come to the body of the prayer, which consists in acts of the theological virtues.

First of *Faith*. I do not mean by that the repetition of the Creed or any statement of one's belief, but rather a look of loving faith. This act is a contemplation of God in some fundamental truth, *e.g.* His love, His holiness, His majesty or, perhaps, quite simply and generally in Himself. Souls vary immensely in their *attrait* in this matter, but perhaps for most it is well generally to contemplate God here in His eternal Being as distinct from His relationship to His creation or His work for man or His dealings with the individual soul.

There follows an act of *Hope*, and here one is concerned with His revelation, His redemption, His grace. In this act one puts one's whole trust in Him and His grace. It is the hope of the Cross, " I thirst." I thirst for God and know that I shall be satisfied, I thirst for the souls of men, that they too may be filled with Him. It is, then, a real act of intercession, a lifting up of the whole world to the Father.

Finally—and this is the apex of the whole prayer—an Act of *Charity*. For the purpose of our thought this may be divided into two parts, though in practice they become almost if not quite one.

S

One should aim here at depth and calm, by an act of the will directing one's whole being to God and holding it in Him.    That is the first part, and from it flows the second—the clear intention to conform one's whole will at every moment to the will of God.

It is clear that this way of prayer is very deep; it is, as it were, the movement of the whole soul, or better, perhaps, the stillness of the whole soul in union with God; the acts of which it consists, although they appear complicated in speech, are of the utmost simplicity, and tend as time goes on to become still simpler and more inexpressible in word.    As the method we have been considering becomes more familiar, the soul is able to rely more wholly upon the Holy Ghost for the form which its acts shall take, and it is difficult to distinguish always between an act of faith and an act of love, when these virtues have become, as they should, closely interwoven in the very fabric of the soul.

One point needs emphasis.    The exercise of prayer we are considering, and indeed all forms of the prayer of acts, as well as the further ways of prayer we have yet to consider, needs time for its exercise.    One of the first marks of any form of advance in prayer is the need which the soul feels for more time for communion with God.    The method of prayer I have sketched consists only of six acts expressed in few or no words; other ways are even simpler; but the soul that uses it will not be content with a bare ten minutes for its exercise; half an hour will probably find it unfinished, and before long an hour will seem all too short.    Almost anyone who prays at all can use a prayer of acts for five or ten minutes, but only souls which are ready for this way of prayer can persist in it without effort on the one hand or day-dreaming on the other for, say, half an hour daily.    To them it is the natural way of approach to God, not merely a bit of spiritual excitement, and continuance in it and ability to use it for a fair length of time are one of the surest signs that a soul is ripe for its use.

# CHAPTER XIX

# CONTEMPLATIVE PRAYER

*Be still then, and know that I am God* (Ps. xlvi. 10).

IT will be helpful to our understanding of those ways of prayer which are the subject of this chapter if we first of all stop to get a general view of the life of prayer from the point which we have now reached. By many people contemplation is confused with ecstasy or hysteria, while by others it is thought to stand outside all ordinary ways of prayer and to be peculiar to certain saints; it is therefore advisable to clear our minds as to what our subject really is and its relationship to what has gone before.

Thought proceeds by a method of abstraction. All existence is an unity, but, since our minds are incapable of containing all that is, we have to split the κόσμος into bits, examine them and put them together again, thus endeavouring to gain some knowledge of the whole. If we are to think intelligibly about anything, for the purposes of our thought, we have to abstract it from its place in the whole and examine it before we can understand it, either in its place or in that whole of which it is part. We are applying this scientific method to the Christian prayer life in these chapters; but before we go further we must remind ourselves that the prayer life is an unity of which all those manifestations which we are considering, as well as those we are not, are connected parts.

Let us return to our definition: " Prayer is the lifting up of the mind to God." In the traditional theology " mind " means not the intellectual faculties, as in the modern use of the term, but the essence or highest part of the spirit, which is made in the image of God; essentially, then, prayer is the fixing, by the will, of the spirit upon God in Whose image it is made. This is truly a simple operation—the simple fixing of the essence of our being upon the simple Being of God—and it is a simple act of the will assisted by the grace which flows from our Lord through His mystical Body, the Church.   A recent author has further defined it as " Loving God in act, so that, one with Him in mind and heart, the Divine Life may communicate Itself freely to us, and through us to the world." [1]   Christian prayer is therefore at once a vehicle and the fruit of the Divine Life.   Prayer, then, we repeat, is an essentially simple thing, so simple that a child may best enter by it into the kingdom of heaven.

But prayer is simple only to the simple and loving, and most of us are very far from perfection in these things.   Some favoured souls, indeed, never lose their childlike innocence, while others attain some measure of simplicity very early, but the majority of souls are extremely complex, at any rate at the beginning of the spiritual life, and often far on in it as well; their wills are divided, their hearts unstable, their intellects proud and their imaginations unruly—they are, as yet, ununified, really beginners in the spiritual life.   For such souls mental prayer has two ends: the spiritual assimilation of the truths of the Christian Faith, and the deliberate lifting up of each power of the soul to God.   These ends are attained by the ordinary Ignatian and similar methods of meditation.

Growth in prayer is growth in simplicity, and as the powers of the soul become united with the will in the act of love which is prayer, their method of operation alters and becomes less deliberate, until they appear to be doing nothing, a fact which often causes much heart-searching to the inexperienced.

The first power of the soul to become thus simplified is usually the intellect.   Some people never need to use their intellect much in prayer, and for them some method akin to the Sulpician is the right beginning, but to those who have to begin in the Ignatian way the Sulpician method represents a distinct advance in prayer.   Here, as has been already pointed out, the intellect is still deliberately used, but in a different way.   In the Ignatian method the intellect worked discursively, we prepared a subject and thought about it, preached ourselves sermons about it;  now the intellect no longer works discursively, but contemplatively— it does not argue, but looks by an act of simple apprehension.

In this simplification the intellect attains its right activity in prayer, an activity which itself becomes increasingly simple. Discursive thought is, to the souls which need it, an important preparation for prayer;  but it is not itself prayer:  in Ignatian

---

[1] Fahey, *Mental Prayer According to the Teaching of St. Thomas Aquinas*, p. 41.

meditation we do not think in order to think, but in order to provide a means whereby the heart may mount to the love of God.  Prayer is not thought, though it may proceed from it; the intellect does not pray by thinking, but by contemplating The business of the soul in prayer is with God, not with its own thoughts; consequently, in course of time, usually before very long, the soul finds that it needs fewer and less varied considerations, the mind is satisfied, and more deeply satisfied, with a simple look at God than it was at first with much thinking.  The weight of prayer has shifted from the mind to the affections; the mind intuitively, and sometimes almost unconsciously, assumes without labour the prayer relationship with God, and the soul enters straight away into the prayer of the heart and will.

We have described the prayer-activity of the intellect as "contemplative," as opposed to the discursive activity which leads up to it.  This is a real and important distinction, but it must not be thought that this way of praying is "contemplation" in its true sense, or that those who practise it are yet "contemplatives."[1]  Contemplative prayer, as we shall see, is something simpler and deeper than this, and springs from a much greater unity of soul than has usually been attained by those whose prayer is of the stage which we are now considering; nevertheless, there is an element of contemplation in all true prayer, and this new mode of intellectual action is a definite turning from thought about God to the apprehension of God by the mind.

Once this simplification of intellectual activity has begun we find ourselves at the commencement of affective prayer.  In this stage the deliberate action of the intellect is reduced still further to a single spring whence the heart's prayer may rise, a single thought satisfying and giving rise to the acts of which we spoke in the last chapter.  But now there occurs a further simplification, for, as the heart becomes more wholly given to the love of God, so it tends to require less variety of acts to express its love and to use not only fewer thoughts, but fewer words, speaking to God in "groanings which" not only are not, but "cannot be uttered."

At the beginning of this stage of the prayer life there is often

[1] We do well to recall the statement of S. Teresa, " I have been striving to become a contemplative for the last *twenty years.*"  (*Way of Perfection,* cap. xvi. 3, p. 90.)

considerable sensible fervour, and the soul, like a young lover, is frequently intoxicated by the beauty and wonder of God. This is quite as it should be, but this sensible intoxication does not last in its pristine exuberance, and it is succeeded by a period in which the soul understands by experience the meaning of Fr. Baker's term "*forced* acts of the will." The point to be observed here is that, despite the loss of fervour, the prayer is still affective; the soul has not ceased to love because it has ceased, for the time at any rate, to enjoy the consciousness of the presence of God. Rather, its love is being tested and its heart purified; if it perseveres (and the great danger of this stage is that of giving up), its love of God will become less emotional, but much deeper; it will learn to desire God for Himself and not for His gifts, and will abandon itself into His Hands more simply, and therefore more wholly. What happens in this way is that the heart gradually disentangles itself from fundamental delight in secondary objects of love and fastens itself simply upon the one perfect object of love, which is God.

Just as there is complexity in discursive reasoning which is reduced to simplicity in contemplative thought, so there is complexity in emotional fervour which is reduced to simplicity in affective prayer.

The length of time spent in these ways of prayer varies in different souls, but, normally, the well-disposed soul should be able to pass fairly soon from meditation to affective prayer, but it may spend years in affective prayer before passing on to contemplation, if, indeed, it ever does so. The simplification of the heart is a far more difficult thing than that of the intellect; for it is in the heart that those fundamental attachments to inordinate desires, to secondary objects of love and to self, take place, so that, while there are generous souls which are able to give their hearts to God in a moment, to most it means a long period of prayer and mortification. This is the reason why the number of Christ's lovers always remains small in comparison with the number of professing Christians.

The Quietists talked a good deal about the pure love of God, but it is at least open to question whether they realised the full implication of the phrase, for the pure love of God, which is the complete simplification of the heart, is only attained in this world by the saints; nevertheless, among souls of good will, a relative simplicity of heart may be and is attained, which produces a way of prayer which is truly contemplative.

It may seem that we have been a long time arriving at the subject of this chapter, and that we have spent overmuch time in treating of matters which have already been spoken of elsewhere; but it has been necessary to attempt to visualise the life of prayer as a whole before treating of its simplest and most ultimate forms, in order that those forms may be seen as parts of the whole, and not merely as eccentric aberrations of a few individuals. There are, indeed, mystical ways of prayer which are the gift of God to His individual lovers; with these we are not concerned, since their discussion belongs to mystical theology; but the ordinary ways of contemplative prayer are the final simplification of prayer at which ordinary souls may arrive, if such be their vocation, by perseverance in mortification, prayer and love, aided by grace and the guidance of the Holy Spirit.

The more simple prayer becomes, so much the more difficult becomes its description; anybody can describe meditation, but it is hard to say what we mean by the prayer of faith. This is due to the fact that the latter is a much more fundamental and less common way of prayer than the former. It is impossible adequately to describe a way of prayer which one has not practised, and if one has practised it, it is impossible to convey by word what it means to the soul; so we are on the horns of a dilemma. Difficulty of description causes endless trouble in this branch of theology: the saints describe the indescribable in different ways, and the theologians cannot agree upon a terminology, neither of which facts need cause us much surprise. In this chapter we propose to leave aside matters of debate, and describe as simply as may be the two forms of contemplative prayer which we know to be practised by ordinary people.

## I. THE PRAYER OF LOVING REGARD

In this prayer " there is a thought or a sentiment that returns incessantly and easily (although with little or no development) amongst many other thoughts, whether useful or no. This dominant thought does not go so far as to be continuous. It merely returns frequently and of its own accord. . . . The prayer of simple regard is really only a slow sequence of single glances cast upon one and the same object. . . . The affections and resolutions show little variety and are expressed in few words." [1]

This somewhat bald statement of fact may be enlarged by the eloquent words of another spiritual writer: "It is no longer the toilsome work of the imagination, the memory, and the understanding, though these faculties are actually occupied, but in a more simple manner. Instead of seeking the truth by the long, painful and roundabout ways of reasoning, they have already completed their journey and have reached its term. The mind, possessing the truth, contemplates it by a direct act, and enjoys it without effort. It is a simple attention, a memory, a look, an intuition. The light has come, the convictions are well founded, the evidence is such, that the things of God are perceived almost as we perceive first principles; we remember, we look, we attend, and this is enough. This does not hinder this view from becoming sometimes more luminous, sometimes weaker and more veiled. By its very nature it is somewhat obscure and confused, because it proceeds mostly by way of general views, not stopping at details, pretty much as we take in at a single glance a whole landscape.

"This simple look is always accompanied with love—a love, it may be, almost imperceptible or all on fire, calm or impetuous, bitter or savoury. This love is even that which is the chief thing in contemplation; it is at once the source whence this latter flows, the term towards which it tends, the fruit which it bears; we look because we love, we look in order to love, and our love is fed and inflamed by looking.

"Love is always accompanied by knowledge. We cannot love God if we do not know that He is lovable, and do not think on this truth; and this knowledge, being somewhat general and indistinct, love also is somewhat obscure and confused. . . . The object of contemplation is God in Himself or in His works; God is the primary object; the things of God are its secondary object. That which charms us in God is His *beauty*, His *goodness*, His *love*. Our Lord has an especial attraction for the contemplative soul. . . .

"Whilst the interior eye remains fixed upon God alone, the will is borne towards Him by a movement of love or by acts: sometimes the soul remains silent in this admiring look and this disposition of love; sometimes it pours itself forth *in a holy*

[1] Poulain, *The Graces of Interior Prayer*, p. 8.

*colloquy*, of love, confidence, abandonment, humility, &c. But always at the end of this prayer of contemplation the soul's union with God is more and more intimate." [1]

Much of what has just been said may be applied to affective prayer in general, and it is clear that this way of praying is simply affective prayer carried to such a pitch of simplicity that it becomes contemplation, a fact which is, in itself, a demonstration of the essential unity of the life of prayer. The important point to notice is the simplicity of the soul's action, which is " really only a slow sequence of single glances cast upon one and the same object." Whatever may flow from it in the way of affections, acts, colloquies or resolutions, this prayer is essentially a simple act of the will, lifting the soul without discourse to the contemplation of God. This accounts for the lack of variety in acts which has been noted in it. Superficially this lack may seem to be an impoverishment of prayer, but it is not so. The soul lacks variety in its prayer not because the prayer is getting thin, but because it is getting deep, and all those acts which before had to be made separately are now becoming merged into the unity of the act of love.

## II. The Prayer of Faith

We have now to consider a way of contemplation which is even more simple and thorough-going than the last; it is, indeed, the highest way of prayer to which ordinary people may be called, and therefore the highest which concerns us. It is a far more distinctly contemplative prayer than that of Loving Regard, for it deliberately drops much which that form of prayer uses. I have thought it best to adopt the name given to this prayer by Fr. de Besse, who derives his teaching from S. John of the Cross, but I adopt the teaching of the old English spiritual book *The Cloud of Unknowing*, which is, in my opinion, the best exposition of contemplative prayer for those who are not called to the mystical degrees.

According to the anonymous author of this work, the contemplative is in his prayer like a man on a mountain top in the midst of two clouds; " the Cloud of Forgetting " below him, blotting out all sight of the world, and " the Cloud of Unknowing " around and above him, through which he presses up to God.

[1] Lehodey, *The Ways of Mental Prayer*, pp. 185 *ff.*

With regard to the first of these clouds, the author counsels his reader to " do that in thee is to forget all the creatures that ever God made and the works of them, so that thy thought or thy desire be not directed or stretched to any of them. . . . Put a *cloud of forgetting* beneath thee, betwixt thee and all the creatures that ever be made. . . . Stalwartly step above them with a fervent stirring of love, and tread them down under thy feet. . . . And if they rise oft, put them down oft: and (shortly to say) as oft as they rise, as oft put them down." [1] This is an abstraction of the soul from all that is not God, a deliberate act of inattention to all but Him, and a recollection of the soul into itself by which all the powers of the soul are gathered up into one.

Thus abstracted and recollected, the soul presses upon the Cloud of Unknowing: " Smite upon that thick *cloud of unknowing* with a sharp dart of longing love; and go not thence for aught that befalleth." [2] Desiring God alone, the soul holds itself steady in Him. This prayer is essentially an act of the will, there is no thought, even of the Divine attributes, and no acts, for the soul can make none, simply " a little blind love set on God." [3]

The great difference between this way of prayer and the preceding lies in its obscurity. The Prayer of Loving Regard was simple but definite, to the extent that it still made use of at least one mental image and definite acts, but the Prayer of Faith rejects both.

It may be asked, Why call this way of praying the Prayer of Faith? In the answer to that question we come to the root of the matter. S. Paul opposes Faith to sight, an opposition which we, with our clear-cut notions concerning the Creed, commonly lose sight of. " We walk," he says, " by faith, not by sight," and when he says that, he is not referring to what we call the Faith, but to that obscure vision of God which may be ours by the infused virtue of Faith. So in this way of prayer, we reach out to God in the Cloud or the Darkness of Faith, not in the clear brightness of sight and, strange to say, we are nearer essentially to God in the dark than in the light.

> One talked with me and I with Him.
> " We know Thou art the Light,"
> I said, " but this is night,
> And our whole world's abrim
> With hideous shadows that shut out the land.

---

[1] *Op. cit.*, capp. iii. v. xxxi.    [2] *Op. cit.*, cap. vi.    [3] *Op. cit.*, cap. xxiv.

We know Thou art the Light,
But this is night . . .
When wilt Thou understand? "
'Twas then He bade me hark,
" Since I have come back from the dead—
Though still the Light, I'm something more,"
He said—
" I am the Dark."

To the soul that is not called to contemplation this may sound perilously near nonsense, but to the contemplative it represents the most fundamental truth of his religious experience; and here we reach the basic fact that no soul can pray contemplatively without God's call and assistance, with its correlative that, having reached contemplation, it is unable to pray in any other way. Contrary to popular belief, contemplation consists, to use a figure of Baron von Hügel's, much more of tunnels than of triumphal arches, and is anything but the sentimental musing that most people believe it to be. It will be well, then, to try to discover what is the condition of the soul to whom this way of prayer belongs, for contemplation is not a matter of choice, but of necessity.

In the first place, there is a still further simplification of the action of the intellect, for, although outside prayer, he can think as well as anyone else, or better; when he comes to praying the contemplative finds that his intellect, apparently, will not work at all—he cannot think, he cannot even contemplate in the sense in which that term has been used above: the mind just seems to go out of action.

Very much the same sort of thing then occurs in the heart, which may seem to be dry, cold and motionless, while the emotions are quite quiet and incapable of affective acts.

The active force is the will, which is strongly attracted towards God and desires Him intensely, " meaning Himself and none of His goods," abandoning itself to Him, holding itself in His will with the utmost simplicity.

It seems as if nothing at all is happening, or at least very little. But are the intellect and heart really inert? No, they are still at work, but, intuitively, almost unconsciously. The discursive reason refuses to act because the intellect is occupied, at last, with God, Who is imperceptible to the discursive reason. This occupation is generally unconscious at the time, though afterwards the contemplative recognises that it has been a reality. This being so, the emotions have nothing to feed upon, and so

the heart seems dry, though it is unconsciously occupied with
God and it is conscious of desiring Him.   The absence of emotional stimulus sometimes produces a sense of separation from
God which is a source of suffering, but the separation is only in
the conscious faculties, and when the prayer is ended the heart
too knows that it has been unconsciously in touch with God in
the Cloud of Unknowing.

The essential factor of this way of prayer is the desire for
God.   " All thy life now must all ways stand in desire, if thou
shalt advance in degree of perfection.   This desire must all ways
be wrought in thy will, by the hand of Almighty God and thy
consent." [1]   This desire is obscure because God is not desired
in any particular way—there are no intellectual phantasmata;
nor is He desired in any particular loveliness—the emotions are
still; but the will desires Him in Whom is all perfection and all
loveliness.   The aim of the praying soul in this way is not intellectual abstraction or emotional enjoyment, but the purified action
of the will reaching out to the living God.   " Bide in this darkness as long as thou mayest, evermore crying after him whom
thou lovest." [2]   The will thus loving is passive under the hand of
God and abandoned to Him, but this passivity is not vacuity,
rather it is concentrated activity: " Smite upon that thick cloud
of unknowing with the sharp dart of longing love; " [3] not the
restless activity of the intellect, nor the equally restless activity of
the emotions, but the still holding of the mind in Him that He
may do what He will.

The real difficulty of this way of prayer is not its simplicity—
though that not infrequently causes the soul to wonder whether
it is praying at all—but its tremendous liability to distraction.   It
may be helpful at this point to describe what commonly happens.

" One sets oneself to pray, say for the regulation half-hour;

" empties the mind of all images, ideas, concepts—this is
commonly done without much difficulty;

" fixes the soul in loving attention on God, without express
or distinct idea of Him, beyond the vague incomprehensible idea
of His Godhead;

" makes no particular acts, but a general actuation of love,
without sensible devotion or emotional feeling: a sort of blind
and dumb act of the will or of the soul itself.

" This lasts a few minutes, then fades away, and either a blank

---

[1] *Cloud of Unknowing*, cap. ii.      [2] *Ibid.*, cap. iii.      [3] *Ibid.*, cap. vi.

or distractions supervene: when recognised, the will again fixes
the mind in ' loving attention ' for a time. The period of prayer
is thus passed in such alternations, a few minutes each, the bouts
of loving attention being, in favourable conditions, more
prolonged than the bouts of distraction." [1]

It will be seen from this that for most people the amount of
distraction in this way of praying is considerable, more considerable, indeed, than we can feel altogether happy about; for
only when conditions are favourable do the periods of recollection
exceed those of distraction. We must try, then, to understand
the causes of these distractions.

The first and most superficial cause is the imagination. We
have already had occasion to note the difficulty commonly
experienced in the control of this faculty. In contemplation the
difficulty is increased, because, since there are no images in this
way of praying, there is nothing upon which the imagination
can be fixed; it is therefore free to wander at will. Much of
this wandering can safely be disregarded; the images buzz about
like flies, and may be disregarded or brushed away without
interfering seriously with the prayer. When, however, the mind
is attracted and the will deflected by them, such distractions
become more than superficial; then they must be gently but
firmly put away, and the will give itself again gently but firmly to
its proper business.

I have repeated the adverbs in the last sentence because gentleness and firmness are of the essence of the matter; impatient fuss
only increases the trouble. Some directors, in dealing with
imaginational distractions, advise that they should be fought,
resisted, prayed about or turned into prayer; but all such advice
gives a false importance to the distraction and provides just that
opportunity which it needs to attack the mind and will. The
right way of dealing with such distractions is to ignore them;
the soul cannot be bothered with them, because it is already
occupied with something far more important, therefore it does
not fight them—they are not worth it—it simply disregards them.
This is true of all ways of prayer, not only the contemplative.

A further and deeper cause of distraction lies in the heart.
It cannot be too clearly realised that what we are in the rest of
life, that we are too in our prayer. When we come to pray we
strip ourselves of all that is merely selfish and earthly, and

[1] Butler, *Western Mysticism* (2nd ed.), p. xlix.

centre the whole of our attention upon God, but it is the same
" I " that works, plays, strips and attends, with its inordinate
concupiscences, desires and loves.   In the world it is easy to disregard these inordinate movements of the heart, but as soon as we
come to prayer it is no longer so, and the more intense the prayer
so much the more inevitable is the pull of those secondary objects
of love and interest.   If we are wholly occupied with God, then
the slightest interest in anything else, whether good or bad, is a
distraction, and it is through these distractions that the soul
learns its own impurity.

These distractions are best dealt with by purifying the intention.   If they lead to a deepened attention to and desire for
God and a purer offering of oneself to Him, they will have been
a blessing in disguise;   they can only be completely cured by
detachment and a pure love of God alone, a state of perfection
to which few attain in this life.   Meanwhile, they may be useful
in stimulating the soul to perseverance in mortification, and
humility, which perseverance will itself help to eradicate them.

There remains a third cause of distraction to be considered.
In Abbot Butler's description of an average prayer-time in this
way, quoted above, it will be noticed that an alternating rhythm
is set up in the soul, prayer and distraction succeeding and, more
or less, balancing one another.   This points to the final cause of
distraction which is simply human imperfection.

Contemplative prayer, for all its simplicity and because of its
simplicity, imposes a great strain upon the powers of the soul,
which they are incapable of sustaining unimpaired for very long.
On the other hand, the soul called to this way needs long stretches
of time for its prayer.   The result is a rise and fall rhythm between
prayer and distraction, differing in different souls and in the
same soul at different times.

To speak accurately, this is but a semi-distraction resulting
from fatigue and the absence of external aids;   it does not disturb
the repose of the will in God.   When it comes it must be endured.
It is a troublesome, humiliating and sometimes painful thing,
but is none the worse for that.[1]

The saints sometimes speak of the pain and suffering of prayer.
Beginners in the spiritual life, if they read such statements, fre-

---

[1] It may be noted here that conditions of over-fatigue, over-strain and over-
fasting are not conducive to good contemplative prayer.   The writer of the
*Cloud* points out that the body must be in a fit state for this way of prayer.

quently disregard them; but if they do take them in they are surprised and bewildered because their idea of prayer is ruminative happiness. The whole question of suffering in prayer is too vast to be considered here, and belongs rather to mystical theology than to ascetical; nevertheless, it must be pointed out that the contemplative soul is also a suffering soul. This fact is not appreciated by our pseudo-mystics and emotional quietists, but should be faced by anyone called to the higher ways of prayer, as it will quite certainly be experienced if the vocation is persevered in. It should be unnecessary to labour the point here after what has been said. Darkness of mind, absence of sensible fervour, distraction, the imperceptibility of the prayer and often of the divine response, the realisation of sin, as well as the hungering desire for God with which the whole is permeated, are all fruitful sources of suffering, as is the deepening union with Christ which comes to the soul that is faithful in this way. Such union is with the whole, the eternal Christ, the Christ of Bethlehem and Calvary, no less than Christ in glory; therefore the sin of the world is felt in Christ, and the soul enters into and takes its part in His offering, and this means suffering.

But along with and because of and in and through this suffering comes joy—the heavenly joy of God's love; a deep joy, not emotional but spiritual; a joy dependent not upon temperament or circumstances, but upon the will of God; a joy which, so far from being selfish, can only be experienced when self is laid aside.

This joy is often, perhaps generally, unconscious so far as prayer is concerned (we are in the region of paradox and must speak paradoxically, ὁ ἀναγινώσκων νοείτω), but it expresses itself in life in a consciousness of activity in God: it is, indeed, the joy of an intense, super-sensible love given and returned and lived, bringing with it the peace that " no man taketh from you."

Further, in this way of prayer we may, if God so will, touch the experiences described in mystical theology as the infused degrees. The life of prayer is, as we have attempted to show, a unity in which the experience of the saint, no less than that of the novice, finds its place; and the break which the theologians envisage between acquired and infused prayer is less radical than would appear. Acquired and infused prayer are, indeed, two distinct things; *acquired* prayer being all those forms to which we may attain, if we be called thereto, by our own efforts, aided by grace and guided by the Holy Ghost, and *infused* those which are the pure gift of God. Nevertheless, it is impossible to say exactly at what point infusion begins, for there is an unexpected element of " givenness " in many prayers which are certainly not technically infused. Differences in opinion among the masters, as well as unity of experience among those who practise it, alike point to the conclusion that the way of prayer before us is a bridge between acquired and infused prayer. In itself it is plainly acquired, but from time to time, sometimes only for a moment, but quite unmistakably, there comes that touch of God to which no man may attain. The loving soul is face to face with the Beloved in the dark.

We have now outlined the progress of the soul from discursive meditation to contemplation and shown something of the essential unity of the prayer life; there remains a word to be said about individual souls. As time goes on the soul grows in prayer, and some souls which begin with discursive meditation do go on to contemplation by all the stages which we have indicated, but others do not. For some Ignatian meditation is the only way; others—the majority—never leave the ways of affective prayer; some who progress from one stage to another occasionally fail to show any signs of others which are theoretically intermediate; while to the few it is given to find and remain in contemplation. In guiding souls one must bear in mind the immense variety in *attrait*, and study to direct the soul not according to theory, but according to its call. The theoretical side of the matter is useful in enabling the director to recognise the state in which the soul is, to direct it wisely and rightly in it, and to save it from losing its way. We need always to remember that the Holy Ghost is the Guide and Mover of the praying soul, which in some part of the way He guides through us, and our guidance must always be in accordance with His drawing, and not our own prejudices or predilections; we must never force a soul out of its way, rather it is for us to lead it in it, and this demands wide knowledge and deep prayer.

# CHAPTER XX

# RECOLLECTION

*Rejoice evermore. Pray without ceasing. In everything give thanks : for this is the will of God in Christ Jesus concerning you* (I Thess. v. 16–18).

In the previous chapters of this part we have been concerned with the Christian prayer-life in all the richness of its several depths and varieties, we have striven to understand how souls pray and how they grow in prayer, but we have considered them only in the specific activity of prayer in the times specially set apart for it. We have now to investigate those movements of prayer which transcend the limits of such times, and inspire and irradiate the common activities of life in the world.

Our Lord " spake a parable unto them to this end, that men ought always to pray, and not to faint," [1] and S. Paul exhorted the Thessalonians to " pray without ceasing." Both Christ and the Apostle of the Gentiles meant exactly what they said ; nevertheless to the novice in the spiritual life continual prayer seems an impossibility, while many people strive after it for years without, apparently, making any progress towards its attainment. The difficulty in both cases is that of departmentalism, the antithetical separation of complementary realities.

To say that two realities are complementary is not to assert that they are identical ; nor does the statement that they are different imply that they are unrelated. Flesh and spirit, work and prayer, natural and supernatural, are different one from the other, but they are complementary ; our difficulty is that we regard them as antithetical. We constantly separate work and prayer, bodily and spiritual activity, natural and supernatural modes of life, and so prayer becomes a separate entity, cut off from the rest of life, and life is but partially, if at all, influenced by religion. This accounts for many of those sad aberrations from the Christian ideal which appear to the critic to be hypocritical, but are not really so.

[1] Luke xviii. 1.

The work of the Holy Spirit in the disciplined soul is essentially that of unification, knitting up the powers of the soul and the departments of its activity into one and bringing all into conformity with the will of God; but that is impossible so long as the soul itself separates its life into water-tight compartments. So long as prayer, work, rest and recreation are separate and unrelated entities, supernatural life in its completeness is impossible.

The soul that really gives itself to prayer finds, as time goes on, that prayer refuses to be confined within the limits of prayer-time. The Beloved desires to accompany it not only in church, but in the world too, not only at such times as it gives itself to Him alone, but also when it is occupied in secular activities; and so there arises a desire for recollection and a love of interior silence at all times which will not be denied. Gradually the barrier between prayer and the rest of life breaks down and all activities begin to be infused with the spirit of prayer, until at last the soul actually does " pray without ceasing."

Recollection is not essentially different from prayer, neither is it prayer diluted, rather it is that practice of the Presence of God (made familiar to us by Brother Laurence's well-known account of it) which makes every act prayer. It is the endeavour to live one's whole life with God and to do everything for love of Him. We can, then, hardly lay too much stress upon its importance to the Christian life. S. Teresa remarks somewhere that " a soul in a real state of recollection is a true paradise," because it walks with God and is becoming more and more united with Him. It is clear that unless there is some degree of recollection the greater part of life is lived without reference to God at all, which is a common, but hardly Christian, state of affairs.

We may define recollection as " continual, loving attention to God "; but it is necessary clearly to realise the implication of every word of this definition.

In the first place, it is *continual* (ἀδιαλείπτως, in the Pauline phrase). Prayer consists primarily in a series of acts, of one kind or another. Public worship and, indeed, all vocal prayer is of this kind, as also are those forms of mental prayer which we have considered in Chapters XVII and XVIII above; but those ways of prayer which we described in Chapter XIX approximate far more to a state of soul than a series of activities. In contemplative prayer the soul is held by the will in the presence of God and is

frequently conscious of very little more than this " holding on ";
it is in a state of attention to God, which may or may not include
definite acts.  Recollection is a similar, though to all but saints
a less intense, state of attention to God; acts may be, and to most
people are, necessary, in order to attain it, but in itself it is a state
or an attitude of soul.  Were it otherwise, its continuance would
be impossible, for we cannot always be making acts of prayer
when we are immersed in our daily work, nor can we always be
consciously thinking of God; but if we are recollected, it is
possible for the soul to be always turned to God even in the most
distractive work.  Its unconscious depths may be truly with God
while the conscious mind is busied with the most engrossing or
commonplace occupations, and in the midst of those occupations
may come at times uprushes of intense realisation of God almost
intoxicating in their strength.

The recollected soul finds God in all things and all things in
God; in those occupations which are miscalled " secular " it
looks beyond the immediate end to the will of God, to which it
seeks to relate not only all its doings, but all its desires and
thoughts.  Without recollection the soul becomes immersed in
the machinery of daily life, caught up in the complex of secondary
ends and separated thereby from God; with recollection,
secondary ends find their place in the κόσμος of the will of God
and the machinery finds a soul—all is done with a supernatural
motive because the soul is continually with God.  The recollected
man is not an absent-minded person, who is incapable of doing
a good job of work, because he is always ineffectively attempting
to say his prayers, when he should be giving his attention to the
matter in hand; rather his work is as good as it can be because
it is done in God and for God.  His recollection is a continuous
state of awareness of God.

Awareness of God brings love, and so recollection is *loving*.
The love of God—Charity—is not an emotional thing, and recollection is not an emotional exercise; rather it is an act of the will,
the desire for God and the intention to do in all things His most
holy will.  The man who is in love orientates his whole being
and his whole life towards the beloved, so is love the dynamic
power of recollection.

But the recollected soul is not in a constant state of ecstasy.
There may be warmth of affection or there may not—its presence
or absence depends upon the state of the soul, circumstances or

the gift of God, and what we may call " affectivity " is accidental
—but the recollected soul is constantly loving God by subordin-
ating its will to His and abandoning itself to Him in actual life.
Without recollection it is impossible for the love of God to
penetrate life at all, apart from those times which are given to
specifically religious activities; with recollection it is possible
for the soul at all times to love and serve, even though it may be
doing nothing more interesting than adding up a column of
figures.

Above all things, recollection is *attention*, and it is important to
understand what is meant by this term, for it is clear that attention
may be of various kinds and that the attention of recollection is
not synonymous with the attention of prayer.   The attention of
prayer is *actual* attention, the deliberate attention of the whole self
to God and to nothing else.   Clearly this kind of attention is
impossible at all times: in some sorts of work and some sorts of
recreation the mind has to be concentrated exclusively upon the
matter in hand; the heart is frequently occupied with the love
of one's neighbour; while at other times the body is wholly
occupied with manual labour or exercise, all of which things make
actual attention to God more or less impossible.   Even under the
most favourable circumstances the soul is unable, by reason of
its weakness and creatureliness, to fix the whole of its attention
upon God at all times.

It should be noted that not all occupations render actual attention impossible; manual and mechanical work often leave the
mind very largely free to occupy itself with other things, a freedom which is commonly used for day-dreaming and thinking
about a variety of unimportant matters; but the recollected soul
can turn such labours into acts of real prayer when it is actually
occupied with God.   The more intellectual one's occupation
becomes, however, even if the intellect is only engaged in directing
the body in a game of tennis, the less possible is actual attention
to God.   Our aim must, then, be to attain to an *habitual* attention
to Him.

This attention is not intellectual, but spiritual, not a tension
of the mind, but a quiet holding of oneself in God.   The
theological meaning of the term " recollection " is just that:
in ordinary language recollection simply means " remembering,"
and the ordinary dictionaries give no other definition, but in
theology it signifies primarily the gathering together of the soul

and its turning inward to God; it is thus synonymous with " introversion " in its theological, as distinct from its psychological, sense.

Almost everyone is conscious, if he really examine himself, that ordinarily he pours himself out too much upon the affairs of this life. There is a right concentration upon temporal affairs and a right giving of oneself to one's neighbour in God, but there is also a squandering of oneself which results in real loss. Seneca has somewhere a remark to the effect that whenever he went among men he was wont to return less of a man than he was before; that is the result of extroversion. The man who would live a spiritual life must so cultivate introversion that he never lose his soul in the distractions of the world. This involves detachment, the recollection of the soul within itself and the habitual attention of the spirit to God.

This leads us to the further meaning of the term " recollection," in which it approaches nearest to the popular sense, which is remembrance of God. If we are truly recollected, the remembrance of God will be always with us; we shall not always be thinking of Him with the mind, but, when the distractive occupation is over, the mind will quietly return to Him and find that it has not left Him.

We can remember or realise the presence of God in two ways: firstly, and more elementarily, we can realise Him as with us but apart from us. Jesus the ever-present Friend and Lord, going with us through life, to Whom we may turn at all times, that is the realisation which turns for many the desert of this world into a garden, the garden of Paradise; while others bear before the eyes of the spirit the image of Jesus crucified, and so their whole life is saturated with the sacred Passion. To others, again, the key realisation is that of God present in all creation. This is right and valuable, but needs to be balanced by another devotion, for by itself it may lead towards that nemesis of spirituality which we call pantheism.

The other way is the realisation of God within us; the soul turning within finds the Master in the depths of its own being and realises Him, sometimes under some mystery of the incarnate life, but more often quite obscurely, as the Lord enthroned in the inner sanctuary. This method of realisation is the deeper of the two, and consequently comes, as a rule, later in the spiritual life; but souls naturally tend to gravitate towards the external or internal realisation of the presence of God, according to their general *attrait*.

Perhaps the deepest and most balanced realisation of God is both external and internal, " the powerful presence within us of an inward Christ pushing us upwards and outwards with a view to join hands with the outward Christ Who is pressing inwards " [1] It is perhaps to this realisation—which is, after all, the realisation of the exact truth—that the deepest souls tend, but as recollection deepens it becomes more obscure and less explicable in proportion to its depth.

It is above all things important that the soul should give itself from moment to moment to the guidance of the Holy Spirit; for just as prayer is His so also is recollection. The soul attains to recollection not by its own efforts, but by its ever-deepening response to the movement of the Holy Spirit.

We must now inquire how recollection may be cultivated, and we find that it is directly dependent upon actual prayer. If the prayer life is weak, recollection disappears, but if the prayer life is strong and fervent, it passes naturally and inevitably into recollection.

Charles de Foucauld, commenting on Mark xiv. 38, says, " We need two things to resist temptation. Firstly, long hours of prayer every day with unchanging regularity.[2] Secondly, constant prayer all the rest of one's time. . . . If we are working at anything in the presence of one we love we cannot forget his presence for a moment. Our eyes are on him constantly and the time passes quickly and happily. It should be the same with our Lord, the Divine Spouse of our souls. Perpetual prayer throughout the day will keep temptations from our souls, the presence of our Lord will drive them away and prevent their harming us. The hours given up entirely to prayer will give us the strength,[3] with God's grace, to keep ourselves in his presence through the rest of the day and give up all our time to what is called ' perpetual prayer.' " [4]

We should notice here the importance of long hours consecrated to prayer daily with inviolable regularity, for it is these which, with

---

[1] Von Hügel, *Selected Letters*, p. 78.
[2] "Longues heures *consacrées* à la prière, chaque jour, avec une régularité *inviolable*."    [3] " La force."
[4] *Meditations of a Hermit*, p. 19. The *Écrits Spirituels* of Charles de Foucauld should be read, if possible, in the original; the English translation is not a good one.

grace, will give the *force* necessary to recollection. Charles de Foucauld literally gave long hours daily to prayer. That is not always possible to persons living in the world, but for all of us it is essential that we give as long as possible to prayer, and that with unfailing regularity, if we are to attain to recollection, for recollection depends upon this.

On the other hand, prayer depends upon recollection, for it is a matter of common experience that the unrecollected soul that has poured itself out upon a hundred occupations and persons finds it almost impossible to give itself to prayer when the time comes, and its prayer becomes distracted and meaningless. In the recollected soul there is a spiritual rhythm of prayer and recollection, and it passes naturally from one to the other, each gaining power and depth from the other.

But recollection is not gained all at once and, especially at first, the soul needs aids to its attainment. To some the imagination is of use, and they find it helpful to picture our Lord present by their side; while others, in whom pictorial imagination is not very strong, will gain no advantage from such a method. In any case the imagination is a doubtful ally, and is apt to fail one just where one most needs help. It should be used, if at all, with great discretion, realising its limitations, and it should never be strained or forced in any way.

A more useful aid is the practice of frequent ejaculatory prayer —the turning of the soul to God by darts of vocal prayer. A phrase of three or four words which is full of meaning for the soul should be used, and need not be varied: in course of time the one word " God " or the sacred Name of Jesus will be all that is needed. The purpose of this prayer is not to say something or to ask for any specific grace, but to centre the soul on God; it should therefore be quite direct and short.

Another useful practice is the deliberate offering of the intention to God at every change of occupation during the day, or when we hear the clock strike. By this means, whatever we are doing, even recreation or rest, may be supernaturalised and directed towards its true end, the unpleasant and painful things of life may be accepted and offered, and all our activity may become prayer.

Definite turning points of the day, such as meal-times, goings-out and comings-in, may be utilised as means of stimulating the memory and recalling the soul to God.

It is also well to cultivate a habit of returning to God whenever the mind is not occupied with any employment. The rush of life often leads us to think that we are far more continuously busy than we are, but if one examines one's life, one finds that there are periods in every day when, though one may be superficially occupied, the mind is doing nothing more important than holding a desultory conversation with itself. If at these times the mind can be habitually directed towards God, so that its converse may be with Him, and not merely with itself, it enters at once into actual recollection. This method of recollection is not so difficult as may appear. When the mind is at work it is like a piece of elastic stretched taut, but when it is released from its occupation it springs back, like the elastic, to its point of rest. If that point of rest is self, as it commonly is, the result is self-pleasing dreaming; if, however, it is self plus the presence of God, the mind acquires the habit of resting in Him and so becomes filled with Him.

As the soul advances in recollection it learns to love silence and solitude, and in them to build up and strengthen its being. There is in this age very little understanding of the true nature of silence or its right use. The world gets steadily noisier and more distracting, and people throw themselves into the noise and enjoy it and add to it, and so become incapable of sustained attention to either thought or prayer. So we find people living with the wireless perpetually turned on, not because they want to listen to it, for it often impedes conversation, but merely because they cannot bear to be quiet even for a moment. All this makes for shallowness of soul and weakness of spiritual apprehension. Religion comes to mean nothing, because the faculties by which God is known have been whirred and buzzed and shouted out of existence.

Noise is a necessity to our present civilisation, but it is an unfortunate necessity, and if the spiritual life is to be cultivated at all it is necessary to oppose to it the love of interior silence; the Christian should never let himself go and become immersed in the noise of the age. The recollected man bears within him an habitual consciousness of the presence of God, and as his recollection grows he learns to live more and more in the silence of the soul, which is constantly turned towards and attentive to God. Attention to God demands interior silence, and those who love it find Him.

We have discussed certain means whereby recollection may be

acquired, but we must remember, at the same time, that the power and love of recollection depend very much upon the gift of God. To the soul which faithfully uses such means as may help it towards continual recollection, and which, above all things, desires and longs for the continual presence of God, the Divine Lover gives an ever-deepening power of recollection, deepening and growing with the life of prayer; for recollection is ultimately the overflowing of prayer into life. Speaking generally, the soul whose way of prayer is meditation finds recollection difficult, an external exercise which has to be perseveringly cultivated, but as its prayer becomes more affective, its acts of recollection become simpler and its colloquies with our Lord easier, until in contemplative prayer recollection becomes habitual and almost, if not quite, continuous—an unrecollected contemplative is a contradiction in terms. In other words, as the habitual action of God in the soul increases, its prayer comes to depend more on His action than its own, and He fills it more and more continuously with awareness of and desire for Him. The awareness is, in some states of aridity, unconscious, but it is there nevertheless, and the soul is recollected and attentive to God present, even though it have no conscious realisation of Him.

It is necessary to add that the attention of recollection is attention to God, and not to self. Some souls who desire to live spiritual lives never get beyond themselves; they become so wrapped up in their own interior that they never give themselves to Him Who dwells there, and so they become self-conscious and their spiritual life artificial; they are pious in the bad cant sense. It is impossible to be too recollected if we are giving ourselves at the same time to the activity which God is demanding of us, but it is quite possible to be too recollected if thereby we are running away from a real responsibility to luxuriate in spiritual day-dreaming. If our recollection is attention to God without thought of self or self-satisfaction, then it is right and healthy and the most precious thing on earth, for it is by men so recollected that God's will is done " in earth as it is in heaven."

# CHAPTER XXI

# LITURGICAL PRAYER

*Wherefore, holy brethren, partakers of the heavenly calling, consider the Apostle and High Priest of our profession, Christ Jesus* (Heb. iii. 1).

WE have, so far, been occupied with the prayer-life of individuals, but our study would be seriously incomplete if we left it at the point we have now reached, for no man is simply an individual, and no prayer-life, however deep, is that of a simple unit. The prayer of the individual finds its completion, not its balance, in the prayer of the Church.

The nature and necessity of liturgical prayer are far too little understood among us, even by those whose spiritual life is nourished by the study of the great doctors of prayer; consequently, on the one hand, some priests exhort their people to " come to church " merely as a duty, without explaining the reason for church-going, beyond linking it up with the divine command, or giving any instruction as to the nature of their prayer when they get there; and, on the other hand, some would-be mystics tend to regard liturgical prayer as superfluous, in view of the absorbing nature of their private experiences. There is also a large body of good people who are the spiritual backbone of the Church to whom the Church's worship means more than they can say, but even they are sometimes a little hazy as to its exact implications.

It is true that the masters of the spiritual life say little about liturgical prayer, and the study of their works sometimes leaves the reader with the impression that private contemplation is the highest exercise of prayer; but so far as this is so it is not that they ignore the Church's worship, but that they take it for granted, since its discussion does not come within the purview of their writings. If we would understand their teaching aright, we must see it always against the background of the Catholic worship which they and their readers practised.

Liturgical prayer has many virtues: it prevents individuals from becoming cranky and self-centred, by keeping them in touch with the corporate prayer of the Church; it prevents prayer from floating away in a mist of sentiment, by attaching it to definite times, actions and intentions; it keeps a balance between vocal and other prayer, which is always necessary; and it is a corrective of quietism, illuminism and other dangerous aberrations of the spiritual life. But all these good effects are entirely secondary to its main purpose, which is nothing less than the uniting of the individual in the Church with her divine Head in the perfect worship of God the Father.

By liturgical prayer we understand that prayer of which the Church's liturgy is the expression. We are not concerned with *any* prayers which may take place in Church, but with the Holy Eucharist and the Divine Office of which it is the centre. Prayer-meetings, Guild Offices, Stations of the Cross, the Three Hours and other devotions of that kind are excellent and valuable in their right place, but they are not liturgical, for they merely express the devotion of those who take part in them, whereas the liturgy is the expression of the devotion of the whole Church. We shall in this chapter be concerned primarily with the Holy Eucharist, and secondarily with the Divine Office, and with nothing else.

The purpose of the Liturgy is not the saying of certain prayers, though prescribed prayers must be said, but the performing of an action of perfect worship to God the Father. This will become clearer as we proceed, but it is necessary to stress the fact that the Father is the object of the worship of the Liturgy, because to many folk the presence of our Lord in the Blessed Sacrament is such a radiantly wonderful fact that it overshadows all other considerations, and their action at Mass stops with the adoration of Him.

It must not be thought that we wish in any way to depreciate the adoration of our Lord present in the Blessed Sacrament; He is present and must be worshipped with lowliest reverence. Nor is it true that in worshipping Him we are separating that worship from the worship of God, for it is impossible to divide the Persons of the most Holy Trinity one from another. Nevertheless, in the Mass Christ is present for the purpose of offering the Holy Sacrifice to the Father, and it is that purpose for which the Church is then gathered together; the action is therefore directed to the Father through the Son, and we must not stop short of the realisation of that fact.

The Liturgy exists for the purpose of worship, not for the comfort or edification of the faithful; we do not therefore take part in it for any personal gain, but to make the most perfect offering to God of which man is capable.    And if we make our Communion and receive Him Who is our perfect joy, still it is not for our own benefit, but that we may be more wholly given to God in union with Him.

The worship of the Liturgy is sacrificial, being nothing less than the offering to the Father of the sacrifice of Christ, which is ultimately the act of Christ Himself.    The detailed consideration of sacrifice and priesthood in general is beyond our scope, and must be taken for granted or studied elsewhere, but we must attempt to gain some understanding of the High Priesthood of Christ, if we are to understand the true meaning of the liturgy.

Our Lord Jesus Christ is the High Priest of Creation, perfect God and perfect Man, Who alone can make to the Father that offering of reparation and worship which can take away the sins of the world, reunite man with God and direct his activity towards its right end.    It was in order to offer this sacrifice that He came into the world a Victim and a Priest.

We commonly restrict the exercise of our Lord's priesthood to three hours on Good Friday, but that is to mistake a part, even though it be the essential part, of His sacrificial ministry for the whole.    Our Lord began to exercise His priesthood from the first moment that He came into the world, and the exercise of that priesthood is still continuing—there is no moment in the life of the Incarnate Son of God in which He is not offering the perfect sacrifice of Himself to the Father: in the manger, in the home at Nazareth, in the ship on the lake, in the towns of Galilee, in the houses of the Jews no less than on the Cross and in heaven Jesus is the High Priest of Creation offering Himself on behalf of the world to the Father.

The essentially godward Intention of the Incarnate life is frequently overlooked.    It is, of course, true that our Lord " came into the world to save sinners," [1] and that the greater part of the last three years of His earthly life was taken up with teaching and working miracles for the benefit of men; nevertheless, the Incarnation was not only philanthropic, but the fulfilment of the will of God.    The author of the Epistle to the Hebrews sums up the point we would make in these words: " Wherefore when he

[1] I Tim. i. 15.

cometh into the world, he saith, Sacrifice and offering thou wouldest not, but a body hast thou prepared me: In burnt offerings and sacrifices for sin thou hast had no pleasure. Then said I, Lo, I come (in the volume of the book it is written of me,) to do thy will, O God. Above when he said, Sacrifice and offering and burnt offerings and offering for sin thou wouldest not, neither hadst pleasure therein; which are offered by the law; Then said he, Lo, I come to do thy will, O God. He taketh away the first, that he may establish the second. By the which will we are sanctified through the offering of the body of Jesus Christ once for all." [1]

The Incarnate life leads up to the great priestly action— the slaying of the Victim on Calvary. This is truly our Lord's own action, though He was slain by His enemies: " Therefore doth my Father love me, because I lay down my life, that I may take it again. No man taketh it from me, but I lay it down of myself. I have power to lay it down, and I have power to take it again. This commandment have I received of my Father." [2] On the Cross Jesus our High Priest " offered Himself without spot to God " [3] for the sins of the whole world.

Just as the sacrifice of Christ did not begin on the Cross, so neither did it end there: the crucifixion was the central, not the final act. The purpose of sacrifice was not the offering of a death, but a life, which fact was symbolised in the sacrifices of the Old Covenant by the offering of the blood of the victim. The author of the Epistle to the Hebrews expressly compares the sacrifice of Calvary with the Sin Offering made by the High Priest for the sins of the people on the Day of Atonement, in which the blood was offered in an unique and especially impressive manner. This offering of the blood is the specifically priestly action in all Jewish sacrifices, to which everything else is preparatory. The preliminary acts vary little, if at all, in the various sacrifices. The offerer brought the victim to the Temple and presented it to the Lord; he then laid his hands upon it, thus identifying himself with it, and slew it. In the case of the Day of Atonement, with which we are particularly concerned, the High Priest made this offering on behalf of the people, and was simultaneously offerer and priest. Then followed the priestly action with the blood, the symbol of immolated new life. In the case of all other sacrifices this was poured on the altar, but in the sin-

---

[1] Heb. x. 5–10.    [2] John x. 17–18.    [3] Heb. ix. 14.

offering it was smeared on the horns of the altar, while on the Day of Atonement the High Priest entered into the Holy of Holies and sprinkled the blood of the sacrifice upon and before the mercy-seat, afterwards returning to put it upon the horns of the altar.[1]

It is plain now that the high-priestly entrance into the Holy of Holies is the action of the Resurrection and Ascension: in heaven our great High Priest eternally offers to the Father the sacrifice of Calvary, the blood of His risen life.

Two quotations may help to make this clear. The first is from Mr. Gayford, whose lectures on Sacrifice have guided my thought on this matter for nearly twenty years. " Professor W. Milligan," he says, " has collected and examined the passages treating of the Blood of Jesus Christ, its meaning and efficacy, and compared with them the corresponding sayings in reference to His Death. The conclusion which he draws is that when the Apostolic writers wished to describe the full effects of the atoning work of Christ they almost invariably prefer to speak of His Blood, rather than His Death, as the means by which He won salvation for us. We need not remind our readers that the word ' Blood ' in itself involves the idea of Sacrifice. It was by a Sin Offering that Atonement was made under the New Covenant as under the Old. But further, ' Blood,' in its sacrificial associations, refers particularly to something which took place after the victim's death, *i.e.* to the altar-transaction, the ' pouring ' or ' putting ' or ' sprinkling ' of the Blood. Also the blood itself was the symbol of the life that *had been through death, i.e.* the risen life. So, the ' Blood of Christ ' refers us to a *sacrificial* work belonging to the *Resurrection-life.* His offering of the blood is fulfilled by something which he does in his Resurrection-state and with His risen Life." [2]

My second quotation is from Dr. Moberly, " As, then, the shedding of the blood is not in itself the consummation, but is the preliminary condition necessary for the consummation, of the symbolic sacrifice under the Levitical law; so when we turn to the essential realities, though Calvary be the indispensable preliminary, yet it is not Calvary taken apart, not Calvary quite so directly as the eternal self-presentation in Heaven of the risen and ascended Lord, which is the true consummation of the sacrifice of Jesus Christ. But of course, in that eternal presentation Calvary is eternally implied. Of that life, the ὡς ἐσφαγμένον,

---

[1] Lev. xvi.          [2] *Sacrifice and Priesthood*, pp. 144-5.

the ' as it had been slain,' is no mere past incident, but it has become, once for all, an inalienable moral element. Christ's offering in Heaven is a perpetual ever-present offering of life, whereof 'to have died ' is an ever-present and perpetual attribute. If 'Calvary' were the sufficient statement of the nature of the sacrifice of Christ, then that sacrifice would be simply past and done, which is in truth both now and for ever present. He is a Priest for ever, not as it were by a perpetual series of acts of memory, not by multiplied and ever remoter acts of commemoration of a death that is past, but by the eternal presentation of a life which eternally is the ' life that died.' " [1]

This " eternal presentation " by our High Priest is the centre of the worship of heaven, and what Christ does in heaven in His risen body that also He does on earth in His mystical body.

It has often been suggested that the worship of the Church on earth is the terrestrial parallel of the worship of heaven; that as Christ offers Himself in heaven, so He gives to His Church to offer Him on earth. Such statements are only partially true; the worship of the Church on earth is not related to the worship of heaven, it is a real part of it; the Mass is not the offering of the Church as an entity separate from Christ, it is the offering of Christ Himself. Christ is not only the Victim, but also the Priest, offering in His mystical Body on earth that sacrifice which He ever offers in His risen Body in heaven. The Church in offering the Holy Sacrifice does so not as an institution or a body of people, but as the Body of Christ; her action is the action of her divine Head through the power of the Spirit; she is the body of the High Priest, performing His High-priestly act.

In this presentation of the sacrifice every member of the Body of Christ has its part. The Mass is not a service which is performed by a priest and his assistant before, but independently of, a congregation of more or less interested individuals. We must remind ourselves that the norm of Catholic worship in East and West is what we call, in the West, High Mass; Low Mass being a necessary concession to convenience which is even now unknown to the Orthodox churches of the East.

In a High Mass, priest, deacon, sub-deacon, servers, choir and people all have their several parts; the celebration of the Holy Mysteries is the work of the body every member of which has to fulfil his own part without which the work would be incomplete.

[1] *Ministerial Priesthood*, p. 246.

The choir is not the people, and the people are not the priest, but even the youngest child has its part in the priesthood of Christ, of Whose Body it is a member.[1]

When the individual takes his part in the celebration of the divine mysteries he is not making his own prayer—he enters into an act of prayer which is going on independently of himself as an individual, because it is the prayer of Christ, our High Priest. Even on earth each Mass is not a separate act of worship, but the taking up, in that particular place, of the ceaseless worship of the Church throughout the world, and is one with the worship of the Church Triumphant—the offering of the " Lamb as it had been slain."

The prayers of the Liturgy are plural, not singular,[2] " we " not " I " (just as our Lord taught us in the fundamental liturgical prayer to say " Our Father " not " My Father "), for they are the prayers of the whole body of Christ. We must realise the universality of the liturgy—that it is not simply the action of the few or many people gathered together in the particular building in which Mass is being celebrated; in the celebration of the holy mysteries that congregation is one with the whole Church *semper et ubique*, the barriers of time and space disappear, the faithful are lifted up to the heavenly places, Christ descends upon the altar, and the Church militant, expectant and triumphant, is one.

In the Liturgy is realised the unity of the Body of Christ, for the Church is an entity; its vital principle is the life of Christ, it is one with Him its head, guided by the Holy Ghost. The individual Christian is not an entity, but a member of this unity, a cell of this living organism which is the Church. He has his own spiritual life, which must be lived and developed, but which can never be developed fully apart from life in the organism.

The collective prayer of the body differs considerably from the separate prayer of the individual, for it is not simply the sum of many individual prayers, but the prayer of an organism which is

---

[1] We have considered High Mass specifically because in it the difference between the various parts of the Body of Christ and their integration can be most clearly seen; it must not be argued from this that Low Mass is in any way incomplete or undesirable in itself, or that in it the individual has a smaller, because less differentiated or vocal, part. There is no essential difference between either method of celebrating the divine mysteries, and the offering of the two or three is as truly that of Christ as the offering of two or three thousand.

[2] I gladly acknowledge my indebtedness for the elucidation of much that immediately follows to Guardini, *The Spirit of the Liturgy*, a small book which amply repays careful study.

more than an aggregation of individuals, the prayer of the mystical body of Christ the High Priest.

Attempts are sometimes made to assimilate the prayer of the Liturgy to that of the individual, but such attempts are really misguided. Services of a popular character (using the word " popular " in its best not its cheapest sense) are necessary to the full expression of individual devotion and must exist side by side with the Liturgy, but the two must not be mixed or substituted for one another. A sensitive soul instantly feels that extempore praying and subjective hymn-singing, while eminently right at a prayer-meeting, are out of place at Mass, though perhaps he may not be able to say why he feels it. The individualist, on the other hand, wants to find in public prayer the direct expression of his own spiritual condition and needs, and to him therefore the Liturgy seems to be generalised, formal and cold: hence arise the experiments we have in mind.

The fact is that individual prayer, even when collective, is one thing, and the liturgical prayer of the Church another, and both are necessary. The Liturgy is not concerned with the individual as such; it is the expression of the worship of the body; hence liturgical prayer is essentially and rightly impersonal. The individual is required to sacrifice his individualism in order that he may enter into the fullness of the Body of Christ. Only as he is humble enough to do this does he find out what worship really is. In liturgical worship one is worshipping God the Father in union with the Incarnate Son, and this worship " through Jesus Christ our Lord " is far deeper than the most beautiful offering of our own which we can make to God the Son, because He is offering it in us who are members of His Body.

The liturgical worship of the Church is essentially impersonal, because it is suprapersonal, and this impersonality is right. The sacred vestments, so far from doing honour to the individual priest, obscure his personality; he is no longer A.B., but Christ's deputy. The priest who attempts to use his personality or consciously develops personal eccentricities at the altar is putting himself before his Lord, and so dishonouring Him; and the layman who worships merely as an individual is doing, in his own degree, much the same thing. The peculiar suitability of plainsong to the Church's worship is not only that it expresses in a beautiful and flexible manner the *nuances* of the sacred text as no other music does, but also that it is entirely

U

impersonal, hence many people who have not really entered into the spirit of the Liturgy dislike it fervently. The individual does not assist in the Liturgy to enjoy himself or to make his offering to God—he does it to unite himself with the offering of Christ, and in suppressing what is merely personal he finds himself in a wide field of spirituality which by its very impersonality unites him to the prayer of the Church of all ages and places.[1]

The prayer of the Liturgy is thus a breaking down of the barriers which separate soul from soul in the Body of Christ. The soul is thereby enabled to share its deepest existence with others without at the same time vulgarising it, to enter into the most intense depths of the common worship in closest contact with its fellow-members while retaining that spiritual modesty which guards for God that inner sanctuary of the soul which is His alone. The prayer of the Liturgy is therefore essentially reserved; it does not seek to express in words the inexpressible or describe the innermost desires or experiences of the soul, but by this very reserve it expresses far more than the more emotional utterances of prayers intended for private use. Everyone accustomed to the habitual and loving use of the Liturgy knows how wonderfully the *sortes liturgicæ* and also the invariable parts of the service supply the needs of the soul and raise it above itself as nothing else does.

Another great characteristic of liturgical prayer is its balance. This is obvious in the arrangement of the cycle of the Christian Year, uniting the Church, as it so wonderfully does, with the Incarnate life of her Head in all its stages and aspects. But there is also a wonderful balance discernible in the actual prayers prescribed, lifting up, as they do, all the powers of the soul into the act of worship.

Balanced prayer needs to be sustained by the spiritual apprehension of the whole faith. Individuals tend to isolate certain truths which appeal to them, and build their spiritual life around these with little reference to those parts of the faith which are less personally luminous; but the liturgical prayers (witness for

---

[1] " Morality of outlook is inseparably conjoined with generality of outlook. The antithesis between the general good and the individual interest can be abolished only when the individual is such that its interest is the general good, thus exemplifying the loss of the minor intensities in order to find them again with finer composition in a wider sweep of interest." Whitehead, *Process and Reality*, pp. 20-1.

instance the Collects) are remarkable for the way in which they are built upon intellectual and spiritual apprehension of the whole body of truth.

Liturgical prayer is founded upon thought in such a way that it sometimes appears almost frigid. It is not so, for it truly contains warm feeling, but that feeling is more usually to be found underlying the thought of the prayer than expressing itself in words. The aspirations of the heart are really expressed, but in a tranquil, reserved, almost incidental way which guards against all emotional excesses.

Further, liturgical prayer issues—as all true prayer must—in the movement of the will, again in a reserved and almost incidental manner. We do not find resolutions or expressions of individual intentions, but rather the identification of the individual will with the Church and the will of God by way of prayer.

The Collect for the Sixth Sunday after Trinity is a good example of this balanced and completely satisfying reserve: " O God, who hast prepared for them that love thee such good things as pass man's understanding (an intellectual statement of truth): Pour into our hearts such love towards thee, that we, loving thee above all things (the movement of the will), may obtain thy promises, which exceed all that we can desire (the heart): through Jesus Christ our Lord (union with the intention of our High Priest). Amen (union with the Church).

It is true that in the Prayer-Book we do occasionally find prayers which are not truly liturgical, but they only serve to throw into higher relief the true spirit of the Liturgy. Such blemishes are found in certain prayers inserted into the ancient framework at the Reformation which reflect the spirit of that age; the forms of liturgical confession being particular offenders in this respect; and it is much to be hoped that a future liturgical revision may produce a return to the more reserved language of the older liturgies. For a congregation which is, for the most part, in a state of grace, to describe itself as " lost sheep," for instance, is an exaggeration which tends to unreality and focusses attention upon the state of an individual soul, which is contrary to the spirit of the Liturgy seeking to direct its whole action towards God. How much more fitting is the reserve and Godward intention of the ancient formula: " We confess to God Almighty . . . that we have sinned exceedingly in thought, word and deed, through our fault, our own fault, our own most grievous fault; wherefore we pray God Almighty to have mercy upon us . . . "

We have dealt in some detail with the specific prayers of the Liturgy; we must now return to the fact that the Mass is essentially not the saying of certain prayers—though these must be said by the Priest—but an act of prayer.   There are therefore different ways in which the laity may assist at the offering of the Holy Sacrifice. We shall consider three chief ways:

(i) The following of the acts and words of the Liturgy exactly or almost exactly.   This is a literal uniting of the individual not merely with the intention of the Church, but with the exact acts and words of the priest, and is a very valuable way of worship, and deserving of encouragement.   It needs no explanation, for it is obvious, but we must enter one *caveat*.   The purpose of the Liturgy is the worship of God in union with the Church and her divine Head, not the edification of the individual—that is incidental.   There is a certain danger of self-centredness in this way of assisting at the Holy Mysteries.   Every parish priest knows the folk who demand to hear every word that he says at the altar, and complain peevishly if they miss anything.

It is necessary to remember that the priest at the altar is addressing God, and not the people (except of course in the epistle, gospel, absolution and blessing).   This is no excuse for slovenly speech—rather it makes such laziness the more reprehensible— but it does mean that shouting and " preaching " are not only undesirable, but definitely irreverent.   In a small church or a side chapel it is quite possible for the priest to be heard without unduly raising his voice, but in a large building audibility is always more or less difficult.   Where this is so the laity—who, after all, are not as a rule illiterate—must be prepared to assist their hearing by adequate use of the printed page.

(ii) Another way of assisting at the Holy Mysteries is by way of mental prayer.   This should not as a rule be recommended to souls whose normal way of prayer is meditation, unless they are using some method akin to that of S. Peter of Alcantara, but it is often valuable to those whose mental prayer is affective and who find the previous method difficult.

There is a danger in the use of this method which must be pointed out.   It is not desirable, unless one is so short of time that the two things must be combined, simply to make a meditation while Mass is in progress.   We come to Mass in order to offer it;

the way in which we assist in the offering may vary, but the offering itself does not; consequently our mental prayer, if we use it, must be directed towards the offering. If this is not fully realised, there is a danger of the soul actually separating itself from the worship of the Mass by its own mental prayer, and so not assisting in the offering at all. It is necessary to remember always that the prayer of the Liturgy is not our prayer, but Christ's, and any method we may use must be directed to the fullest union of ourselves with that prayer. This is not fulfilled if we simply make a meditation with an act of adoration thrown in at the Consecration.

The best ways of using this method are three. First to turn each part of the sacred action into affective prayer. This has been done very admirably by Fr. Roche in his *Mysteries of the Mass in Reasoned Prayers*, which is a book that has been found extremely useful by many souls. Something of the same kind is intended by the prayers of most of our devotional manuals, but the difficulty in their use lies in the fact that they usually provide prayers of some length to be said, rather than short acts to be used.[1]

The following scheme of acts appropriate to each part of the Liturgy may be found helpful:—

| | |
|---|---|
| Preparation, Kyries: | Contrition. |
| Collects: | Petition. |
| Epistle, Gospel, Creed: | Faith. |
| Offertory: | Self-oblation. |
| Prayer for Church Militant: | Intercession. |
| Preface: | Union with Church, saints and angels. |
| Consecration: | Adoration. |
| Communion: | Communion (actual or spiritual). |
| Post-Communion Prayers: | Thanksgiving. |
| Gloria in Excelsis: | Praise. |
| Blessing: | Recollection. |

Another way of praying affectively is to prepare one thought, idea or text of Holy Scripture beforehand which can form the basis of our liturgical acts.

Contemplative souls sometimes find that the only way in which they can assist in the offering is by a simple act of adoration and

---

[1] But cf. note on p. 211 *supra*.

love, by which they unite themselves to the sacred offering
without using the medium of words, either liturgical or other.

(iii) The third way of assisting at the Holy Mysteries is by
intercession. Whatever method we may use, it is important that
we should have a definite intention for which we assist at the
offering, something or somebody in particular for which we pray
in union with the sacrifice of Christ, and in this method one
simply holds this intention up to God at each point of the sacred
action. A great wonder of the Holy Sacrifice is that our Lord
allows us to offer Him, to plead His sacrifice and apply it to
individual things and needs. Those who really intercede know
that the offering of the Holy Sacrifice is the apex of all their
intercession; but, unfortunately, most people have very little
grasp of what intercession should mean and the place it ought to
hold in their spiritual life; consequently the Mass is often used
too exclusively for themselves. It is of great importance that
people should be led to make of it a real intercession.

We have considered the Liturgy proper, which is the offering of
the Holy Sacrifice; we must now add a note on the extension of
the Liturgy in the Office. The Mass is of obligation to all
baptised Christians, for in it the Church takes her part in the
offering of the High Priest. The Office is not of equal obligation,
being the devotional extension of that offering—it is of obligation
only to priests and religious; but it is a privilege which is offered
also to the laity, and which should be used by all.

The Office is secondary to the Mass, and depends upon and
centres around it, but it should not, for that reason, be thought
unimportant. S. Benedict was so much alive to its importance
that he called it *Opus Dei*—the Work of God. Apart from the
Mass it loses much of its meaning, but used, as it is intended to be
used, to link up the whole day and the whole life with the Holy
Sacrifice, it is of the greatest possible value.

It may be said that private prayer is sufficient to link up life
with the Mass, but that would be to take up too individualistic a
standpoint. The unique feature of the Office is that in it the
whole Church is ever praying as a whole, for the Office is truly
liturgical.

We need not repeat what has been said as to the true character
of liturgical prayer, but we must point out that the Office should
be kept distinct from popular congregational devotions. Much
is gained by doing this. Popular devotions may well take place

after Evensong, but the atmosphere of the two things should be quite distinct.

The structure of the Office should be noted. It is built up on the Psalter, the whole of which is said once a week according to the Breviary and once a month according to the Prayer-Book. There is a great devotional value in this complete recitation of the Psalter, which the devout and leisured laity should be encouraged to make the most of. Those who can only come occasionally— say to Evensong on Sundays—miss much of this recitation, but they should not therefore be deprived of what they may have. The popular custom of saying one Psalm only is liturgically indefensible and devotionally impoverishing. The Psalms are the great storehouse of prayer, and their devout recitation does an immense amount for the building up of the spirit of prayer; any undue abridgment of this part of the office is therefore to be deprecated.

Secondly, the Lessons. The Office is the great regular opportunity for people to hear the Word of God, and now that so little Bible-reading is practised at home the lessons of the Office have an added importance.

Thirdly, the great Christian Canticles which train the soul in pure praise.

And lastly, the Collects, gathering up the petitions in the words of the Mass, link up the whole action of liturgical prayer.

The structure of the Office is definite and simple, as all true liturgical structure is; its matter is of the greatest value to the praying soul; but most of all it keeps the prayers of the individual sweet with the living breath of the Church of God.

PART V

# CHAPTER XXII

# PERFECTION

*Be ye therefore perfect, even as your Father which is in heaven is perfect* (Matt. v. 48).
*God is love* (I John iv. 8).

WE are approaching the conclusion of our study of the elements of that wonderful complex of divine action and human response which we call the spiritual life. We must therefore ask what end the spiritual man, aided by grace and moved by the call of God, seeks to attain.

The complete and costing practicalness of the spiritual life should require no demonstration to the reader who has followed us thus far; nothing is further from the truth than the popular notion that fervent religion is merely idle dreaming whereby the introvert seeks to live in an imaginary world far removed from reality and the " hard facts " beloved of the extrovert: that practical thing, then, must have a clear purpose and end.

That purpose is nothing less than perfection—the formation of a perfect soul leading a perfect life—and its end is the Beatific Vision of God. We are so accustomed to mistaken and partial views of religion that this sounds a somewhat Utopian ideal to put before weak and sinful souls, perplexed with the problems of our twentieth-century civilisation; nevertheless, it is that which our Lord puts before us uncompromisingly in His saying: " Be ye perfect, even as your Father which is in heaven is perfect." The perfection of God is, indeed, a staggering thing to contemplate as a human possibility, yet that saying was not addressed to a few favoured, specially pious and sheltered persons, but to the disciples in general, by Him Who " knew what was in man." In spite, therefore, of his obvious sinfulness and weakness, man is not only capable of attaining perfection, but is created and redeemed in order that he may do so. Perfection, and nothing less, is the end which we must seek to attain if we would follow and serve Christ, and this is true for every baptised man, woman and child: it is not the ideal of the few, but the vocation of all whom our Lord has made one with Himself in His Church.

A perfect being is one which fulfils the end for which it was created. S. Thomas Aquinas puts the matter succinctly when he says: " *Unumquodque dicitur esse perfectum inquantum attingit proprium finem, qui est ultima rei perfectio.*" [1] That is true whether one is speaking of men or angels or motor-cars. Everything is created or made for some purpose; in so far as it fulfils that purpose it is perfect, and it is imperfect by just so much as it falls short of that fulfilment. Christian Perfection, then, so far from being an unpractical ideal, is simple realism, since man was created by God for a purpose.

The end for which we were created is union with God: as S. Augustine says in a famous phrase, " *Fecisti nos ad Te et inquietum est cor nostrum, donec requiescat in Te ;* " [2] and S. Thomas Aquinas, " *Ultimus hominis finis est bonum increatum, scilicet Deus, qui solus sua infinita bonitate potest voluntatem hominis perfecte implere.*" [3] We are created by God for God, and no merely created good is finally and completely satisfying; our *summum bonum* is union with Him.

This union is only perfectly attainable in Heaven, but the Christian life on earth is a foretaste of and preparation for the Beatific Vision. Union with God is potentially ours in Baptism, deepened by Holy Communion and actualised by prayer; the Christian life faithfully lived is, therefore, a progressive growth in that union with God which is the purpose of our creation. In this world we are pilgrims towards the heavenly Jerusalem, of which we are already citizens, and our perfection depends upon our approximation here and now with the heavenly life of union of the whole being with God.

Our Lord not only bids us be perfect, but be perfect " as our Father which is in heaven is perfect." Christian perfection is the most complete participation in the perfection of God which is possible to a creature; consequently it is no merely human perfection we are seeking, but the image of the divine. Man was created in the image of God so that a real union might be possible between God and creation. His perfection is that of a being like unto God, living with the life of God given to him in the sacraments; if he is to be perfect, he must be perfect as God

---

[1] IIa. IIae, Qu. clxxxiv., Art. 1. "A thing is said to be perfect in so far as it attains its proper end, which is the final perfection of the thing."

[2] *Conf.* I. i.

[3] Ia. IIae, Qu. cxi., Art. 1. "The final end of man is uncreated good, that is to say God, who alone is able by his infinite goodness perfectly to satisfy the desire of man."

is, and the divine perfection is summed up by S. John in the one word Love. The essence of perfection is, therefore, Charity.

Growth in perfection is growth in Charity, which alone unites the soul with God. In heaven we shall have no need of Faith, for we shall see God face to face; Hope will come to an end, for we shall have attained that which we desire; but Charity will only then come to its full fruition. The perfect man is he who loves God and is filled with His love, for therein is union.

" If ye love me keep my commandments," [1] said our Lord to His disciples, and the commandments are simply the exercise of love. " Thou shalt love the Lord thy God with all thy heart, and with all thy soul, and with all thy mind. This is the first and great commandment. And the second is like unto it, Thou shalt love thy neighbour as thyself. On these two commandments hang all the law and the prophets." [2] " All our perfection consists in a state of love and an entire conformity with the divine will." [3] Love issues in obedience, and obedience is the exercise of love.

The Christian virtue of Charity is not self-regarding; we desire to possess and to be united with God, and to that end we seek to keep His commandments. The pursuit of Christian perfection, therefore, consists in growth in holiness; because we love God we seek to cultivate the virtues, not because we wish to be thought virtuous, but because they are pleasing to Him; and, further, because we love God we seek to love our neighbour for Him.

The soul is not an individual entity which can live its life in isolation; it loves God as a creature, as a member of the human family, as a member of Christ, and it has its responsibilities in each of these connections. Its service of love is part of the service of the world, the human family, the Church; its end is bound up with theirs, its perfection is part of the perfection of creation, and its loving service of God involves also the loving service of its neighbour. The service of God is fundamental, the service of man springs from it and may take very varied forms, but the soul that is striving perfectly to love God must, as a consequence, love its neighbour also.

The essence of perfection is love of God and one's neighbour, which involves as a consequence the sacrifice of self-will. The soul that desires to possess and be united with God must be

---

[1] John xiv. 15.                          [2] Matt. xxii. 37–40.
[3] Augustine Baker, *Holy Wisdom*, p. 542.

empty of self, and must desire that possession and union not simply because it is infinitely desirable, but because it is the will of God for it. Hence the necessity for mortification, which finds its place as an act of love, and not simply as self-discipline. Perfection, then, involves the direction of the whole self and the whole life towards God. The details will vary with each soul, but the end in all cases is the same. In the next chapter we shall be concerned with the three Ways or stages of the spiritual life, but it will be well here to point out that the details of each Way vary. The perfection of the Purgative Way consists essentially in the extirpation of sin and the settling of the soul in virtue, along with the spiritual assimilation of the truths of the Christian religion. The perfection of the Illuminative Way consists essentially in the acquisition and practice of the virtues, growth in prayer and the actualisation of sacramental grace. The perfection of the Unitive Way consists essentially in contemplation, the acceptance by the whole being of that union with Himself which God gives as He will, and the unifying of life in Charity. The perfection of the beginner differs considerably from that of the saint. We may say, then, that perfection at any moment consists in the most perfect correspondence to its end of which the soul is capable at the moment. The pursuit of perfection is progressive, and there never comes a moment in this life in which one may believe oneself to have attained; nevertheless, if one is making the most loving response to God of which one is capable at the moment, one is, to that extent, relatively perfect, *i.e.* in the way of perfection which leads to the heavenly Jerusalem.

Those who are pressing on towards perfection are not only pleasing to God, they are also of the greatest value to the world (though the world does not always recognise that fact), for they are fulfilling the purpose of creation. The divine plan for humanity is fulfilled by consecrated souls, and His kingdom comes through them. G. K. Chesterton has, I think, a remark somewhere to the effect that it is untrue to suggest that Christianity has failed, for the simple reason that it has never been tried. This, of course, must not be interpreted literally; nevertheless it contains a truth, for if every member of the Church were perfect, *i.e.* fulfilling the purpose for which God created him as perfectly as he is able, the whole world would be brought to the feet of God.

Our Lord is Himself absolute perfection, and we shall attain to our perfection by deepening and living in that unity with Him

which is ours by the sacraments, by the imitation of His most
holy life, and by the life of prayer. We must assimilate Him,
learn of Him and live with Him if we are to attain that perfection
which He would see in us, for He is the way, the truth and the
life of His people, and we, having no perfection apart from
Him, with Him can do all things. The ideal of perfection for
the Christian is, then, to be so united with our Lord that we can
say with S. Paul, " I am crucified with Christ: nevertheless I
live; yet not I, but Christ liveth in me: and the life which I
now live in the flesh I live by the faith of the Son of God,
who loved me, and gave himself for me." [1]

It is the duty of the parish priest to set before his people, of
whatever sort they may be, the fact of perfection as the end of
life, and to refuse to allow them to remain content with anything
less. The Prayer-Book Catechism has its own excellences, upon
which we need not dilate here, but one cannot but admire the
directness with which the Penny Catechism of another communion plunges us at once *in medias res*, so that the child who
learns it finds the right orientation of life at the very beginning
and cannot forget it, whether he rises to it or not. The pertinent
questions and answers are these:—

" Who made you?
" God made me.
" Why did God make you?
" God made me to know Him, love Him and serve Him in
this world, and to be happy with Him for ever in the next."

That is the acceptance of perfection as the end of life for every
child of God, and it is that acceptance to which we want to lead
our own people. Duty is a fine conception which has produced
fine characters, but by itself it is not enough; it is philosophical
rather than religious, and it needs to be co-ordinated with the
knowledge, love and service of God through union with Jesus
before it can be completely adequate. The call to perfection and
the love of Jesus is characteristic of the best and truest strains of
Catholicism and Evangelicalism alike, and is much in need of
enunciation to-day. It calls to the depths of the soul, and many
generous-hearted boys and girls who would respond to it turn
away from the Church because they do not hear it. To most of

---

[1] Gal. ii. 20.

our people fervent religion is the fad of the few, whereas it should be the life of the many.   When perfection is rightly and naturally taught, the spiritual life is seen to be, not a visionary ideal, but the ordinary life of workaday Christians, and Charity becomes the most natural thing in the world.

# CHAPTER XXIII

# THE THREE WAYS

*Eschew evil, and do good: seek peace, and ensue it* (Ps. xxxiv. 14).

THE spiritual life divides itself naturally into three parts or Ways, called traditionally the Purgative, Illuminative and Unitive. It will be our business in this chapter to discuss each of these three Ways in some detail, but before doing so it will be well to make some general remarks on the whole subject.

The three Ways correspond to reality, and are in no way arbitrary; nevertheless, it is quite possible for a director to use his knowledge of them arbitrarily in dealing with souls. We would emphasise the fact that there is no rule-of-thumb method of training souls; every soul is different and, though we may be perfectly certain which Way it is in, we are sure to find that at some point or other it refuses to fit into any cast-iron intellectual scheme and demands special treatment. Every soul has its own spiritual history and temperamental peculiarities, and the workings of grace vary infinitely, and must be studied individually: there is, for instance, a considerable " no-man's-land " between the Purgative and Illuminative Ways where certain characteristics of both appear to exist simultaneously in the same soul, and a similar state may often be found between the Illuminative and Unitive Ways. Great damage may be done by a director who forces the soul to practise the exercises of one Way to the total exclusion of the other in such cases. One must be prepared for great diversities between souls, and sometimes considerable over-lapping between the Ways; the distinctions which we rightly make in classification are not absolute, and it is a great mistake to treat them as though they were; nevertheless, rightly used, our classification is of the greatest practical assistance to the director.

In ordinary speech a " way " signifies a path whereby we go from one place to another; the Ways of the spiritual life are not, therefore, permanent states in which the soul abides for life—

they are the different parts of the path whereby the soul travels on its journey heavenward. It is true that many souls who sincerely desire to give themselves to God never get beyond the Illuminative Way in this life, while others do not progress beyond the Purgative, but the director should beware of assuming that because a soul is in a certain Way when he takes charge of it, it will remain permanently in that Way, for even in the Unitive Way there are many degrees and much possibility of progress. It is the director's business to study the soul in the light of his knowledge of the Ways in order that he may help it to follow the guidance of the Holy Spirit in the Way He would have it go.

Some souls are in too great a hurry to arrive at the highest stages, and imagine themselves to be mystics before they have made any serious attempt at self-mastery; they will probably have to be kept for some time at the steady grind of the Purgative Way; others, through slackness, lack of knowledge or nervousness, fail to progress when they should do so, and need to be taught and encouraged to go on. The director should know the Way himself, and also when to apply the rein or the spur.

## I. THE PURGATIVE WAY

This is the Way of beginners in the spiritual life and, as its name implies, its primary purpose is the purification of the soul.

The foundation of the whole spiritual life is a sincere conversion of the soul to God. We have already said something about conversion,[1] and need not repeat ourselves here; it has, as has been said, many forms, and must not be expected to issue at once in the all-consuming love of God which we find in the saints, though, especially in the young, it will probably result in considerable sensible fervour for a time. The primary effect of conversion from which the Purgative Way begins is the desire to accept God as our Lord. The soul at the beginning of its way knows very little about God—real knowledge of Him is to come —but it knows enough to desire to choose Him, and it has taken the first step in the way of Charity, which, we have seen, is the essence of Perfection.

This is the way of the servants of God; deep intimacy with God is yet to come, but He is recognised as Creator, Master and King, and the soul desires to respond to His love, to worship and to serve Him.

[1] cf. pp. 159 f. supra.

There are many kinds of beginners in the spiritual life, varying from those who have kept their baptismal innocence free from any serious stain, to those who have been newly converted from a life of serious sin. With some a drastic purgation from affection to mortal sin is necessary, with others, only a gentle detachment from venial; but all, if their spiritual life is to be securely founded, will need to face the fact of sin from the point of view of God, and to refuse it because they have chosen Him.

The primary aim of the Purgative Way is the production of real penitence, for this will do more than anything else to detach the soul from sin and turn it to God. With less generous souls the motive to penitence will be largely fear of the wrath of God, and the fact of that wrath must be faced by all. Popular religion degrades God's love to mere good-nature, and refuses to believe in any vital way in His holiness and inevitable wrath against sin, and it is sometimes quite difficult to persuade souls to recognise these facts; nevertheless, they are fundamental and may not be glossed over.

The motive of fear is, however, an inferior one, and in generous souls gives place before long to a deepening realisation of the love of God and a hatred of sin, not because they will be punished for it, but because it is rebellion against that love. Penitence through fear is a necessary stage to most souls, but it is a preliminary one—it must lead to the perfect penitence of love.

Real penitence does not come all at once. Souls converted from a life of serious sin have come to a full and efficacious penitence, else were there no conversion; but the same souls later in life would be the first to admit that that penitence, overwhelming though it was, was but the beginning of a far deeper experience which came with a deeper knowledge of God and self, together with a costing living of the Christian life. Progress in the Purgative Way brings a deepening of penitence through just these things.

A soul that is becoming penitent realises the necessity of a real self-knowledge. It desires to love and serve God truly, and as that desire grows it realises more and more the malignity of the concupiscence within and the necessity, if this malignity is to be overcome, of knowing itself as it is in His sight. At this stage the habit of daily self-examination needs to be formed.

This is a habit which many souls never attain; there is no doubt that it goes very much against the grain of the natural man and that its acquisition demands much perseverance; nevertheless, it is of great importance, and the sooner it is begun the better.

Self-examination is of two kinds, general and particular. The general examen, with which we are now concerned, consists in an examination of one's conscience with regard to sins of all kinds. We have already dealt with this in a practical way, and it is only necessary here to point out the great value of its daily use. The examen need not—indeed should not—take long, and it should be made in the closest possible union with the Holy Spirit, Who alone can show us what He would have us know of ourselves. It is a short, business-like proceeding, in which we learn with some measure of precision how well or how badly we have served God in the day past. To sentimental people whose main idea of religion is just feeling good such a proceeding seems unnecessary, but those who desire to serve God well will realise that it is simply common-sense. The man of business who seldom if ever makes up his books is hardly *au fait* with his finances, and should not be surprised if his neglect of a necessary precaution finally lands him in the Bankruptcy Court; if he is wise he will make up his books daily. Daily self-examination is just as necessary to the soul that desires to serve God well. It does not lead to scrupulosity and undue preoccupation with self if wisely practised, rather it is a guard against these aberrations; it is the soul that does not use regular self-examination that becomes self-absorbed, never quite sure where it is or what it is doing; the regular examen gives to self-scrutiny its proper place in the exercises of the spiritual life.

The particular examen consists in the regular and careful examination of conscience in regard to one particular leading sin which the soul is striving to overcome or one key virtue that it is seeking to acquire. This practice is clearly of great value in the Illuminative Way, and further on in the spiritual life, too, but it should not be recommended in the Purgative, for the soul does not yet know itself well enough to use it wisely, and may easily become obsessed with the idea of self-examination.

Great wisdom is necessary in guiding souls in these matters; the purpose of this exercise needs to be made clear to them, for they must not on any account be frightened or weighed down with the idea of endless examens. Its purpose is not to compile dreary lists of sins, but to arrive at a real knowledge of oneself as one is in the sight of God, taking count of one's good deeds as well as of one's bad ones. In the sight of God one naturally sees one's sins, imperfections and failures most clearly, and it is right that this should be so, in order that one may know what to amend; but self-examination reveals something more than one's own sinfulness and weakness, namely, the wonder of the grace of God.

The Purgative Way is not by any means an easy one, and along with real penitence there often go increasing temptations. The soul has good desires, but it is not yet stabilised in virtue, and the attraction of the world, the flesh and the Devil is commonly strong; its love of our Lord is yet fitful, alternating with periods of weariness and tepidity, and it is from time to time tempted, often severely, to give up the hardness of the narrow way. The Slough of Despond, the Hill Difficulty, the Valley of Humiliation, Vanity Fair are all met in this way, and the soul needs much encouragement if it is to persevere valiantly. " A large part of the life of every priest with a cure of souls is spent sitting on a stone near the top of the Hill Difficulty encouraging pilgrims. For the Hill Difficulty is the grind of the whole thing which none of us can escape, the grind of resisting sin, of turning a deaf ear to temptation, of sticking to the necessary rules, the grind of the early morning alarum, of monotonous days, the grind of helping people about their weaknesses, of seeing their sufferings, a grind disfigured by the failure of losing one's passport through sins of infirmity and sins of surprise, of having to climb down to find it in penitence and to climb back again forgiven once more." [1]

The soul is striving for self-mastery in order that it may rise superior to the sin for which it is learning to sorrow, and it has need then of real self-discipline and mortification upon which its advance largely depends; only as it learns self-discipline and mortification will it be able to combat adequately the fatal attractions of concupiscence and the reactions against the spiritual life which are bound to come, and so attain that stead-fastness in the love of Christ by which it arrives at the next stage of its journey.

Self-discipline is greatly assisted by the making and keeping of a wise Rule of Life. To the novice this sounds a very forbidding and complicated thing, but it should be neither. The soul that tries to live without rule never really forms habits of virtue or

---

[1] Mackay, *The Pilgrim's Progress in the World To-day*, pp. 32–3.

learns to live the Christian life as it should; for without rule the whole of the conduct of life depends on the whim of the moment, instead of being regulated with regard to the will of God, and the soul never knows for certain what to do next.

In the business world office hours are regulated with care, otherwise there would be much waste of energy and little would be accomplished; in the spiritual sphere the Religious knows well the necessity of rule and time-table, and the same sort of regulation is necessary in the Christian life in the world.

It is impossible to draw up a rule or rules which would be suitable for everybody, or even for certain classes of persons, because no two persons are alike; the rule must be an individual one drawn up in consultation with the director.  The hours of work will probably be fixed by external circumstances, but times for prayer, worship and the reception of the sacraments must be settled, as well as periods of recreation and sleep, and there will also be some understanding with regard to almsgiving and works of charity.  A rule full of meticulous detail is a weariness to the flesh and usually defeats its own end; a wise rule should cover the whole of life so as to bring every activity within the will of God, but it must be simple, easy to remember and not too difficult to keep.  It is well, too, that it should be a minimum and not a maximum rule.  Generous souls frequently want to bind themselves to perform all the offices of religion which they would do on their best days; then they have a bad day and the rule goes by the board and has to be picked up again with great difficulty and some shame.  It is much wiser to make a rule which is well within one's power to keep and from which there is no reasonable excuse for departing, and on one's good or less busy days add to it such things as the Holy Ghost may suggest.

So far the Purgative Way has shown itself to consist of hard negative things—penitence, self-knowledge, mortification—and these things are necessary and can never be dispensed with if the spiritual life is to be well founded; but the Purgative Way has its positive side as well, though this is not always recognised as it should be.  In this Way the soul should be acquiring those convictions of the truths of the Christian religion which turn them from intellectual propositions of assent to spiritual truths whereby to live; there should, then, be much rumination of and meditation on those truths.

One is sometimes surprised and saddened by the sudden lapse

into unbelief of a soul which has been well instructed in the truths of the Faith and regular in its practice of religion. Such lapses are generally due in the first instance to the influence of friends, unwise reading and like causes, but they are made possible by the fact that the truths of the Faith have been to the lapsing soul only so many alleged facts to be proved or disproved intellectually, instead of spiritually experienced realities.

There is need, then, in this way, of regular meditation; and meditation of some kind by which the truths of the Faith are spiritually assimilated, is the normal way of prayer of souls at this stage of their development. Souls should, as a rule, be encouraged to continue in meditation until these truths are so assimilated that they become part of the fibre of the spiritual life.

Many books of meditation outlines exist which can be adapted to the needs of individuals, but when the soul is ready for it, it is well to lead it to make a Retreat on a definite scheme of meditations, such as those suggested by S. Francis de Sales in *The Devout Life*,[1] which may lead it deliberately to choose the service of God. A similar Retreat is also necessary for beginners who have got beyond the beginning if they have not really grasped these fundamental truths or if they have become slack and aimless, for until they have faced and chosen God they are likely to make but little progress.

Apart from meditation, the soul's prayer at this stage will probably be mainly vocal, and for this a book will be necessary, at least sometimes; and for persons of sufficient education the personal collection of prayers is invaluable.

The danger of prayers recited out of books is that they are easily regarded as formulæ which must be said in their entirety; they may thus actually stifle real prayer. The soul that feels it must get through a certain prescribed number of set prayers at a given time is depriving them of their value and binding upon itself a burden which it should not carry; its attitude should rather be that at a particular time it will pray, and that it will use certain known and loved prayers in so far as they help it to do so, using its own words and keeping silence as it is drawn.

[1] *The Devout Life*, Part I, capp. 9–18. The Meditations suggested are: 1. Creation. 2. The End for which we are created. 3. The Benefits of God. 4. Sin. 5. Death. 6. Judgment. 7. Hell. 8. Paradise. 9. Election and Choice of Paradise. 10. Election and Choice of the Devout Life. The Exercises of the First and Second Weeks of S. Ignatius are similar, though more elaborate, and are directed to the same end.

At this stage the soul can sometimes well make use of periods of quiet to learn to be silent with God. Even in the most elementary conversation the talk is not always on one side, and the soul may well learn now to be leisurely in prayer with increasing attention to God. It is much better to give a certain length of time to prayer than to settle with oneself to say certain prayers; that time can be variously used, but while it lasts, even if it be but short, the idea of time should be quietly excluded from the mind, and the soul should feel quite free to speak or to listen as it is led.

The soul needs to be strict with itself in regard to prayer in this way. It has to acquire the habit of prayer and to learn not to give up when it does not want to pray; it has not yet acquired that love of God which draws it to pray even in times of dryness. Indeed, it has not yet fully discovered what prayer is, and regards it as one of its spiritual exercises rather than its life; consequently it has often to urge itself to its devotions and break by force through the barrier of disinclination which separates it from God. The director has need of much patience in instructing it as to the true nature of prayer and encouraging it to overcome self in this matter. It is true that, especially at the beginning, there is often much sensible fervour in this way, but it is seldom constant. It comes from time to time for the encouragement of the soul, but it is too sensible and the soul too little stabilised for it to last. Fervour should be accepted thankfully and used well, but not relied upon as a constant factor in the spiritual life; advance in spirituality can only be attained by hard work and faithfulness in prayer.

What has just been said with regard to prayer is true also with regard to the use of the sacraments. It is often a real mortification to drag oneself to Confession when one does not want to go, or to get up early on a cold morning when one is tired in order to make one's Communion, and one has to use force with oneself; but the soul that only uses the sacraments when it feels inclined will soon turn aside from the spiritual life.

Further, in this way the soul should be steadily, and often by hard labour, cultivating virtues. It has the Infused Virtues to make its own, and there are others—notably humility and the virtues opposed to its favourite sins—which need deliberate attention. The purification of the soul is, indeed, far more radically performed by the effort to acquire virtue than by the effort to overcome sin; the latter is essential, but it needs to be directed towards the former if it is to be successful; consequently, even in the Purgative Way, the soul should not rest content with the struggle against sin, but stretch out beyond that to the conquest of the virtues which God wills to give it.

It cannot be said too frequently that it is in this stage that the habits of the spiritual life are formed, and these have to be acquired; supernatural habits of prayer and virtue have to be deliberately opposed to the existing natural habits of self-pleasing, and the soul has to learn to walk, and continue walking, worthy of the vocation wherewith it is called.

It is necessary to point out that the formation of habits is essential to the spiritual life. Many people have a horror of forming spiritual habits, owing, mainly, to a fear of formalism; irregularity and infrequency in prayer and the use of the sacraments are thus made into virtues, whereas they are very much the reverse. Formalism is a great evil to be avoided by every possible means, for it takes the very heart out of religion; but formalism is not the result of habitual prayer and sacrament, it is caused by the absence of love and desire for our Lord. The formal soul is mechanical whether it has formed spiritual habits or not, because its religion is based merely upon the observance of certain practices; the loving soul cannot become mechanical so long as it loves, for as its love grows so its desire for our Lord in prayer and sacrament grows, and habits are formed which keep it near to Him. It is a mistake to advise people to pray only when they want to, only to make their Communions when they feel like it and their Confessions when they have committed some great sin which gives their conscience no rest, for such counsel makes religion dependent upon the will-o'-the-wisp of sensible fervour, and prevents any real intimacy with our Lord.

Perhaps the most essential habit to be acquired is that of doing everything, however dull and ordinary, for love of God. This is the sanctification of all life and the secret of its happiness; it helps one to do unpleasant things cheerfully and enables one to do uncongenial work not merely for one's employer or to gain one's livelihood, but because it is God's will for one at the moment, and is thus the secret of contentment and a peaceful spirit.

The length of time during which souls remain in the Purgative Way varies from a few months in generous and innocent souls to many years in recidivists; there is no absolute rule, and the director must be guided by the state of the individual.   There is no absolute dividing line between the two Ways, and it will frequently be found that a soul which in one respect is in the Illuminative Way in another is equally certainly in the Purgative. The exercises of the one Way should, therefore, not be substituted for those of the other altogether at one specified time; rather the soul should move according to its growth when and as it is ready.

## II. The Illuminative Way

This is the way of devout souls who have made some advance in the spiritual life.   Hitherto they have been advancing in loyalty to Christ their Lord and Master, now He says to them, " Henceforth I call you not servants; for the servant knoweth not what his lord doeth: but I have called you friends; for all things that I have heard of my Father I have made known unto you." [1]   Souls in this way are admitted into that friendship with Christ for which the Purgative Way has been preparing them; loyalty has deepened into love.   The entrance upon the Illuminative Way marks a real advance in Charity and the commencement of the truly interior life, for the soul is now beginning to know what it may mean really to love God, and those practices of devotion which it has been acquiring are becoming the natural expression of the spirit.

(1) The first characteristic of this Way is the beginning of a new and deeper love of God.   There has probably been fervour in the Purgative Way, sometimes intense fervour, but it has been spasmodic, and there will have been long periods of time when it has been really absent; in the Illuminative Way there will also be bursts of similarly flamboyant fervour from time to time, but simultaneously there will be growing an habitual love for our Lord, which, though quieter, is more truly fervent, and prayer on the whole will contain much sensible devotion.

In the Purgative Way there is at times great delight in prayer, in Holy Communion and in the services of the Church, but the delight is primarily in the thing done or the experience gained; the Lord is loved indeed, but for His gifts.   In the Illuminative Way the gifts are loved because they are the means whereby the

[1] John xv. 15.

Giver grants intimacy with Himself. Christ is loved in the gift, rather than the gift on its own merits. In the Purgative Way the soul and its Lord are, so to say, two separate entities between whom there is from time to time correspondence; in the Illuminative Way the soul is learning to live with its Lord and really to love Him; it is beginning to learn that what it *does*, which was its primary occupation in the earlier stage, depends upon what it *is*, and that what it is depends upon that intimacy with Christ to which it is now giving itself.

(2) The second characteristic of this Way is the deepening of the infused virtue of Faith.

"The servant knoweth not what his lord doeth," but " all things that I have heard of my Father I have made known unto you." This way is called Illuminative because in it our Lord is, through love, developing in the soul the power of spiritual insight and a real knowledge of the things of God. The ways of God with souls are wonderful and, not seldom, unexpected, and one of the greatest joys of a director is to observe the, often very rapid, advance in spiritual perception of souls in this way. Sometimes one finds souls with very little capacity for thought who, through contact with our Lord, have developed what can only be called a *sense* of God, by means of which He enlightens and guides them and keeps them in touch with Himself, so that their life is irradiated by faith and joy. This insight is independent of intellectual capacity [1] and is often found in its full beauty in simple folk, but where it is combined with an acute and profound intellect we have the greatest type of Christian character. The spiritual insight which comes by love is not a substitute for intellectual effort to those who are intellectual, but its guide and completion;

---

[1] " All reasonable creatures, angel and man, have in them, each one by himself, one principal working power, the which is called a knowing power, and another principal working power, the which is called a loving power. Of the which two powers, to the first, the which is a knowing power, God who is the maker of them is evermore incomprehensible: but to the second, the which is the loving power, he is, in every man diversely, all comprehensible to the full. Insomuch that one loving soul alone in itself, by virtue of love, may comprehend in itself him who is sufficient to the full—and much more, without comparison—to fill all the souls and angels that may be. And this is the endless marvellous miracle of love, the working of which shall never have end, for ever shall he do it, and never shall he cease for to do it. See, whoso by grace see may; for the feeling of this is endless bliss, and the contrary is endless pain. . . .

" In the love of Jesu there shall be thine help. Love is such a power that it maketh all things to be shared. Therefore love Jesu, and all thing that he hath it is thine . . . Knit thee therefore to him, by love and by belief; and then by virtue of that knot thou shalt be common partaker with him and with all that by love so be knitted unto him." *The Cloud of Unknowing*, cap. iv.

for them the two works must go on simultaneously and harmoniously, they must not cease to think because they love, nor to love because they think; rather, because of their love God will become the " Master-light of all their seeing " and in Him they will see truth.

(3) The third characteristic of this Way is the deepening of the infused virtue of Hope. In the Purgative Way Hope is usually not very strong, and there will be times when the fight against sin is very difficult, when the odds seem overwhelmingly against the soul and it comes perilously near to despair. At such times the director has to work hard to produce the least flicker of Hope. Now, however, Hope begins to become a reality to the soul, for the love and knowledge of God are beginning to issue in that confidence in His love which leads to that certain trust in Him which is Hope.

The foundation of this Way is, therefore, the triad of the Infused Virtues, and as the soul gives itself to their exercise it is led to the fourth characteristic of the Way, which is the deliberate imitation of Christ. The soul is now, through Faith, Hope and Charity, becoming more and more centred upon Jesus, and this results in an increasing desire to become like Him.

(4) The fourth characteristic of this Way is the imitation of Christ. We had occasion in a previous chapter to make a long quotation from Dr. Moberly in which occurred the following words: " Consciously or unconsciously, love is imitative. What I am really in love with I must in part be endeavouring to grow like : and shall be growing like, if the love is really on fire, even more than I consciously endeavour. What I am really in love with characterises *me*. It is that which, I, so far, am becoming." [1] That is deeply true of this Way, in which the soul is becoming more and more in love with Christ and desiring above all things to please Him and be like Him; it therefore seeks to model itself upon Him and its life upon His.

This is the inspiration of the deliberate practice of virtue which is the work of the soul in this Way. It does not see virtues as detached objects of desire, but, loving Christ, it seeks to reproduce in itself those virtues which it sees in Him.

The imitation of Christ is not a vague general thing which comes by desire—it has to be deliberately practised, bit by bit and virtue by virtue. At first the soul has need to concentrate on

[1] *Atonement and Personality*, p. 147.

those virtues which form the likeness of Christ in it—simplicity, humility, love; then those in which it is notably deficient; then the rarer virtues which it sees in its divine Model; and in doing this it should not hurry restlessly from one to another at its own will, but place itself in our Lord's hands, that He may guide it to produce the virtues He would see in it. There should be an increasing co-operation between our Lord and the soul in this matter. If the soul tries to produce virtues in its own strength and at its own fancy, it may, if it perseveres, produce some virtue, but such virtue will be weak and partial, the soul's strength and hope in this way are that Christ Himself is guiding it and helping it to be like Him. All really depends upon a close intimacy with the Master and a ready willingness to obey His call and follow His leading.

From time to time the soul will probably suffer much temptation to self-assertiveness and uncharitableness, and it will, if it is to be like its Lord, need to learn to love men in Christ as He loves them. Supernatural Charity towards one's neighbour is a rare virtue which, among Christians, should be a common one; if the soul becomes so absorbed in its duty towards God that it has no care for its neighbour, instead of becoming beautiful with the love of Christ it will merely become hard and selfish. Charity towards and service of one's neighbour are essential to the following of Christ, and the soul has to learn to go about doing good with its Master. This means being Christ to men—a simple but difficult thing. It does not necessarily mean good works and social service, though it may do so, but rather being like Christ in the ordinary human relationships of one's state, and it can widen out to the whole world from that foundation. It is much harder to be Christ-like at home or in one's place of business than in self-chosen surroundings, but it is also far more meritorious; and Christ-like love of humanity will come from the Christ-like love of those, often trying, people among whom our lot is cast. Charity to one's neighbour is a command laid upon us by God, and a notable following of Christ, and is as possible to a permanent invalid as to the busiest social worker, being, indeed, the way in which we let our light, which is Christ the Light of the world, shine before men.

(5) The fifth characteristic of this Way is a deeper love of prayer. The friend of Christ naturally wants to be more often with Him than His servant, and realises that only as he knows our

Lord better will he become more like Him; so the soul now strives after longer times of prayer, and finds it can use them better than it used to do. Its manner of prayer also changes. If, hitherto, it has been using with profit one of the methods of prayer described in Chapter XVII above, or some method like them, it will probably find that it tends to think less and love more, until its normal method may be like that of S. Sulpice.

This is a healthy and right progression; the soul will at first still meditate, but not by way of thinking about things or preaching itself sermons. Its favourite subject will probably be the gospels, and it will seek simply to look at and love our Lord as He reveals Himself in them, drawing into its own heart and bearing in its own hands the virtues which it sees in Him.

In process of time discourse in prayer will become less necessary and finally impossible, and the soul will pass to affective prayer pure and simple, which is the normal prayer of souls in this Way. This advance should not be checked when it shows itself as a clear leading of God, but, equally, it should not be pressed before the soul is ready for it, on the ground that souls in this Way must pray affectively. There is no must about it; it is possible, though uncommon, for a soul to reach contemplation by discursive meditation or vocal prayer alone, and these Ways must not be regarded as necessarily too elementary for advancing souls. What needs to be realised is that the Illuminative Way is a Way of growth in which prayer commonly progresses in the direction indicated. There is a real danger of souls who have a notable devotion to our Lord becoming proud through thinking themselves persons of advanced spirituality, whether they are indeed so or not.

Mental prayer in this Way tends to become less wordy, and the value of words tends to change, but this does not mean that all vocal prayer must be abandoned. A balance must be kept between vocal prayer and wordless, or nearly wordless, prayer, or the spiritual life becomes stunted. For priests and Religious the foundation of this balance is to be found in the Divine Office, which, rightly used, is both vocal and contemplative and in any case supplies a nucleus of vocal prayer. Persons living in the world often find great help also in the regular use of at least some part of the Divine Office; it may be quite a small part—Evensong, Compline, Prime or Sext—according to devotion and opportunity, or for persons of devotion and leisure perhaps the whole. The point to remember is that the use of the Divine Office must be regular, and that the soul should not bind itself to use more than devotion and time allows.

If the soul has been using vocal prayer well in the Purgative Way it has probably evolved a method of its own which meets its needs fairly completely. This should be quite freely altered as the soul grows and finds adaptation necessary, but it should not be put away merely because in mental prayer words are beginning to become an embarrassment. Vocal prayer will probably follow mental in becoming less varied—it may reduce itself to a few loved and tried forms; on the other hand, the soul may need to find expression more freely in word; in either case vocal prayer, outside the Office, will tend to become more affective and aspiratory, and this should be encouraged.

With the deepening practice of prayer goes increased love of it, and there springs up in the soul a desire for silence and solitude which is probably new to it. In the Purgative Way the soul has been actively engaged in laying foundations by the exercises of purgation, and the love of Christ has not yet laid hold of it in the way that makes for silence; in the Illuminative Way the friend of Christ begins to love being with Him more than anything else in the world, and consequently desires to increase his times of prayer when he can be alone with Him, and this alone-ness with Christ is becoming a primary necessity of his life. This does not mean that he is developing an anchoretic vocation or an active dislike of the society of his fellow-men, but simply that his spiritual life, which hitherto has been cramped by pre-occupation with the world, is now opening out into fullness. The soul in this Way, even though it be constantly occupied with necessary worldly business, will need to increase its time of prayer and approach the altar more frequently; it will want to detach itself from the noise of the world that it may listen to its Lord, and the practice of Retreat will become of immense value. Recollection and interior silence will now begin to be loved, and the soul will want to be with Jesus not only at prayer, but also in the streets and workshops of the world.

It is sometimes thought that a serious practice of the prayer life is only possible to people of leisure, and that working folk must be content with the exercises of beginners, but this view is certainly mistaken. The working man called by our Lord to His friendship will find times for prayer in all sorts of ways if he is in earnest—dropping into church for a while on his way to or from work or in the lunch hour, using odd scraps of time on omnibuses or walking along the street and in a variety of other ways. Some ingenuity will be necessary and much goodwill, coupled with suggestions from his director, but the thing can be done.

Every parish priest knows that it is difficult, if not impossible, for some people to pray in their homes, and it is necessary to encourage them to use the church for this purpose; this encouragement should not only take the form of teaching and exhortation, but also of making the parish church the real spiritual power-house of the parish. We must thank God that now almost every parish church is open for prayer at least some time during the day; but, alas, not every parish church is the home of the people. One has visited churches which, so far from inviting people to pray, really dissuade them from doing so by their coldness (spiritual and sometimes physical) and stiffness; others suffer from hosts of budding organists whose energy, though commendable in itself, makes prayer an impossibility; others again, though open all day, are closed as soon as the workers return home; there are yet too few still, dim shrines of prayer filled with the peace of the Presence of God, into which one can slip unnoticed and be at home.

The sixth characteristic of this Way is the beginning of a real sacrifice of self. In the Purgative Way the soul is learning to make sacrifices; this and that has to go because it is incompatible with the spiritual life, and with more or less of a struggle and often many set-backs, this and that has gone or is going; now it is self-love and self-will that are laid at the feet of the Master.

As the love of Jesus increases so, to the generous soul, self comes to matter less and less. The way of love is the way of sacrifice, and the soul gradually realises that " He must increase, but I must decrease "; [1] self has to be quietly put out of the way, that Christ may be all in all.

At this stage the problem of the double will is particularly acute. The soul is increasingly desiring and intending to will the will of God, but it is at the same time powerfully attracted by the attachments to creatures which yet remain unmortified, so that self-will is still strong. At first the competition between self-will and the will of God is seen in large and obvious matters, but as mortification does its work it becomes more interior and subtle,

[1] John iii. 30.

and is found in motives and minor selfishnesses. In the greater matters, as in the Purgative Way, self has to be fought directly and positively, but as time goes on it is more effectively put in its proper place by the deliberate exercise of humility.

" I am He that am aught, thou art she that art naught," said our Lord to S. Catherine of Siena, and the realisation of one's own nothingness is fundamental to advance in the spiritual life. The exercise of humility leads one not to fight or argue with, but simply to drop self, because, in comparison of God, self is of no importance.

To the unmortified soul self is the centre of the universe; it does what it feels inclined to do, it regards other people from the point of view of their pleasant or unpleasant effect upon itself, and the will of God is strictly subordinate to its own desires. With the mortified soul it is just the other way about: God is the centre of its being, and so, since there cannot be two centres, self is quietly dropped. As mortification progresses, self has less and less ascendancy and is less spoken and thought of, until the soul becomes almost selfless.

Progress in this way of sacrifice depends upon mortification, which must become deeper, more complete and more fully willed. If the soul is to give itself wholly to God there must be a desire for discipline and mortification. At first this desire will doubtless be weak, and sometimes fearful, but it will grow as love grows, because the soul will realise the necessity for the removal of all obstacles to the love of God. Mortification will now become more interior, and the soul will strive to accept ever more willingly the discipline of the daily trials of life, realising that, as Père de Caussade says, " God teaches the soul by pains and obstacles, not by ideas." This will lead to a deeper *abandon* of self to God. Indeed the whole purpose of mortification is to form

> A heart resigned, submissive, meek,
>   My dear Redeemer's throne;
> Where only Christ is heard to speak,
>   Where Jesus reigns alone:
>
> A heart in every thought renewed,
>   And full of love divine;
> Perfect, and right, and pure, and good,
>   A copy, Lord, of thine.

That is the whole burnt-offering which God would have of us and which the soul in this way desires to give Him.

Y

This leads to our last characteristic, which is a deeper penitence. When Christ is known as Friend, the struggle against sin changes its character. Evil is no longer resisted merely because it is evil, but hated because it hurts Him; and penitence becomes not merely sorrow for particular sins, though it still is that, but much more sorrow for one's whole part in the sacred Passion. Sin is seen and repented of in the light of Calvary, which becomes an ever-present fact. For this reason the soul will seek to avoid not only great sins, but the least touch of evil, which is becoming truly repulsive, and it will seek in all things, however small, to please Christ. The struggle therefore becomes at once more interior and more intense; more interior because the initial battles have revealed something of the mass of evil within, of which the overt sins against which it is struggling are but symptoms; more intense, because it is now directed against the so-called minor sins as well as major infidelities.

This demands a deepened knowledge of self and perseverance in wise self-examination. As time goes on, the method of daily self-examination should become flexible, searching and simple. The use of questions should by now have become less necessary, and the soul should be able to see its leading sins and virtues by means of a rapid but searching look at the day past.

At this stage the practice of the particular examen will be found useful by most people. This consists in a simple but careful inquiry day by day into one particular leading fault, and it goes hand in hand with the cultivation of the virtues. If, for instance, one is attempting to cultivate humility, it helps greatly to know what are one's falls into pride, and what one is really doing in regard to them; advance in humility and watchfulness against pride thus go together to establish the soul in virtue.

The particular examen should be directed against a leading fault, while at the same time one is trying to practise the opposite virtue. Such faults should be attacked one at a time for as long a period of time as may be necessary to make some headway against them. Of course this does not mean that while we are attacking our worst sin we are allowing all the rest to flourish undisturbed, but that, while we are resisting all sins that may show themselves, we are directing the attack towards the capture of one position in particular. Temptations are not isolated units, but are commonly interrelated, and the conquest of one often brings with it the conquest of others connected with it; and the knowledge of one which comes by particular examen often reveals others whose existence has been hitherto unsuspected.

The subject of the particular examen should not be chosen at random, but carefully and with prayer.   The method is extremely simple, and consists of two parts: the Prevision, which should form part of the morning prayer, and the Examen, which should take place in the evening.

The Prevision consists in placing before oneself the virtue one seeks to gain and the sin to be overcome; then a glance at the day coming, noting the probable danger points and temptations; followed by a resolution and prayer for grace.

The Examen consists of an inquiry as to how the resolution has been kept during the day past and the motives which have led to any breaking of it, accompanied by an act of contrition.   Neither Prevision nor Examen should be over-prolonged—a few moments should be sufficient in each case.

As a rule, souls remain in the Illuminative Way for some considerable time, and many never get beyond it; clearly, then, it contains many varieties of souls, and there is room for great advance in it.   In our description we have had chiefly in mind the beginners in this Way, but they will not always be beginners— they will, if they be truly friends of Christ, attain to real, and perhaps great, holiness of life and depth of devotion.

It may not perhaps be unnecessary to add that this Way has dangers of its own, for the Devil does not commonly leave alone those whose feet are set on the way of salvation.   As the soul becomes more interior so does temptation become more subtle, as the soul becomes more disciplined with regard to the world and the flesh so do the spiritual temptations increase, as the obvious sins decrease there come movements of pride and self-satisfaction. Not all souls that enter upon this Way persevere; there is, however, no cause for panic so long as the soul has true humility with regard to self and complete trust in God.


### III. The Unitive Way

This is the Way of Christ's lovers, and represents, in its highest manifestations, the climax of Christian perfection in this life.   It is seen in its fulness in the selfless charity and complete union of the saints, but it would be a mistake to confine it to them.   There is considerable variation between souls in this Way, and even the saints, like the stars, differ from one another in glory; there is no absolute criterion, from the human point of view, of sanctity. We may legitimately make a distinction between the Unitive Way and the Unitive Life. A way, as we have remarked above, is a path whereby we go from one place to another, but the saints have arrived at the summit of perfection and have, presumably, no further need of a path; theirs is the Unitive Life. There are, however, other souls whom our Lord has been pleased to call to some degree of union and who, if they are faithful, may confidently hope to advance beyond their present state, even though they have no expectation of arriving at heroic sanctity without a special grace; these souls are on the Unitive Way.

The dividing line comes between the lower degrees of contemplation, which we have already considered [1] and shown to be common to those whom Christ calls to the contemplative life, and the higher infused degrees of contemplation the consideration of which belongs to mystical theology. The Unitive Way with which we are concerned lies between the two dark nights of sense and spirit, or perhaps it would be truer to say it is the Way of the dark night of sense.

Spiritual writers are agreed that the Unitive Life of the saints is wholly given by God to those whom He calls, and may therefore not be desired or prayed for by ordinary folk, but accepted with humility if it be granted; but the Unitive Way of ordinary contemplation is open to all who through charity, mortification and prayer are ready to enter upon it, should they receive the call of God to do so.

The whole subject bristles with difficulties and is variously interpreted by different authorities, but, since this is but one part of a book which aims at being non-controversial, we shall not attempt to reconcile different theories, but content ourselves with presenting what seems to us to be the truest explanation of the matter.

What we have called ordinary contemplation is the fullest development of the normal devout life, and is therefore open, as we have said, to all; it does not, however, follow from this premiss that all will attain to it, for its attainment depends upon three factors which are not always present.

(1) The first of these factors is the absence of obstacles.

(a) The final obstacle with many folk is their own temperament;

---

[1] cf. cap. xix *supra.*

there are Marthas in this world as well as Marys, and it is improbable that the one will ever develop into the other, nor is there any reason why she should, for the soul whom our Lord intends to find its perfection in the active exercises of the Illuminative Way will find it there, and not in contemplation. S. Teresa is rather bewilderingly clear on this point. " With the help of divine grace," she says, " true union can always be attained by forcing ourselves to renounce our own will and by following the will of God in all things. . . . Our Lord asks but two things of us : love for Him and for our neighbour : these are what we must strive to obtain. If we practise both these virtues perfectly we shall be doing His will and so shall be united to Him." [1] Union with God is, therefore, possible in the Illuminative Way as in the Unitive, for it depends upon perfect Charity and abandonment ; and the active temperament, though not called to contemplation, is not deprived of the possibility of that union.

(b) Another obstacle is lack of the necessary dispositions ; the soul which is not advancing in Charity and detachment and is yet unmortified is not ready for the Unitive Way, for it is held up in the advance to perfection. The soul at the entrance to the Unitive Way has need for great Charity and much mortification, and the lack of these things constitutes an obstacle which must be removed before the soul can advance a step.

(2) The second factor in the attainment of ordinary contemplation is most crucial, for it is nothing less than the call of God, and the director needs to satisfy himself as to this. It is difficult to suggest tests which would be valuable beyond the signs of the Unitive Way mentioned below ; there are, however, a few danger signals.

(a) Of these the most common is sentimentalism. This is often temperamental, but by the time the Unitive Way is really reached the soul should have made sufficient progress in mortification to have got its sentimentality in hand, if not conquered. A fruitful cause of this bugbear is ignorance ; many people think contemplation is just a beautiful dream in which one does nothing but enjoy God. This leads straight to Quietism, with all its great dangers.

(b) Another danger-signal is rashness and self-satisfaction. The statement that " men," or more often women, " rush in

---

[1] *Interior Castle*, Mans. V, cap. iii, 3, 7.

where angels fear to tread " is especially true of contemplation; the claim to be a mystic and a desire to talk glibly about spiritual experiences are always suspicious signs.

(c) A third warning is absence of spiritual suffering. God tests those whom He calls to the Unitive Way by suffering of different kinds, and it is very rarely, if ever, that a soul attains to this Way without it; it is therefore necessary to look for some signs of the night of sense or other pain in souls which seem to be drawn this way.

The call, when it comes, usually does so gradually and inevitably, the soul hardly knowing what is taking place and often in doubt as to the rightness of its state. It should be reassured and guided step by step and encouraged to place itself wholly in the hand of God, Who will guide it far more than the director, who often has only to watch and see that it does not go wrong.

(3) The third factor is the movement of the Holy Spirit. There is a real distinction between acquired or active and infused or passive contemplation, but we cannot draw a straight line and say that all on one side of it is acquired contemplation which the soul has won for itself, and all on the other infused and the pure action of the Holy Spirit. In all degrees of prayer there is an interaction between the soul and the Holy Spirit without Whom all prayer is impossible, and moments of passivity in which the soul is raised to contemplation are possible even in vocal prayer. The prayers of Simplicity and Faith are truly acquired, inasmuch as they are modes of prayer which may be practised and are under the control of the will, but that movement of the Holy Spirit which we call infusion is also present, certainly in the prayer of Faith, making the supernatural act of contemplation possible. As the soul advances in contemplation, the will is more closely identified with the movement of the Holy Spirit, and the degree of infusion increases, but in ordinary contemplation there are always times when it has to fall back on simply acquired prayer.

It is clear, then, that although contemplation is open to all as the fullest normal development of the devout life, not all attain to it, some because of their own fault and some because they are not called thereto in this life by the wisdom of God. There should therefore be no straining after contemplation on the part of those who have no call, and such should not feel aggrieved as though they were unfairly treated by God, for they have the possibility of a union with Him which, though different is none the less real, and of a perfection through Charity which is not inferior to that of any saint.

In the Illuminative Way the soul has learned to walk with Christ as Friend, and in process of time this experience of our Lord has become more interior, until it has become a real communion with Christ within. There is a great change here which is characteristic of the Unitive Way when it becomes habitual. The external, transcendent Christ is not lost, neither is the soul absorbed into Him, but, as the soul learns true introversion, this same Christ is known and worshipped as immanent within the soul itself. Our Lord must always be known under both modes, exterior and interior, but the devotional *attrait* of souls tends to find Him more easily in one mode than the other: and as the soul grows towards contemplation and its own interior life develops, so its deepest experience of Him is within. This leads to the habitual interior union with Him and with the Holy Trinity through Him which is characteristic of the Unitive Way.

Union with God, Who transcends all things, comes about through what Barbanson [1] calls the " experimental knowledge of God " immanent in the soul, and it is this knowledge which the soul acquires in the Unitive Way.

We must now seek to discover the chief marks of a soul in this Way, the first of which is Charity.

(1) We have seen that Charity is the essence of perfection and that each step in the soul's advance is marked by the deepening of this fundamental virtue; with the entrance upon the Unitive Way the love of God which has hitherto been becoming the chief virtue in the Christian character becomes actually unique, the virtue towards which all the rest converge and of which they are manifestations. The will being united with God by Charity, Charity is the motive power of life. This produces a fundamental simplification in life and prayer; the soul becomes unable to practise any virtue separately, for that virtue is simply a manifestation of Charity, [2] while in prayer it becomes incapable of making forced acts of the virtues because they all become acts of love.

This does not mean that the virtues disappear, but that, through Charity, which has at last reached its rightful pre-eminence, the soul operates in a different way.

---

[1] *Secret Paths of Divine Love, varr. locc.*

[2] It is at this stage that the maxim of S. Augustine " *Ama et fac quod vis,*" which is so dangerous where charity is imperfect, becomes a sure guide, and an explanation of why the saints may do what we cannot.

The virtues are now no longer actively sought and practised; the soul has entered upon the intuitive possession of the gifts of the Spirit and, willing to love God in all things, the gifts find expression in action, and everything is seen and done in God.

This uniqueness of Charity does not come about all at once, indeed it cannot come about so long as certain antecedent conditions are absent. (*a*) There must first of all be a considerable self-mastery. This is the way of the strong, not of the weak and sentimental who are yet babes in Christ; and the strength necessary to it is not the aggressive, self-assertive strength of the superman, but the humble strength of the soul that has faced itself as it is in God's sight, and through patient mortification has killed the " old man " that the " new man may be raised up " by the grace of God. It has mastered self by losing, not by exaggerating, self.

(*b*) Secondly, there must be complete detachment from creatures in themselves. Only as this is thorough can the soul give itself wholly into the hands of God.

(*c*) The third condition is abandonment to the will of God. This is not a nerveless, negative thing, but a flaming desire that the will of God shall be done in all things. It is this which completes detachment and makes it healthy. We love the world rightly when we receive it, purged of its dross, from the hand of God; we love our fellow-men rightly when we love them in God, and only as we give ourselves to the will of God can we serve them rightly. Detachment which is not a self-regarding thing does not prevent us from loving our neighbour; rather it makes love possible, for only as we are detached from our selfish predilections and wholly given to the will of God can we love in God.

(2) The second mark of a soul in this Way is habitual recollection. In the Illuminative Way the soul has been becoming more recollected and has deliberately striven to become so; now it is conscious of a fundamental recollection which, though not always conscious, is yet always there. It desires to possess God always and never to depart from His presence; it has no bits of life which it wants to keep for itself, for it lives its whole life in God's sight. Recollection in the earlier Ways was occasional; it had, indeed, been growing in continuity, but it was mainly conscious and dependent upon deliberate intention and the absence of engrossing occupations; now it is very largely unconscious, one may almost say " conscious-unconscious," the result of the soul being con-

stantly set towards God; and it is there whatever the soul may be doing.

(3) The third mark is a radical change in prayer, for the soul now enters upon contemplation. In all true prayer the soul is in the hands of the Holy Spirit, but in contemplative prayer the divine guidance is much more evident; it is therefore a mistake to exhort people to pray contemplatively as though it were their own act, for this way of prayer is only possible to those whom God leads to it, and we must therefore consider the signs of His leading.

(a) The first of these signs is a somewhat unexpected one, for the soul finds itself lost in aridity. The popular idea of contemplation is that of a blissful state of communion with God at which one gradually arrives by a process of evolution in fervour, but the reality is indeed far otherwise; for the soul when it enters upon this advanced way of prayer finds that, so far from increasing in fervour, all the fervour which it has hitherto possessed seems to depart, and it is left with nothing but dryness. There have, of course, been times throughout its spiritual life when its fervour has departed from it and the spiritual life has been merely a grind, but those aridities have been due either to its weakness and immaturity or to sin and, if it has been faithful, the clouds have passed in time and the sun of fervour has shone again. At all times in the spiritual life there is a sort of rhythm alternating between fervour and dryness in which one or the other has preponderated, but now fervour seems to depart and aridity to become habitual, and the soul not infrequently looks back to days that are past as those in which it was happy with God, and contrasts them sadly with its present exile.

There is an aridity, common in the Purgative and Illuminative Ways, which is the fault of the soul; it may be too weak to sustain the effort necessary to keep its spiritual life constantly at its highest point, or concupiscence may drag it away from God to desire lesser goods. The result in either case is loss of fervour; but the aridity of which we are now thinking cannot be accounted for by the soul, for it is the action of God.

It is important that the director should be able to distinguish the aridity of the Unitive Way from that of the others and we may note certain distinguishing marks :—

(i) The soul is unhappy in its condition, which it feels is

z

exile from God, and looks vainly for some sin in itself which will account for it.

(ii) It constantly recurs to the thought of God in a sort of arid recollection, having no real interest in anything apart from Him.

(iii) It finds itself unable to pray as it used and, apparently, does nothing when it attempts to pray; nevertheless, it desires prayer more and more.

Where these signs are present with the further evidences of God's leading which we are about to consider, the soul is being led by God, and should be encouraged to persevere.

The reason for this aridity will become clearer as we proceed. It is not due to any real absence of God—though that is what it feels like—it is not a punishment for sin, nor is it an abnormal state; rather the soul is in God's hand more completely than ever before, and the Lord is leading it by the way of the wilderness. The soul is not going backward, as it almost always thinks it is, but advancing, and this fact should be made clear to it again and again.

(b) The second sign of God's leading is a certain inability of the soul to help itself. It cannot pray as it used, though it wills to pray, and it cannot practise virtues as such—it can only love God in everything that it does, which is a more perfect way of life, though, at any rate at first, it is harder; for it is more difficult to give oneself at all times to the will of God than to seek to exercise one's own will rightly.

The prayer of this Way has been considered above, in the chapter on Contemplative Prayer, but there remains a difficulty concerning self-examination which must be touched on here.

Hitherto self-examination has doubtless been a fairly straightforward, if unpleasant, exercise; now, however, the soul, though conscious more than ever of its great sinfulness, finds that the more it strives to examine itself the less it can see. Under these circumstances the director should guard it from scrupulosity and discourage any preoccupation with self. If the soul is truly in the Unitive Way the love of God is its constant motive, and it will know at the time when it has sinned against that love; its self-examination should then be the simplest gathering up of its sins, known and unknown, and casting them in general into the fire of God's love. A spiritual writer has well said: " Too much particularising of our defects is distractive, it being sufficient to examine the performance of our duty and obligatory actions, or if any notable defect have carelessly crept upon us; all other defects being more profitably wrapt up in a generality, and so cast into our Saviour's Passion, than particularly stirred up, which would but in a manner raise up a new dust in the soul. (Concerning) the anxious looking upon the defects in themselves and in their peculiar matter or object; it is better and safer to turn the eye of our soul from the matter in particular unto God Almighty, humbling ourselves before Him, and with loving reverence craving pardon of Him." [1]

The deliberate practice of virtues is now becoming impossible, because the soul is learning to live intuitively in the power of the gifts of the Spirit and all things tend towards the love of God.

(c) The third sign is that obscurity of soul which has been treated of in our section on the Prayer of Faith. [2] It is unnecessary to add anything to what has been said there, except to notice that, although He seems to be absent, God is really nearer to the soul than ever before and he is acting more powerfully on it when it seems to be accomplishing nothing itself except the holding on to God with the will.

(d) We have seen that the Unitive Way is the perfection of Charity. There are moments when the soul experiences a realised possession of God through love, but these are of short duration and of uncertain occurrence; normally the love of God shows itself in intense desire for Him, " evermore crying after Him Whom thou lovest." This desire is the fourth sign of God's leading, for to the souls whom He calls by this Way He gives a pure desire for Himself alone, compared with which the natural desires are as nothing. The soul longs for Him Who alone can perfectly satisfy it, and therefore hates sin, which keeps it from Him, and seeks in all things to place its own will in His. Its desire is for God and not for His gifts; for God and for nothing outside of God.

These signs of God's leading are the characteristics of that first dark night of the soul, which S. John of the Cross calls the night of sense. Some confusion has crept into this subject owing to the fact that S. John himself appears to place the night of sense at the beginning of the Illuminative Way, whereas in practice one finds

---

[1] Leander a San Martino, " A Memorial," in Augustine Baker, *Holy Wisdom* pp. 558–9.　　　　[2] cf. pp. 265 *ff. supra.*

that it occurs at the beginning of the Unitive.   The Saint's words are these, " Souls begin to enter the dark night when God is drawing them out of the state of beginners, which is that of those who meditate on the spiritual road, and is leading them into that of proficients, the state of contemplatives, that, having passed through it, they may arrive at the state of the perfect, which is that of the divine union with God." [1]   It seems clear that his division of the spiritual life differs from ours, the " state of beginners " being for him our Purgative and Illuminative Ways, *i.e.* everything below contemplation; the " state of proficients " being our Unitive Way, and his " state of the perfect " that way which lies beyond the second dark night of the spirit characteristic of saints and elect souls, with which we are not concerned in this work.   S. John of the Cross, then, does actually place this dark night exactly where we find it, as we should expect him to do, and the difference is only one of terminology.

The dark night of sense is not nearly such a complicated or rare phenomenon as many folk imagine it to be.   " The night of sense is common and the lot of many . . . the spiritual night is the portion of very few." [2]   To some souls it is a vague discomfort, to some acute agony; some find their way in it without much difficulty, others are perpetually distressed; to some the darkness remains dark, to others it is clearer than the light.   Whatever may be its precise form to the individual, it has a twofold effect, for firstly by suffering, aridity and darkness it purifies the soul of attachments to earthly things as such, and then, having detached it from these, it attaches it in a spiritual and selfless way to God, Whom it loves.   It is therefore the way to that peaceful union with God which is the end of the spiritual life.

[1] *Dark Night of the Soul*, Book I, cap. 1.
[2] S. John of the Cross, *op. cit.*, Book I, cap. viii.

# CHAPTER XXIV

# THE GUIDANCE OF SOULS

*Behold now, there is in this city a man of God, and he is an honourable man ; all that he saith cometh surely to pass : now let us go thither ; peradventure he can show us our way that we should go* (I Sam. ix. 6).

FROM time to time in the course of our discussion we have had occasion to refer to the priest as the director of souls; it may therefore be useful to conclude our study by a short discussion of the responsibility of the parish priest in this most important matter. An adequate discussion would require a book to itself, and will not be attempted here; we shall confine ourselves to a few suggestions in barest outline.

In our first chapter we found that the *differentia* of the Christian life is that it is a participation in the life of God, given by the Holy Spirit dwelling in us, in virtue of the merits of Jesus Christ. If this is so, it follows that an essential part of the ministry of every priest is the guidance of the souls committed to him in their response to the Holy Spirit and their willed participation in that life. Spiritual direction is not the close preserve of a few experts, but an essential part of the responsibility of every priest with a cure of souls.

A priest is a man sent forth to bring men home to the Heart of God, his primary mission is therefore one of conversion; but where that mission has been accomplished, he has to face the further responsibilities of training and guiding souls in the spiritual life. This guidance will take different forms in different cases, but every soul needs it: it is not enough merely to exhort our people to be good, to say their prayers and frequent the sacraments, they look to us for guidance in these matters, and such guidance is of the essence of the pastoral office.

In a general congregation the only direct incentive to the Christian life which many people get comes to them through sermons, whence also they obtain their guidance in spiritual things; so that if the Sunday sermon is barren of spirituality,

333

as it not infrequently is, " the hungry sheep look up and are not fed."

We are not here concerned with Homiletics, but we must point out that what most people rightly look for in our sermons is not fine preaching, topical fireworks or intellectual essays, but, as they say, " something to think about during the week," *i.e.* spiritual guidance. The preacher's business is not to be sensational, nor should he be content to " say a few words " about nothing in particular—his true aim is to teach his people the Faith and how to live by it as simply and plainly as he can.

Confirmation classes and addresses to parochial guilds afford unique opportunities not only for explaining the Faith, but also for continuous training in the spiritual life, and we can hardly give them too much care and thought. It is to be feared that some priests regard these things as rather troublesome disturbances of the normal parochial round, but they are rather the means whereby we may train our young people in real devotion to our Lord; the seed-beds of the Church, to which we should give the best that is in us.

The inner circle of the more devout is a part of his congregation which the priest often thinks can take care of itself, but he should not forget that in the midst of His ministry to the multitude our Lord gave Himself to the intensive training of the Twelve upon whom he founded His Church. We shall be wise, therefore, to give Lent and other courses for the more devout which shall provide them with real training in the more fervent and costing devotion to our Lord for which they should be ready. The reason why the devout often become so trying is that they do not receive the guidance which they need, and so, instead of growing in self-oblation, they merely become self-absorbed. The inner circle should be the spiritual power-house of the parish, not a clique of somewhat pharisaical *élite*.

The means of spiritual guidance which we have so far considered are of great importance, but it is in his dealings with individuals that the priest will be called upon to guide souls most intimately. Individual work is difficult and exacting, but it is impossible to exaggerate its vital importance, and it is here especially that the priest can be the guide and father of his people if he really gives himself to them.

In his visiting the priest finds that his advice in spiritual matters is constantly sought, often by most unexpected people,

and it is his privilege to deal with a variety of doubts and difficulties. He may feel sometimes that this does not lead anywhere,
but if he always gives of his best he may find that his words go
farther than he thinks. We must not depreciate the value of this
sort of ministry, for it is not only of use in itself, but it not infrequently leads on to more detailed and continuous guidance.

Besides those who come to him for occasional help in spiritual
matters, there are also those who are more particularly his
children, whose confessor or director he is, and we must now
endeavour to make clear the difference between these two
offices.

As confessor the priest's relationship to his penitent is that of
spiritual physician and, so far as counsel is concerned, his
business is to deal with the matter of the confession and prescribe
remedies. As director, he has an even graver responsibility,
for he has to take cognisance not only of the matter of a confession, or even several confessions, but of the whole spiritual
life of the soul, and show it the way in which it should go in
prayer, mortification, the practice of virtue—indeed, in every
department of its life.

" Direction is the art of guiding souls so that they shall respond
most readily to their graces. . . . It implies a settled relationship between director and directed, not merely by way of giving
and seeking advice, which would still leave open the private
judgment of the one directed, but rather a relationship resulting
from prayer and careful search in which the soul has found the
' guide of souls ' upon whom it feels it can depend. Being sure
of this, the soul has adopted the avowed intention of obeying the
counsels of that friend."[1]

It is a matter of the greatest importance to a soul seeking
perfection that it should be directed in its way by a wise priest
learned in the spiritual life, but, unfortunately, such a priest is
not very easy to find; we have, indeed, many confessors, but few
directors. The parish priest must not expect to direct all his
penitents as a matter of course, for some of them have perfectly
good reasons for going elsewhere, and it is of the greatest moment
that a soul should be directed by the priest whom it believes to
be the right one for itself; but he should be capable of directing
ordinary souls rightly, and should know the limits of his own
capacity well enough to send those whose way he does not

[1] Gilbert Shaw, *Some Notes on Terminology*, pp. 22-3.

understand to a more expert priest. It is vital that there should be experts in spiritual direction who can deal with exceptional souls, but the majority of souls are not exceptional, and should be able to find what they need at home if their clergy would take the science of the spiritual life seriously and study to become directors of souls.

It is a mistake to think that long interviews of direction and rigorous cross-examinations are constantly necessary in this work. Once the director has visualised the state of the soul and decided upon its way, it is not generally necessary to do more than deal with questions and difficulties as they arise, except at long intervals or when a change occurs in the spiritual state of the soul; most of the director's work can be done at occasional interviews or, in case of necessity, even by correspondence. Some directors exact a great deal of spiritual account-keeping from the souls who commit themselves to them, and require from them an obedience similar to that which a Religious gives to his Superior, but such requirements are an abuse of the director's office which is most cramping to the soul. The relationship between director and directed is that of father and child, not superior and subject, a distinction which should always be borne in mind.

The guidance of souls is not easy; rather it is an exceedingly delicate task, and makes great demands on the character of the priest himself: we must therefore attempt to visualise some of the chief qualities which the director should seek to acquire.

The priest's whole ability to guide souls depends upon his being a man of God. Spiritual guidance can only be undertaken by one who is himself humbly seeking to live with and for God: a worldly priest, though he may be popular, is incapable of this work; nor is it sufficient merely to have a good knowledge of human nature nor to be well up in the latest theories of psychology. The direction of souls is the work of the Holy Spirit, and the priest is simply the human medium through whom the Spirit works; the director's primary qualification is not anything of his own, but fidelity to the love and will of God. His work is so delicate and difficult that he may well despair of doing it at all in his own power, and he needs to live in constant dependence upon the grace of his ordination, and to correspond to that grace by constant prayer, holding himself and his spiritual children within the Divine will.

As regards himself, the director should aim at a very real and fundamental detachment from all things and people in themselves. Instances are common, far too common, of priests who, often with the best possible intentions, attach souls to themselves rather than to God, with disastrous consequences when the inevitable break comes. The relationship between confessor and penitent or director and directed is so intimate, being concerned with the deepest things of the spirit, that it creates a real bond between them, and when that bond is truly spiritual and in God, it is right and good; the difficulty is that it is apt to become, on the penitent's side at least, something merely emotional. This can be counteracted by real detachment on the part of the priest, who should also train his child in this fundamental austerity.

Further, the director needs to be disciplined with regard to his personal ascendancy over the soul he directs. The exercise of spiritual authority demands the greatest humility, and all temptations to substitute one's own will for that of the soul must be strenuously resisted. The director's business is to direct, not to bully; he has to develop the soul's personality, not to subject it to his own; he will need to beware of directing too much and of subjecting souls under his care to vows and rules which cramp their initiative.

Again, the director needs a reverence for the Holy Ghost so great that he never puts himself in the way of the Divine guidance. When one sees a soul opening out and developing, it is so easy to attribute that result to one's own careful direction, instead of seeing in it the work of grace; then, perhaps, one increases one's counsel with a view to making the soul what one wants it to become oneself, without reference to the will of God; but one has no right to do that. It is no part of the director's business to make all his spiritual children contemplatives, or to force all of them to meditate in his particular way or to follow his particular rule of life; it is for him to visualise the Spirit's leading and will with regard to the individual, and to show that soul how best to correspond with that leading and will, quite irrespective of his own plans and prescriptions.

Sometimes with advancing souls the director's best course is simply to watch and make occasional suggestions, for with them the Holy Ghost often does His work more or less directly; in such cases the director must be content to remain in the background until he is needed.

The director should never forget that he is the father of the spiritual children whom God gives him to cherish and guide. We have considered the fundamental detachment which must be if the relationship between father and child is to be in God, but that detachment must not issue in a hard coldness, but in a spiritual love, which is purged, indeed, of selfishness and emotion, but warm with Charity.

The director's love for his spiritual children is shown first of all in the compassion of his Master—that compassion which is a real entering into the soul's life and sufferings, the understanding which comes by Charity. It is essential to the soul that it should be understood by its director, and such understanding can only come by compassion.

Compassion should produce patience. People, even holy ones, are often extremely trying, fussy and exacting, but if the director is to be of any use at all, he must be patient, and he can be so if his compassion and understanding are real.

These qualities should be accompanied by zeal for the salvation of the souls committed to us. Patience alone may develop into *laissez-faire*, zeal alone may become feverish, but together they produce a balance of soul characteristic of the true guide of souls.

Charity must be accompanied and illuminated by knowledge. The soul is a delicate organism, and ignorance and clumsiness, even when well-intentioned, may do a great deal of damage.

The director needs to fit himself for his task by careful study. He is not a psycho-analyst, and some knowledge of psychology, though useful, is not an adequate equipment. The priest treats souls on the spiritual, not the psychic level, and what is important for him is an adequate knowledge of the four closely related branches of theology—dogmatic, moral, ascetical and mystical. Of these we would stress the importance of the third, which should be studied not in little modern books, but in the works of the proved masters. If one is to train souls in the spiritual life, one must know what that life is and how souls may cultivate and grow in it, and this means careful study of ascetical theology.

But this knowledge must not be merely theoretical—there must also be practical experience. The director should not be a sign-post, which points out the road without travelling along it; his most valuable knowledge of the spiritual life comes through his own attempts and failures, and he cannot guide others in a life which he is not living himself.

Lastly, the director needs wisdom, which is firstly the gift of God and secondly the result of knowledge. Wisdom consists essentially of two elements; an instinctive understanding of what is right for the soul one is directing, and that instinctive quality called tact (or more technically though less graphically " discretion ") in dealing with it.

Finally, one should pray much for one's spiritual children. Nothing is more beautiful in the letters of that great spiritual director, Abbot Marmion, than the way in which he says over and over again *Je prie beaucoup pour vous*. Those words may well be the motto of the guide of souls, whatever form his guidance may take, for it is by prayer, even more than by counsel, that he can bring and keep them close to the Heart of God.

# BIBLIOGRAPHY

## I. PATRISTIC AUTHORS

### (E.T. = English Translation.)

S. Basil: *Regulæ.*
    E.T. *The Ascetic Works of S. Basil,* Lowther Clarke, 1925.
S. Augustine: *Enarrationes in Psalmos.*
    *Sermones.*
    *Epistolæ.*
    *Confessiones.* E. T. various editions.
Ps.-Macarius: *Homiliæ.*
    E.T. *Fifty Spiritual Homilies of Macarius the Egyptian,* A. J. Mason, 1921.
Cassian: *De Institutis Cænobiorum.*
    *Collationes.*
Ps.-Dionysius: *De Divinis Nominibus.*
    *De Mystica Theologia.*
    E.T. *Dionysius the Areopagite on the Divine Names and the Mystical Theology,*
        C.E. Rolt, 1920.
S. Benedict: *Regula,* ed. Butler, Cambridge, 1912.
    Trans. anon., S.P.C.K., 1932. (A Pax Book.)
S. John Climacus: *Scala Paradisi.*
S. Gregory the Great: *Regula Pastoralis.*
    *Moralia in Job.*
    *Homiliæ in Evangelia.*
    *Homiliæ in Ezechielem.*
S. Bernard: *De Diligendo Dei.*
    *The Book of S. Bernard on the Love of God* (Latin and English text), E. G.
        Gardner, 1916.
    *Sermones in Cantica Canticorum.*
    E.T. *Sermons on the Canticle,* S. J. Eales, 1896.
    *De Consideratione.*

## II. CLASSICAL AUTHORS

S. Thomas Aquinas: *Summa Theologica,* Pars IIa.
    E.T. ed. Dominican Fathers. 9 vols.
Thomas à Kempis: *The Imitation of Christ.*
Blosius (Louis de Blois): *Works,* ed. Bertrand A. Wilberforce. 7 vols., 1925–30.
Barbanson, Constantine: *The Secret Paths of Divine Love,* ed. Dom. Justin
    McCann, 1928.
Hilton, Walter: *The Scale of Perfection,* ed. Dom E. Noetinger, 1927.
Anon.: *The Cloud of Unknowing,* ed. Dom Justin McCann, 1924.
Baker, Augustine: *Holy Wisdom,* 1876.
    *Confessions,* ed. Dom. Justin McCann, 1922.
    *Inner Life of Dame Gertrude More,* ed. Dom Benedict Weld-Blundell, 1910.
Law, William: *A Serious Call to a Devout and Holy Life.*
Taylor, Jeremy: *Holy Living.*
    *Holy Dying.*
S. Peter of Alcantara: *Treatise on Prayer and Meditation,* ed. Dominic Devas,
    1926.

S. Teresa: *Life*, ed. David Lewis, 1910.
    *Way of Perfection*, ed. Benedictines of Stanbrook, 1925.
    *Interior Castle*, ed. Benedictines of Stanbrook, 1921.
S. John of the Cross: *The Ascent of Mount Carmel*, ed. David Lewis, 1906.
    *The Dark Night of the Soul*, ed. David Lewis, 1916.
    *The Spiritual Canticle*, ed. David Lewis, 1909.
    *The Living Flame*, ed. David Lewis, 1912.
S. Ignatius: *Spiritual Exercises*, ed. Longridge, 1919.
    do. ed. Rickaby (with supplementary volume, *Waters that go Softly*), 1923.
de Berulle, Cardinal: *La Direction Spirituelle*, Paris, 1926.
S. Francis de Sales: *Introduction to the Devout Life*, ed. Allan Ross, 1924.
    *Treatise on the Love of God*, ed. Canon Benedict Mackey.
S. John Eudes: *The Reign of Jesus*, 1925.
de Caussade: *Abandonment to Divine Providence*, Exeter, 1921.
    *On Prayer*, 1931.
Grou, Jean: *Manual for Interior Souls*, 1892.
Scupoli, Laurence: *The Spiritual Combat*.

### III. MODERN AUTHORS

Bremond, Henri: *Histoire Littéraire du Sentiment Religieux en France depuis la fin des Guerres de Religion jusqu'à nos jours.* 10 vols., Paris, 1923.
    E.T. (first two volumes only), 1929–30.
Butler, Abbot Cuthbert: *Western Mysticism.* 2nd edition, 1927.
Chautard, Dom J. B.: *The Soul of the Apostolate*, 1928.
de Besse, Ludovic: *The Science of Prayer*, 1925.
    *Light on Mount Carmel*, 1926.
Frost, Bede: *The Art of Mental Prayer*, 1931.
Guardini, Romano: *The Spirit of the Liturgy*, 1930.
Knox, Wilfred L.: *Meditation and Mental Prayer*, 1927.
Lehodey, Dom Vital: *Le Saint Abandon*, Paris, 1930.
Manning, Cardinal: *The Internal Mission of the Holy Ghost.*
Maritain, Jacques and Raissa: *Prayer and Intelligence*, 1928.
Marmion, Abbot Columba: *Christ the Life of the Soul*, 1924.
    *Christ in His Mysteries*, 1925.
    *Christ the Ideal of the Monk*, 1926.
Thibaud, Dom Raymond: *Un Maître de la Vie Spirituelle.* Maredsous, 1929.
    A Life of Abbot Columba Marmion containing many of his spiritual letters and a careful study of his teaching.
Ullathorne, Abp. W. B.: *The Endowments of Man.*
    *Groundwork of the Christian Virtues.*
von Hügel, Baron Friedrich: *Eternal Life*, 1913.
    *The Mystical Element of Religion*, 1908.
    *Essays and Addresses.* 2nd Series, 1926.
    *Selected Letters*, 1927.

### IV. HANDBOOKS

Tanquerey, Adolphe: *The Spiritual Life*, 1930.
Lehodey, Dom Vital: *The Ways of Mental Prayer.* Dublin, 1924.
Saudreau, M. le Chanoine: *Degrees of the Spiritual Life.* 2 vols., 1907.
    *The Life of Union with God*, 1927.
Poulain, A.: *The Graces of Interior Prayer*, 1904.
Beaudenom, M. le Chanoine: *Pratique Progressive de la Confession et de la Direction.* 2 vols. Paris, 1905.
    *Les Sources de la Piété.* Paris, 1908.
Farges, Mgr. Albert: *The Ordinary Ways of the Spiritual Life*, 1927.
Desurmont, Achille: *La Charité Sacerdotale.* 2 vols. Paris, 1925.
de Journel, Rouet and J. Dutilleul: *Enchiridion Asceticum.* Fribourg, 1930. A valuable collection of patristic extracts.
Pourrat, P.: *Christian Spirituality.* 3 vols., 1922–7. An historical survey of the teaching of the great writers and schools of spirituality from the time of our Lord to the seventeenth century.

# INDEX

PRINTED IN GREAT BRITAIN BY RICHARD CLAY AND COMPANY, LTD., *Bungay, Suffolk*